Other Books By James Braha:

Ancient Hindu Astrology for the Modern Western Astrologer

How To Be a Great Astrologer: The Planetary Aspects Explained

Astro-Logos, Language Of Life: The True Story of a Man and the People and Planets Around Him

Transits of the West Dasas of the East

HOW TO PREDICT YOUR FUTURE

By James Braha

Hermetician Press / Hollywood, Florida

Hermetician Press
P.O. BOX 1961
Hollywood, Florida 33022

Transits of the West—Dasas of the East: How to Predict Your Future

Cover design by Lyndel Opozda
Copyright free illustration by Gustav Doré

ISBN 0-935895-05-1
Library of Congress Catalogue Card Number: 93-080114

Printed in Hong Kong by Liang Yu Printing Factory, Ltd.
Mr. Eric Hui (852) 560-4453

First Printing

1 2 3 4 5 6 7 8 9 10 15 20 25

To Vashti, my wife

The most extraordinary combination of
heart and mind I have ever known

With love and admiration

ACKNOWLEDGEMENTS

I would like to express my thanks to those who have helped with this book, as well as friends and supporters who have made my astrological journey richer and more fulfilling. I am deeply indebted to Nancy Ross Gilius, my editor. Her diligent and painstaking work has added immensely to the clarity of this book. Furthermore, her patience and caring are an inspiration. To Sheppard Root, my typesetter, for his expertise and precision as well his valued friendship. To my dear friend Emmett Walz, who understands my vision of astrology better than anyone and whose words of encouragement during times of frustration are more meaningful than he knows.

To Bob Fitzpatrick, Mike Donnely, Frank and Phil Grant, and the other members of the South Florida Sterling mens' group I have attended weekly for over seven years. Their comaraderie and support is a continual source of strength and joy. To my Hindu astrology mentors R. Santhanam in Delhi and P.M. Padia in Bombay.

To Marcos and Jane Tobal, Richard and Paula Houck, Sam Zimmerman, Ginger Chalford, Lynn Hertsgaarde, Terry Therion, Barbara Zeitlin, Jolie Martin, Toni Lefler, Charles Braha, Liz Karabatzo, Virginia Letter, Sheldon Epps, Mimi Mukherjee, Lucy Clark, Thor Thorgeirsson, Steve Niemela, Patrick Bosold, Moira Collins, Rudy and Brigitte Gillmann, Walter Gillmann and Karen Pomsar, Jerry and Kisan Greiff, Howard Dugan, Shane Dugan, Dennis Harness, Dennis Flaherty, Dan Buls, Lans Peterson, Jim Leonard, Lisa Hawley, Joy Billings, Lilly and Ashley Braha, Herb and Carol, and Marco and Jasmine.

To Eric Hui, my printer in Hong Kong for his quality workmanship, patience, and fine character. And to Kerry Breitbart for his friendship, warmth, and compassion over the past twenty years. My heartfelt thanks to all.

Transits lie at the heart of western astrological prediction. Ever since my beginning days in astrology, I have been frustrated by the lack of good material on transits. Like every dedicated student, year after year I searched for books that could explain my current or future transits. Year after year, I found the same few texts on the bookshelves. In a field as vast in size, profound in implications, and rich in diverse opinions as ours, it is incomprehensible that there are only three or four serious, comprehensive books about transits available today. Students of astrology need differing opinions and viewpoints. We also need the material to be presented in different ways. And most importantly, we need greater depth and wisdom in the explanations of each transit description.

In this body of work, I have tried to present more than the surface effects of each particular transit. Transits are profound because they reveal a person's inner experience as well as what may occur externally. Transits represent the growth processes of an individual. They depict nothing less than evolution in action. How magnificent! As Robert Hand, to my mind the greatest living exponent of astrology in the western world, says in his excellent book, *Horoscope Symbols,* "The primary value of astrology is as a symbolic description of the human psyche. To me, astrology best describes what we are like inside. It relates to external events only insofar as they arise out of what we are and how we behave."

The main purpose of understanding a particular transit is to be able to bring light and consciousness to whatever internal process is occurring. Individuals who have a clear awareness of what nature is doing, a clear understanding of what is happening within themselves, are better equipped to handle whatever situation they encounter. I have tried in this book to provide information about each transit in a way that the reader can directly relate to. My intention is that my descriptions of transits will help the reader to understand the opportunities for growth that they represent, and that this understanding will help the reader take full responsibility for his or her own evolution. Only then can a person take full advantage of a transit.

It is crucial to understand that, despite my authoritative writing style, the knowledge in this book is in no way intended as gospel truth.

Because part of my background in astrology is in the ancient Hindu predictive system (also known as Vedic astrology), I have chosen to write in a style similar to that of the ancient sages. I do this for the simplicity, directness, and power it delivers. For astrological writings, I have found no other style as effective. My purpose in astrology is to serve others in their growth toward fulfillment and perfection. Though it may appear so to some, I am not interested in fortune telling. Indeed, in my astrological practice, I consider myself a humanistic, or counseling, astrologer. I have, however, misgivings about the writings of most humanistic astrologers.

Many modern astrological writers try to "protect" the reader by using ambivalent words and soft-pedaled knowledge, so that the essence of their message is lost or rendered impotent. Ironically, this kind of writing has arisen in response to readers who wish to abdicate responsibility for their own lives by taking astrological explanations as absolute truth. However, when astrological writings are watered down, we dramatically slow the growth of the entire astrological field! What astrologer does not know some brilliant astrological disciples who have given up on the star language because they could not find decisive, powerful material? In a field as infinite and complex as astrology, writing authoritatively is clearly risky. But how can power be achieved without risk? I take this risk because I believe that for the student to learn, he or she must have a clear view of what is on the teacher's mind.

This is my third textbook in which I continue with the ancient Hindu writing style which employs the masculine gender exclusively and for which I feel the need to apologize sincerely. It does not become easier for me with time to compromise the feelings of women, though I do so in favor of providing the clearest, most powerful, and direct teachings I can. As explained in my aspect book, *How To Be a Great Astrologer,* I feel that most astrological reference texts leave the reader begging for a deep, visceral experience of archetypal knowledge. This problem is largely overcome, in my opinion, by the use of the forthright ancient Hindu writing style. The exclusive use of masculine gender, however, not only disturbs female readers, but it perpetuates the damaging, imbalanced energy of our culture.

This point is made clear by Robert Hand in *Horoscope Symbols* in which he discusses the Moon—the planet symbolizing women: "Astrologers have seemed not to understand the Moon as well as the Sun, and not to accord it quite the same importance. This is due to something within our culture that has manifested as sexism, but in reality goes much deeper. Our culture has lost touch with the power of yin. We strive to go out into the world, to grab it by the throat, and thus to master it.

We do not understand the way of waiting and of learning to fit in to become a part of the whole. ...It is not enough that the female sex gain political equality with the male if the yin principle does not also gain equality with the yang. Man as well as woman is yin, and both are yang. As long as we act as if the yin is not an equal principle, we face life as half-beings, incomplete and out of touch with nature."

When the time finally arrives that I can afford to do so, the text you now read will be available in two versions. One will be the same text in your hands, and the other will be the same information, only the "*hes*" will all be "*she*s," and "*his*" will be transformed into "*her*." Until then, I sincerely beg the reader's indulgence.

Although I present the material in this book in a decisive tone, I do so only to deliver information and concepts clearly and precisely. Astrology is not, as far as I am concerned, an absolute science. Do not expect that every transit description in this book will necessarily correspond to your experience or to that of a particular client. Aside from the fundamental correctness or incorrectness of my delineations, when it comes to astrology (as most astrologers would admit) sometimes the magic works and sometimes it doesn't. The fact that the following transit descriptions are fairly traditional, in keeping with essential planetary and house symbolisms, and the fact that much of the information is based upon my own personal experience does not necessarily mean that my transit descriptions will match every person's particular process.

This is more than just a disclaimer. It is an acknowledgement of the elusiveness of the miraculous but sometimes inexplicable discipline we are dealing with. Astrologers should always use wisdom, intuition, discretion, and knowledge of the client's way of functioning. Common sense comprises almost half of the predictive process. Also, please bear in mind that the explanations throughout this text are actually descriptions of planetary symbolism, even though I relate all transit descriptions to "the person" (i.e. "When transiting Jupiter conjuncts natal Venus, the person is lucky in love matters."). That is simply my teaching method. If every astrology client in the world were as agreeable and accommodating as "the person" in my books, our search for knowledge could end right here!

I pray that the information in this book will be helpful. That it will be studied, assimilated, and incorporated in professional birthchart interpretations. But most of all, I pray that the material will be improved upon by future writers. This is more than rhetoric; it is a call for action. Today, more and more specialized astrology books are being written while the basics are being neglected. Clearly, astrologers are not well

4 served. Powerful astrological interpretation requires deep understanding of the fundamental influences. This is gained best by building upon the work of our elders.

There is a profound statement in Stephen Arroyo's book *Astrology, Karma, and Transformation* that has reverberated in my consciousness since I read it in 1979: "If you understand one factor in the chart *thoroughly*, it will lead you to the center from which all emanates.... As Albert Einstein remarked, if you penetrate to the core of anything, you will eventually encounter the deepest reality and truth." Let us seek to penetrate the core of astrology before delving further into endless complexities. God bless.

September, 1993

Part One
Transits of the West

Transits are the passages of planets in the sky in relation to your natal horoscope. In order to use this book it is necessary to either own an ephemeris (a book listing the daily positions of the planets, the Sun, and the Moon), an astrological calendar, or a printout of your transits for the year from a mail order astrological computer service. Finding your transits using an ephemeris is very easy, but for those who would rather purchase their yearly transits, I have listed a few reliable companies in the back of this book in the chapter titled "Services." Simply send accurate birth data (birth date, place, and time—as close as possible within minutes) and the required fee.

To determine your transits using an ephemeris or astrological calendar, you must know the symbols for the twelve astrological signs and understand that each sign is comprised of thirty zodiac degrees. Also, the symbols of the aspects should be learned. First, the symbols of the zodiac signs and aspects:

Aries	♈	Libra	♎
Taurus	♉	Scorpio	♏
Gemini	♊	Sagittarius	♐
Cancer	♋	Capricorn	♑
Leo	♌	Aquarius	♒
Virgo	♍	Pisces	♓
Conjunction	☌	Square	□
Trine	△	Opposition	☍
Sextile	✶		

A transit occurs when a planet in the sky aspects, or reaches a point that corresponds to or forms a relationship with, a planet in the natal horoscope. For each of the planets, this book describes five major transits. They are as follows: the conjunction, an exact aspect; the square, a 90° aspect; the opposition, a 180° aspect; the trine, a 120° aspect; and the sextile, a 60° aspect. As an example, let us say that the planet Venus occupies twelve degrees of Libra in a person's natal horoscope (the birthchart based on a person's date, time, and place of birth). If Uranus reaches twelve degrees of Libra, then this means that transiting Uranus conjuncts (forms an exact aspect with) natal Venus. If Uranus comes to twelve degrees of Capricorn, which is ninety degrees away from the twelfth degree of Libra, then transiting Uranus squares (forms a ninety degree aspect with) natal Venus. If Pluto occupies twelve degrees of Gemini, then this means transiting Pluto trines (forms a 120 degree aspect with) natal Venus. And so on.

In this book, transits of the slower moving planets (Jupiter, Saturn, Uranus, Neptune, and Pluto) are analyzed because they are the ones which cause or correspond with the more significant occurrences in a person's life. The transit descriptions in this text generally begin to take effect when a transiting planet comes within one degree of its exact transiting aspect. The effects continue until about one degree AFTER the exact transit. (Some astrologers consider a transit finished after the exact transit has been made. I allow an extra degree mainly to take into account the precession of the equinoxes, which is explained in the chapter titled *The Two Zodiacs*.)

For example, if transiting Saturn is coming to a conjunction of the Sun in five degrees and sixteen minutes of Leo, then the person will feel the effects from the time when Saturn reaches four degrees and sixteen minutes of Leo until it reaches six degrees and sixteen minutes of Leo. This is called a one degree orb (one degree on *both sides*). The effects of transits, however, are sometimes felt earlier than one degree before the exact transit. In fact, many astrologers use a four or five degree orb for outer planet (Uranus, Neptune, and Pluto) transits. In my experience, outer planets do generate a noticeable effect well before their exact degree of transit that is worth recognizing. During this time, the person can go through the internal or psychological changes that lead up to the major life changes that occur when the transit reaches its one degree orb.

Although there are five major planetary aspects (some say six because they include the 150 degree quincunx) all having distinct discernable traits, I have treated squares and oppositions (the "hard" transits) as identical and have done the same with trines and sextiles (the "soft" transits). I have done this because the effects of transiting squares and oppositions and transiting trines and sextiles are so similar. Most texts which describe the hard transits separately manage to say the same things about both transits using different words. The same occurs when they describe soft transits separately. However, in order to make accurate predictions and give clients a thorough understanding of what to expect from a particular period, astrologers must bear in mind the essential differences of the aspects.

The transiting conjunction is the most powerful transit, and it can be either positive or negative, depending upon the two planets involved. For example, transiting Jupiter conjunct the Moon is a happy period because both planets are benefic and have a soft, harmonious nature. Transiting Uranus conjunct Mars, on the other hand, can produce a volatile time because intense Uranus and malefic Mars simply do not blend well. When analyzing any transit, whether a trine, sextile, square, or opposition, I recommend reading the transiting conjunction description first in order to understand the natures of the planets and how they interact together.

Opposition transits tend to produce effects which involve others in the person's life. The person will encounter difficulties with some individual who resists or opposes him or her. A predicament ensues that feels like a win-lose situation in which only one party can prevail. The person tries to win through battle, negotiation, or compromise. Transiting squares, on the other hand, are more difficult because they create dilemmas wherein the person is thwarted by his or her own unconscious, unhealthy attitudes and behavior. Because these problems do not manifest through some other individual, the person may be completely baffled as to the source of his or her troubles. A good deal of time may pass before the person even considers looking inward.

Transiting trines and sextiles are less similar to each other than squares and oppositions in that sextiles are much weaker than trines. Transiting sextiles only represent an opportunity to gain benefit. In other words, the person must take action to make the indicated positive effects happen. Transiting trines, however, produce gains, profits, and opportunities that fall into the person's lap. During a time, the person adopts an attitude of optimism and impartiality in the areas signified by the transiting and natal planets involved. The person is open to harmonious forces of the universe headed his or her way. Unfortunately, the effects of transiting trines and sextiles often pass by completely unnoticed by the person. The periods of transiting trines and sextiles are characterized by such grace, ease, and peacefulness that the person may become lazy, passive, or self-indulgent. Furthermore, if the planets involved in the transit are comfort-loving by nature (Moon, Venus, Neptune, etc.), then the transit is unlikely to produce intense effects.

The transits described in this book are written with western astrology and the tropical zodiac in mind. However, practitioners of Hindu astrology may also wish to use this section of the book. It is my experience and deep conviction that astrologers who use both Hindu and western astrology have a profound advantage because they have more information about an individual in terms of both psychology and karma. Hindu astrology (sometimes called Vedic astrology or *jyotish*) excels in its predictive ability and western astrology excels in its psychological and humanistic descriptions, but each system is capable of predicting both behavioral patterns and karmic events. Therefore, by using Hindu and western astrology side by side (employing the RESULTS of the systems but never mixing the techniques), the astrologer has a double wealth of knowledge on which to draw. However, those who wish to practice only Hindu astrology can still benefit from many of the descriptions which follow.

To do so, however, requires some explanation about the meanings of the houses, most of which are primarily the same but a few of which are different. And, for astrologers who practice both Hindu and western astrology, there is a serious question of which chart (Hindu or western) to use when analyzing the transits of Jupiter and Saturn through the houses. (Since I do not advocate using Uranus, Neptune, and Pluto in Hindu astrology, I do not perceive these as an issue, and I recommend using their transits strictly from the western chart and the tropical zodiac.).

While it occasionally happens that a planet transits the same house in the Hindu and western chart at the same time, very often the transits may be several months or a year or more apart. In other words, Saturn may transit the tenth house of a person's western chart in January of a particular year and not enter the tenth house of the Hindu chart until many months or even a year later. Since the transit produces the same results in either chart, which one should the astrologer use? My observations, personally and professionally, lead me to conclude that a particular transit works in either of the charts and that the effects become greater when the transiting planet passes through the same house in both charts. For instance, in the example above, the person would begin to experience noticeable tenth house Saturnian effects in January, when Saturn entered the tenth house of the western chart. Then those same effects would increase or intensify later on, when Saturn makes its way to the Hindu chart tenth house.

These conclusions, the reader may note, are at variance with my findings on the effects of natal planets in houses that differ in a person's western or Hindu chart. As I have stated in previous texts, when a planet occupies a different house in one's western and Hindu birthchart, it is the Hindu planetary chart position that reveals objectively verifiable results and the western shows only psychological or behavioral effects. This is, I believe, how the famous Gauquelin research studies could have proved cadent planets (planets in the third, sixth, ninth, and twelfth houses) to be the strongest of all, in direct opposition to fundamental astrological teachings that have, over the ages, maintained that angular planets (planets in houses number one, four, seven, and ten) are the strongest, and cadent planets, the weakest. Many, or most, of the cadent planets Gauquelin studied would probably have been angular had he used the Hindu charts of the individuals involved.

When studying transits, I recommend that astrologers who use both Hindu and western astrology should base their predictions on the period when the transiting planet enters the first chart (whether Hindu or western) and then expect an increase of intensity when it enters the same house in the other chart.

Occasionally, house meanings in the Hindu system differ from the western meanings. Those differences are as follows: second house (ruled by 3rd house in western)—writing, education, poetry, teaching, speech, and counseling; second house (4th in western)—family life; third house (5th house in western) music, dance, and drama; fourth house (5th in western)—the heart; fifth house (4th in western)—the stomach; fifth house (3rd in western)—the mind; twelfth house (8th in western)—sexual pleasure.

Another important phenomenon for astrologers to know about transits is a peculiar but consistent effect that occurs just before a transiting planet leaves a birthchart house for the last time. For some reason, when a planet nears the final degree of a house cusp, it often gives powerful results relating to the fundamental nature of the transit. For example, when Saturn transits the second house, there may be money problems or financial restrictions for approximately two-and-a-half years, to which the person gradually becomes accustomed. Just before the planet leaves the house for the last time, however, the person's difficulties may suddenly intensify. It is almost as if the planet is an intelligent force making one last attempt to drive home the message it has been trying to teach for the entire period. Incidentally, the duration of this last thrust can be fairly long in the case of slow-moving planets. For example, a transit of Pluto through the sixth house may hover between the sixth and seventh house cusp for a year or more, at which time the person experiences powerful sixth house transiting Pluto effects. He or she may become more consumed by daily work than ever. Or the person may have sudden health problems that cause him to adopt a healing regimen or physical fitness program.

In the chapters of Jupiter and Saturn transiting the twelve houses, I have included brief descriptions of the effects these transits generate in the Hindu chart. Although Hindu transits work in essentially the same way as in western astrology, much additional information is revealed because transiting planets throw aspects onto other houses while in transit. In Hindu astrology, Jupiter always throws an aspect onto the fifth, seventh, and ninth houses FROM THE POSITION OF ITS TRANSITING HOUSE. Saturn always aspects the third, seventh, and tenth house FROM ITS TRANSITING HOUSE. (If this is confusing for newcomers, it will quickly become clear after reading a few Jupiter and Saturn transits through the houses.)

I have included these tidbits just to pique the reader's interest in Hindu astrology. While many will find some accuracy in the delineations, THEY MUST NOT BE USED PROFESSIONALLY UNLESS THE ASTROLOGER ALSO KNOWS THE HINDU CHART OF THE PERSON INVOLVED. This is important because, as mentioned above, a planet may transit a particular house of the western chart for many months before entering the same house of the Hindu chart. In such cases, all information revealed from the transiting aspects to additional houses will be erroneous until the Hindu transit catches up with the western transit.

Finally, astrologers may note that I have not analyzed transits to birthchart angles. This is because conjunctions to the angles will function in much the same way as my descriptions of planets transiting the angular houses (one, four, seven, and ten) but with more intensity and for a much shorter period of time. As for transiting squares, oppositions, trines, and sextiles to the angles, I simply do not pay much attention to them in my own work. I do acknowledge their influence, however, and am not suggesting that they are insignificant. They are simply beyond the scope of this work.

THREE MISUNDERSTOOD HOUSES

The transit descriptions in this book are fairly traditional, in keeping with fundamental meanings of the planets and houses. Some of my explanations vary in tone or intensity from standard texts, however, because I have given greater priority to certain significations which other texts ignore or neglect. These discrepancies are greatest in my treatment of the eighth, eleventh, and twelfth houses, and therefore an explanation is appropriate.

Birthchart houses always bear a resemblance to the signs they are naturally connected to (i.e. first house = Aries, second house = Taurus, third house = Gemini, etc.), but this connection varies from house to house. In my experience, the eighth house has a significant connection to the sign of Scorpio. As such, I have treated the eighth house as much more than merely the house of death, the partner's wealth, inheritances, and sex. The eighth house, like Scorpio, represents the mysteries of life, one's desire nature, and spiritual experiences or psychological transformation leading to liberation or enlightenment. In order to thoroughly understand the eighth house, one must grasp exactly what these transforming experiences are about. Before proceeding, I would like to mention that while my explanation of the eighth house may vary from certain standard texts, the information is neither new nor revolutionary. It is just that most written material on the subject has been so inadequate. I believe the reason this has occurred is because the eighth house is a spiritual house, and spiritual realities have held low priority and have been hardly understood in the West. I also believe that because the eighth house is the house of mysterious affairs, its meaning has remained a mystery.

The eighth house is diametrically opposed to the second house, both in the birthchart scheme and in meaning. The second house rules possessions, money, holdings, and material assets while the eighth house significations are antithetical to these—namely the soul, the spirit, and everything nonmaterial. As a person experiences a planet transiting his or her eighth house and tunes in to the nontangible, though very real, soul and spirit, he or she feels an increase of inner freedom and psychological liberation (psyche means "of the soul"), which is the most profound significance of the eighth house. People commonly **13** experience major personal transformations when transiting planets pass through the eighth house. This invariably happens through a process of suffering (specifically emotional death-and-rebirth experiences), which is caused by the person's attachment to unhealthy, unattainable, or otherwise inappropriate desires. Eventually, as the pain becomes more and more acute, the person realizes that the only solution is to relinquish his or her attachment to the particular desires and to surrender control in the matter. The person stops trying to get his or her way through manipulation and coercion and adopts an attitude of acceptance and openness. This produces inner freedom and reconnection to one's very essence that then often leads to striking intuitive, mystical, or spiritual experiences.

In the transit descriptions of the eighth house, I have also made many references to astrology, metaphysics, and occult subjects. Most modern western astrology texts do not mention a particular house as ruling astrology although one might assume the eleventh house to be significant because it corresponds to the sign Aquarius, which rules astrology. But in my experience, eighth house transits produce significantly more interest in astrology and occult subjects than eleventh house transits. (Interest in metaphysical subjects always occurs when the outer planets transit the third, ninth, and twelfth houses, but those houses are not intrinsically connected to occult knowledge.)

The reason for this is clear. Metaphysics is by nature mysterious or hidden (an eighth house signification), and it is a subject which deals directly with the soul or spirit in relationship with earthly living. During an eighth house transit, the person learns astrology, psychic subjects, and metaphysics in order to reunite with his or her soul, so he or she can let go of everything that is not the self and experience freedom from attachment. Bear in mind that the eighth house is the house of death, which even though it seems final, is actually an experience in which one temporarily disengages from the world and reunites with the soul and spirit. I say temporarily because astrology embraces the doctrine of reincarnation. If death were considered final in the astrological paradigm, it would be governed by the twelfth house—the last house in the birthchart. Instead, it is freedom from attachment that is the essence of the eighth house, and metaphysical subjects clearly support this purpose. It is also worth noting that in Hindu astrology the eighth house represents astrology, psychic ability, intuition, and occult or secret subjects.

My descriptions of planets transiting the eleventh house are also somewhat different from other texts, more in the significance of the house than in content. I believe the eleventh house is more meaningful than most western texts explain. To some degree, my feelings have arisen from experience with Hindu predictive astrology, but they are also the result of viewing the birthchart houses from a spiritual and holistic perspective.

What makes the eleventh house of the western system profoundly significant is its implied rulership of happiness. Unlike Hindu astrology, a very technical system which predicts happiness by the condition of Venus and the fourth house and which is the product of a spiritual culture that. considers happiness a completely independent function (that is, unrelated to things like success, possessions, benefits, etc.), in the western world happiness is directly connected to whether a person can fulfill his or her desires. Westerners live by a more worldly or material philosophy, where free will reigns supreme (note that in the western system the most important planet is the Sun—the planet of willpower—as opposed to Hindu astrology's dominant Moon), and therefore happiness depends almost entirely on one's ability to fulfill major desires, goals, and wishes. When a planet transits the eleventh house of the western chart, the person begins to deeply examine, and sometimes fulfill, his or her most important ambitions. The person suddenly pauses from activity to consider what will bring real happiness and contentment. This is an intimate and discriminative process, but it does not mean that before the eleventh house transit the person was pursuing a random or haphazard path. Now the person just sees matters from a different perspective. Previously, the person has been involved in all kinds of activities and now he or she discovers whether such activities bring happiness or not. And if they do not, the person going through an eleventh house transit wonders, then what will?

To grasp the significance of the eleventh house, it is necessary to understand the purpose of life. Nearly all religions and spiritual teachers proclaim that the purpose of creation is happiness. They all state, in one way or another, that God (or nature, or supreme being, or supreme intelligence) manifested material existence in order to enjoy itself (in other words, to create happiness). It is not at all accidental that eleventh house significations—major goals and wishes (and therefore happiness)—come before the twelfth and final house of the zodiac, which, as I describe below, is the house of enlightenment or final liberation. In order to fulfill God's infinite plan, a person must gain a degree of relative happiness or worldly fulfillment. This is the significance of the eleventh house. Having obtained this fulfillment, a person can then move on to the twelfth house matters of enlightenment or final liberation.

In dealing with twelfth house transits, traditional astrological texts speak mainly of effects on the subconscious mind, psychological growth through therapy, hidden fears and complexes, self-undoing, confinement or imprisonment, intuition, and escapist tendencies. As a house with spiritual overtones, occasionally meditation and mysticism are mentioned. In this book, I have treated the twelfth house as the representation of enlightenment (nirvana or higher consciousness) and final liberation, and I consider this the most important and essential meaning of the house. The twelfth house, being the last house in the birthchart scheme, reveals the ultimate experience and purpose of human existence. This final, spiritual purpose of life is a return to God, nature, or the eternal energy from which we were created. This return to our immortal and divine selves is what the word religion once meant: "re," meaning again, "ligio," meaning source. Although religion has come to mean ritual and devotion, its original meaning referred to an experience of returning again to the source. This kind of religious experience is the essence of the twelfth house and Pisces.

Different cultures call this ultimate spiritual reunion by different names. In India, the term is *moksha*, meaning final liberation, and it is clearly ruled by the twelfth house of the horoscope. In the West, it is called enlightenment and is generally understood to be what Christ called "the kingdom of heaven within." The West, however, has almost entirely ignored the spiritual realm in favor of science and materialism. Consequently, the twelfth house of the western birthchart has become so misunderstood as to warrant this disturbingly accurate statement in *Horoscope Symbols* by astrologer Robert Hand: "There are few traditional interpretations of the twelfth house that one could really look forward to experiencing."

During a twelfth house transit by a major planet, anything in a person's psyche and inner being that impedes his or her reunion with the source comes to the surface in order to be processed and purged. Although such experiences are almost never pleasurable, the resulting freedom is. In fact, final liberation is said to be a state of unending bliss —obviously something more rewarding than anything any other birthchart house has to offer!

I would also like to make a distinction between the liberating effects of twelfth house transits and those of the eighth house. During an eighth house transit, a person suffers from undue attachment to unhealthy or inappropriate desires and eventually relinquishes life-damaging behavior brought on by the need for control. This leads to freedom and, occasionally, to mystical experiences. During a twelfth house transit, a person is compelled to confront problems, unhealthy behavior, fruitless relationships, or any condition which holds him or her back from the source or

16   from a genuine experience of self. (Until one's consciousness and nervous system are ready for full enlightenment, a person can only enjoy a taste of liberation, and this is experienced as a harmonious state of well-being and naturalness.) During eighth house transits, the person gains freedom from attachment. During twelfth house transits, the person returns to the source of creation.

It would be wonderful if transits worked as expected all the time, every time. They do not. Although transits are perhaps the simplest and most reliable predictive indicators, their accuracy depends upon many factors. When analyzing transits it is crucial to consider the natal strengths of the planets involved, the signs and houses they occupy, and especially the natal relationships of the two planets involved in the transit. For instance, if Saturn and the Sun form an exact trine in the natal birthchart, then even the normally discordant transiting square of Saturn to the Sun will produce benefit. Likewise, if the Moon and Neptune form a tight square or opposition in the natal chart, then even the normally harmonious transiting trine of Neptune to the Moon will likely bring problems and suffering. Although the transiting aspect carries its own inherent harmonious or discordant dynamics, it must also stimulate the person's characteristic handling of the planetary energies involved.

In the Sun-Saturn example above, the Sun-Saturn trine in the natal chart reveals that the person is quite responsible, disciplined, efficient, and purposeful. How then can a transit of Saturn square or opposite the Sun suddenly bring difficulties associated with authority figures, duties, and responsibility? Unless natal birthchart factors are weighed and considered as thoroughly as possible, predictive accuracy of planets transiting planets will be very arbitrary. The influence of the natal chart cannot be overemphasized. As Stephen Arroyo says in his book, *Relationships and Life Cycles,* "That is why... *most* books on transits are almost worthless. Even the better books are only useful as rudimentary guidelines."

Even more important, transits are generally subordinate to larger birthchart factors, namely progressions (in western astrology) and dasas (pronounced dashas) and bhuktis (pronounced booktees) in Hindu astrology. For example, a person with transiting Pluto conjunct the Sun whose progressed horoscope reveals a square aspect of the same planets (Sun square Pluto) can expect to experience a dramatic episode or circumstance that will change his or her life forever. Not so for a person with transiting Pluto conjunct the Sun whose progressed chart is inactive.

In Hindu astrology, dasas and bhuktis give a broader picture of a person's life. Dasas and bhuktis are periods and subperiods during which a person's life is influenced by a particular planet. (In order not to assign causative power to planets, it is perhaps more appropriate to say that the person's life corresponds to the symbolic representations of the dasa or bhukti planet.) Dasas are based upon the exact degree of the natal Moon position and are somewhat like progressions, except that their effects are more obvious and long-lasting. Dasas give the overall picture of a person's life for many years. Hindu philosophy teaches that the normal span of human life is 120 years. (The reason humans do not live this long now is because we are living degraded, spiritually bankrupt lives filled with stress and strain, impure air, toxic foods, and so on.) Therefore the dasa scheme is comprised of nine dasas, one for each of the seven original heavenly bodies (Uranus, Neptune, and Pluto are not used) and Rahu and Ketu (the North Node and the South Node) totalling 120 years. One can be born at any point within any dasa period. For example, a person might be born with five months of a six-year Sun dasa left. After the Sun dasa, the dasas follow a prescribed order as follows: Moon, ten years; Mars, seven years; Rahu, eighteen years; Jupiter, sixteen years; Saturn, nineteen years; Mercury, seventeen years; Ketu, seven years; Venus, twenty years.

Each dasa is then broken down into subperiods of the same nine planets. For example, Jupiter dasa begins with Jupiter dasa Jupiter bhukti for two years, one month, and eighteen days. Then comes Jupiter dasa, Saturn bhukti for two years, six months, and twelve days. Then Jupiter-Mercury, then Jupiter-Ketu, and so on. Effects of bhuktis are subordinate to the effects of the dasa, which is more powerful and pervasive in its influence. For example, during a Mercury dasa a person can expect a happy and successful seventeen-year period for educational affairs, communications, and all intellectual matters if Mercury is natally well-placed and well-aspected (or at least unafflicted). Also, the seventeen years of the dasa will be good for the significations of the houses that Mercury rules. For instance, if the person has a Sagittarius ascendant, then Mercury, which rules Gemini and Virgo, governs the person's seventh and tenth houses—marriage and career. This means that the person's marriage and career flourish during the whole dasa. However, if the person comes to a bhukti (subperiod) of an afflicted planet, then there will be troubles in the areas of life ruled by that particular planet. But the person's difficulties will only last throughout the few months or few years of the bhukti and will not, generally, overshadow the benefits of the dasa. More on how dasas and bhuktis work is explained later.

Because dasas and bhuktis are both broader in scope and more pervasive in their effects than transits, transits are easier to evaluate in light of a person's dasa and bhukti. The intensity of a particular transit, as well as its positivity or negativity, is more obvious if one knows the operating dasa-bhukti at the time. For example, in the two years of Richard Nixon's downfall, between late 1972 and late 1974, the most difficult transits occurring were Saturn conjunct Pluto, Uranus square the Sun, and Saturn opposite Mars. A transit of Saturn through the tenth house also occurred, but this is not inherently difficult. From the transits, no one would have predicted that his life and career would suddenly deteriorate so intensely. From the dasa, however, anyone could see monumental problems on the horizon. In Nixon's natal Hindu chart, his most afflicted planet is Mercury, which is less than one degree away from malefic Mars. In Hindu astrology, if two planets are within one degree of each other they fight a "planetary war," and the planet in the later degree loses and becomes completely powerless. Such is the case of Nixon's Mercury. Nixon entered the Mercury dasa in November 1970. The first period, Mercury dasa, Mercury bhukti, lasted until April 1973 when the president's problems were under way. Because Mercury dasa lasts seventeen years and had only just begun, the possibility of his problems being alleviated was minimal.

An even better example of how transits are secondary to dasas and bhuktis occurred in my horoscope during the writing of this book, somewhere around the middle section. Transiting Jupiter made a conjunction to natal Venus in the fourth house of my chart. Venus signifies love and the fourth house governs home and mother. Venus in my chart is afflicted natally, but is not in a particularly negative relationship with natal Jupiter. Transiting Jupiter conjunct natal Venus is one of the most harmonious transits of all. Naturally then, by analyzing the transit alone I would expect positive, or at least satisfactory, effects in the areas of love, home, and mother. Unfortunately, however, my current dasa-bhukti was Rahu-Venus, and Venus is the most afflicted planet in my Hindu chart—being two degrees away from malefic Mars and only one degree away from an exact opposition with malefic Rahu. (In Hindu astrology, planets are considered essentially benefic or malefic in the aspects they make with other planets.) Because of the dasa-bhukti, I would have problems with all matters relating to Venus and the fourth house. During the six or seven days that transiting Jupiter formed its conjunction with natal Venus, I was turned down for a home mortgage and experienced more severe problems with my mother than I had in years. On top of that, I experienced major disruptions in my love relationship. Dasas and bhuktis always take precedence over transits. Transits, very often, are simply timing indicators for predictable effects of dasas and bhuktis.

The second half of this book, "Dasas of the East" is about Hindu dasas and bhuktis. I have included the section for two reasons. The first is to introduce Westerners to this new, profound material. I say "introduce" because it is impossible to master dasas and bhuktis without having a thorough grasp of natal Hindu birthchart analysis. The second is to provide more information for those astrologers studying Hindu astrology. It has been eight years since the publication of my text, *Ancient Hindu Astrology for the Modern Western Astrologer,* and I am now taking the opportunity of sharing more knowledge. Those who are unfamiliar with Hindu astrology should read the dasa section in this book in a light, easy way to become familiar with what Hindu astrology has to offer. If this whets the appetite, you may want to go on to the three or four easily understandable books written by Westerners now available on the subject. (See the service chapter in the final page of this book to order my text, *Ancient Hindu Astrology for the Modern Western Astrologer.*)

One final note. Indian astrology is known by three names. Vedic astrology, Hindu astrology, or *Jyotish. Jyotish* is the Sanskrit name and it means "the science of light." The term Vedic astrology refers to the astrology as taught through the Vedas, the Indian body of knowledge which predates religion and is said to have been cognized by sages or enlightened beings. Hindu astrology simply means Indian astrology as practiced by the majority of Indians—the Hindus. I prefer the term Hindu over Vedic because I believe that too much of original Vedic astrology has been both lost or mixed with western concepts. Several terms used in Indian astrology are of Greek origin, which strongly implies that the purity of Vedic astrology was damaged by invading cultures. The term "Indian astrology" would be perfect for western use if it were not for confusion with American Indians.

♃

When Jupiter transits the first house, the person feels optimistic, cheerful, and content. He is lucky for approximately one year and may receive tributes, promotions, gifts, and courtesies. Others now behave kindly to the person, and his relationships are pleasant and fruitful. Desires meet with little resistance, and the person succeeds easily and abundantly. It is an excellent time to approach powerful or influential individuals. If the person has been seeking a pay raise or advancement at work, he may now attain his goal. Opportunities continually arise and the individual should take advantage of them.

For approximately one year, the person is fortunate, protected, and blessed. His faith in God is strong and he enjoys a special sense of appreciation. His religious, spiritual, and devotional tendencies increase. He is favored by gurus, mentors, or teachers of philosophy and higher knowledge. He gains any knowledge, education, and wisdom he seeks. It is a good time for self-improvement and all kinds of growth. If the person deals with the public in any way, he may now become better known or even famous. His confidence, buoyancy, and enthusiasm are infectious. People are attracted to his happy spirit, and his leadership ability is increased. In competition, the person wins against peers and associates.

Individuals who are particularly jovial or Jupitarian to begin with gain tremendous abundance and fortune now. However, such individuals must be careful not to indulge in excessive pleasure, diversions, or hedonistic activities. They must beware of conceit, egotism, or becoming carried away with their own infallibility. The person may gain weight when Jupiter transits the first house. In his exuding optimism, he expands his activities as well as his sphere of influence. He begins many new endeavors that have an excellent chance of success. There may be interest in travel, law, and philosophy. The person enjoys his friendships, as he is now the focus of everyone's attention and goodwill. There is more joy, contentment, fun, and serenity in his life. He feels secure and gains in honor and prestige. Investments and speculations produce good results, and the person benefits from whatever risks he takes.

In Hindu predictive astrology, when Jupiter transits the first house, it simultaneously aspects the fifth, seventh, and ninth houses. The aspect to the fifth means the person experiences great creativity and mental harmony. Relationships with children are favored, and conception of a child is possible. Jupiter's seventh house aspect indicates the possibility of marriage or an important new love relationship. The aspect to the ninth house signifies travel, auspicious religious experiences, attainment of higher knowledge, and good luck.

When Jupiter transits the second house, the person experiences a joyful sense of abundance and worthiness. As a result he attracts significant financial gains and material possessions; he discovers resources wherever they are to be found. It is a happy period in which the person feels he is getting tangible benefits as a result of his own virtue. If the person is not materially oriented, then instead of acquiring money, he creates rewards that are appropriate to his value system. During the previous Jupiter transit (of the first house), the person received praise, accolades, favoritism, and luck in general because the time had come for him to appreciate his own particular form of divinity. In this transit the person gets to experience the blessings that the physical universe has to offer, in their most basic form. The person feels secure, protected, and cared for. He is not plagued by feelings of scarcity or doubt. He feels good about himself and expects to receive his due. All money matters are favored, and the person profits from business dealings, speculations, and occupational investments. He may receive pay raises, pensions, stipends, or other monetary benefits.

In Hindu predictive astrology, the second house governs family life, education, knowledge, and writing, in addition to wealth. Therefore, the person now enjoys happy domestic life and expands his education. He may begin new studies or return to school. Or he may decide to give out knowledge through teaching or writing. It is an excellent time for those in literary or intellectual professions. As Jupiter transits the second house, it simultaneously aspects the sixth, eighth, and tenth houses. The favorable aspects to the sixth and tenth houses mean the person succeeds easily in his work and career. The aspect to the eighth house brings wealth through partnerships and joint finances. The person may borrow money with little restrictions or difficulties.

$$\text{♃}$$

When Jupiter transits the third house, the person's mental faculties and cognitive abilities sharpen. Knowledge grows and the person is able to absorb and assimilate new information easily. It is an excellent time for studies, training programs, and examinations. The person feels mentally receptive, optimistic, and enthusiastic. He becomes interested in many different subjects. He may become fascinated with books or any sort of literature, and he may write articles or engage in publishing endeavors. He communicates well and enjoys writing letters, diaries, and journals. If the person is a teacher or writer, or pursues an intellectual profession, he flourishes in his undertakings at this time. He is open-minded now, and he is mentally bright and cheery.

The person is very energetic and active within his immediate surroundings, and relationships with his siblings and relatives are favored. The person may enjoy the company of his brothers and sisters, or receive benefits, blessings, and advantages from them. He is constantly making short journeys within his neighborhood. He interacts more with friends, neighbors, and relatives than usual and enjoys variety and "spice of life" for approximately one year.

In Hindu predictive astrology, the third house is unrelated to the mind (which is represented by the fifth house). The third house is said to govern courage, adventures, energy, and the fulfillment of daily desires, as well as publications (but not writing or teaching) and siblings (except for the eldest, which is an eleventh house matter). Thus, the person now fulfills his daily desires with ease. He is able to run errands all day long without getting tired or meeting with frustrations and delays. He accomplishes his objectives, meets his goals, and still has energy left over. It is a time of incessant activity wherein the person pursues his interests and promotes his endeavors powerfully and effectively. He enjoys many adventures.

The third house also rules the fine arts (music, dance, singing, and drama) in Hindu astrology. Thus, the person attends more plays, operas, movies, or musical events at this time and derives great pleasure from them. If he is involved in dramatic arts by profession or as an amateur, then this transit may be a time of profound creativity and success.

However, painting, drawing, and crafts are not affected now because they are governed by the fifth house.

As Jupiter transits the third house, it simultaneously aspects the seventh, ninth, and eleventh houses. The aspect to the seventh house means the possibility of marriage or a significant new love relationship. The ninth house aspect signifies good luck, long-distance travel, and favorable experiences with religious teachers or institutions of higher learning. Jupiter's glance on the eleventh house means positive group activity and good rapport with friends. It also indicates benefits from the eldest sibling and financial gains from "side ventures" other than one's daily means of support.

When Jupiter transits the fourth house, domestic life is favored. The person finally locates surroundings perfectly suited to his needs and temperament and feels a sense of balance and stability. He is likely to move to a new apartment, house, or city. Nature supports his endeavors and the person may find exactly what he wants at a price he can afford. Even if the person does not intend to live on the land he acquires, he will gain from real estate investments. The person may refurnish his residence, or make other renovations and home improvements. He now obtains great pleasure from landscaping, gardening, farming, or any hobby involving the earth. He may also feel strong emotional attachments to his material belongings.

The person becomes interested in long-term security and with ensuring the well-being of his family. He feels safer and more protected than ever in his habitat and optimistically begins to build a base for the future, from a position of abundance. He may concentrate on collectibles, possessions, property, or any fixed assets which help provide future security on earth. The person feels strong and satisfied. He enjoys seclusion and solitude more than before, and has little need to venture far from his abode for status, recognition, and public purposes. He feels strong and enjoys inner peace. He has a sense of belonging and is happy and secure within his familial traditions. He enjoys wonderful social gatherings in his home and may use his residence for spiritual or philosophical purposes. He may engage in traditional religious rituals and services at home or experience his dwelling place to be a spiritual haven.

The person gains happiness and benefits from his family. He gets along well with his mother and profits from his association with her. It should be noted, however, that in certain cases the relationship with the mother may actually appear to worsen rather than improve. In rare instances where the person has tolerated an abusive relationship with a cruel or dysfunctional mother in the past, he may decide to break off relations altogether. This occurs because the person now feels such optimism about a pleasurable and healthy relationship that he can no longer endure what he knows he does not deserve. Similar seemingly negative effects involving the spouse and father may occur when Jupiter transits the seventh and tenth houses, respectively. And, to some extent, the same is possible with friends and siblings when Jupiter transits the eleventh and third houses. As the fourth house represents endings, the person feels satisfied about things that come to their natural conclusion.

In Hindu predictive astrology, the fourth house represents happiness, the heart (rather than the stomach), conveyances (cars, boats, planes, etc.), educational degrees, and comforts (jewelry, toys, accessories, stereos, etc.), as well as land and homes. Therefore, during Jupiter's fourth house transit the person is happy and content, and he is successful in obtaining cars, homes, ornaments, educational degrees, and the "toys" of the current society. When Jupiter transits the fourth, it simultaneously aspects the eighth, tenth, and twelfth houses. The aspects to the eighth and twelfth houses bring interest in astrology, metaphysical studies, and spiritual growth. The eighth house aspect also signifies good results with wills, legacies, joint finances, and money from "unearned" means (lotteries, insurance benefits, etc.). The twelfth house aspect gives the possibility of travel to remote foreign countries for spiritual purposes, along with beneficial experiences in such lands. Jupiter's glance on the tenth house means career success and expansion of one's influence in the professional sphere.

When Jupiter transits the fifth house, artistic endeavors are favored. The person is creative, imaginative, original in his behavior, and self-expressive. If the person is an artist by profession, he is likely to experience one of his most significant and prolific years. The person welcomes pleasure, joy, and fun into his life as never before. In his soul and spirit he feels free of the usual constraints of responsibility, discipline, and obligation. He attends many parties, celebrations, and festive affairs. He enjoys romance for the sheer infatuation, excitement, and passion of it and may create a love affair of pure merriment. He may visit nightclubs, dance halls, bars, or other means of entertainment on a frequent basis. He also gains great pleasure from sports or competitive activities.

All activities involving children are favored, including a strong possibility of pregnancy or childbirth. This transit is very gratifying and fortunate for teachers and parents. The person enjoys a year of happiness, popularity, and individual purpose. He is optimistic about taking risks, and is confident that all will be well no matter what the outcome. He feels powerful in his individuality and strong in his ego. He functions from a position of abundance, and, as a result, his social interactions are extremely successful. He feels a healthy sense of self-love, dignity, and deservedness. His will power is very strong now, and he may feel comfortable about the possibility of leadership, fame, or recognition. Speculations are favored, and the person does well in gambling, stocks, or investment undertakings.

In certain cases, where Jupiter is afflicted or overly powerful in the natal chart, the person must beware of engaging in excessive pleasures, too much partying, or other hedonistic recreation. Individuals who habitually abuse alcohol or drugs must be especially vigilant.

In Hindu predictive astrology, the fifth house rules kingship, the mind, mantras, and "poorvapunya" (past-life credit), as well as the significations already described above. Therefore, the person is mentally happy and spirited. He may take an interest in mantras, hypnotism, or other spiritual techniques. He will sense the destiny and purpose of his existence and realize what he deserves, for better or for worse. When

Jupiter transits the fifth house, it simultaneously aspects the ninth, eleventh, and first houses. The aspects to the first and ninth houses indicate very good luck and favoritism. There will also be general good health and well-being, as well as ninth house benefits of travel, higher knowledge, and blessings from spiritual teachers. The favorable aspect to the eleventh house means good results with groups, friends, and the eldest sibling. The person has an easy time fulfilling major goals and desires, and opportunities are consistent and abundant.

$\gimel$

When Jupiter transits the sixth house, the person thrives on work, self-improvement, and self-healing. It is a time for personal growth and development of one's particular methods, practices, and routines. The person succeeds in his daily job, and his work meets with little resistance or criticism. He enjoys even menial tasks or detail-oriented assignments; technicalities and normally tedious jobs don't bother him. His projects and endeavors are stress-free. The person gets along well with co-workers, bosses, and employees. He feels enthusiastic about his job, and his working conditions may improve at this time. The person's efficiency and precision grow stronger and he may now become more specialized in his work. If the person decides to seek new employment, he is likely to succeed in his quest.

The person is capable of strengthening his body and healing deficiencies or health problems. He can obtain good medical care easily. It is an excellent time to begin a new diet or fitness regimen. However, traditional astrological texts report a strong possibility of gaining weight during this transit. Therefore, the person should be careful not to let overconfidence about his health lead to overindulgence in sweets or other cravings.

The person reflects upon his routine and on the mundane details of his life. He may decide to purchase a new wardrobe. If the person is motivated toward service projects, he may offer his time. It is also an excellent time for personal development in any area of the person's choice.

In Hindu predictive astrology, the sixth house rules enemies and competitors, as well as the significations mentioned above. Therefore, when benefic Jupiter transits the house, the person is not bothered by rivals, opponents, or jealous people. Neither is he likely to be accused in court cases. As Jupiter transits the sixth, it simultaneously aspects the tenth, twelfth, and second houses. The favorable aspects to the tenth and second make this a good year for wealth and career expansion. The person also benefits from education, knowledge, or any literary undertakings. And he succeeds in doing good deeds for society at this time. Jupiter's glance to the twelfth house means the person is not plagued by unexpected debts and expenses. Growth is plentiful, and he makes very good progress on the spiritual path. Travel to remote foreign countries for spiritual purposes may occur at this time.

$\gimel$

When Jupiter transits the seventh house, the person has opportunities for fruitful partnerships and love relationships. His happiness comes from sharing life with another person. He attracts persons of the opposite sex, and learns much about himself in the process. He may be attracted to special, wealthy, famous, or spiritual persons. Or he may become interested in someone from a foreign country or of a different philosophy or background. It is a time of optimism, enthusiasm, and expansion of one's social boundaries. Relationships begun at this time generally produce happiness and good fortune. However, it should be noted that for many people this transit coincides with divorce or the ending of a relationship. If the person has been enduring an abusive or life-damaging relationship with no improvement in sight, then he now realizes he deserves better and begins to see ample opportunities to have his needs met properly. Some individuals involved in difficult partnerships of course find that their situations improve at this time, but many do not.

The person is favored by others. At the very beginning of this transit, when Jupiter exactly conjuncts the descendant and opposes the ascendant, the person may establish an important spiritual relationship with a teacher, mentor, guide, or guru. His consciousness may be raised or expanded as a result. The person may obtain support from wealthy benefactors or philanthropists. In any event, there is significant fortune, opportunity, and luck in one-on-one associations with others. Regarding love opportunities, the person is now captivated by someone whose honesty, integrity, and principled character he can respect and honor. During this transit, the person has a sense of fairness in relationships. He sees his mate's point of view, and takes such feelings into account. He is not obstructed by ego issues, and, through observing his partner he learns new ways of responding to life.

The person is diplomatic, and he experiences peace and harmony, and a powerful sense of appreciation. Love comes quite naturally to him now. He is sociable, generous, affectionate, and capable of intimacy. In Hindu predictive astrology, when Jupiter transits the seventh house, it simultaneously aspects the eleventh, first, and third houses. The third, seventh, and eleventh houses are considered "desire" houses (because they correspond to the air signs—Gemini, Libra, and Aquarius). Thus, the person effortlessly fulfills his daily desires and major goals. He has tremendous energy for daily errands and minor tasks throughout this transit. Relationships with siblings, both younger and older, are favored, as are friendships and group activities. Jupiter's glance to the first house means promotions, advancement, good luck, fortune, and a measure of spiritual development. In the Hindu system, the seventh house represents passions, and therefore the person can expect strong sexual desires and cravings, which he now fulfills effortlessly.

When Jupiter transits the eighth house, the person experiences a degree of unity and oneness with the world around him. This is a spiritual transit during which the person feels connected to people and absorbed in his experience without feeling undue attachment to either. He is liberated, for approximately one year, from his usual identification with his desires. That is, his happiness and stability do not depend on the success or failure of anything external. The result is a sense of genuine freedom. The person is freed from undue sensitivity and the need to control experience in order to avoid pain or suffering. He feels emotionally resourceful and resilient, open to others, and unafraid to be vulnerable. And he maintains his power and dignity while merging his identity and individuality with others, especially loved ones.

The person's values change from personal to universal, from possessing to sharing. As the person surrenders his own individual needs and wants in favor of a value system that provides for all, he is rewarded by the possibility of financial gains from wills, legacies, and money from "unearned means." The person is favored in all matters of joint finances. He may succeed in obtaining loans or grants, and it is a good time to negotiate alimony payments or pensions. The person makes money through his partners, insurance companies, lotteries, and inheritances. Since the eighth house relates to sex in Western astrology, the person is likely to have positive sexual experiences during this transit. He is not plagued by scarcity in the sexual realm, and he is able to appreciate the beauty, joy, and holiness of sexual pleasure. He may feel his consciousness expand and experience the most wonderful merging with his lover through the surrender of orgasm.

Occult and spiritual endeavors are quite favored at this time. The person may visit psychics, astrologers, or anyone who can help him uncover secret, hidden knowledge. Or the person may conduct his own research into metaphysical subjects. Because the person is free from his usual attachments, fears, desires, and complexes, he is able to delve deeply into issues which he might normally feel sensitive about. Therefore, it is an excellent time for healing or transforming afflicted features of the personality. The person may now see death as a natural experience and confront his mortality with a sense of hopefulness. He may consider the reality of astral travel, reincarnation, or immortality. Intuition is strong now, and the person feels peaceful and serene about such talents.

In Hindu predictive astrology, when Jupiter transits the eighth house, it simultaneously aspects the twelfth, second, and fourth houses. The aspect to the twelfth house means a year of growth, spiritual development, bargains, sexual enjoyment, and the possibility of travel to remote foreign countries for spiritual purposes. The aspect to the second house indicates good luck in earning wealth and favorable educational experiences. The fourth house glance signifies that the person may move or obtain a new home or new car. He benefits from his mother, and their relationship brings happiness at this time.

When Jupiter transits the ninth house, the person expands his boundaries, both literally and philosophically. He explores new religions, ideologies, and paradigms, which broaden his awareness. He learns as much as possible about foreign affairs and previously unfamiliar ways of living. He travels to other cities or countries, where he is successful and productive in his endeavors.

The person may now engage in consciousness expanding techniques, New Age seminars, or other self-development programs. It is a time of idealism and mental optimism. The person learns about the purpose of existence and the truths of life. He perceives life in a macroscopic way and enthusiastically contemplates his faith in God. He does well in writing or publishing. It is an excellent time to write a book or any important literary endeavor. Activities with teachers, mentors, and religious figures are very favored. Individuals pursuing a spiritual path may enjoy a period of great jubilation, joy, and bliss with their guru. Spiritual growth is enhanced, as life experience is now augmented by higher knowledge. The effect is integrating, and powerfully enriches the person's sense of judgement, wisdom, and discernment. Because he sees the whole picture, he is better able to measure priorities, fathom consequences, and draw appropriate conclusions. He now understands how to balance his intuitive faculties with his logical and reasoning powers. There is an understanding between heart and mind.

The person may do well in business dealings involving import-export. He may also do well with foreigners. He feels inspired and should take his ideals and visions seriously. He may now be somewhat prophetic in perceiving the future. He reflects on morals, ethics, and principles, and may involve himself in noble causes. He may enthusiastically promote freedom or a particular religion. He benefits from, and greatly enjoys, religious ceremonies and rituals.

In Hindu predictive astrology, the ninth house represents luck (as well as the significations described above), and is considered the best house of the birthchart. Therefore, the person experiences good fortune, happiness, and blessings during this period. He is favored by his spiritual preceptors and is protected from harm. In South India, the ninth house is taken to represent the father (because the father also functions as a spiritual teacher). Therefore, activities involving the father are favored, and the person gains benefits from him. When Jupiter transits the ninth house, it simultaneously aspects the first, third, and fifth houses. The aspect to the first house means good health, promotions, favoritism, and general happiness. The third house aspect indicates the ability to fulfill daily desires. Associations with all siblings except the eldest bring benefits. Jupiter's fifth house glance signifies pregnancy or childbirth, favorable experiences with children, successful investments, and mental exuberance.

When Jupiter transits the tenth house, the person gains in status, reputation, and fame. He becomes known for what he does or who he is. It is an excellent time for career advancement, promotions, and expansion of professional activities. The person receives publicity without asking, and he should take full advantage of the opportunity to broaden his sphere of influence. He may win awards or gain major recognition. His actions meet with little resistance, and he has the respect and support of peers and the public. He is definitely favored by authority figures and government officials.

New ventures or careers flourish at this time, but the greatest rewards come to those who have been working towards realization of specific career achievements. The person feels confident, a clear sense of purpose, and a positive attitude toward success. He is in touch with his life calling. Accomplishments made during this time are important and of lasting value. To the extent that the person identifies with his career or role in society, he now feels his life validated. Knowing that he makes a tangible difference in the world around him uplifts both his spirit and psyche. There is an element of self-actualization brought about as the person sees a measure of his individual purpose come to undeniable fruition.

The relationship with the father brings joy and happiness, and the person has a deep sense of appreciation and gratitude for his father's love. Their bond is strengthened and the person may receive benefits, gifts, or profits from the father.

In extremely rare cases, it is actually possible for the relationship to deteriorate. This may occur if the father is dysfunctional to the point of abusiveness. Because the person now feels hopeful, optimistic, and deserving of happiness from his father, he decides he is no longer willing to tolerate mistreatment. He may therefore sever or significantly detach himself from the relationship. Such cases, however, are unique and scarce and certainly not to be expected.

In Hindu predictive astrology, when Jupiter transits the tenth house it simultaneously aspects the second, fourth, and sixth houses. The aspects to the second and sixth houses make this an excellent time for financial benefits, good working conditions, and success in all practical matters and worldly affairs. Health is strong, and the person is not bothered by enemies and competitors. Education is favored and family life prospers. The fourth house aspect means the person is happy and content, and he benefits from his mother as their relationship flourishes. (Unlike western astrology, the fourth house always rules the mother and both the ninth and tenth houses always represents the father.) Educational degrees are forthcoming. The person may obtain land, homes, and cars or other conveyances (elephants, boats, planes, etc.). He also acquires jewelry, comforts, stereos, and the current "toys" of the culture. The combined effect of Jupiter's influence on the tenth and fourth houses indicates religious or spiritual pilgrimages.

When Jupiter transits the eleventh house, the person realizes the fulfillment of important goals and ambitions. Whereas Jupiter's transit of the previous house bestowed status and recognition from the outside, the person now understands the significance of achieving, or having just previously achieved, long-held fundamental desires and aspirations. He feels deeply satisfied by his successes. If the person has remained true to his ideals over the years, then he now feels profoundly rewarded. He finally accomplishes the goals which touch him the deepest—the goals which bring him most happiness.

Opportunities for prosperity and new endeavors abound. The person gets to concentrate on as many different interests and ambitions as he desires. He has good perspective and knows exactly what will bring him happiness and what will not. Friendships are more favored than ever. The person appreciates his friends, and he enjoys an excellent social life. He makes new acquaintances and has continuous opportunities to expand his connections and his day-to-day company. He may associate with religious, spiritual, or foreign friends. Or he may receive gifts, presents, or donations from friends. He will benefit and derive pleasure from all types of group activity at this time. The person has a sense of belonging, and he functions well in organizations, associations, fraternities, and the community at large. He may especially enjoy participation in spiritual or philosophical groups.

Although he is enjoying the fulfillment of personal goals during this transit, the person can also help society now. His detached intellect and idealism combine to produce a realistic humanitarian vision. He understands what is needed and is sensitive to how society works. And he has the skill to instigate reforms that will stick.

In Hindu predictive astrology, the eleventh house governs gains and profits from side ventures, as well as the significations described above. Therefore, the person may prosper during this transit. He also benefits from his eldest sibling, another feature of the eleventh house in the Hindu system. When Jupiter transits the eleventh house, it simultaneously aspects the third, fifth, and seventh houses. The aspects to the third and seventh houses mean the person has non stop energy to accomplish daily tasks and errands. There is opportunity for marriage or a significant love relationship. (The likelihood is strongest, of course, if Saturn does not simultaneously aspect the seventh house.) Finally, he fulfills all desires, small and large. Jupiter's glance to the fifth house means possible pregnancy or childbirth, and favorable relationships with children. The person may also receive gifts or benefits from his children. Investments and speculations now bring rewards, and the person is of a happy, exuberant mind. He is creative, imaginative, and original.

When Jupiter transits the twelfth house, the person relinquishes his petty concerns in favor of higher consciousness and spiritual integration. Now that Jupiter has passed through the eleventh house and the person's most intimate desires and ambitions have been fulfilled, he assimilates all the good that has occurred and feels a sense of completeness. The person feels spiritually and psychologically whole. The grip of his emotional and mental boundaries begins to loosen, and he is less affected by his usual fears, complexes, and attachments. It is a time of self-healing, and the person confronts phobias and neuroses that have intimidated him in the past. He gains insights into problems stemming from childhood or even from previous lifetimes. He now has faith in the higher forces of nature and believes that his needs will be met in due course, so he does not fret. He is at peace and approaches life with a feeling of abundance.

The person has a better understanding of the purpose of life. He understands the evolutionary process and he knows he is here to purify his soul and perfect his being. He is less concerned with acquiring and winning, and more concerned with spiritual growth. It is an excellent time for religious happiness and the study of God or other concepts of infinity. Meditation, introspection, and the quest for spiritual liberation are powerfully favored. The person may wish to retreat to a monastery or ashram. If he does so, he can expect happy and fruitful results. The person feels selfless, charitable, and magnanimous. He may volunteer for hospital work or other goodwill activities. He may even travel to developing countries to help the needy.

The person feels intrinsically connected to the universe and is relieved of his sense of separateness. He also becomes cognizant of his subconscious mind. Because he is in touch with nature and his own instincts, the person is protected from serious harm. (Certain astrological texts declare that the person prevails over his enemies.) He may uncover secrets and mysteries within his psyche, and have deep spiritual experiences for approximately one year. His intuition is strong, and the person is able to comprehend the meaning and symbolism of his dreams. Occult endeavors bring happiness, and the person may perceive spiritual dimensions beyond his normal awareness. He also feels especially inspired by art and music.

In Hindu predictive astrology, Jupiter's transit through the twelfth house means that the person makes great progress on the path to enlightenment. He also may visit remote foreign countries for spiritual purposes. He gets bargains and incurs no unexpected debts nor expenses. Finally, he enjoys sexual pleasures and sleeps on luxurious beds. When Jupiter transits the twelfth, it simultaneously aspects the fourth, sixth, and eighth houses. The aspect to the fourth means the possibility of obtaining land or moving to a new home or apartment. It also indicates benefits and luck with the mother. Educational degrees are favored, and the person may get jewelry, ornaments, and other comforts. He may get a new car, plane, or boat. The aspect to the sixth house means the person is not bothered by enemies or competitors, and his health is good. He enjoys his daily work and gets along well with his bosses and co-workers. Jupiter's glance to the eighth house symbolizes money from partners, wills, legacies, and other unearned means. The person visits astrologers, palm readers, and psychics. Or, he may engage in his own astrological or occult studies.

When Saturn transits the first house, the person is drawn inward to work on his personality, character, and internal makeup. He tries to perfect his most essential way of being, and roots out character flaws, shortcomings, and weaknesses. This is an excellent time for introspection, contemplation, and honest self-evaluation. However, it is a tedious and difficult period for worldly matters; no matter how much energy the person expends towards outer accomplishments, he experiences little support of nature. Indeed, the opposite is the case. The person is unlikely to receive awards, promotions, or significant advancement. He must proceed with caution, prudence, and discretion. Because his actions so readily meet with resistance and opposition now, the person is continually thrown back onto himself to examine his motives and reflect upon individuality. He should not look for significant achievement other than the behavioral and psychological gains he makes.

Although Saturn's transit of the first house is a very poor (actually absurd) time to launch new ventures, it is one of the finest periods for the person to learn about his ultimate objectives and desires. Therefore, he does very well in restructuring his existence and modifying the direction of his life. However, he is well-advised to be patient about results and should not expect his current actions to bear too much fruit for some years. Throughout this transit, the person feels pressured to come to terms with his identity and to do the right thing regarding his life. In other words, he is compelled to act in accord with his individual purpose and calling. And while he may feel frightened or overwhelmed, the person is now in the proper frame of mind to accept full responsibility for his destiny. Despite the unyielding tension and pressure the person feels during this transit, he has an unusually objective perspective and is free to rethink, rechoose, and reembrace the life he chose in this incarnation. The task may not be painless, but the opportunity is profound.

This period favors all efforts at personal discipline and psychological integration. The person may succeed in transforming his personality, correcting bad habits, and beginning new practices and customs. His body may demand attention, and it is an excellent time to start exercise programs, fitness regimens, necessary diets, and so on. The person makes serious advances in psychological work, counseling, or therapeutic techniques. He may feel that his growth is slow, tedious, and perhaps even imperceptible. However, the changes now occurring are genuine, lasting, and meaningful. The power of one's consciousness directed on the self cannot help but bring about maturity and self-knowledge. By the time this transit is over, the person is older, wiser, and more objective about himself. He relinquishes long-held illusions, fantasies, and deceptions about his identity and personality.

Health-wise, the person may feel tired, lifeless, and lacking in vitality. He should get plenty of rest, exercise, and fresh air, and maintain a healthy lifestyle. If he indulges in poor living habits during this period, he will certainly pay a price. The person should avoid overworking and excessively stressful situations. It is a good time to take calcium for the teeth and bones. The person may be criticized or reprimanded about his appearance and should now consider exactly what image he wishes to project to the world. For those who are overweight, it is an easy time to thin out. Because he feels serious and somber during this transit, the person should include plenty of recreation and entertainment in his life.

In Hindu predictive astrology, Saturn's transit of the first house means the person receives no favors from others and may suffer from lack of confidence. It is a time of little luck, abundance, or fortune. As Saturn transits the first house, it simultaneously aspects the third, seventh, and tenth houses. The tenth house aspect combined with the first house influence strongly indicates little chance of advancement in worldly matters. The aspect to the third house signifies restriction in fulfilling daily desires, difficulties with siblings, and low vitality. Saturn's glance on the seventh house means restricted opportunities for new love relationships and obstacles or strife in married life. During these approximately two-and-a-half years, the head is susceptible to injury or affliction.

ħ

When Saturn transits the second house, the person concentrates on wealth, possessions, and self-worth. After Saturn finishes its passage through the first house, and the person has defined exactly who he is, he now moves on to examine what he is worth, and what, of all the world's assets, he deserves to own. Though the intense personal pressure of the last two-and-a-half years subsides, this period also brings a good deal of self-analysis and self-examination. The main difference is that while self-worth and deservedness are sensitive and intimate issues, the person is now more outwardly directed. He is consumed with financial pressures and requirements. He focuses mainly on making money, meeting expenses, and, if he is lucky, collecting his share of material benefits. Therefore, this transit is experienced as a very practical time. The person finds himself engaged in a quest for financial security.

The person should be made aware that there is a deeper significance to his pursuit of wealth. Though he appears simply to be responding to circumstances, he is, in fact, being driven to confront confidence issues. The connection between his self-worth and the wealth he is able to create becomes obvious now. Income is very likely to be restricted, and the resultant financial pressure causes the person to look deeply into his feelings and beliefs about himself. When he cannot meet expenses, he questions his fitness and worth. This transit makes the person take responsibility for creating a healthy sense of self-worth. Certain individuals make more money than ever before during this period as a result of a true self-confidence and diligent, effective efforts to gain wealth during several previous years.

For those who habitually ignore the concept of affluence or neglect material needs, these two-and-a-half years may be extra difficult. The person may suddenly find himself struggling under the weight of debt, deficits, and old bills. He must now squarely face the importance of money in his life. Some people decide to place great attention on earning wealth, either to gain a greater feeling of security or to ensure freedom and independence in the years to come. In any event, financial responsibility is essential now. This is a poor time for gambling, get-rich-quick schemes, or high-risk investments. The person should especially avoid extravagant spending. He should work on building resources and creating a solid foundation of capital. He must learn the value of receiving proper rewards for his efforts and decide exactly what part money plays in his priorities. By the end of this transit, the person realizes that before he can enjoy any of life's pleasures, he must first be able to meet his basic financial needs and feel good about himself. For this reason, the transit is a profoundly important one.

In Hindu predictive astrology, the second house represents education and family life, as well as money matters. Therefore, the person suffers domestic troubles, difficulties in school, and meager earnings. He may also have problems with the right eye. As it transits the second house, Saturn simultaneously aspects the fourth, eighth, and eleventh houses. The fourth house glance means restriction or tediousness with homes, cars, comforts, happiness, mother, and educational degrees. The aspect to the eighth house indicates loss, or little profit, from joint partnerships and insurance companies, and potential problems with the reproductive system. Occult studies are not much favored at this time. Saturn's aspect on the eleventh house restricts financial success from side ventures. It also means the person does not fare well with his friends and acquaintances, and he has a very difficult time fulfilling important long-term goals and desires.

♄

When Saturn transits the third house, the person delves deeply into knowledge and tries to learn all he can in order to better his existence. This is a time of profound focus and concentration in school or any kind of career training. The person may conduct research, analysis, or other investigative projects. His thinking will be deep, profound, and serious. He must, however, beware of depression and a somber attitude. Recreation, amusements, and hobbies can counter the person's laborious, concentrated mental activity.

Saturn's transit of the third house signifies an unusual drive to reach out and connect with others. The person may encounter obligations and responsibilities with siblings and relatives. He will feel a powerful need to communicate with friends, peers, and loved ones. The person is compelled to extract all manner of detailed truths and to share his findings with those who will listen. He writes more letters, messages, and bulletins than ever before. Or he may explore the possibility of writing in magazines and journals. Such activities may not flow with great spontaneity, but they spring from a sense of urgency, importance, and purpose.

The person's daily habits and attitudes now demand attention. He suddenly views his experience with microscopic perception, and everything seems to slow down. The person witness his behavior with more detachment than usual and observes that many of his actions and undertakings do not produce all that he wants and deserves. While the quantity of his life feels retarded or restricted, the quality of his life is about to make serious (even if inconspicuous) progress. He begins to examine everything outside himself in a fresh and objective way. Now that Saturn has passed through the first two houses of the birthchart, and the person has handled his most important personal and private issues, he is ready to confront the world around him. He spends these two-and-a-half years determining what information he needs in order to live successfully. And then he vigorously educates himself.

The person makes excellent use of the plentiful knowledge that comes his way. He is capable of structuring his ideas and opinions better than ever. Educators, intellectuals, and those who use their minds to earn a living may feel burdened by this transit, because the mind is strained. But this period brings powerful insights, and the person improves his cognitive power in a way that benefits him profoundly in the years to come. Health-wise, the lungs and nervous system are vulnerable. The person feels a great responsibility toward his environment. He should do his best to avoid worrying, although he must constantly deal with minor details, trivial matters, and unimportant problems.

By the time this transit is over, the person has grasped the need for precision and has learned to think. He has strengthened his rational mind and significantly increased his ability to function objectively. As a result, he is more flexible and able to function within the often paradoxical world in which he lives. He is also ready for Saturn's transit through the fourth house, when he will shift his attention from knowledge to a more instinctual experience of his heredity.

In Hindu predictive astrology, the third house represents energy, willpower, and the ability to fulfill one's daily desires. Therefore, the person has difficulty accomplishing simple goals and minor tasks. He works diligently but feels as if he is spinning his wheels. He is, in fact, learning how to make the most efficient use of his energy, as minor obstacles interfere with his intentions for two-and-a-half years. During Saturn's transit of the third house, it simultaneously aspects the fifth, ninth, and twelfth houses. The aspect to the fifth means tedious experiences with pregnancy, children, and investments. The aspect to the ninth indicates restricted luck and travel, difficulties with religious or spiritual teachers, and hardship in gaining any higher knowledge. Saturn's glance on the twelfth house signifies many debts and expenses, misfortune with remote foreign countries, and strong discipline to pursue "moksha" (enlightenment or final liberation).

ħ

When Saturn transits the fourth house, the person spends two-and-a-half years building the foundation for his future success and achievement. It is a time of slow, concentrated effort to ensure one's ultimate security in the material world. This is one of the least rewarding transits of all for increase, gain, promotion, and all outer signs of accomplishment. The person is engrossed in a natural state of introversion and introspection. He lives life from the perspective of ancestral values, hereditary talents, and security/survival concerns. The person is focused on his most fundamental nature and instincts. He should now be seeking to plan, build, organize, structure, and save. If he is expecting abundance, luck, and prosperity, he is likely to be sorely disappointed. (In ancient Hindu astrology, as Saturn passes through the fourth house, it simultaneously aspects the first, tenth, and sixth houses. The aspects to the tenth and first powerfully inhibit gain in the world).

Difficulties involving the person's habitat and living conditions may surface at the onset of this transit. The person directs his attention to the home space and residential location. He must now make all necessary improvements to his home and car. Situations arise which guide the person to consider whether he lives in the area best suited to his nature and needs. Now is the optimum time to learn lessons and responsibility about land, homes, and property. If the person moves during these two-and-a-half years, he will likely do so out of a sense of duty, and the move may seem burdensome. Moves during Saturn transits occur only out of definite purpose and necessity, and happen less frequently than when Jupiter transits or aspects the fourth house. (In Hindu astrology, Jupiter aspects the fourth house at least every three or four years. However, a relocation may be blocked if Saturn simultaneously aspects the house.) Moves during Jupiter influences produce buoyancy, happiness, pleasure, and luck, while Saturnian moves generate security, safety, and a solid ground for one's future base of operations.

The person's major concerns are personal and intimate, and he now works diligently to safeguard his future peace and tranquility. He is sensitive to domestic issues and family needs. He may have problems or increased responsibilities with his parents, but more likely with his mother. This transit may be somewhat unfavorable to his mother's

50 health if she is old, sickly, or chronically ill. Expansion of public life or community affairs are not much favored. In western astrology, the fourth house relates to family life and genetic inheritances, and so on. Therefore, this is an excellent time to engage in psychological healing techniques.

More than ever before, the person has access to memories of his upbringing and early childhood. He begins to realize how his individuality, personality, and psyche has been shaped by his background, his parents, and his ancestors. As this awakening occurs, the person reflects, clarifies, and begins to take responsibility for all his inherited, unconscious behavior so that when Saturn reaches the fifth house (creativity, self-expression, and pride), he has the wherewithal to differentiate himself from others and develop his ego to the fullest. He takes stock of his origins, confronts his internal fiber, and makes some of the greatest personal and psychological advances of his life. Planets transiting through the fourth house bring a person in touch with his innate, instinctive being. Transformations made during this period occur on a very subtle core level, and produce lasting, tangible effects.

In Hindu predictive astrology, Saturn's transit of this house is an arduous one, as already mentioned above. As it moves through the fourth, it simultaneously aspects the sixth, tenth, and first houses. As a result, restrictions, obstacles, and delays in health, daily work, career success, promotions, and any type of personal luck or favoritism occur. It is a good period to engage in discipline, self-control, spiritual austerities, and organizational assignments. Unlike western astrology, the fourth house in Hindu astrology rules the heart rather than the stomach. Therefore, Hindu astrologers predict vulnerability or difficulties involving the heart, while western astrologers are on the lookout for stomach ailments during this transit.

When Saturn transits the fifth house, the person explores the uniqueness of his spirit. His energy and intensity are now focused on personal creativity and self-expression. The purpose of his existence becomes his biggest concern. During this remarkably important transit, the person discovers his most essential talents and abilities—those which differentiate himself from others. Now is the time for the ego to reveal itself to the soul and psyche, so that the personality emerges as a unique and specialized spark of the Divine. It is an excellent time for gaining self-knowledge and self-understanding through introspection, self-analysis, and all methods of soul-searching. The person may exercise authority as well as express himself artistically. Individuals involved in the arts, sciences, and literary professions may experience profound results during this time as they now come into contact with their deepest creative resources. Such persons should consciously strive to make the most of this period.

Although profound progress and breakthroughs can now be made, Saturn's transit of the fifth house is neither easy, pleasurable, nor fun. Indeed, the opposite is true. The person feels serious, somber, and burdened by the weight of responsibility. Development of potential and mastery of one's god-given talents is necessary now. The person has a hard time enjoying himself and may need to be reminded to "lighten up" and schedule recreation in his life. He must beware of overworking.

The fifth house in Western astrology relates to love affairs and love received. Therefore, Saturn's transit brings up issues of deservedness and the person's ability to receive love. The person may undergo what feels like "fated" experiences with his partner. The person feels vulnerable in the realm of love and is driven to contemplate the meaning of these affairs and incidents. For those who find themselves suffering at the hands of their partner, it is an especially important period. Unlike one's ordinary experience of repaying past-life debts, the person now has the perfect psychological temperament to gain strikingly accurate insights and conclusions about what he deserves and what he does not. The person is extremely objective in perceiving the ramifications of his past actions and behavior.

Many individuals during this transit feel unloved, unappreciated, and lacking in energy, enthusiasm, and confidence. In such cases, the person must confront the whys and wherefores of the matter and make whatever changes are necessary. Such effects are, of course, due to the person's subtle, innermost feelings about himself. This is one of the best transits of all for transforming one's pride, dignity, self-respect, and self-worth. It is also a time to consider one's potential and likelihood for fame and leadership. The person evaluates his standing in the world. He may feel a very strong sense of determination and willpower, and feel compelled to follow his own instincts, desires, and heart at this time. However, all forms of gambling and speculation should be avoided, as Saturn's passage through the fifth house dampens one's buoyancy and luck in such matters.

There may be also restriction, burden, difficulties, and grief through children and youngsters during this transit. Women should beware of unwanted pregnancies or abortions. Health-wise, the heart may be vulnerable or under pressure. Traditional astrological texts report that there may be love affairs with older or authoritarian individuals. They also say that the person may produce creations (artistic or otherwise) which are extraordinarily long-lasting.

In Hindu predictive astrology, as Saturn transits the fifth house, it simultaneously aspects the seventh, eleventh, and second houses. The aspects to the seventh and eleventh houses (considered "desire" houses) temporarily limit the person's ability to fulfill his ambitions and cravings. He may have difficulties with groups and friends, and he may encounter restrictions or problems with his spouse. If the person is single, he has fewer opportunities for creating a beneficial love relationship at this time. Saturn's aspect on the second house means financial delays and obstacles, which are in turn exacerbated by the weakened eleventh house (the house of "gains and profits through side ventures").

Concerning the meaning of the fifth house there are a few distinctions between Hindu and Western astrology. The Hindus know the fifth house as ruling the mind (intellect) and the stomach. Therefore, the person's thinking is subject to depression, seriousness, or pessimism. His body is vulnerable to stomach (not heart) problems. In Hindu society, marriages are traditionally arranged at a very young age, so there is no threat of karmic, burdensome love affairs unless the person breaks the rules and engages in extramarital activities. However, married life and one's emotional needs may certainly be thwarted or harmed, as mentioned earlier, due to Saturn's "glance" or aspect to the seventh house. The fifth house is also known as *poorvapunya* or past-life credit, as well as kingship. Therefore, this is an important time for remembering one's destiny and considering the possibility of leadership or politics.

ħ

When Saturn transits the sixth house, the person learns the value of daily work. He also becomes accountable for his health, appearance, and habits. Circumstances may arise which require the person to work harder, longer, and more diligently than any time within the past twenty-nine years. He improves upon habitual methods and procedures and finds better ways to accomplish his goals. He is more organized than ever.

He may experience difficulties and frustration at the hands of co-workers, employers, or both. The person will likely have to work harder than those around him. Yet, he receives conspicuously little acknowledgement or appreciation. Misdeeds or shoddy work will be immediately noticed, and the person cannot avoid censure. At times he may even be unjustly reprimanded. His task during these two-and-a-half years is to become conscious, perceptive, and wise in the workplace, a realm characteristically comprised of habit, routine, and constricted focus.

The person may find himself working at a job which is tedious and restrictive, a job incapable of generating fulfillment and satisfaction. In certain cases, the person decides to quit, choosing unemployment over monotonous, unstimulating work. However, such a response is only wise if the person is seriously seeking a better situation. If he is merely trying to avoid pressure and struggle in the workplace, he may lose valuable lessons and experiences and be less successful for years to come.

During this transit, the person becomes extremely discriminating. He begins to examine all of his habits and private rituals. He may rapidly develop a strong sense of patience which allows him to plan and design his life more efficiently. Practical matters such as health, diet, and clothing are especially important at this time. For individuals who do not wish to focus on details and mundane concerns, life will feel tedious and tiresome. However, this is the perfect time to take responsibility for health and all personal concerns. This is Saturn's last passage through a "personal" house, and the person must strengthen and fortify himself for Saturn's transit through the final six houses which affects public life, community matters, and his relationship to society at large.

Fitness regimens and exercise programs are now appropriate. Any weak or vulnerable bodily functions may immediately break down at the onset of this transit in order to be finally corrected. The person should address chronic illnesses in a serious, committed way. Although health matters for some may be difficult and demanding during the entirety of these two-and-a-half years, by the end of this transit the person may have completely transformed his relationship to his physical well-being. In short, the person becomes aware of his responsibility for taking care of his body. This is a good time for organization, skill, efficiency, service-oriented concerns, and the study of medicine or any other healing methods. However, the person may have troubles with servants, maids, and subordinates.

In Hindu predictive astrology, as Saturn transits the sixth house, it simultaneously aspects the eighth, twelfth, and third houses. The aspects to the eighth and twelfth houses bring difficulties with sexual enjoyment, debts and expenses, and wills and legacies. It is not a good time to borrow or spend money. Also, spiritual and occult studies are not much favored. Saturn's aspect on the third house, in the Hindu system, means difficulties and frustration with siblings, as well as limited energy to fulfill one's daily desires and ambitions.

♄

When Saturn transits the seventh house, the person learns to take responsibility for his love life. His marriage, or primary love relationship, will be the most important arena for his growth during the next two-and-a-half years. During this time, the person defines the most essential and specific needs of his heart. He learns the true meaning of flexibility and learns to compromise with his cherished one. The person is called to task for inappropriate or unloving conduct which would previously go unnoticed or unchallenged. All of his limitations, restrictions, and imperfections in the area of the heart are laid bare by circumstances and his partner, so that the person may now improve his behavior. During this period, the person is unusually objective about his shortcomings in such matters, and is more than willing to mend his ways. He feels a deep and profound sense of responsibility toward his partner at this time.

Saturn's transit of the seventh house is an unequivocal time for commitment or recommitment to one's spouse or partner. If the person is involved in an easygoing, noncommitted relationship, he now determines whether to deepen his involvement or to eliminate it altogether. He perceives his domestic life especially clearly and practically at this time. If his situation is a hopeless one, with no harmonious future in sight, the person becomes quickly aware that he must end his predicament. Saturnian pressure, disturbing tension, and the simple desire to "do the right thing," guides the person to take necessary action.

When Saturn, the planet of karma, transits the seventh house, the person is forced to confront whatever lessons are needed in the area of love. Some individuals experience a time of few or no love opportunities at all, and feel profound loneliness. Though such effects could be the consequence of negative actions from past lifetimes, this is not usually the case. Most often, the person is being blatantly pressured to take responsibility for creating love by socializing, or else suffer the consequences of his self-induced isolation. During this transit, other persons may find that they are best suited to a monastic or single life. And those who are involved in extramarital affairs or improper situations may now be found out.

Single individuals who are seeking a committed relationship may now find themselves in one of the most serious and intense love relationships of their lives. Some realize that it is now time to lower unrealistic standards or relinquish certain requirements and finally materialize their goal. Therefore, marriage is a distinct possibility. Others in this situation, however, are foiled by deep-rooted problems which require counseling or therapy. In these cases, the person attracts a partner by whom he is profoundly captivated. He feels certain he has found the perfect soul mate, the one he is destined to marry. Unfortunately, the mate is ultimately unsuitable and exists only in order to reveal the person's inadequacies in the realm of love. Because of the person's extreme desire to have his special partner and because of the intense pain which is generated, the person may finally obtain the outside help which has been long needed.

This transit often brings karmic relationships which feel predestined and which are highly significant to the person's overall growth process. The person's ability to love may be tested to the limit. He may be attracted to older, authoritarian lovers. Traditional astrological texts report that because Saturn is now crossing the horizon of the birthchart, the person enjoys a more public existence or begins an upward climb towards career goals. By the end of this transit, the person understands love as something much greater than mere emotions, sensations, or a happy state of mind. This is an excellent time to deal squarely with issues of "scarcity consciousness" (chronic feelings of being undeserving or unworthy) in love matters.

In Hindu astrology, as Saturn transits the seventh house, it simultaneously aspects the ninth, first, and the fourth houses. The first house aspect means the person feels personally restricted for two-and-a-half years. He is unlikely to be favored, win awards, or enjoy promotions. The aspects to the ninth and fourth houses signifies difficulties or limited fulfillment with travel, religious or spiritual teachers, land, homes, and the mother.

♄

When Saturn transits the eighth house, the person purifies his desire nature and his use of power. He is pressured from outside forces to contemplate his motives as well as his methods of achieving goals and attaining fulfillment. Manipulative or domineering habit patterns will be exposed and attacked by others, and he must now root out such tendencies. This period is potentially a time of great emotional vulnerability. The person is extra sensitive to criticism and feels compelled to correct any compulsive or obsessive features of his character that are founded upon deep attachments and unconscious desires. These two-and-a-half years may bring significant psychological pain, depending upon how willing the person is to deal with trust and control issues. The person now undergoes a seemingly interminable ego death-and-rebirth process, during which he must relinquish all unhealthy or inappropriate passions and cravings. He may feel his individuality being curbed or pressured out of existence. By the end of this transit, much of his personality is transformed, and the person is healthier, more psychologically balanced, and emotionally freer. Having purified his desires, the person is less bound by unconscious, worn-out motives and behaviors. He now begins to prepare for Saturn's transit of the ninth house, where his search for meaning, significance, and a sound life philosophy is unfettered by trivial preferences and ignorant cravings.

During Saturn's transit of the eighth, the person learns lessons about sex and procreation. The person may experience temporary sexual dysfunction or difficulties in his sex life. Because of these effects, he decides to pay conscious attention to his physical passions and their impact on himself. The person now feels a sense of discipline and duty in a previously instinctive, organic realm. He may wish to investigate the field of sexuality, as well as examine his own bodily abilities and carnal techniques. The person is more aware than ever of the power of sex. He is conscious of the effects of his sexual activities on himself and others. During this period, he may be celibate, or at least very deliberate in the use of his sexuality. The person realizes the potential energy drain of sexual carelessness or misconduct. If he is involved in a physically unsatisfying relationship or marriage, sexual matters will worsen at the onset of the transit until he addresses the issue and makes necessary adjustments.

For these two-and-a-half years, the person acutely feels his mortality. He ponders the fact that human life is temporary and can end at any moment. The issues of death and the afterlife suddenly become important. Though this transit may coincide with the death of friends or relatives, such occurrences are not a foregone conclusion. However, if death occurs within the person's circle, he will certainly be summoned to attend the funeral and eager to comply. As a result, the person gains knowledge, wisdom, and a degree of preparation for death and dying. It is now time to earnestly reflect on the mysteries of life and matters of the soul. The person gains significant spiritual growth and may directly experience metaphysical or occult incidents.

Saturn's transit through the eighth house is generally an unfavorable time for money from partners or gains from wills, legacies, insurance companies, and lending institutions. If at all possible, the person should be alerted BEFORE this transit to organize his financial affairs and to eliminate all past debts, monetary obligations, and undesired economic partnerships. Affairs stemming from joint finances and previous borrowing may bring feelings of burden and stress at this time. It is a very poor time to borrow money or undertake new financial risks or ventures. Instead, the person should attend to his financial responsibility within existing partnerships. The person should update his will, clarify his economic situation, and inform his loved ones of all necessary information, facts, and figures they would need in case of his death.

During this transit, the person has more patience, persistence, and perseverance for research and investigation. He becomes infinitely more aware of other people's values, principles, and standards, and he learns how to peacefully coexist with them. By the end of this transit, the person will have eliminated certain ineffective or life-damaging habit patterns.

In Hindu predictive astrology, as Saturn transits the eighth house, it simultaneously aspects the tenth, second, and fifth houses. Therefore, there may be difficulties, delays, and obstacles in these realms. The person has a hard time expanding his career and increasing his wealth. Investments are not favored, nor are dealings with children. This is a time of responsibility, discipline, and preparation for one's duty in worldly matters.

ħ

When Saturn transits the ninth house, the person searches for the meaning of life. He tries to understand the significance of existence and discover where he fits into the larger scheme of things. The person spends approximately two-and-a-half years defining his beliefs, values, and morals. He engages in serious discussions regarding religion, philosophy, and all kinds of higher knowledge. During this transit the person will be especially discriminating in his choice of gurus, mentors, and spiritual teachers. He does not accept the views and opinions of others blindly, and he may challenge people frequently. There may be significant disappointment, disillusionment, or frustration in the person's religious or spiritual life. His heroes and idols may collapse under close scrutiny.

The person will travel long distances for serious, philosophical, or spiritual purposes. The person is now committed to finding truth. His faith will be tested. He may undergo ordeals, trials, and tribulations that test his values and morals. The person will delve deeply into all the wisdom he has gained throughout life. His task at this time is to bring his most substantial ingrained spirituality into his daily life. His ability to translate faith into action will be challenged. He will rigorously examine his concepts of right and wrong. He may face difficulties, delays, or obstacles in foreign countries in order to broaden his perspective and to learn the underlying reasons for customs and practices of other cultures. Or karmic problems may occur while traveling due simply to negative actions committed in previous lives.

During this period, the person will have aspirations to expand his awareness, knowledge, and experience. More than this, he may feel a profound yearning to spread his influence far and wide. He may travel to foreign countries for business or professional interests. The person will feel pressured to disseminate any knowledge, information, or writings he has been previously procrastinating over. Publishing (or promoting any message or material) may not be simple, but the person is now committed to the process.

The person seeks an intense and concentrated learning experience. He may return to school or any serious training program. He wants to master whatever practice or profession he has been working on for the previous several years. He wants to discover the most realistic and practical methods for his work, his beliefs, and his philosophies. This is his final opportunity to perfect his abilities and expertise and to put them into fruitful action. He is (unconsciously) getting ready for Saturn's transit of the tenth house two-and-a-half years from now, when he can gain the greatest professional authority, reputation, and prestige.

In Hindu astrology, as Saturn transits the ninth house, it simultaneously aspects the eleventh, third, and sixth. Therefore, the person experiences difficulties in the realms ruled by these houses. Due to the malefic aspect thrown onto the third and eleventh, there will be delays, obstacles, and complications with all siblings, younger and older. Since the third and eleventh are the desire houses, the person experiences temporary difficulties and setbacks in fulfilling his goals and ambitions. Saturn's aspect on the sixth house indicates stress in the workplace and pressure on the person's health for two-and-a-half years.

When Saturn transits the tenth house, the person takes responsibility for his life calling and becomes accountable for previous career efforts. He gets rewards, promotions, and credit for the good he has done; criticism, demotions, and condemnation for ineffective or damaging professional actions and little response at all for inertia and inaction. This is a very important transit because the person becomes very sensitive to his status and position while receiving feedback from the world. He is committed to determining his position within society and his precise role in his chosen vocation. During these approximately two-and-a-half years, the person is able to see his career performance more realistically than ever. If he has been living under any delusions or misconceptions about his efficiency, he now comes face to face with the truth of the matter. It is very important to note that the person does not necessarily reap either excessive praise or rejection. In many cases, very little happens externally. But what does happen is of utmost importance to the person. Because he is now so committed to his calling, he analyzes all feedback fully. He contemplates whether his achievements and accomplishments are valid and whether he truly deserves what he has reaped. He wants to achieve his true status and fulfill his personal destiny.

If the person has worked diligently toward career goals for some time, he now stands a very good chance of making a big impact. He may receive a leadership or organizational position because his superiors suddenly recognize and appreciate his wisdom and experience. Certain individuals reach the peak of their professional life at this time. But this is more probable during Saturn's second or third transit of the tenth house (during the person's later years). It is important for the person to have organized his personal life well before this transit, because his career responsibilities seriously increase now. He may be downright compulsive in working on career goals and taking advantage of his newfound worldly influence. Therefore, he must be careful not to offend family, friends, and loved ones by his neglect. Rest assured that the person's workload will be great, and his time most precious.

This transit brings a certain degree of grace and naturalness due to Saturn's connection to Capricorn, the "natural" ruler of the tenth house.

62   However, this period almost always brings frustration as well. Unfortunately, no one, in charting the course of his dreams, responds flawlessly to every obstacle along the way. The person now finds out exactly where he has miscalculated or failed, and why. The good news is that he is crystal clear about who he is (because he understands his place within society) and what he must do in the future to fulfill his goals. The bad news is that any unrealized professional ambitions bring special disappointment because the person intuitively realizes that this is a culmination period for his career.

Ultimately, this is a time of powerful personal integration. Because the person is so much more detached and objective about the significance of rank, honor, and status, he can properly determine what he is willing to do to achieve them and what he is not. He discovers his real commitment in life, (despite any claims he has made), by observing society's response to his performance. The person works diligently and unrelentingly, and, remarkably, he is not emotionally affected by success or failure. Therefore, the person can do his best, most efficient work ever. Furthermore, he is exceptionally disciplined, organized, and purposeful now. During Saturn's transit of the following house, the eleventh, the person will define his personal goals and ambitions —that which will make him the happiest. But before he can do so, he must understand explicitly and dispassionately where he stands in the world and what rewards he has gained for the efforts he has made.

If the person has been extremely responsible and effective in his past career activities, then he is recognized and acknowledged by his bosses. Otherwise he may have difficulties with them or suffer misfortune on their behalf. In rare cases, where the person has gained prominence and success illegally or immorally, this transit may bring public disgrace or downfall. As the tenth house represents the father, the person should take care of any unresolved issues or concerns with that parent now. At the beginning of this transit, the person may experience some discord, restriction, or limitation from his father. The father may begin to behave strictly or severely. Or he may withdraw emotional support. Such behavior is especially difficult if the transit occurs during early childhood. In cases where the father is old or in failing health, Saturn's tenth house passage does not help matters. Astrologers who consider the tenth house to represent the mother and the fourth house to govern the father may want to apply the above description to the mother.

In Hindu predictive astrology, when Saturn transits the tenth house, it simultaneously aspects the twelfth, fourth, and seventh houses. The twelfth house aspect means more debts and expenses than usual and the possibility of loss from thieves and robbers. The person enjoys sex less. He may have difficulties in remote foreign countries. Saturn's fourth house glance indicates problems or restrictions associated with the person's mother. The mother's health may suffer, and there are obstacles or difficulties with cars, land, and the home. Saturn's aspect to the seventh house signifies less happiness in married life, or, for single individuals, little opportunity for marriage or a satisfying relationship.

$$\hbar$$

When Saturn transits the eleventh house, the person takes responsibility for his ultimate life vision. His focus shifts from such practical matters as career, financial success, and his impact on the world to the more essential concern of what will really bring him fulfillment. Now that Saturn has passed through ten houses, including the zenith or peak of the chart, the person has experienced nearly all manifestations of life. It is finally time to draw conclusions regarding happiness, contentment, and fulfillment. The person realizes that his bliss does not necessarily come from the achievement of logical or rational desires. Having worked on so many different realms of life in previous years, his perspective is greater than ever. He observes that, beyond the workings of his intellect and reasoning power, he has a simple knowingness about what he really wants from life. Priorities for a meaningful existence become remarkably clear.

While it may seem odd, in terms of sequence, for consciousness to shift from such important issues of the previous several houses (influencing the masses, contributing to the world, religion, philosophy, godliness, and spiritual teachings, etc.) to examining personal goals and aspirations, there is actually good reason for such change. According to religions, the purpose of life is happiness—the enjoyment and appreciation of God's masterful creation. Now that the person has confronted the various conditions of life and performed the right and necessary actions, he pauses to consider the most crucial consideration: "What do I want to achieve by my existence?" He now perceives life through the eyes of opportunity rather than those of obligation. The person begins to design his life according to his ultimate ambitions and long-range objectives. He determines how to break away from anything that does not support his greatest vision.

During the approximately two-and-a-half years of this transit, the person takes stock of his friends and the groups he associates with. Problems, irritations, frustrations, and annoyances in these areas may intensify, and the person is compelled to deal squarely with them. He cuts off detrimental friendships or those which are more work than they are worth. Solid, rewarding friendships become stronger as the person sees the value of comrades whose commitment and loyalty are great. He may also make friends with older, authoritarian, or ascetic individuals. At the same time, the person defines and sets limits on the group activities which are most suitable to him. He decides which groups to become more involved with and which ones to eliminate. In certain cases the person may take on group leadership or assemble his own club or organization.

As the person gains clear vision of his most intimate and important life goals, he simultaneously focuses on his relationships with others. This is the perfect time to do so because friends and groups exist largely as a support system for one's values, interests, and desires. Friends and groups vanish when they are no longer helpful to one's purpose.

The person also begins to think of how to best create an ideal society. He may donate time and resources to community interests or become involved in public issues. He is concerned with humanitarian issues and may be more altruistic than ever. Throughout Saturn's entire transit of the eleventh house, the person is of an idealistic and visionary mind. He is decidedly more mental in his approach as his greatest responsibility and obligations lie in planning the future.

In Hindu predictive astrology, Saturn's passage through the eleventh house means difficulties with friends, groups, and one's eldest sibling. Side ventures bring little profit, and one's major goals and desires are delayed and obstructed. As Saturn transits the eleventh, it simultaneously aspects the first, fifth, and eighth houses. The aspect to the first house indicates lack of promotion, advancement, or favoritism, as well as potential minor health problems. The fifth house glance means a poor time for investments, a serious or somber mind, and problems with children or an inability to get pregnant. Saturn's eighth house aspect brings obstacles involving joint finances, is a less favorable time for occult studies, and causes vulnerability of the reproductive system.

When Saturn transits the twelfth house, it is time to experience life from a spiritual perspective and to integrate the growth of consciousness resulting from all the previous transits. Now that Saturn has passed through the other houses of the horoscope, the person must take stock of his accomplishments, achievements, and failures. He contemplates the meaning of his experiences, and seeks to discover his place within universal existence. This transit is decidedly unlike any other, and unless the person is quite mystically, spiritually, and emotionally healthy to begin with, he is liable to feel confused or puzzled for approximately two-and-a-half years. The soul and psyche are engaged in a process of assimilation and no amount of rational or logical analysis can ease or accelerate the procedure. The person simply must call on his deepest spiritual and intuitive resources and surrender his attachments, his ego, and his petty individual preferences to the higher part of his nature.

Enlightenment, or evolution of consciousness, is an experience whereby one's boundaries expand in order to appreciate the universality and oneness of all things. And while the result is blissful, the process is often unfamiliar and uncomfortable. Faith is one's only ally. As the person reaps the spiritual consequences of his life experience, he is well-advised to have faith in the universe and enjoy whatever expansion of consciousness occurs.

As Saturn is now finishing its cycle of the twelve houses, the person finds himself reviewing his past years and attempting to complete all unfinished projects and undertakings. It is a time of endings, resolutions, and conclusions—not new beginnings. There is very little support from nature for major new enterprises and undertakings. Further, the person feels a powerful natural tendency to go within, to mentally retreat from the world. His attention is clearly focused on the inner self.

This state of introspection continues for almost five years, through Saturn's passage of both the twelfth and first houses, but Saturn's transits of the twelfth and first are like night and day. During the twelfth house transit, the person abdicates whatever he can of his small self (individuality) in order to attain as much of his higher self (universality) as possible. When Saturn transits the first house, the person returns to **67** work on his individuality, diligently building his personality anew, using all the expansion of awareness gained during Saturn's twelfth house transit. The more inner growth and spiritual integration the person accomplishes during Saturn's twelfth house sojourn, the greater his perfection of personality will be when Saturn transits the first.

Among other things, the twelfth house represents secrets, all that is hidden, and the subconscious mind. Therefore, this Saturn transit is the optimum time for clearing up psychological problems and all kinds of deep emotional obsessions, complexes, or phobias dating from childhood and even, perhaps, from past lives (represented by the twelfth house in western astrology). The person is compelled to confront his demons. Though he may be comfortable with his own peculiar fears and neuroses, he now realizes that it is time to put his spirit and psyche in order. Some individuals will seek out psychological therapy, while others may go to ashrams, monasteries, or convents. Inner healing is now extremely well-facilitated as the person's boundaries expand to find new definition. Old, worn-out mental constructs disintegrate so new ones may arise, although the rebuilding process may feel very slow.

A great deal of dream activity during these two-and-a-half years reveals deep and hidden information. Individuals involved in analyzing their dreams now have abundant material. Mystical, spiritual, and occult studies are favored at this time, and much progress can be made in these areas. Certain people may find themselves wishing to do healing work or service-oriented endeavors.

In Hindu predictive astrology, Saturn transiting the twelfth house indicates difficulties with the left eye and large, unexpected debts and expenses, or both. It also means problems or frustrations in activities involving remote foreign countries. It could bring sexual dysfunction or lack of sexual pleasure. As Saturn transits the twelfth, it simultaneously aspects the second, sixth, and ninth houses. The aspects to the second and sixth cause restriction in the practical matters of wealth and daily work. There may also be hardships involving health, education, servants, employers, or employees. Saturn's ninth house aspect reveals difficulty gaining higher knowledge, problems with gurus or religious teachers, and restricted luck in general.

When Uranus transits the first house, the person awakens to a compelling sense of responsibility about his individuality, self-expression, and need for unconditional freedom. He is remarkably present and conscious and realizes that the only way he can maintain his integrity is to live moment by moment, uncompromisingly true to himself. He is consumed with the need to fulfill his own interests and preferences and to function with independence and authenticity. For the next seven years (approximately), an enlightening process of personality and character transformation takes place. During this time, there is a unique opportunity for the person to experience life on his own terms, without undue influence from his past history or from the expectations of society, friends, and loved ones. He is able to relinquish old habit patterns, psychological characteristics, and rigid routines in order to create a new pattern of behavior. His behavior starts to reflect his real essence, as he ruthlessly eliminates perfunctory habits and superficial conduct. Uranus, the higher octave or vibration of Mercury, causes the person's rhythm of experience to accelerate. The person feels alive, invigorated, and significantly detached from his usual emotionality and sensitivity.

The person is receptive to self-improvement and evolutionary progress. He is willing to do almost anything in order to go beyond his usual limitations and expand his boundaries. This transit promises a great deal of excitement and adventure throughout. The person is open to all kinds of untried interests and activities. Endeavors in the area of human potential are especially favored, as are occult studies, psychic phenomenon, and any secretive subjects hidden from normal view. The person enjoys topics which are innovative or ahead of the times. He is especially interested in science and any knowledge that elucidates the laws of the universe and the workings of nature.

The person must beware of rebellious or radical behavior, especially when Uranus is within two or three degrees away from the ascendant (this generally occurs at the beginning of this transit, on and off for the first year or so). The person may be erratic, extreme, and fanatical. Even if he acts responsibly, he is very likely to experience changes in some significant personal relationships as he restructures his behavior and priorities. Now that his main concern is to fully concentrate on his own desires and pursuits and to realize his personal potential to the fullest, the people around him may be surprised or upset. They may also be threatened by his emerging independence, new image, and somewhat altered lifestyle.

These years bring great creativity, inventiveness, and originality. The person experiences sudden, unexpected opportunities and adventures. He continually meets eccentrics, geniuses, and exciting people who provide stimulation and insight. The person is clearly unconcerned with security, stability, tradition, and ritual. He is thrilled with growth, change, permissiveness, and asserting his own will. He enjoys upheaval, revolution which generates positive results, and the transformation of worn-out systems and structures. He may surround himself with friends and acquaintances who are young, liberated, and freedom-loving. The person himself may appear younger and more inspired. He is aware of his personal power and ready to put it to use. He trusts his own feelings and opinions and will not be dominated or intimidated. He needs to create his own destiny. The person goes on instinct and impulse, and he may have many clairvoyant experiences. In his excitement and newfound confidence, the person may overextend himself, however. Therefore, he must beware of stress, which can lead to spasms or other minor health problems.

When Uranus transits the second house, old and worn-out self-assessments are shattered, as the person breaks boundaries in the realms of worthiness, confidence, and self-worth. For approximately seven years he gains insight into his own merit. The person's perception expands to comprehend more complexity and to include a far greater variety of factors when evaluating himself and his personal needs. As a result of this liberating internal process, he experiences a newfound freedom from his belongings and possessions. Because he is more creative and inventive when evaluating himself, and because he now has a measure of detachment and can see himself more objectively, he realizes he has been identifying himself with what he owns. As Uranus, the great illuminator, sheds light on the second house issues of values, the person begins to consider the importance of human experience over human ownership. And although the experience may feel revolutionary, being begins to take precedence over having.

The person is less concerned with material security, stability, and protection and more interested in personal development, experimental undertakings, and exciting risk-for-reward endeavors. Sudden major fluctuations in finances, resources, and properties are likely to occur intermittently throughout this transit. If the person is conscious of his desire to grow and to experience new ways of being, these events will not be as surprising or disturbing as they might be otherwise. It is not likely to be the easiest or most peaceful of times, since Uranus is fallen in Taurus, the earthy, material, and preserving sign which is the natural ruler of the second house. But the opportunity exists to incorporate more enlightened values into one's belief system. And the opportunity to free oneself from the limiting restraints of earthly bonds and attachments, and all kinds of practical concerns is also strong. Ultimately, tremendous spiritual gains are to be made when Uranus transits the highly personal second house.

The person can make money through new and interesting sources of income. He may become bored with his means of making money or irritated by lack of financial growth potential. Now is a good time for a change of approach to money making. Financial dealings involving astrology, science, innovative technologies, or any occult field are favored. Because there may be big ups and downs (great profits and/or great losses) in the person's finances, he should diversify his holdings and be wary of investing all his assets in any one enterprise. Individuals who are normally extremely conservative with their resources may now feel a desire to throw caution to the wind and go for exciting, radical, or highly imaginative investments. On the other hand, speculative types may consider behaving with more financial consistency and stability. The person's relationship to the physical universe is being transformed and reconstructed as his self-perception and self-appreciation is adjusted. New values are constantly coming into play.

When Uranus transits the third house, the person has a break-through in his ability to think. He awakens to a highly conscious, independent, and stimulated intellect. He is receptive to new theories, philosophies, and interests and is unusually original and creative. Mental rhythms increase dramatically, and his mind functions with acute dexterity and flexibility. During these approximately seven years, the person experiences enlightening insights, realizations, and revelations. He is mentally and psychologically inspired. He finds himself unaffected by the beliefs and opinions of peers, the consensus of society, and the prevailing beliefs of humankind. The person thinks for himself. He trusts his own interpretations and conclusions and asserts his unique perceptions and impressions.

Great improvement can now be made in all facets of life as the normal boundaries and limitations of the rational mind expand. However, an individual may make the most profound gains in the areas of occult knowledge, mysticism, and spiritual evolution because these are directly connected to, and intrinsically dependent on, unbounded consciousness. The person does not necessarily become devotional, religious, or particularly interested in the Divine, but rather, he spontaneously opens up to the higher realities of life. Universal laws and underlying principles of existence become perceptible and important. Truth is a very high priority during this transit. Spiritual paths that emphasize the intellect, such as Zen or *gnana* yoga (the yoga of discrimination), are supremely favored, and the person may eradicate mistakes of the intellect (incorrect or delusional thinking which retards ones spiritual evolution and growth to perfection) in the quick of an instant. The person is able to correct psychological misinterpretations swiftly and painlessly, with detached and objective intellect. He does not maintain attitudes and beliefs for emotional or egotistical reasons. There is a strong possibility that the person will begin to study astrology, tarot, yoga, and psychic or mystical subjects. Even if he has never given much thought to these fields, he may now inquire seriously into them. He enjoys research, analysis, and investigation, as his mind is lively and dynamic. He does well in the fields of science, electronics, computers, or technology.

Because he is no longer influenced by conventional thought, the person is capable of inventions, discoveries, and innovations of all kinds. He simply ignores the limits and restrictions of what is supposed to be possible and what is not. Old mental habits are relinquished, and the person sees things anew. He relies on intuition and mental instinct. There may be clairvoyant experiences or flashes of genius. The person excels in his ability to handle details, and he is constantly traveling within the community, enjoying the variety of life and diversity of thought around him. This is a time of delight for intellectual individuals and philosophical souls. The person savors his mental freedom. He interacts more with siblings, neighbors, and relatives. He is exuberant about communicating the new information and insights coming his way.

The person may feel mentally restless, impatient, or irritable. He may have a rebellious temperament or willful demeanor. There is an acute ability to distinguish and discriminate during these years. It is a profound opportunity to perceive issues anew, to delve deeply into alien knowledge, and to restructure attitudes, beliefs, and one's practical, day-to-day philosophy of life.

When Uranus transits the fourth house, the person feels, at the core of his being, an intense desire to dislodge himself from past conditioning. The foundation of his existence undergoes a profound transformation for approximately seven years. The person suddenly notices the conflict between the deep, essential needs of his soul and any mechanical behavior he unconsciously adopted as a child. Uranus transits to any angle of the birthchart bring about a pronounced need to assert independence, individuality, and creative self-expression. But the fourth house passage is particularly significant. During this period, the person disengages himself from outmoded, superfluous security and survival mechanisms he has learned from parents and ancestors. He becomes increasingly aware of how much of his life and major decisions have been influenced by genetics, culture, tradition, and heritage. He is now bursting with energy to eliminate conditioned behavior and take full control of his own life and destiny.

The person is excited about change and impatient with habit and routine. He is unconcerned with stability and security. Rather, he does whatever it takes to restructure his environment and create a base of operations that will allow him to fulfill his true needs. He gains constant insight into his internal resources and makeup and he modifies his behavior appropriately. He wants tangible evidence that his outer life is consistent with his inner being. Self-integrity is of utmost importance now, and compromise, in any way, shape, or form will only bring frustration or suffering. The person's thrust is outward, and his energy is dynamic and powerful. He is ready for new experience.

Because the fourth house represents endings and Uranus symbolizes fluctuation, this period is very likely to correspond with major life change. Old personal ties and worn-out structures will be broken. The person's vitality and vigor will help him through the changes, but he will also need to be extremely flexible and adaptable. He has a great opportunity to rid himself of any feelings of being a victim. If he is ever to take responsibility for the direction of his life, it is now. He is in touch with his deepest core energy, and his psyche is illuminated. Changes during these years occur at a most integral, fundamental level. By the end of this transit, the person functions differently than he did at the start.

The person's domestic life may be rocky. He may experience significant ups and downs with his parents, most likely with his mother. His mother may be more excited, unsettled, erratic, or changeable. She may also be more open-minded, detached, or objective. She may awaken spiritually. The person may concentrate on home improvement or move to another home, apartment, city, or state. He may use his home for exciting spiritual gatherings, occult teachings, revolutionary intentions, creating inventions, or meetings to promote enlightenment. The home space is not a model of stability now, and therefore it is wise to have one's habitat well insured. Buried treasure or money under the mattress is at risk. Because the fourth house in western astrology relates to family life, the person's domestic harmony may be affected by excitement, stimulation, unrest, or instability. In extreme cases, divorce is possible. But this occurs as a result of dramatic internal transformation, not merely domestic ups and downs. Divorce may occur during any powerful Uranus transit if the person has not been true to himself or if he has been out of touch with his real needs and desires.

Because the fourth house represents extremely personal matters, including inherited traits and old, primordial conditioning, it is impossible to predict exactly what concerns may surface. Each individual has his own peculiar gestalt. Rest assured, however, that the person will have to confront very intimate core issues which have remained unconscious or suppressed, whether intentionally or not, for many years. Fortunately, the person is now especially capable of confronting such matters, as Uranus' transit of any angular house gives an abundance of spiritual resourcefulness in the form of discrimination, nonattachment, and objectivity. There is a profound ability to live in the moment. The person may alter his relationship to tradition, ritual, and ancestral values. He may become interested in farming, mining, archeology, or innovations relating to land. Domestic and maternal instincts are subject to change or upheaval, as are all aspects of family life. There is less concern with emotional security, devotion, and sentiment. The same is true of possessions, collectibles, and fixed assets.

It should be noted that for children (especially before the age of six), this transit may be difficult or disturbing. The child's security is likely to be shaken if his mother behaves too erratically, or if the family moves to another city or state. Furthermore, the child may suddenly feel detached from his mother or father, and this may be the first time he sees that parent in an objective light.

When Uranus transits the fifth house, the person has a dramatic awakening of spirit. His innermost being is aroused and enlivened, and he wants to express his individuality with all the excitement and enthusiasm at his command. This is one of the best periods of all for artistic endeavors. The person is abundantly creative and original. His imagination is fertile; he is in touch with his uniqueness and inner child. He feels unaffected by the opinions of others and does not censor himself. The person feels a profound sense of freedom, and his actions reflect this. He takes risks and follows his heart. He pursues whatever course of action strikes his fancy. The person articulates his ideas clearly. He avoids compromising his integrity. He asserts his individuality, takes pride in his creativity, and is unattached to the outcome of his actions. He is thrilled to be alive!

During these approximately seven years, the person takes fun and pleasure to their extremes. He experiences the ultimate meaning of enjoyment. It is not merely that he pursues more entertainment, recreational activities, or love affairs. And it is not that he is necessarily more prosperous or successful in his undertakings. But he is, quite simply, intensely stimulated by life. He loves his life and is thoroughly aware that the greatest opportunity of human experience is to live fully, passionately, and without reservation. It is now time for him to participate in the play of creation and even contribute a verse. During the transit of Uranus through the fourth house, the person gained insight into his soul—the underlying essence of his existence and that which is eternal, unbounded, and connected to all. Now he awakens to his spirit—the manifestation of his individuality in the world of action. The person is dynamic and experimental, and he no longer feels vulnerable, undue self-restraint, or oversensitivity.

While this transit generates extreme creativity, artistic expression, and originality or genius, it brings a potential downside. Uranus is in its detriment in Leo, the corresponding sign of the fifth house. Thus, the person may act carelessly and imprudently. He may alienate others by his audacity, impudence, or intermittent egotism. Worse, he may indulge excessively in pleasure. He does not respond to parental or authoritative advice, and he is unconcerned with the concepts of caution, discretion, and conservative judgement. He must beware of unwise partying, hedonism, and stimulants. Finally, the person is likely to create difficulties in love affairs because of his erratic, inconsistent behavior with his partner or his demands for unconditional emotional freedom. Though exciting or titillating love affairs are likely now, this is an unfavorable time for anything but short-term romance. Commitment may feel unnatural, and the person may attract lovers who are unprepared or unable to settle down. He may pick partners who are unusual, unconventional, or very different from himself. Certainly, the person should expect the unpredictable in his love affairs during this transit.

Married individuals, whether tempted to engage in extramarital affairs during this transit or not, are also much affected in the area of love and romance. Sexual stimulation is at an all-time high, and the person is more uninhibited, unconventional, and experimental in his sex life. Although the eighth house represents sex in western astrology, the fifth house influences such matters because of its connection to passions, romance, and so on.

There is likely to be a strong interest in speculations or gambling. However, the person should be careful in these realms. Investments are subject to great fluctuations, and the person should be aware of the risks involved before pursuing them. If the person has children, he may have disturbances or disruptions in his relationship with them. His children may act oddly, irrationally, or without great balance. Or, on a more positive note, they may awaken to spiritual or occult subjects. Or the person may now gain knowledge about his children's behavior and insight into the nature of their relationship. He is also more objective and dispassionate about them.

In the final analysis, this transit has great power, and it can be used to good advantage if the person is mature, serious, and dedicated at the outset.

When Uranus transits the sixth house, the person awakens to the possibility of self-improvement and purification. He is especially stimulated in the areas of health, diet, dress, and daily work. The person may take an interest in health foods, alternative healing methods, or any human potential endeavor which purifies the body, energizes the organism, and enriches physical well-being. The person is fascinated with learning all he can about the underlying laws and principles of his bodily functioning. He is constantly gaining insights about his health, and this period marks a breakthrough in his ability to focus on fitness and to take dynamic action in this realm. Dietary changes and healing techniques adopted during these years result in rejuvenation and physical refinement. The person feels excited about purifying his body.

His relationship with his daily work is transformed. While Uranus passed through the fifth house, the person spent approximately seven years thoroughly enlivening his spirit and creativity. Now his task is to integrate all the vitality he has gained into his everyday existence. He is consumed with bringing originality, inventiveness, and excitement into the workplace. He craves freedom to develop new working methods and products, and he can barely tolerate the routine drudgery of which most jobs consist. He is imaginative and inspired at work, and his innovative attitude contributes to his success.

Ultimately, however, this is one of the most frustrating and tedious of all Uranus transits, whether or not the person responds well to Uranian energy. Sixth house affairs (daily work, self-improvement, health, diet, service to others, etc.) are almost entirely dependent upon discipline, routine, and system. Uranus epitomizes the opposite of these qualities and even symbolizes an explicit abhorrence for rules, regulations, and restriction of any kind. The person suddenly loathes conventional methods, predictable chores, and the mediocrity of his habitual tasks. His patience at work is taxed to the limit. Unless the person's job is extremely creative, stimulating, or unrestricted, he is liable to feel imprisoned at work for approximately seven years. Time may slow down to a standstill!

The person is unhappy about having to obey his employer, and he may become rebellious or defensive. If working conditions are oppressive or abusive, he may become somewhat of a revolutionary, influencing and inciting co-workers. He asserts his will and lets his opinions be known. He sees greater possibilities and potential at work, and may feel frustrated by conservative, unprogressive employers. There is a strong possibility of changing employment both at the start of this transit and throughout the entire period. The person may pursue occupations such as astrology, science, the occult arts, computer programming, or electronics. Inventors, individuals who are involved in futuristic innovations and projects, and those already involved in the above-mentioned fields can make great advances during this transit. However, the person needs latitude and freedom within his work at this time. Indeed, if given the chance, he might prefer to work alone.

Because the person takes great interest in personal fitness and health matters, he may consider entering any of the healing professions now if he is predisposed toward this area. Regarding his own physical well-being, he may suddenly be subject to nervous ailments, spasms, or other health problems when Uranus strikes the sixth house cusp. Such illnesses may be the impetus for the person to delve deeply into the healing process. Because the sixth house relates to dress, the person may purchase a new wardrobe or begin to wear more exciting and dynamic clothing. Strange things may occur with co-workers and subordinates. If the person is in a high position, he should keep a close watch on his maids, servants, or any domestic attendants. The person may dramatically excel at detail-oriented endeavors now. However, he only considers such tasks bearable if they help him advance toward his greater vision.

Although this transit can be significant and productive in the areas already mentioned, the overall feelings it generates may be frustration, tedium, and oppressiveness in daily life. Theoretically, it would seem that Uranus would greatly enliven the boring realms of routine tasks, disciplined efforts, daily work, and other repetitive activities. But in practice, more often than not, the person simply feels supreme impatience, even nagging, perpetual tension about his everyday existence. The reason for this is not completely clear. One possible explanation is that the sixth house corresponds to the pure and perfectionist sign of Virgo. Perhaps the enlightening energy of Uranus simply incites too extreme a yearning for a condition which does not exist within relative existence.

When Uranus transits the seventh house, the person has a breakthrough in his marriage or primary love relationship as old, rigid, ineffectual ways of relating are eliminated once and for all. During this transit, the person gains freedom, excitement, and profound insight in his love unions. He becomes assertive, innovative, and uninhibited about fulfilling his needs in relationships. For approximately seven years, the person investigates the intricacies of mating and experiments with his own desires in this realm. He now has the necessary detachment and objectivity to analyze this highly personal, instinctual area of his life. He sees his partner in new ways. He is excited about courtship and romance, whether he is married or not.

This transit is extremely important because it transforms both the person's bond to his mate and the way he relates to others. These transformations will affect his relationships for the rest of his life. It is crucial to understand the period completely in order to reap maximum advantage and to avoid the pitfalls. Make no mistake, there are few energies as incongruous as Uranus and the seventh house. Uranus represents independence and autonomy, while the seventh house governs union or partnership. The combination is about as suitable as a bull in a china shop. The obvious result of all this is sudden endings (and new beginnings) of close relationships. However, such incidents, if they occur, are absolutely not the essence of the transit—they are the external result.

The real purpose of the transit is to bring freedom, honesty, integrity, and consciousness into the person's primary love partnership and to liberate him from intolerable relationships that have been held together solely because of obsolete commitments. He now has the opportunity to be with his spouse as if for the first time and to renegotiate the terms of their union. In short, he gets to choose freely whether or not to renew his love contract (emotionally speaking of course). The person's marriage is likely to be seriously tested. And the test cannot be passed by fraudulent or counterfeit measures. During this entire transit the person is consumed with the need to function honestly with his mate and to fulfill his own needs and passions. Under no circumstances will he now hide his feelings or pretend to be happy in order to please his partner. His need for love is at stake, and to fulfill it, he maintains his principles with uncompromising integrity. For some individuals, standing up to their mates may not be the easiest course, but the person is proud to finally reveal his true feelings. There may be significant life changes and restructuring of relationships during these years. If the person behaves with awareness and responsibility, it is an invigorating, empowering, and enlightening time. The person is extremely present, vivacious, and animated, especially when Uranus transits the descendant (the cusp of the seventh house) at the beginning of the transit. This occurs on and off for approximately one year in most cases.

The person's mate may suddenly behave differently, shattering common bonds and accepted boundaries, and thereby compelling the person to feel a great gulf between himself and his partner. If the person's sense of separateness is caused by the partner, he may become upset at his vulnerable position. His happiness in love may appear to rest in his partner's hands. The challenge in such a situation, and it is not an easy one, is for the person to understand that he is *ultimately* (directly or indirectly) accountable for the changes in his partner's behavior that now affects their relationship. In order to maintain both his power and his sanity, the person must determine what part he played in creating the stressful situation he's in. Because of the karmic blending that occurs when two individuals relate to one another, one person is never the sole cause of something affecting both parties. Even where there is a victim and a perpetrator, both are responsible. When Uranus transits the seventh house (or slightly prior to the transit), the person may unwittingly send out powerful messages, behaviorally or telepathically, letting his partner know that it is time to dramatically alter their relationship or end it. His partner's actions simply become the natural consequence.

For obvious reasons, certain individuals feel victimized by their mates during this transit. Unfortunately, the more the person tries to control his mate, the more he suffers. The wise person flows with nature, adopts a nonresistant attitude, and accepts the evolutionary changes taking place. As astrologer Isabel Hickey used to say, "You cannot control Uranus experiences, but you can control your reactions." The person should do his best to appreciate that he is permanently shattering rigid, obsolete ways of functioning. As a result, his future relationships will be marked by greater freedom, creativity, enthusiasm, and originality. For better or worse, his present ones will never be the same again.

The person meets fascinating and exotic individuals during this transit. He comes into contact with astrologers, occultists, scientists, inventors, and strange or eccentric people. Relationships begin and end suddenly, and the person should not necessarily seek to make long-term commitments. He should beware of partnerships with erratic, unstable individuals. In love affairs he may attract exciting, free-spirited types who are very different in age or background. The person's greatest thrill comes from his new associations and the liberating effects they generate. Business partnerships are also potentially subject to major change.

In cases where the person's primary relationship erupts when Uranus exactly crosses the descendant, the final outcome of the situation will not be clear until the *last* conjunction to that cusp. Usually Uranus hits the descendant, continues in its forward motion, then backs up again conjuncting the descendant, and eventually resumes its forward motion, hitting the cusp for the third and last time. Each "hit" produces a discernable and predictable flare-up of the situation. However, the initial conjunction is the most severe. Finally, it may be mentioned that because the seventh is the first nonpersonal house in the cycle of the chart, it is considered to have a bearing on public life. The person may find himself more outwardly directed and more prone to dealings with, or recognition from, society. It is a favorable effect for those who desire to influence or benefit from the masses.

As always, when Uranus crosses an angle of the birthchart, it is time to experience independence, individuality, and self-expression in a dynamic, integral way.

When Uranus transits the eighth house, the person awakens to the power, potential, and intensity of his being. He is in touch with his deepest resources and taps into his abilities in an exceptional way. Research of any subject is favored, but the real essence of this transit is the person's ability to understand the laws of the universe, his own soul, and the soul's relationship to the universe. This does not mean intellectual study, of course, but direct experience—insights into and enlightenment about one's *real* nature. As this occurs, the person is liberated from the intense grip of ego identification, and he senses the futility of trying to possess or control ever-changing features of existence. He naturally begins to relinquish some of his unnecessary desires and deep attachments.

This transit is subtle, but very powerful, because the person gains greater flexibility about change and transformation. He begins to confront and embrace the weak aspects of his personality, rather than resisting or withdrawing from them. For approximately seven years he learns spiritual skills in the science of being and art of living. He gives up certain habits of control, fears, and manipulative behavioral patterns. Important spiritual growth takes place as the person grasps the absurdity of identifying with anything but his true nature—the infinite, unbounded being within. Uranus is exalted in Scorpio, the sign corresponding to the eighth house, and therefore this transit operates smoothly, without the usual abrupt, shocking effects of Uranus. However, it should be noted that the person's transformation occurs on a largely internal and perhaps unconscious level. Inner freedom is a natural state which arouses little attention or fanfare. But rest assured that something quite good, behaviorally or psychologically, is happening. The person experiments with new concepts of reality. He now begins to comprehend the true meaning and value of power. He may inquire seriously into the nature of death, astral travel, or reincarnation. He is less plagued by jealousy, revenge, and possessive emotions than before.

Because the person opens up to a broader, more spiritual, and evolutionary experience of life, his value system is bound to change. Thus, this period coincides with the death of some long-held beliefs. These changes vary for each individual, and there is no way to predict beforehand exactly what transformations will occur. The person can be expected, however, to be perfectly ready to surrender his past in order to forge a new future. He feels that one portion of his life is over for good, and there is no looking back. Regenerative forces are extremely strong now, and the old is quickly replaced by the new. The person is in touch with his potential and is eager to redesign his life. It is, to a large extent, the end of one era and the beginning of another.

There will be excitement, creativity, and experimentation in the person's sex life during these years. The person is sexually stimulated and less inhibited or self-conscious about such matters. He has a sense of detachment and can therefore overcome sexual dilemmas or difficulties more readily now. Because the person's attention is less on himself and more on union, his experience of orgasm entails greater freedom and surrender. His consciousness is expanded, and he is more receptive to unbounded, universal energies. Occult and metaphysical studies are greatly favored, and the person may succeed in secretive endeavors. It is an excellent time for deep investigations of astrology, tarot, science, and all sources of power.

The eighth house rules inheritances and joint finances. As a result, the person may now receive unexpected monies from wills, legacies, insurance companies, and other "unearned" means. But this, of course, is only likely if the natal chart promises these benefits from birth. There may be sudden fluctuations or disruptions involving monetary partnerships. Therefore, the person should be extra cautious and prudent about whom he deals with financially or borrows money from. Stability and security in this area are unlikely during this transit, as the person is unconventional, individualistic, and experimental in his joint financial dealings. However, although he may take more risks or incur unusual debts, he gains all kinds of knowledge and insights about the values of others. He becomes aware of his financial responsibilities to others.

This period generally brings very strong intuition, or, for some individuals, striking psychic episodes. Such experiences may be linked to past-life memories, astral entities, or other unexplained phenomena. The person is now in touch with the mysteries of nature. He is for the time being relieved of ordinary possession consciousness. He undergoes transformations in character and evolutionary growth with grace and ease. It is an exciting time of self-renewal.

Although the eighth house represents death, here it brings mainly the possibility of continual ego deaths and rebirths, as well as the end of worn-out behavioral patterns or ineffectual character traits. Personal transformation is indeed a death of sorts. As for physical death, this transit alone does not particularly indicate the person's death or that of any loved one. But if death does come now, it is likely to be sudden and quick.

When Uranus transits the ninth house, the person makes profound breakthroughs in his understanding of life. He continually gains philosophical insights and contemplates the meaning of existence from the broadest possible perspective. He is excited about religions, philosophies, spiritual truths, and any knowledge that illumines the higher laws and realities of life. The person no longer accepts traditional teachings and dogmas without question. Instead he trusts his own feelings and observations. Obsolete, rigid viewpoints and beliefs are demolished as the person passionately investigates new, progressive, and revolutionary paradigms. The person is open, inspired, imaginative, and idealistic. Above all, he maintains uncompromising integrity in his search for truth and meaning.

During this transit the person's social value system is transformed forever. As he investigates the world and draws his own enlightened conclusions about existence, his world view shifts. New systems of reality require different strategies and approaches. The previous Uranus passage (of the eighth house) brought insights into and liberation from the person's own deep-rooted attachments and behavioral attitudes. Breakthroughs occurred in personal, psychological, and behavioral freedom as well as plain old spiritual growth. Now, however, the person is focused on higher knowledge, universal truths, and age-old wisdom. The knowledge he gains now will eventually be brought to bear in his relationship with the world at large. The person examines his own principles, morals, and religious beliefs as he rethinks and reshapes his own unique life philosophy. But the overall ramifications of this transit are social, impersonal, and collective. To understand this it is necessary to consider the difference between the Uranus transits of the third house (the "lower mind") and the ninth house (the "higher mind").

When Uranus transits the third house, the person becomes receptive to sciences which break the boundaries and limitations of "normal" consciousness. His interest in astrology, metaphysics, tarot, yoga, and other New Age studies grows as the mind expands to embrace more subtle realities. During the ninth house Uranus transit, the person shows an interest in the same subjects, but the information he gains has a different meaning and significance. Unlike the intellectual growth the

86   person experienced during the third house transit, this expansion of the intellect is more profound as it affects every future action! The ninth house is extremely purposeful, and it is no accident that its significations (philosophy and higher knowledge) directly precede tenth house matters (one's life's calling and worldly activities). Suffice it to say that the more conscious and enlightened the person becomes in his ideology and philosophy, and the greater integrity he experiences regarding his personal beliefs and convictions, the more profound impact he will have on the world around him and the evolution of humanity as a whole. Thus, the ultimate use of the ninth house Uranus transit is for the person to investigate and experiment with truth and come to the most real and empowering understanding of reality that he can. His future, as well as the future of the world, depends upon it. The doctrine he ultimately chooses affects everyone and everything.

There may be a great deal of long-distance travel during this approximately seven-year period. The person may attend college, night school, or other institutions of higher learning. He may have dealings with foreigners or decide to study in a foreign country. He is open to progressive teaching techniques and revolutionary educational practices. As the person experiences change in his religious ideas and beliefs, he may abruptly forsake idols and mentors. He may come into contact with exciting, brilliant, strange, or eccentric teachers and gurus. As his perception of the world broadens during these years, he may become interested in law or social change. Intuition may be strong now, especially the ability to predict societal or public events.

The person may have insights and realizations about his ideals and visions. If he has previously been unrealistic or utopian in his thinking, the person may now become more reasonable and pragmatic. If his thinking been too mundane all along, he may finally wake up to a higher reality and find his vision expanding. The person may also scrutinize his belief in God. His faith, whether great or small, may fluctuate.

Authors, lecturers, and promoters of higher knowledge may find this transit exhilarating. The person is summoned to foreign countries to present his message or to translate his written material in other languages.

When Uranus transits the tenth house, the person makes break-throughs in his career as boundaries and restrictions are suddenly annihilated. He approaches his professional life afresh and feels inspired to redesign his worldly activity or life's calling. Unlike before, he is detached from his usual need for status and recognition. He is not concerned about consistency, conformity, or living his life to please others. Thus, he begins to test his most intimate, heartfelt desires about his vocation. He is excited and stimulated about all aspects of his career during this approximately seven-year period. New professional opportunities constantly arise and the person makes unpredictable, perhaps even heroic, career changes. However, there may be serious fluctuations in the person's rank and position. He is no longer thrilled about accepting orders from superiors if they differ even slightly from his own viewpoints and standards. As a result, he may have to start at the very bottom of a new business in order to maintain his integrity and to honor his newfound courage.

The person is poised to break away from monotonous projects and mundane practices, and he can make remarkable progress and expansion at this time. He may abruptly end one segment of his career and begin a brand new phase. The Uranus transit to the zenith of the birthchart (the tenth house) is extremely powerful, and the person is well advised to trust his feelings and desires and to make the most of his present awakening. All Uranus transits to angular houses bring about significant change, dynamic action, a profound sense of independence, and a compelling urge to express one's unique talents. Because the tenth house specifically symbolizes the person's mission and professional activities, he now has an ideal chance to demonstrate his. There is absolutely nothing to hold the person back from pursuing his own ideas and concepts. He overcomes inner censoring mechanisms generated by rules, regulations, and society's notions of what is or is not possible. Now is the perfect time for inventions and modernizations and to take whatever risks are necessary to further one's special calling.

The person may encounter difficulties or disputes with bosses, officials, and supervisors because of his independent, individualistic attitude. He may also quarrel with his father for the same reason. There is a strong possibility that the person will suddenly experience his father as an unstable influence. Therefore, this transit is a delicate one if it occurs during early childhood. If the father's behavior becomes unpredictable, irregular, or erratic, the person may feel he has very little control or power within their relationship. On the positive side, however, the person's father could begin to show an interest in metaphysics, mysticism, astrology, or New Age disciplines. He could also become more liberal, open-minded, enthusiastic, and uninhibited. In rare cases, where the father is very old or in failing health, the Uranus conjunction to the midheaven may coincide with the father's death. It should be noted, incidentally, that many astrologers consider the tenth house to represent the mother rather than the father, perhaps depending upon who is the main authority figure within the household. Astrologers who believe so may apply the above information to the person's mother instead of the father.

Although this transit signifies great potential for professional progress and career transformation, it is not necessarily comfortable, harmonious, or even welcomed. Uranus is not a particularly compatible influence with the house that corresponds to the earthy, material, and status-conscious sign of Capricorn. There will be continual ups and downs in the person's career, and unless he enjoys the thrill of living moment by moment in his professional life, he may be sorely irritated. This is a time of expansion and development rather than contentment and complacency. There is plenty of vocational growth and evolution, but not necessarily reward or acknowledgement. The person may enjoy some recognition during this transit, but it is almost entirely irrelevant to him emotionally and psychologically. Therefore, the person's task is to flow with nature and not try to hold on to any agenda of accomplishment he may previously have drawn up.

Individuals who have pursued astrology, metaphysics, occultism, or mysticism as an important hobby may now feel compelled to practice professionally. If the person considered sharing his psychic or spiritual knowledge in the past but restrained himself because of fears or "practical" concerns, his days of holding back are over. There will not be a better time to begin. The same is true of would-be inventors and scientists. Those who are involved in public careers now have enormous ability to incite, inspire, and stimulate their constituencies. If the person aspires to be a revolutionary of the people, then his time has definitely come. Whatever the person's calling, he now approaches his work in a dynamic and vital way, with little concern for the opinions and sentiment of the world. Because he feels detached from society and approaches his vocation objectively, he is able to embrace his true calling more passionately than ever. He may, however, surprise or shock establishment forces in the process.

When Uranus transits the eleventh house, the person breathes new life into his ultimate goals and ambitions. He reflects on the nature of personal fulfillment as he gains continual flashes of insight into what will really make him happy. Long-held fundamental dreams and visions change. This transit exists to break up erroneous or misguided aspirations the person may have embraced in his pursuit of contentment. It is an exciting time wherein the person recognizes the importance of gaining happiness, of doing real justice to the magnificent opportunity of life. To fulfill his purpose in God's creation, he must now experiment, investigate, and awaken to his own means of gaining relative (earthly) bliss.

The person makes breakthroughs in his evolutionary process as he reflects on his life's purpose. Thus, he is liberated from a vast array of mental concepts, philosophical doctrines, moral principals, vocational callings, and social teachings that he may have accepted as explaining human existence. The more insight and illumination he gains about his fundamental aspirations, the more powerful, profound, and integrated the rest of his life will be (assuming he is willing to take action). This is a very important and powerful transit, because the person also awakens to his social role, within his community and the world. As he becomes interested in improving society, he contemplates the possibility of humanitarian work and social or cultural reform. As the person learns what makes him happy, he is simultaneously inspired to build a better future for everyone. He experiences the connection between personal happiness and collective well-being.

As the person gains insights into his ideals and revises his goals and ambitions, he is compelled to rethink his friendships and group memberships. The person may find that his old friends and groups no longer fit in with his new direction. Further, he may simply rebel against the conformity or conservatism of his previous associates. The person feels free to create happiness for himself, and he may want to be around more fun-loving, exciting, stimulating people. His new companions may be quite different than his previous ones. He may associate with unconventional, independent, or highly spirited types. His new friends may be conspicuously spiritual or occult-minded. They may even practice astrology. Because Uranus transits often generate events beyond one's

control, the person may lose certain friends, or undergo strange occurrences with friends, for no apparent reasons.

Uranus is the ruler of Aquarius, and Aquarius is the corresponding
sign of the eleventh house. Therefore, Uranus passes through the
eleventh house with grace and coherence, or natural integrity.
Furthermore, Uranus and Aquarius imply strong scientific, metaphysical,
occult, and New Age overtones. The person may become involved in
groups advocating humanitarian or revolutionary progress. He may join
dynamic or innovative educational societies. There will be significant
personal progress because the person is more conscious and deliberate
in pursuit of his goals. He enjoys a more vibrant, exciting social life. He
may embrace new hopes and wishes or feel his old ones tremendously
revitalized. His chances of living a life with more pleasure, satisfaction,
and fulfillment are infinitely greater by the time this transit is over.

When Uranus transits the twelfth house, the person's unconscious mind is liberated, and many of his fears, neuroses, and psychological boundaries are brought to light and conquered. During this extremely spiritual transit, the person suddenly becomes aware of major factors that have been repressed within his psyche. As the person deals with these issues, he grows in inner freedom, as well as in detachment from the superficial and mundane in life. He confronts the truth rather than continuing to neglect his relationship to the Source or Creator, which is what happens when he suppresses painful or unpleasant psychological problems. He examines inner obstacles that have previously kept him from knowing his true nature and overcomes them. He wakes up to his unity and oneness with everything. During the transits of Uranus through all the previous houses, the person gained insight into himself and his relationship with the world. Now he awakens to something more significant. His individual soul is reconnected to the creative source of the universe.

Individuals working on growth of consciousness will gain solid advancement toward enlightenment (nirvana). However, there are two very important points to consider. First, the effects of this transit may be extraordinarily subtle—there is nothing more natural or inherent than inner freedom and unity. Indeed, the more spiritually and psychically healthy the individual is, the less commotion he will be likely to stir. Which brings us to the second point. The person's quality of consciousness has great bearing on the effects he will experience during this transit. If the person has ignored his true spiritual nature in the past, magnified his fears, and suppressed psychological problems with great intensity and rigidity, then he could now have major difficulties.

In such cases, sudden, surprising incidents expose secrets or dilemmas that the person has struggled to conceal. The person no longer has the power to control what his subconscious mind finally wants to confront. But if he is willing to face his experience honestly, he now has an ideal chance to relieve himself, once and for all, of many internal burdens.

During these years, the person is dealing with core issues directly affecting his evolution, spirit, and soul. Psychotherapy or other counseling undertaken at this time will have an extraordinary impact on the person's well-being for the rest of his life. The person begins to have flashes of insight into the destructive effects of any suppressed emotions. Few or no barriers now separate the conscious mind from distressing childhood memories or even from past-life impressions that have a damaging effect on the mind in this incarnation. The person feels restless and rebellious about his psychological limitations. He is unwilling to compromise his spiritual wholeness any longer. He may take up meditation, psychic investigation, hypnosis, or any self-development technique which promises to heal his ailing or vulnerable spirit. Dreams may be prolific and especially revealing at this time. The person is in touch with his "higher self" and he may dispel "mistakes of the intellect" (incorrect or delusional thinking which retards one's spiritual evolution and growth to perfection) quite readily now. Although Uranus' transit of the twelfth house has no specifically religious or devotional overtones, a spiritual rebirth of sorts may take place during this approximately seven-year period. The rebirth, however, occurs as a result of conscious attention to one's personal complexes rather than any instantaneous spiritual "conversion." The effects are highly personal, intimate, and sometimes subtle to the point of etheric.

The person will have strong intuition and psychic experiences, and he should trust such impulses. This transit is magnificent for artists, musicians, and anyone who relies upon inspiration in their daily work to transform abstract energies into concrete expressions. The imagination is completely unobstructed. The person can draw upon personal impressions residing within his psyche, as well as collective images from the beginning of time. Creativity is strong. By the end of this transit, the person has been honest with himself. In doing so, he has had the good fortune to discover the real meaning and essence of freedom. He is psychically liberated and ready to make the most of the first house Uranus transit, during which time he begins a profoundly conscious period of personality and character transformation.

When Neptune transits the first house, the person lives in his emotions, instincts, and impressions instead of in the rational side of his being. He relinquishes his fierce grip on the reality he sees through his senses and opens up to more ethereal, mystical, and spiritual energies. His senses are temporarily heightened, and his boundaries expand enormously as he experiences the whole of life rather than merely its physical form and structure. His perception is altered, and he may become aware of subtle or intangible dimensions. The person feels connected to all of existence. During these approximately fourteen years, the person behaves like a sponge, constantly absorbing the vibrations in his environment and empathizing deeply with those around him. He has no feelings of separateness, and he feels appreciative or grateful. His devotional and idealistic nature is awakened, and he is no longer completely satisfied with the material side of life alone. During this very spiritual transit, intuition, inspiration, and introspection are all very strong.

Although these years bring great potential for spiritual growth, deeper and more profound perception, and a better comprehension of the wholeness of life, this transit is not particularly easy. The influence of Neptune's qualities—ephemerality, intangibility, and illusiveness—can seriously weaken a person's assertiveness, self-esteem, and self image, as well as his grasp of the physical and practical. Therefore, the transit is especially hard for individuals who are ordinarily indecisive, uncertain, or lacking in stability or confidence. The person can expect some confusion, particularly in his personality. He lacks objectivity and his experience does not necessarily correspond to external reality. He finds himself merging with everyone and everything. He is especially emotional and may be unable to discriminate well. He must beware of exaggerated perceptions and subsequent inappropriate choices. The person wants to please everyone and create perfection, harmony, and bliss. He knows no boundaries. He may be in danger of being exploited or taken advantage of. The person is optimistic, gullible, and enthusiastic. He is especially generous and he sacrifices his own desires to help others. During this transit, the person must remember, above all, that much of what he believes to be real may actually be his own projection.

94   The person's imagination is active at this time. Music, painting, and all artistic endeavors are strongly favored. This is one of the best times to begin practicing meditation or studying any facet of mysticism. The person is more capable of prayer and surrender than before, and he readily experiences the celestial, the divine, and the sacred. The person feels egoless, and anything is possible now in the realm of religion and God. Dissatisfaction with ordinary existence and a longing for higher consciousness or final liberation characterize this transit.

The physical body may be extra sensitive during these years, and the person should be careful not to eat old or contaminated foods. He should do his best to eat pure foods which do not cause toxicity or contain poisons. Drugs of any kind will have extraordinarily powerful effects. Individuals with addictive personalities are at risk during this transit and should direct their escapist tendencies toward enlightenment and the transcendent, rather than hallucinogenics or alcohol.

Traditional astrological texts warn of potential scandals or secretive affairs. They also report that the person experiences major changes in the way he relates to others, partly because he is more impressionable and empathetic and partly because he is so affected by his subconscious mind.

When Neptune transits the second house, the person loosens his grip on his attachment to possessions in order to explore greater possibilities in the material world. His personal values and ideas about money change dramatically. Although the person suddenly begins to think in terms of affluence, almost paradoxically, he no longer feels so connected to his earthly treasures. He approaches money and possessions with philosophical, idealistic eyes and feels no need to function practically and reasonably toward them. For spiritual-minded individuals this transit brings an awakening of consciousness to internal prosperity, the wealth present within the soul. The person makes spiritual progress by distinguishing between changeable and therefore ultimately insignificant resources and invaluable, everlasting ones. For others, this period simply brings about a great quest for riches, although they will likely be elusive.

The person dreams about what is financially and materialistically possible. He thinks in grandiose terms about what he is worth, what he deserves, and what belongings he should own. However, the person should be extremely careful to differentiate between reality and wishful thinking. There is a danger of engaging in highly speculative endeavors, gambling enterprises, or get-rich-quick schemes. The person needs to discriminate between deceptive or fraudulent deals and genuine financial opportunities. He is especially vulnerable because he is so influenced by his imagination that he fails to evaluate risk clearly. Hard-earned capital may be easily dissipated during this transit. But of course, as always, all birthchart factors must be considered.

During these approximately fourteen years, the person's confidence, certainty, and security undergo serious analysis and change. This occurs quite naturally as the person suddenly finds himself unable to gain confidence from his possessions. Such effects may also occur, or be exacerbated by, his financial status which is very likely to fluctuate dramatically during this period. The person must recognize that healthy self-esteem and inner strength arise spontaneously from a balanced, well-nurtured psyche. Property and belongings simply will not fill the void the person feels about himself. Ultimately, the person engages in a subtle but important and powerful examination of meanings and values.

If he is strong and healthy enough to surrender to the experience and confront the reality of the human situation (where true stability can only come from within), then he will emerge victorious, free to enjoy living, or being, rather than owning. In this case, the person gains the greatest confidence of all, confidence born of freedom from attachment. In other words, he is free from the psychological consequences of loss or gain. Unfortunately, however, many individuals undergoing this transit do not achieve such an understanding. They simply feel confused, upset, or pained over difficult or changeable finances and the resulting loss of personal confidence.

The person gets a chance to determine his highest ideals and intentions regarding money. Traditional astrological texts report that the person can make money through artistic or spiritual endeavors during this transit. They also mention possible chaotic, secretive, or mysterious financial affairs.

When Neptune transits the third house, the person's mind expands to perceive more subtle, ethereal, and transcendental realms than he ordinarily experiences. The person adopts a new attitude and approach to everyday living. He relaxes the grip of his intellect and begins to think with his heart and soul. He favors his intuition and feelings over rational and analytical examination. He broadens his perspective and tries to see the whole picture. Mental boundaries and limitations disappear, and the person may take an interest in astrology, metaphysics, meditation, or mysticism. This is one of the best periods of all for prayer and devotional activities. The person is influenced by his imagination, inspirations, and fantasies. He is mentally idealistic, optimistic, and visionary. He thinks in terms of supreme achievement rather than satisfactory, passable results. He focuses on theories, abstracts themes, and profound universal issues.

Although this period is spiritually powerful, especially because the mind is so unaffected by boundaries, minor details, and daily concerns, many facets of the person's practical life suffer. The person temporarily loses much of his mental objectivity and discriminative powers. He may be gullible, sentimental, and impressionable. He may have a hard time concentrating and may forget trivial errands and inconsequential tasks. Daydreaming becomes a favorite pastime, and the person finds himself confused on more occasions than he would like. Relationships with relatives, especially siblings, may be significantly impaired, and the person must beware of miscommunications, misrepresentations, or deceptive dealings within his family. In extreme cases, siblings may act strange, weird, or secretive for no apparent reason. The person is also at the mercy of mysterious affairs with neighbors or others in his immediate environment. He is more affected by his fears and particular neuroses than usual. Because he suddenly loses so much control of his daily affairs and mundane existence, the person may begin to feel insecure, unprotected, and occasionally downright unstable. The nerves are under attack, and the person should take care to get plenty of rest and recreation.

On the positive side, these approximately fourteen years are excellent for creativity, artistic expression, and ingenuity. The mind is flexible, adaptable, and open, and the person feels anything is possible. He responds to spiritual and psychic things, and is able to discern subtle truths with his feelings and emotions. Constant and important personal insights throughout Neptune's entire transit of the third house make this an excellent time for the study of psychology.

In order to make the most of this period, the person could pursue mind expansion, astrology, psychological development, prayer, or highly imaginative writing. At the same time the person must strive for accuracy, mental clarity, careful negotiations, and decisions based on proper analysis rather than emotional projection. If possible, the person may wish to delegate those tasks requiring precision and analysis to loved ones, associates, or employees.

When Neptune transits the fourth house, the person embarks on a psychological though largely unconscious quest to discover his essence. He relinquishes patterns of behavior that have provided security in the past in order go beyond surface behavior and arrive at the core of his soul. This is an extremely powerful and profound transit, subtle though it is, for the spiritual seeker in pursuit of self-knowledge. Neptune is exalted in Cancer, the natural or corresponding sign of the fourth house, and, as a result, the person is exceptionally aware of his feelings, instincts, and perceptions. He has an excellent opportunity to experience his true nature, unaffected and undisturbed by childhood conditioning and the influence of society. The person courageously lets go of what is safe and comfortable so that he can determine exactly what sustains his existence and allows him to function as a stable individual in an ever-changing universe. If the person is ever to find his roots, it is now. This is an excellent time for introspection, meditation, and psychological inquiry.

The person may experience some form of dissolving or slowly disintegrating breakdown within his home space. This can mean deterioration of his home or land, especially gas, oil, or water leakages, or it may manifest as domestic problems with his spouse, parents, or family. The person should avoid storing valuables at home and make sure his property is well protected and insured. He should periodically check for termites or other things that could erode the foundation of his house. Strange or weird incidents may occur in the home, especially at the onset of this transit. A family member may begin to behave oddly or indulge in alcohol or drugs. At some point during these approximately fourteen years, the person may decide to use his home for spiritual purposes. Or a spiritual person may come to visit and stay in the person's home.

Transits to angular houses always bring about an increased influence of the transiting planet. Thus, during Neptune's transit of the fourth house, the person's idealism and devotion increase significantly. If the person is at all spiritually inclined, he is likely to become engrossed in mystical endeavors, ego renunciation, or the pursuit of enlightenment. The person has powerful intuition now, and psychic or supernatural experiences come naturally. Through such experiences, the person learns viscerally of his immortal, everlasting soul. Artistic endeavors are greatly favored. The person is imaginative and creative, and has clear access to his inner resources. He functions from his heart and is sensitive to his environment. He is appreciative of Mother Earth, the myths of the land, and the traditions brought to him by his parents and ancestors.

Certain individuals undergoing this transit may be especially moody. They may be uncomfortable with psychological changes that occur when latent or repressed childhood memories surface. The person may have problems with his mother, who is subject to peculiar or eccentric behavior. His mother may become interested in religion, spiritualism, or devotional life. She may unintentionally withdraw emotional support, which could be quite devastating if this transit occurs during early childhood years. In cases where the mother is very old or in failing health, this transit does not help matters. In rare cases, the mother may become mentally unstable. There is also a possibility that the person will have to take care of one or both of his parents, even to the extent of taking them permanently into his home. Astrologers who consider the fourth house to signify the father rather than the mother may wish to apply the above to the father.

When Neptune transits the fourth house, the person contemplates his highest vision of home life. He explores all possibilities and generates many ingenious ideas for his dream house. If this transit comes toward the very end of life, however, the person is likely to live peacefully and spiritually in restful, hermit-like seclusion.

When Neptune transits the fifth house, the person's ego is dissolved so that he may directly experience the highest qualities of human life: selflessness, compassion, benevolence, generosity, and sublime spiritual love. The person sacrifices his individual needs and preferences in favor of others. In romance, he learns how to love another person selflessly, rather than for what he stands to gain. His passions and infatuations in all areas are suddenly motivated by admiration, devotion, worship, and idealism. He is more considerate and thoughtful when pursuing the pleasures and enjoyments of life. Please note, however, that this transit is generally difficult unless the person is extremely spiritual, humble, altruistic, and egoless by nature. Since most people today, especially Westerners, live for ego gratification and the development of their own particular talents and abilities, the tendencies of this period can be at cross purposes to the person's goals. With self-expression and individuality no longer dominant, the person surrenders his confidence and pride. As astrologer/author Robert Hand constantly points out, Neptune is in no way friendly or favorable to the human ego; Neptune epitomizes everything alien to individuality, but the fifth house, the arena of creativity and self-expression, represents a person's distinctness, speciality, and uniqueness. The combination of Neptune and the fifth house is in many ways as incongruous as it gets.

For individuals who are excessively proud or conceited, these approximately fourteen years can be hellish on the psyche. Aside from the weakening of self-confidence and assertiveness which the transit naturally brings, the person's poise and dignity may be adversely affected by poor investments, overly emotional or unrealistic love interests, and an impaired grasp of practical matters caused by a departure from practical thinking. Individuals who are prone to hedonism or excess may have to be careful during this transit. The person may develop strong urges for alcohol or drugs, or he may go overboard in partying. Love affairs during this time are not much favored, mostly because they are not what they seem. The person is so emotional that he may idolize members of the opposite sex or fall in love with his image of someone rather than the real person. His imagination works overtime. It is also common during these years to fall in love with someone who is married, unavailable, mysterious, strange, weird, or mystical and devotional. On the more positive side, however, the person may get an exquisite taste of romance, exoticism, or spiritual love even if the relationship is not long lasting.

The person should avoid gambling and speculations. Investments are likely to be unstable, erratic, fraudulent, or deceptive, even though they may appear incredibly fortunate. Relationships with children are subject to confusion or chaos. Because he is functioning too emotionally, the person must make an effort to see things objectively. His children may behave strangely or unconventionally. They may begin to engage in spiritual, metaphysical, or mystical movements. In extreme cases the children may take drugs or alcohol.

All forms of artistic or creative endeavors are powerfully favored. The person is as inspired and imaginative as he will ever be. His creative fantasies are easily materialized, and he is not at all bothered by an inner censoring mechanism or any mental restrictions. If the person is a musician, filmmaker, photographer, or magician, this may be one of his most prolific periods.

The person sees life in more grandiose, majestic terms at this time. His sense of appreciation is dramatically heightened. As he lets go of his pride and feelings of personal superiority, the person experiences an important sense of unity with the rest of the human race. He discovers the illusory nature of his individual identity, and realizes that we are all the same in spirit. The person becomes perfectly willing to sacrifice his own desires in order to support others. This does not mean that he takes an interest in aiding or improving society, but that he sees himself in everyone he meets and therefore empathizes with them. These years are characterized by a utopian or romantic freedom of spirit, a yearning for a kind of unattainable bliss, and a willingness to give one's all for another. Although this transit does not help with worldly progress (unless the person is an artist), the person is forever enhanced because of it. His generosity, compassion, and perspective on life are richer and broader by the end of this phase. Neptune transiting the fifth house opens the person's heart such that it can never completely close again.

Traditional astrological texts report that the person may experience sexual dilemmas, unwanted pregnancies, and an intense longing for idyllic love. In love, he should expect to give more than he receives during these years.

When Neptune transits the sixth house, the person loses his workplace discipline and restricted focus at work, and begins to feel inspired, imaginative, idealistic, and visionary in his daily job. He now sees the real purpose of work as an opportunity to serve individuals in a way that profoundly affects their lives. He feels an urge to apply the selflessness he gained when Neptune transited his fifth house to the most routine activities of his daily life. Unfortunately, however, unless the person has great control over and choice about his employment, he is liable to experience these years as a period of slavery at worst or drudgery at best. The person feels no desire whatsoever to engage in mundane, methodical tasks that simply profit the organization and its investors. If he cannot directly see his work making a significant difference in the lives of others, he remains frustrated, discouraged, or upset. Although this transit can certainly bring great benefits, growth, and expansion, as all Neptune transits may, it is a difficult one because of the incongruous natures of Neptune and the sixth house. Neptune is an unbounded, infinite, and formless influence while the sixth house is a highly technical or specialized one, encompassing discipline, habit, system, and minute attention to detail. Neptune, the ruler of Pisces, is in its detriment in Virgo, the sign corresponding to the sixth house.

There may be health problems at the beginning of this transit, especially caused by poisons, toxins, or spoiled foods. The body is especially vulnerable now, and illnesses develop slowly and insidiously. Diseases and afflictions are more difficult to diagnose than usual, and the person should get more than one or two medical opinions lest he be wrongly treated. He must beware of stress, strain, and overwork. Emotional balance plays a major role in the person's vitality and fitness, and he must therefore be observant and attentive to psychological well-being. He should take immediate action if there are any physical or mental weaknesses, deficiencies, or disorders. Otherwise, matters are almost certain to decay or disintegrate, as that is the way Neptune energy operates. More than ever, the person may heal himself through natural remedies, mental affirmations, creative visualizations, and behavior that is consistent with the laws of nature. The person may engage in special diets for health purposes or spiritual evolution. He may decide to become a vegetarian. Drugs and alcohol have a very bad effect on the

104   system during these approximately fourteen years. Even prescribed medicines may be more powerful than expected.

On the positive side, this is one of the best times to begin a career in medicine, nursing, or spiritual healing. The person is intuitive and insightful about health matters. He is interested in self-improvement and can make great advances if he is diligent and acts upon his vision. The person now considers the spiritual and holistic value of his daily tasks and chores. His work must have meaning, must not harm even one entity, and he must perform to the best of his ability. He has little, if any, patience for details and particulars unless he sees that they serve a larger purpose. If the person's daily work supports his ideals, he will work selflessly and unrelentingly toward his goal. No hardship is too great as long as his task is worthwhile.

The person may experience strange or peculiar difficulties with maids, servants, employees, or co-workers; deception, illusion, or betrayal are possible. Mysterious or odd work conditions may lead to disappointment, discouragement, and dissatisfaction. In extreme cases, the person may be required by his boss to lie or cheat on a regular basis.

Individuals involved in music, art, and photography may find these years productive for their craft. They are able to make their creative visions a reality.

When Neptune transits the seventh house, the person loses his objectivity about relationships so that he can appreciate ideal love and perfect partnership. He suspends rational analysis in this realm and begins to function from the depths of his heart. He is inspired, romantic, passionate, and devoted toward his loved one. However, he is unrealistic and impractical, making it difficult for him to understand his mate's intentions and motivations. The person is vulnerable to illusion, deception, fraud, and disloyalty in both love and business partnerships. He may experience more confusion, misrepresentation, and miscommunication in important close relationships than usual for approximately fourteen years. The person projects all kinds of ideal qualities onto his lover and is willing to sacrifice almost anything to be with that person. His imagination is overly stimulated, and he may therefore be unable to create a relationship that is equal. Many individuals unwittingly set themselves up for disappointment or disillusionment in their primary love relationship. Obviously, the person can benefit from the advice of friends and relatives about the suitability of his partners during these years. In extreme cases, the person is liable to painfully discover that the loved one of his dreams is not what he believed all along.

The person may be attracted to unique companions who are extremely different from himself. Partners may be idealistic, mystical, devotional, and highly religious. Or they may be prone to taking drugs, alcohol, or other activities which lead them to altered states of consciousness. In some cases the partner may simply be strange or weird. There is also a chance that the spouse or loved one may suddenly begin to exhibit Neptunian qualities. That person could start to behave strangely, take hallucinogens, engage in mysterious activities or secretive love affairs, or all of the above. In such cases, the person experiencing the transit should contemplate his own behavior to determine whether he is giving out signals to prompt his mate to act differently.

On the positive side, the person feels a spiritual and psychic bond with his partner and greatly appreciates being in the relationship. He feels the great joy that comes from loving another person wholeheartedly and unconditionally. He wants to give and give, and then give more. As he merges more and more with his mate, he is spared any nagging sense of separateness or selfishness. The person grasps the essence of peace, harmony, love, and compromise. He has little, if any, inclination to argue or fight as a negotiating ploy. He may form a partnership or marriage with a spiritual leader, religious figure, or a guru. During these years the person is especially sensitive to issues of fairness. He wants to do right by others and is sympathetic, understanding, and diplomatic. He does not want anyone's feelings to be hurt. The person is in touch with the higher qualities of his nature.

Transits to angular houses always produce significant effects of the planet involved. Thus, the person now exhibits or experiences Neptunian qualities: abundant idealism, devotion, or spiritual urges. He may be like a sponge, readily absorbing the positive or negative vibrations of his environment. Traditional astrological texts say that this is a poor time for lawsuits or dealings with attorneys. They also say that it is a typical time to fall in love with a married or otherwise unavailable person.

When Neptune transits the eighth house, the person releases control of his desires and cravings and begins to experience more inner freedom. The person subconsciously sets aside worn out aspects of his own agenda as he is freed from long-standing personal boundaries. This is a time of internal change and growth of consciousness, a time of psychic liberation. The person relinquishes emotional attachments, ego identification, and compulsive behavior arising from psychological imbalance.

Although this brings great evolutionary growth, a troublesome, annoying, and difficult situation remains. During these approximately fourteen years, the person loses his grasp on his personal desires and motivations. His broader perspective compels him to operate within a spiritual context; he is moved by the needs of his soul, his being, and true destiny rather than by what feels good or appears rewarding on the surface. This can be disconcerting. Suddenly, and for no apparent reason, the person has trouble maintaining any desire that does not fit perfectly with nature's plan for his growth and development. Many conscious and deliberate desires simply lose their power, whether the person likes it or not.

This period signifies a new era or rebirth. However, the changes are not outwardly obvious. Death, reincarnation, astral experiences, and everything connected to the secretive, mysterious, or hidden side of life are now experienced and appreciated. In his ideals, visions, and inspirations, the person is so (consciously or unconsciously) identified with evolution, universal laws, and natural energies, that his values automatically become higher. He is more spiritual, intuitive, genuine, and metaphysical. He understands what is real and important in this ever-changing, illusory world in which we live. If death occurs to a close friend or loved one, the person will be profoundly affected or deeply disturbed. He accepts death as a natural phenomenon at this time, but he is acutely aware of the loss of contact with a kindred soul.

Neptune's transit through the eighth house is a good time to engage in therapy or any healing method that frees a person from obsessions, fears, and psychological limitations. The person is better able to distance himself from his cravings, and he flows with change easier than usual. Traditional astrological texts report that this period is bad for joint finances and money from wills, legacies, inheritances, and other un-earned means. In fact, these years may find the person experiencing financial difficulties with money in general. The person's higher self is simply more interested in evolution and concerns of the soul than worldly affairs. In certain cases, there may be sexual dilemmas or lack of interest in sex, although it is also possible for the person to suddenly idealize the sex act or correlate eroticism with the Divine. The person is emotionally sensitive, open, and deeply vulnerable for approximately fourteen years. Subtle evolutionary growth is taking place whether it is obvious or not. The person's desire nature is transformed. But he does not lose his desires, he loses his identification and attachment to them.

When Neptune transits the ninth house, the person is inspired and idealistic about religion, philosophy, and higher knowledge. He feels a powerful sense of devotion and is committed to the experience of nirvana or higher consciousness. He wants to know the ultimate truth. He longs for a philosophy that transcends ordinary thinking and explains the dilemmas and discrepancies of everyday life. He is looking for the meaning of human life, and he may relinquish rational convictions in favor of a comprehensive belief system. He is open to all religions and doctrines, even those from foreign countries. No philosophy is too strange, as long as it provides the mystical or spiritual experience he now feels so ready for.

The person may become a disciple of a guru or join a spiritual movement. Prayer and all other forms of communication with God are extremely favored during these approximately fourteen years. The person is unrestricted in his thinking. He is intellectually open, impressionable, and vulnerable, and may take to the path of meditation, contemplation, or monkhood. In terms of spiritual experience, anything is possible. The person is as inspired about God as he will ever be, and he may therefore have sublime experiences that he will remember for the rest of his days.

Long distance travel for spiritual purposes is favored during this time. However, the person should beware of deception or fraud in his contact with foreigners. The person's judgement may be negatively affected due to an overly optimistic or gullible attitude. In extreme cases, he could be duped by false gurus or religious charlatans.

While this transit is generally quite favorable and smooth, the person must do his best to avoid spiritual arrogance and extreme philosophical opinions. In his newfound belief system or religious path the person may feel saved, and therefore judge others harshly or become overzealous in trying to recruit his companions. There is a tendency to fall prey to cults, sects, and panaceas of all sorts. The person's vision is so unrestricted, and he functions so much on faith, that simple discrimination may be lacking. For individuals who were engaged in religious or spiritual life before this transit, these years may bring a culmination of bliss, ecstasy,

110 splendor, and heavenly joy. A universal, all-encompassing sense of wisdom, freedom, and reverence for the divine may envelop the person. Along with this comes prophetic ability and an understanding of life that affects the person forever.

When Neptune transits the tenth house, the person relinquishes his quest for rank, position, and status in favor of work that contributes significantly to the world. He gives up his personal goals for more universal goals and humanitarian ends. During these approximately fourteen years, the person's attitude toward his profession undergoes a subtle but definite transformation. He no longer sees his career as merely a livelihood and an individual path. Suddenly he becomes aware of the enormous opportunity to transcend his personal agenda and do something great for others. He is extremely idealistic about his professional life and wants to scale the heights of his own potential. The person feels as if he has been marking time in his career and must now take action to make his ultimate dreams and visions a reality. He lets go of his sense of professional obligation and commitment, and concerns himself with his supreme calling. It is as though his entire life's work has built up to this important time.

Although the person is poised to make profound progress in one of the most important and vital areas of his life, this transit is by no means easy. For one thing, Neptune is fallen in Capricorn—the corresponding sign of the tenth house. For another, Neptune in the tenth represents an ethereal influence in an earthy and practical house. The person functions from his heart in an area of life which demands discrimination, logic, and proper judgement. There may be confusion, disorientation, and fear about confronting one's calling. The person is sensitive and vulnerable in his career and must beware of deception from managers, supervisors, or anyone who is threatened by the person's potential. If he is engaged in a profession he is unsuited for, his position may slowly disintegrate to the point where he is forced to retire or resign. Scandals are possible, as is the collapse of structures upon which lifelong career ambitions have been built. The person must be careful not to lie or cheat, or he will quickly pay the price.

This is an excellent time for would-be artists, musicians, dramatists, and other creative types. It is also a typical time to engage in volunteer work, humanitarian projects, or any venture which serves to uplift society. Healing work is especially favored, as is a career in religion, astrology, metaphysics, mysticism, or spiritualism. The person must

112   follow the dictates of his heart and soul if he is to maintain any contentment during these years. Should he continue to pursue an old, worn-out profession, as many people do, he will have no peace—only nagging frustration, discouragement, and depression born of resignation. The person must summon up his courage and act upon his ideals. While he may tell others he is confused about which career move to make, it is more likely that he is simply scared to make a new and far more significant commitment in his career than he has ever made. The person has to surrender control over his career and maintain faith in nature. The person needs to choose what he intuitively knows is right, whether or not it seems logical. The person should think in terms of making a contribution and achieving perfection rather than making a practical choice.

The person may suddenly have difficulties with his father, especially if the father is old or in failing health. Either the father begins to act weird, or he consciously or unconsciously withdraws his emotional support. In more fortunate cases, the father pursues devotional, mystical, or spiritual interests, while in other cases the father may indulge in alcohol or drugs. If this transit occurs during early childhood, the effects of the father's behavior on the psyche and emotions can be serious and damaging.

Whenever major planets transit angular houses, the planetary energy involved is more powerfully expressed. Thus, the person may be more idealistic, dreamy, romantic, and devotional. He is more gullible, particularly in career matters, and he may be more sensitive, vulnerable, and impressionable. He is less interested in fame and reputation and more concerned with performing good deeds which aid society and bring out his greatest talents. In very rare cases, the person may engage in a spiritual quest.

When Neptune transits the eleventh house, the person becomes idealistic and hopeful about his dreams, visions, and goals. He is able to visualize substantial personal accomplishments without any fear of failure. There is abundant positive energy, and the person has no fears or doubts of success. The grander his vision, the more enthusiastic he is. Unfortunately, however, he is so optimistic that he loses his normal sense of discernment and discrimination. He overlooks the details and work involved in making any goal come true. He is therefore subject to disappointment or disillusionment in the end. This transit is better for gaining a sense of ambitions than actually realizing any particular goal. Now is the time for the person to use his imagination to fantasize about what will make him happy and fulfilled. The person no longer censors ideas about what is possible, and he is open to all opportunity. He is now innocent and enthusiastic about life's potential and promise.

Because the eleventh house corresponds to the sign of Aquarius, the person begins to envision utopia for all. He dreams of a humane world and may contribute his time and efforts to helping his community. He feels warmth and compassion towards people. If the person enjoys groups, he may join charitable or philanthropic organizations, but more for altruistic than social motives. Or he may be attracted to spiritual movements whose main purpose is to save the world or uplift others. The person's choice of friends may go undergo a major change. First, old friends may begin to behave differently. They may act strangely or they may suddenly lie. The person should be on guard against deception from his friends. Second, the person may start to fraternize with spiritual, mystical, or religious individuals. He may also meet many artists. In extreme cases, or instances where the eleventh house is afflicted at birth, the person associates with alcoholics, drug addicts, or weird and unstable individuals.

These fourteen years provide an opportunity to expand a person's dreams and aspirations and to explore what he can do for the good of society. The person's association with groups and friends can be enriched if he remains true to his highest vision while maintaining discrimination and wise judgement.

When Neptune transits the twelfth house, the door to God and the infinite is opened. It is time to enjoy the goal of human existence—higher consciousness. The person turns inward, withdrawing his attention from external creation. During this introspective period of approximately fourteen years, the person consciously or unconsciously seeks to reconnect his soul with the universe, God, and nature. The person has ended his years of devotion to worldly affairs and is now ready to savor the consciousness that he has gained. His attention falls back onto his inner experience rather than on the flash and glitter of fulfilling individual desires. Thus, he begins to feel innocence, wholeness, faith, and spirituality. He functions from completeness, satisfied with what he is—not what he has. He feels little separation, isolation, or alienation, although he may feel a powerful urge to retreat from the commotion of society.

Neptune is at home in the twelfth house, the house corresponding to the sign of Pisces, which is Neptune's ruler. Therefore, the person has great access to his unconscious mind, as well as past events which he may have unwittingly ignored or suppressed. Important childhood recollections or enjoyable past-life remembrances may surface. This is a good time for psychological cleansing and healing. The person feels compassion for both himself and others. His intuition operates powerfully; he may even feel divine guidance. It is an excellent time for meditation and contemplation; mystical experiences are quite possible. Spiritual initiations are favored, as are charitable endeavors. The person finds meaning and value in his earthly existence. A person with a high level of consciousness or clear intellectual understanding of spiritual values will feel that he has come home.

In certain cases, especially where the person is closed to religion, faith, or spirituality, this period may bring confusion, disturbance, or frustration. Such a person is unable to understand or appreciate the direction his instincts now spontaneously take. He is uncomfortable letting go of control and he fears confronting the unknown. He believes that a psychological state which lacks explicit boundaries is dangerous or unhealthy. The person may become upset as he takes stock of his past experiences. He may be disturbed by his past failures or inadequacies.

The person feels more sensitive, vulnerable, and tender-hearted than usual.

Because Neptune is very much at home in the twelfth house, all twelfth house matters flourish. Now is a favorable time to engage in volunteer work and to perform service to relieve suffering. If the person is an artist or musician by profession, these years will be most prolific. The imagination is fertile and productive, and the person is able to tap into creative ideas and impressions from his own past as well as from the collective unconscious of society. The person is empathetic, generous, and concerned with universal peace and harmony.

P

When Pluto transits the first house, the person experiences a rebirth of vital energy, willpower, and raw potential. Suddenly, for no apparent reason, he feels an intense urge to make use of his abilities, especially those which have previously remained dormant. The person has reached a point in his evolution where he is tired of holding in his power and influence. At the very beginning of this transit, when Pluto sits exactly on or very close to the ascendant, (which may occur on and off for an entire year), the person feels like an active volcano ready to erupt. His vibrational rate increases and he feels more alive and intense. His presence expands, and he becomes more vibrant and magnetic. The person is the embodiment of evolution in action, leaving behind his old, worn-out inhibitions in favor of creativity and self-expression.

The person should be made aware, however, that it is crucial to engage in dynamic action, take a new direction, or become a positive leader. Pluto represents pure potential; its intense energy regenerates the organism. The person may now make phenomenal advances in whatever area he wishes, if he is willing to make use of his talents and gifts. Unfortunately, many individuals feel as if something spectacular will spontaneously happen, and they merely wait in expectation. The person must take hold of his newfound power as readily and comfortably as he can and direct it in whatever way he deems suitable. Pluto's transit of the first house is an opportunity of a lifetime. In eighty years, Pluto will only transit three to six houses, and the ascendant is one of the most significant aspects of the birthchart. This period should not be wasted.

During the next twelve to thirty-one years, depending on the sign Pluto is transiting, the person undergoes an important restructuring of his personality. He is continually receiving feedback from others on how to improve his character, temperament, and image. Because he is more sensitive and vulnerable than usual, he may feel hurt by criticism, but he is committed, whether consciously or not, to balancing his personality and perfecting himself. He may experience the death and rebirth of his ego or psyche many times as he purges old habit patterns. He is guided or, in some cases, forced to let go of certain inappropriate behaviors that create discord in the environment. The person is extremely conscious of his actions and motivations, and during these years he functions on instinct and guts. He is as true to himself as he will ever be, and he is **117** practically incapable of self-deception or pretense. Because this period can bring such enormous growth and development, close relationships may change significantly or end. However, this is more likely during the first year or two of the transit, when Pluto hovers near the ascendant.

As the person comes into his power and his unconscious becomes conscious, he may find that certain friendships or love relationships do not support his new approach to life. The evolutionary leap the person now experiences may bring along with it power struggles and ego clashes. The person should be careful to try not to dominate others or subject them to his will, but to make his position known. His level of personal integration and self-actualization increases, and he has greater self-control, resourcefulness, and vitality. He feels his individuality heightened and intensified. The person senses that his time has arrived, and if he is willing to take action, he will find that it has.

Certain individuals feel a desire to get to the core of their existence and perfect themselves. The person may therefore take an interest in self-development and study occult subjects such as astrology, yoga, and other techniques that explore hidden dimensions. These disciplines now bring powerful results and rapid evolution. The person's progress is dynamic and apparent. His intuition is more obvious and accurate, and he feels a sense of connection to nature and the universe. His charisma and sex appeal intensify. He is more persistent, bold, determined, and assured. By the time this transit is over, the person has transformed his personality and gained tremendous self-knowledge. In more fortunate cases, the person embraces his destiny and begins to make a powerful impact on the world.

P

When Pluto transits the second house, the person experiences a major transformation of his values and his resources. He feels a sudden compulsion for security and protection, and he wants to gain great riches—mainly tangible but, in some cases, spiritual. During Pluto's transit of the first house, the person embraced his personal power, overhauled his personality, and revitalized his self-image. Now he examines those possessions—both psychological and physical—upon which he bases his confidence. During these years the person is very sensitive about his self-worth. He is enormously committed, whether consciously or not, to determining exactly how valuable he is and what he deserves to own. The person undergoes a painstaking process of ego death-and-rebirth connected to his confidence and self-worth. If his sense of self-worth is strong and healthy to begin with, he has a good chance of gaining great wealth at the beginning of this transit. In many cases, however, the person's belief in himself is in such serious need of improvement that he spontaneously loses the bulk of his assets and is forced to rebuild his entire financial structure from scratch. During this process the person confronts the real issue at hand—his feelings about himself.

The person spends between twelve and thirty-one years, depending on the sign Pluto is transiting, discovering what he values most, what will provide the best, most stable, and worthwhile existence. Some, especially spiritual seekers, will find that material assets are unimportant. The person comes to realize that real security comes only from within, and he may therefore decide to use his wealth mainly for furthering his evolution. Other, more worldly and materially-minded individuals, become intense and emotional about wealth. The person feels attached to his resources and belongings and tries to use them to bolster his self-assurance. Power struggles over money or possessions are likely, and the person is wise to carefully examine his behavior in this realm. It is easy to be ruthless and power-hungry now, but such conduct will have negative consequences. Pluto is in its detriment in Taurus, the corresponding sign of the second house, and this transit is therefore more difficult than most. The person is not at all comfortable at having to purge himself of long-held values and to renovate basic financial structures. Nor does he find it easy to analyze his feelings of confidence and self-esteem.

On the positive side, if the person has always wanted wealth, he can make his dream come true now, especially if he has been working toward such ends for some time. During this transit some individuals suddenly become wealthy. The person may reap monetary rewards of past-life efforts and finally fulfill his financial destiny. Whether or not the person's financial status changes significantly, this period is an ideal time to enjoy the physical universe to the fullest. The person appreciates art, beauty, and all earthly delights. The person may enjoy pleasures, comforts, commodities, and collectibles more than ever before. Traditional astrological texts mention that Pluto's transit through the second house may indicate earnings from metaphysical or spiritual endeavors. The main purpose of these years, however, is for the person to determine an appropriate set of values that will support a fulfilling and evolutionary existence.

P

When Pluto transits the third house, the person's conscious mind is energized and his ability to communicate is transformed. The person discovers enormous potential for self-expression and intellectual power for delving deeply into all areas of investigation. He probes the depths of his rational mind in order to find truth and to discover new perspectives. He examines his habits and becomes thoroughly aware of his mind. He wants to understand his psychology and the paradigms by which he lives, as well as the underlying laws of the universe. The person is ready to begin studying astrology, yoga, metaphysics, or any previously unfamiliar philosophy that elucidates the practical workings of creation. The person is open-minded and his mind functions better than ever.

Concentration improves dramatically, and the person finds that he has excellent abilities to evaluate situations and solve puzzles or problems. It is an ideal time to be begin meditation, contemplation, prayer, or affirmations. The person can now imbue his thoughts with feeling thereby increasing his creative power. If he is interested in healing himself through psychology or psychotherapy, he will succeed with ease. He is alert, aware, and conscious, and his discrimination and perception are acute. Willpower improves, and the person is serious and resolute about his goals. He is likely to accomplish the goals he has formed in his mind. If the person is a psychologist, counselor, teacher, or researcher by profession, these years may well be his most productive and prolific. Writers, lecturers, and those involved in communication will also benefit tremendously from this transit. The person's ability to communicate is significantly enhanced, and he moves others with his speech in ways never possible before.

The person thinks more deeply, and he may have profound thoughts. He is hungry for all the knowledge he can get, especially information about the basics of human existence. He spends time and energy contemplating the customs, conventions, and habits of everyday living—things he previously took for granted. He examines how and why he functions within his environment. He questions everything in hopes of finding the ideal path for an efficient and fruitful life. And he is more than willing to surrender his old beliefs in favor of more suitable ones. The person may feel a strong urge to return to school or to begin a teaching career.

Dealings with siblings are now important and significant. The person is sensitive and vulnerable to the influence of his brothers and sisters, and he is powerfully affected by them. Although he begins to function more emotionally towards them, he should resist the temptation to try and control or dominate them. He should be careful of power struggles, confrontations, and competition with them. During these twelve to thirty-one years, depending on the sign Pluto is transiting, the person has a unique opportunity to deepen his bond with siblings and to experience greater passion, depth, and emotional fulfillment in his relationships with his brothers and sisters.

By the end of this transit, the person is much more knowledgeable about life, especially the practicalities and fundamentals of everyday existence. His mind is more seasoned and skillful. He has learned, perhaps painfully, to let go of extreme opinions and inflexible or unreasonable attitudes and beliefs. Traditional astrological texts mention that the person may experience intense effects during short distance travel.

P

When Pluto transits the fourth house, the person turns his attention deep within in order to create inner stability, security, and a basis for lasting contentment. He tries to establish the strongest foundation possible for his outer activity. Toward this end he engages in a process, whether conscious or not, of distinguishing his own reality from that which he absorbed from parents and society. During Pluto's transit of the third house, the person examined truths affecting his daily existence. Now he must discover those inner truths which directly affect his happiness and reasons for living. The person is extremely sensitive and vulnerable during these years because his attention rests deep within his soul rather than in the outer environment. He scrutinizes his unconscious for hints of old conditioning and habit patterns that no longer serve any positive purpose. Childhood experiences and memories are analyzed, processed, and put aside. This is one of the best periods of all to engage in psychotherapy, counseling, or other forms of healing. Changes happening now occur at the deepest level of the human psyche.

The person is very intuitive now. He behaves instinctively and feels close to nature. He wants to get to the core of things and may therefore begin to investigate metaphysics or the occult. If he is involved in spiritual pursuits before this transit, then he will find this period extremely beneficial for his progress. He can let go of deep childhood attachments, root out neurotic tendencies, and come face to face with his soul. Pluto transits of angular houses bring enormous power and potential which may be used in any way the person desires. The person now has the ability to command authority, influence others, and to express himself strongly. He has a profound opportunity to take charge of his destiny and to increase his personal integrity.

Domestic life may be intensely affected, especially at the beginning of this transit. The person suddenly feels emotional and moody about his home space. Within his home, he feels a need to control his experiences as well as his furnishings or physical surroundings. His habitat becomes very important, and if the person is living in an unsuitable or inappropriate house or city, he may immediately decide to move. It is also a favorable time to make important home improvements. In certain cases, the person's house or land may be subject to serious disruption or upheaval due to forces completely outside of his control. If he has ambitions to build a house or to create a resource center, community foundation, or any establishment for universal welfare, then the time may have finally arrived. He now has the inner resources and strength to make his dream a reality. This is also a good time for activities involving archeology, farming, or ecology.

The person's mother may go through big changes during these years. Her health may be affected, especially if she is very old. Or she may experience other serious problems. She may suddenly try to dominate, manipulate, or emotionally smother the person. This transit is therefore more difficult if it occurs during early childhood. A child undergoing the transit becomes extraordinarily sensitive to his mother and home environment, and he may experience great frustration that his parents have such enormous power while he has almost none.

By the end of these approximately twelve to thirty-one years, depending on the sign Pluto is transiting, the person has thoroughly explored all issues involving inner strength and security. He has confronted psychological weaknesses and eliminated ideas which he previously and mistakenly relied upon for stability, fortitude, and equilibrium. In order to do this, the person goes back to his roots, examines his lineage and family traditions, and makes whatever adjustments are necessary.

P

When Pluto transits the fifth house, the person feels an urge to express his individuality and vitality. Life becomes more vibrant, passionate, dynamic, and meaningful. Now that Pluto has finished its transit of the fourth house and the person has separated himself from his family and the values of his ancestors, he is ready to show the world exactly who he is and what he can do. He becomes conscious of his destiny and is inspired just to be alive. He functions from his ego and individualized spirit. His power, dignity, and authority are derived from his sense of self. The person begins to think naturally of the possibilities of fame, recognition, and acknowledgement. During these twelve to thirty-one years, depending on the sign Pluto is transiting, the person may produce more artistic works than at any other time in his life. He lives life intensely and he is more connected and committed to each moment than ever before. He does not tolerate resignation or censorship within himself, and he is an active player rather than a passive observer. It is an intense and stimulating time to be alive.

The person's sexual and procreative energies are very potent now. Children born at this time will be exceptional in some way, and the person's behavior toward his children is intimate, attentive, and dutiful. He becomes deeply attached to his children and forms very strong bonds with them. He may have experiences with them that change his life forever. The person's offspring may win awards or be singled out for acknowledgement. In extreme cases, the person's children may endure serious unexpected difficulties.

Intense love affairs, full of fervent passion, cravings, and infatuation teach him significant lessons and bring transformation. Or they may cause upheaval or even experiences of death and rebirth of the ego. The person becomes obsessed with his lover and tends toward possessiveness. Some married individuals become fascinated by an outsider. The person is driven by his lustful appetites and may experiment sexually. He reaches heights of pleasure previously unknown. Individuals who are prone to abuse alcohol or drugs should guard against excessive indulgence during this period.

The person is extraordinarily creative and expressive. Artwork that the person produces during this transit will be profound and apt to move the emotions. The person has more cathartic experiences than usual. He may feel a strong urge to gamble or speculate. It is an excellent time to engage in dramatic activities, and professional performers may enjoy some of their greatest performances. The person feels himself to be the center of attention, and he gains a good deal of recognition. Leadership comes naturally now, and the person gains a strong sense of pride, self-respect, and dignity. His ambition and willpower increase along with feelings of importance. He is able to follow his heart and to act on his impulses.

During this period the person has one of the greatest opportunities of his life to go forward with his aspirations and to fulfill his destiny. Pluto is exalted in Leo, the corresponding sign of the fifth house, and therefore this transit is more beneficial and smooth than other Pluto transits. The person should not take his inspiration, vibrancy, and gusto for granted. He may never again experience such profound creativity, self-expression, self-confidence, and connection with his individual spirit for such a sustained period of time.

P

When Pluto transits the sixth house, the person transforms his physical body. Chronic weaknesses, disorders, or infirmities suddenly arise in a conspicuous and troublesome way so they can be handled once and for all. For perhaps the first time, the person takes responsibility for his health and well-being. He has both the desire and the ability to focus wholeheartedly on healing any malfunctioning part of his anatomy. The person goes on special diets, participates in fitness programs, and tries various rehabilitative techniques. His regenerative power is acute, and in time he may actually achieve near-perfect health. This twelve to thirty-one-year period (depending on the sign Pluto transits) brings about the most sustained period of self-improvement the person will ever know. He is concerned not only with purifying his body, but also with improving other parts of his life. Wherever he places his attention, he makes remarkable progress.

The person suddenly discovers tremendous organizational aptitude and analytical ability. He begins to focus directly and microscopically. He succeeds in detail work and excels at technicalities, complexities, and tasks that demand precision. However, as his ability to discriminate grows, he must beware of the tendency to judge people. Though his analyses are quite accurate, they may cause more harm than good if allowed to affect personal relationships. Furthermore, the person may create nervous disorders or psychosomatic illnesses if he cannot distance himself from the objects of his criticism.

In his daily job, the person is driven. He feels compulsive about work and may experience extreme perfectionist tendencies. Some individuals function like workaholics and need to be reminded about rest and recreation. At the very beginning of this transit, the person may change jobs if he is bored with his current work. He looks for work which is meaningful. The person suddenly feels a craving to serve others. For those who are interested in working in the health field, this is an excellent time to begin. The person's healing abilities intensify. He also tries to fix any inefficient systems or operations in his work. He works harder, more patiently, and more painstakingly during these years than at any other time in his life.

The person may have intense or tumultuous experiences with employers, employees, maids, or servants. He feels emotional and vulnerable in the workplace and wants to maintain complete control and power there. He does not react well to authority or criticism at work. He wants to be his own boss and may change jobs many times until he finds an appropriate environment for his talents. These years find the person more concerned with practical rather than theoretical or philosophical matters. He is picky and committed to purity. The person may become extremely aware of his appearance and purchase a completely new wardrobe. He experiences a major physical transformation which may cause his self-image to be altered accordingly. Some individuals may suddenly become interested in small pets or veterinary work. There is also a possibility of working with hotels, inns, restaurants, resorts or any enterprise which serves the people. This is Pluto's last transit below the horizon before entering the public houses. It therefore represents the person's last opportunity to make personal changes.

P

When Pluto transits the seventh house, the person's marriage or primary love relationship is transformed forever. The person's love life becomes intense and powerful now. If he is single at the beginning of the transit, then the person soon encounters relationships of enormous emotion, passion, and vulnerability. If he is already married or committed, then his existing relationship may undergo dramatic growth and change. Chronic problems, tensions, or deficiencies within the partnership surface in order to be dealt with appropriately. The person becomes extraordinarily conscious in love matters and can barely tolerate the thought of a mundane, uneventful, or uninspiring relationship. He now craves excitement, passion, eroticism, and extreme stimulation. Many individuals who have been living in unsuitable or decaying relationships end them at the beginning of this transit. If the person cannot find a way to infuse vitality and spirit into his marriage, and if he and his partner cannot communicate with extreme candor and honesty now, then the person decides to cut his losses and move on.

In cases where the person does not wish to face the truth of an inadequate relationship, he may be forced to do so because of bizarre or uncontrollable circumstances caused by his partner. His partner may behave independently or irrationally or seek a love affair outside the relationship. It is also possible that the person himself falls deeply in love with another person. He may meet someone he believes is his soul mate or someone he has known in past lives and feels destined to be with forever. At any rate, the days of relating in a routine, systematic, predictable way in love are over. The person feels deeply and intensely now, and he undergoes many cathartic experiences. Ultimately, he learns how to share intimately and how to give and receive love. He also learns about fairness, equality, compromise, and respect for his partner. His main goal is to merge as completely as possible with his mate, and it is through this that his personal growth takes place. He will endure many upheavals, disruptions, and power struggles in his primary relationship during these twelve to thirty-one years. But by the end of this transit his skill in relating to other people is dramatically improved, and he behaves with more depth, intensity, and profundity in love matters for the rest of his life.

Pluto's transit of an angular house brings a surge of personal power and an opportunity for the person to take control of his destiny. He stops censoring himself and holding back his power and becomes willing to assume authority and let his presence be known. Because the seventh house is the first above the horizon of a birthchart, the person's attention shifts toward the public. He is therefore more successful and effective in business, social activities, and anything involving the community and general populace. At the beginning of the transit, when Pluto opposes the ascendant on and off for approximately one year, the person is affected spiritually. Old, worn-out features of his personality are purged as a more expanded awareness dawns. As his awareness grows, his behavior becomes more compassionate towards all.

It is an excellent time to find a guru, guide, or mentor. The person forms alliances with important and powerful individuals who are to have a tremendous impact on his future. He is sensitive with his partners and may have psychic, mystical, or supernatural experiences with them. In certain cases, the person may marry a spiritual teacher. He is attracted to extremely intense, forceful, and influential people during these years. He must be careful, however, not to choose a mate who is domineering, jealous, manipulative, overly emotional, or volatile. A relationship with such a person will only bring great suffering and heartache during these years. In extreme cases, the person's partner may die or disappear, causing the person both terrible pain and tremendous growth. The first year or so of this transit, when Pluto opposes the ascendant, is an excellent time to engage in therapy or self-healing work. Traditional astrological texts say that the person must beware of lawsuits or intense confrontations with known enemies.

P

When Pluto transits the eighth house, the person experiences the greatest growth and personal transformation of his life. He feels deeply committed to spiritual evolution, and toward this end he subconsciously allows himself to become extraordinarily vulnerable and sensitive. Evolution requires surrender, and during this transit the person is able to give up deep-rooted attachments which no longer serve him. This period may signify the end of an era of personal values and priorities. The person expands his psychological boundaries, and he is less driven by his ego and individual desires. He is more affected by spiritual impulses and desires that spring from deep in his soul. The person has almost infinite ability to examine his relationship with the universe, God, and nature. He may have many mystical, psychic, or supernatural experiences and develop a deep interest in astrology, metaphysics, or the occult. He begins to analyze the mechanics of nature, and as he does so, he better understands the nature and consequences of his own desires. His mind becomes clearer, and he feels as if he is cleansing himself of everything extraneous, unnatural, or superimposed on his true nature. He makes subtle but profound spiritual progress, whether he knows it or not.

Pluto functions well in its transit of the eighth house because the eighth house corresponds to Scorpio, the sign owned by Pluto. However, the person may experience struggle, stress, and pain if he resists change or tries to hold on to old, worn-out ways. He has immense regenerative energy and sexual potency. He also has access to the power of his soul. His resourcefulness knows no bounds. The person may never be as willing to confront such deep personal issues for such a sustained period of time. He is committed to rooting out neurotic or life-damaging behavioral patterns and altering habits that he has lived with for a very long time. He is, laudably, more concerned with growth than comfort and therefore does not suppress issues or try to live in the past. He analyzes his use of power and any tendencies to control or manipulate others.

During these twelve to thirty-one years, the person wants to find answers to the mysteries of life. He learns about death, astral travel, the immortality of the soul, and, possibly, other planes of existence. He may take an interest in reincarnation or in techniques that help people to die peacefully and with dignity. In some cases, he may have intense experiences involving joint finances, financial partnerships, or inheritances, wills, and legacies. The person learns about the values of others, and because of this, he may find himself wishing to help others. He may begin to experiment sexually, and these years may bring more sexual passion than any other time of life. The person loses himself completely in the experience of orgasm and feels a profound connection with God and the universe when he unites with his lover. He is in touch with his emotions and ambitions. He takes any criticism or disapproval to heart and tries to perfect himself and find his proper path. Much of his unconscious becomes conscious, and this entire transit represents a significant and karmic period of change, renewal, and rebirth.

P

When Pluto transits the ninth house, the person becomes consumed with the meaning of life. He spends the next twelve to thirty-one years investigating one or more religions, philosophies, or ideologies. When Pluto passed through the eighth house, the person examined the laws and mechanics of nature; he discovered answers to the questions of how the individual and the universe interact. Now he faces the *why* of existence. Having already investigated the mechanics of nature, he is now left with only one realm to investigate—the realm of God.

This is an expansive and optimistic period in which the person seeks truth, expands his vision, and explores new ideas. He is consciously focused on prophecy—inspired declarations of divine will and purpose. The person's dedication to discovering the meaning of life is so strong that these years bring inspiration and direct experience of God. He feels genuine devotion for God. This is a wonderful time for gaining knowledge, wisdom, and guidance. Intimate contact with gurus, mentors, and teachers is especially favored. Although the eighth house is more connected to occult and metaphysical subjects, Pluto's transit of the ninth house often brings initiations into metaphysical disciplines. However, the person learns these practices as part of a whole religion, philosophy, or doctrine. Isolated bits of knowledge with no connection to a complete, all-encompassing ideology are irrelevant to the person now.

The person may travel to foreign countries and continents more during these years than at any other time of his life. Travel expands the person's awareness of foreign cultures and their customs. The person may study abroad, or in certain cases, visit foreign lands to spread his own teachings. The person is exceptionally influenced by foreigners.

The biggest problem the person faces during this transit is an obsession with his newfound religion. He may behave fanatically, constantly trying to enlighten others to his truth. This may happen because the person is now having powerful and fulfilling inner experiences that color his perception of reality. Even though his speech and actions spring entirely from his heart, his friends do not experience what he does and therefore will not necessarily see things his way.

The person's world view shifts dramatically. At the very beginning of Pluto's journey through the ninth house, the person's understanding of life may be called into question in a distressing way. He is forced to inquire deeply into the meaning of life, and this results in new ideas as well as new directions. He enjoys plunging deeply into serious discussions and wants to learn all he can. He may decide to join a spiritual movement, ashram, or religious order.

By the time this transit ends, the person has developed his faith and experience of God. He has broadened his view of life and gained wisdom, better judgement, and a practical understanding of the meaning of human existence. This period may include intense conflicts in the areas of law, publishing, and institutions of higher learning.

P

When Pluto transits the tenth house, the person becomes consumed with his individual purpose and mission. He embraces his career as never before and his desires for professional success intensify. Now that Pluto has completed its ninth house journey and the person has thoroughly investigated the meaning of and purpose of life, he can forget about universal issues and concentrate on his own goals. He realizes that since all existence is being perfectly cared for with great orderliness, his job is to make a contribution to the world in the best way he can. Pluto, the most powerful and intense planetary influence discovered to date, is now at the zenith of the birthchart. This great planet transiting the most powerful angle of the horoscope brings the person a remarkable opportunity to exercise his power for the good of humankind.

The person thinks in terms of universal welfare, as well as the realization of his own potential. If he has previously ignored healing abilities, suppressed spiritual powers, or avoided any activity connected to human potential or consciousness raising, then his time of procrastination is over. A better time to come to the rescue of those in need does not exist. The person is well received by the public, and he gains recognition almost effortlessly. His genuine desire to serve allows him to quickly cut through obstacles and red tape. If the person is involved in an unfulfilling or inappropriate profession at the start of this transit, then he can expect to change careers soon. Individuals who have been unsure of their career path up until now begin to investigate their options more seriously than before.

The person may become famous or receive honors. However, he must be careful not to hurt others or engage in ruthless behavior to fulfill his desires. Because he wields so much power, the person's motives are important. If the person acts unethically, he will pay the price with interest. Certain individuals are subject to career upheavals, public disgrace, or the destruction of their career. Even in these cases, however, the person still has the wherewithal to pick up the pieces and start over from scratch. This is an excellent time to improve one's systems and to firmly establish a business or undertaking. The person has tremendous determination, creativity, and commitment. He is resourceful in his activities and generates new ideas instinctively and intuitively. He uses emotions and feelings rather than just objective analysis to guide his success.

The person's relationship with his father may become intense or undergo major disruption. The person suddenly becomes extremely sensitive and vulnerable in his father's presence. The father may begin to act weird, compulsive, or obsessive. He may begin to dominate, manipulate, or coerce the person. Or he may become interested in higher consciousness or mystical activities. In extreme cases, the person's father may die or disappear. If this transit occurs during early childhood, the effects could be quite detrimental and long-lasting. The person's masculinity and sense of power can be dramatically affected by his reaction to his father's behavior. Astrologers who consider the tenth house to represent the mother rather than the father may wish to apply the above information to the mother.

The person senses that his time for recognition has arrived. He wants to fulfill his ambitions and purpose and is therefore open and flexible in his professional life. Leadership skill increases, and the person has the power to change the existing order of society. If the person feels that something extraordinary is about to happen in his career, he should not wait for it to happen, but take direct and decisive action.

P

When Pluto transits the eleventh house, the person becomes passionate about finding what will make him happy. Now that Pluto has transited the tenth house, and the person has done his best to satisfy his career goals, he is free to concentrate on his own enjoyment of life. His goals and ambitions may change noticeably, especially if his prior behavior has been motivated by duty, responsibility, and obligation. Now is the time to live for opportunity, enjoyment, and personal gratification. The person begins to consciously design his life around his instincts, impulses, and feelings. He becomes conscious of his most genuine desires and ideals, and he is deeply committed to attaining them.

As the person's aspirations change, so do his choice of friends and group associations. He now meets influential individuals who will have an effect on his life for years to come. He is suddenly attracted to intense, emotional, and passionate people. He may become fascinated with spiritual persons and those who spend their energies in consciousness-raising or human potential work. The person feels sensitive and vulnerable with friends and may now experience upheavals or disruptions with them. He must be aware of the tendency to dominate or manipulate others, and he should not allow others to boss him around. He can expect life-damaging friendships and alliances which no longer serve any purpose to end. The person takes complete responsibility for his friendships.

As he becomes clear about his own dreams, the person simultaneously wants to help society and improve his community. Now that he is on track about his personal happiness and fulfillment, he is free to think about larger issues and take up causes to improve the world. The person may join or establish humanitarian groups, welfare societies, mystical organizations, or spiritual movements. He may take a serious interest in science or any discipline that explains things from a statistical or empirical viewpoint. He is inventive and innovative and attracted to information, facts, and knowledge. He may champion freedom, independence, and equality, and pioneer progressive or revolutionary systems. He is more social than before and may work diligently for the justice and the good of all.

There is controversy over Pluto's exalted and fallen positions. Some say Pluto is exalted in Leo, while others say Pisces. If Pluto is exalted in Leo, then its fallen placement is Aquarius, the corresponding sign of the eleventh house. This is possible because Pluto is far too intense, deep, and emotional to function compatibly with detached Aquarius and the lighthearted eleventh house. Therefore, the person may find these years stressful, especially if he is uncomfortable with intense, passionate, and demanding friendships and groups. Also, individuals who are unable to create happiness and fulfillment may experience this transit as a painful or frustrating time.

P

When Pluto transits the twelfth house, the person enters a sustained period of inner growth, spiritual awareness, and reconnection with his source. His attention turns inward, and he probes the depths of his being in an attempt to root out problems, fears, phobias, complexes, neurotic patterns, and deranged thinking caused by disturbing incidents from his past. The person is not merely working on self-improvement or better psychological health—he wants to experience his true, unbounded, immortal nature. This is the time for him to regain his birthright as an integral part of this vast, infinite creation. The person engages in the most profound process of assimilation he will ever undergo. He evaluates all of his previous experiences in terms of his relationship to the universe. The person relinquishes his passion and his desire for worldly pleasure in favor of serenity, contentment, and completion. He instinctively feels it is time for a cessation of activity, commotion, hustle and bustle.

The person has access to his subconscious mind and previously repressed information. He has excellent results with dream analysis or deciphering personal mysteries. His task now is to liberate any aspect of his soul which is confined, obstructed, or bound by wrong thinking or injurious attitudes. He seeks enlightenment. Meditation, or any techniques that raise consciousness and promote awareness, are favored. As Pluto's transit through the twelfth house progresses, the person feels his soul expand tremendously, and he no longer feels restricted by society's boundaries. He becomes more intuitive and psychic and is receptive to knowledge and information coming from other planes of existence. He appreciates occult or metaphysical subjects and may benefit profoundly from astrology, tarot, or psychic readings. He may have many mystical experiences.

The person is interested in growth and healing. If he attempts psychotherapy now, he gains great self-knowledge. He reexperiences old traumas with a minimal amount of pain, and their impressions are purged from his psyche forever. He may remember past-life experiences and handle their lingering effects once and for all. The late astrologer Isabel Hickey theorized that Pluto is exalted in Pisces, the corresponding sign of the twelfth house. Whether it is actually exalted in Leo or Pisces, Pluto definitely functions powerfully in its twelfth house transit. The person's imagination is extremely fertile and active. He has access to all past impressions, not only his own but also those of the collective unconscious. The person feels connected to the universe and all its creatures, and he is therefore very compassionate toward the suffering of others. He wants to heal the world and may consider serving in a hospital, prison, or charitable institution.

Because Pluto now transits the final house of the horoscope, the person is able to make accurate judgements and draw appropriate conclusions about the significance of all his experiences and the purpose of life in general. He feels a sense of connection to nature and creation and begins to view life from the broadest perspective possible. During these twelve to thirty-one years, the person transcends his individuality, directly experiences spiritual wholeness, and feels contentment in his soul. He lets go of his compulsions and obsessions with his relative, ever-changing, earthly existence and tries to merge with the infinite. By the time this transit is over, the person is ready for Pluto's transit of the first house, where he will utilize all the conscious awareness he has gained to work on perfecting his personality and character.

♃

When transiting Jupiter conjuncts the natal Sun, the person is optimistic, enthusiastic, and successful in whatever he does. He feels buoyant and confident, and all his actions are supported by a feeling of abundance. It is an excellent time to approach employers, government officials, or any authority figures. The person is lucky and favored now. He is protected from accidents and harm. He may obtain promotions, benefits, financial grants, and the patronage of whomever he contacts. During these five to ten days (in rare cases sixty days), nature is definitely supporting his efforts.

The person's willpower is strong, and he feels healthy, alive, and vibrant. If he is recuperating from past illness, he recovers swiftly and vigorously now. He feels cheerful and may experience special and plentiful opportunities. Recognition, approval, and fame are forthcoming. There are benefits and favors from men. The person gets along very well with his father. A woman undergoing this transit benefits in her love life. The person has a sense of freedom, fun, and adventure. He believes that everything will go well, and he therefore triumphs in almost all undertakings. It is a good time to initiate new projects and enterprises. The person should schedule any negotiations, agreements, or contracts for this period.

The person must be careful not to indulge in excessive food, drink, or sensual pleasures. He must guard against laziness, especially since he feels so prosperous and fortunate. As great as transiting Jupiter conjunct the Sun is, the person should not necessarily expect good things to happen of their own accord. He should take action and "make hay when the sun shines," as the saying goes. The person makes progress in business and his sales ability increases dramatically during this transit. His propensity for leadership is expanded, and suddenly he is very popular. His social life improves. Educational and philosophical pursuits are favored, and the person broadens his perspective. He feels better about religion, and he experiences an earnest and gratifying faith in God. If the person has dealings with gurus, spiritualists, or religious teachers now, he may have experiences with them that he remembers forever.

The person is happy and content, and he wants to share his good feelings and abundance. He may be impulsive about gambling or speculating, but he should be careful in this area, especially if the speculations go beyond this short-lived transit. If the Sun is severely afflicted or in a highly unfavorable condition in the natal birthchart, then Jupiter's transit to the Sun may only increase the inherent difficulties or problems.

$$\text{♃}$$

When transiting Jupiter squares or opposes the natal Sun, the person is overly expansive in judgement and action. He feels so lucky and favored that he abandons discretion. The person acts too spontaneously and impulsively. He forgets his limitations, is very ambitious, and thinks constantly of freedom and adventure. He may overextend himself in any or all areas of life during these five to ten days (or, in rare cases, sixty days). Expectations run too high and the person must try to be tolerant and patient. He should avoid gambling, speculation, risky endeavors, or financial ventures which seem too good to be true. The person behaves in a somewhat shallow or superficial manner, and needs to think in more practical, down-to-earth terms.

The person's ego swells, and pride may become a problem. He feels he deserves a raise or promotion, and he may demand attention and recognition. Trouble with bosses or authority figures is therefore possible.

Spiritual growth is favored as the person broadens his viewpoints and philosophy. The opposition aspect is more favorable than the square for religious or spiritual experiences. However, caution is advised lest the person offend his teachers and mentors by rash, reckless, or frivolous conduct. There may be a tendency toward laziness, carelessness, or sloppy work because the person feels he can do no wrong at this time. He may spend too much, think too big, and promise more than he can deliver. He must curb extravagance and conceit.

In some cases, the person may indulge in excessive food, drink, or other sensual pleasures. In order to use this transit wisely, the person should aim for internal growth, expansion of faith, and balance between physical and spiritual values. Despite the generally negative nature of this transit, the person feels happy and delighted with himself. Problems that occur at this time are relatively minor and are social in nature. Individuals in very powerful positions, however, could misuse their authority or squander resources or large amounts of money.

When transiting Jupiter trines or sextiles the natal Sun, the person is cheerful, optimistic, lucky, and confident. He functions from abundance and therefore fulfills his wishes easily. He is energetic, vibrant, and exceedingly creative. This is an excellent time to begin new ventures and expand one's activities. The person is popular and respected. He may receive promotions or be the object of favoritism. Opportunities are plentiful, and the person should take advantage of his fortune while it lasts. There are wonderful experiences with the father and men in general. A woman undergoing the transit may therefore benefit in her love life. Health is good, and the person enjoys sports and other outdoor activities. He is joyful and of very good humor. He feels charmed and blessed.

The person may do well financially. He may win prizes or suddenly make money from investments and speculations. It is a good time for taking risks, if they are not unreasonable. Travel for fun or spiritual purposes is possible. The person feels a strong sense of religion and faith, and he is peaceful and content. There is good intuition, and the person is protected from harm. He is patient, tolerant, and compassionate toward others. His social life improves, and others support him.

Although this transit is excellent for success, the person should not expect wonderful things to happen automatically. He should act on his impulses and pursue his goals with vigor. Because the person feels so content and lucky, he may be lulled into a state of complacency for these five to ten days (or, in rare cases, sixty days). If he is a public figure, he can make great use of this period by presenting his new ideas and proposals. His confidence is inspiring, and fame or recognition follows. The person gains benefits, favors, gifts, and advancements as a result of good deeds he has performed in the past. The transiting trine aspect is more powerful than the transiting sextile. The transiting sextile only represents the opportunity to make the above effects a reality.

When transiting Jupiter conjuncts the natal Moon, the person feels happy, safe, and protected. He suddenly becomes emotionally secure and psychologically healthy. For the next approximately five to ten days (or, in rare cases, sixty days) he feels comfortable about himself and is easily able to demonstrate his affections to others. Family life improves, and the person is open, flexible, and available to friends and loved ones. He charms others effortlessly and feels no need to defend or protect himself. People are completely at ease around him. The person behaves with great softness, generosity, and kindness. He is compassionate, loving, and understanding and, immediately reaps the rewards as others spontaneously return his attention.

This is an excellent time for parties and social gatherings. The person is in good spirits, and he maintains a happy, outgoing mood. Anything involving the home environment is favored. Domestic life is pleasant, and the person receives special favors and benefits from women. He may meet a woman who will figure significantly in his life or help him gain wealth. A man undergoing this transit does well in his love life now. The person's relationship with his mother improves, and he may mend past hurts and injuries with her. He feels great contentment during these days, and gets his needs met with almost no resistance at all. He is lucky. It is a very favorable time for vacations, recreation, hobbies and diversions. Travel and amusing adventures work out smoothly and enjoyably.

The person may receive visits from old friends and acquaintances. He may have beneficial contacts with foreigners and foreign friends. Religious activities, especially devotional ones, are extremely favored. The person's faith in God is great, and he is optimistic that all will turn out well in the end. He is successful in his dealings with the public. Business sales may improve, especially if the person deals with women. This transit sometimes means that the person is too indulgent in sensual pleasures. He must therefore beware of gaining weight if he has a weight problem. Also, certain individuals go overboard with emotionalism or sentimental feelings. However, this period brings good fortune spontaneously. Home improvements go well and are advisable.

If the Moon is severely afflicted or in a highly unfavorable condition in the natal birthchart, then Jupiter's transit to the Moon may only increase the inherent difficulties.

2 ♃

When transiting Jupiter squares or opposes the natal Moon, the person is overly affected by his feelings. He is drawn to sensual pleasures and may indulge excessively in food, drink, or whatever he believes will satisfy his cravings. The person lacks discipline, restraint, and moderation, and he tends toward extravagance. He may squander his energy and resources. He has little willpower and too readily caves in to his weaknesses. He is seeking emotional security. The person is in danger of using poor judgement or making impulsive decisions. He must guard against laziness and try not to procrastinate or perform sloppy work.

The person is sentimental, amorous, and mushy. He may give his affections too easily or inappropriately. He needs prudence and common sense. Minor problems with women may be caused by unrealistic expectations, unfulfilled promises, and exaggerated forms of behavior. The person may have difficulties with religious or spiritual teachers, especially due to misplaced or irrational devotion, but this is more likely during the square aspect. Jupiter's opposition transit to the moon is generally beneficial in the spiritual realm and also brings benefits in or opportunities for love relationships. The person is optimistic and enthusiastic. He must beware of spending too much or overextending himself. The effects of "hard" Jupiter-Moon transits are generally rather minor, but individuals who are unstable or overly emotional by nature may experience significant difficulties. It is certainly a detrimental time for people who are perpetually undisciplined or who indulge regularly in excessive alcohol, drugs, or other life-damaging diversions.

Domestic activities are not much favored, because balance and poise are lacking. Highly emotional or otherwise agitated feelings in relationships are now exacerbated. During these approximately five to ten days (in rare cases, sixty days) the person is vulnerable, impressionable, and prone to overreacting. He should consider issues carefully, try to maintain a sense of equanimity, and beware of excessive spending. Certain astrological texts mention the possibility of sudden problems caused by habit patterns or behavioral traits of the unconscious mind stemming from the distant past.

♃

When transiting Jupiter trines or sextiles the natal Moon, the person feels contented, peaceful, and completely comfortable with himself. He is lucky and prosperous. However, unless there are more powerful transits also occurring, he should not expect much to happen externally. The person has little ambition or outward thrust and is rather complacent or, in some cases, just plain lazy. It is a fine time for parties, recreations, social gatherings, and entertainment. The person may enjoy vacations, holidays, and restful or diversionary hobbies during these approximately five to ten days (in rare cases, sixty days).

Domestic experiences are favored, as are relationships with women. A man undergoing this transit benefits in his love life. He is kind and compassionate in his dealings with others and is favored and adored for such behavior. Women undergoing this transit may feel an especially loving bond with their female friends, and it is an excellent time for female camaraderie.

Religious and spiritual activities go very well, as the person feels a subtle but profound faith in God and nature. He is appreciated by the community at large and may succeed in all public endeavors. Home improvements can be successfully undertaken, and family life is smooth, pleasant, and enjoyable. The person may enjoy cooking or taking care of his loved ones. Friendships are very gratifying at this time. The person is full of warm feelings, and he feels grateful for his existence and all of life's wonderful opportunities. Farming and agricultural enterprises are productive and successful. The person maintains high ethical and moral standards. The transiting trine aspect is significantly more powerful than the transiting sextile. The transiting sextile only represents the opportunity to make the above effects a reality.

$\bf 2\!\!\!\!\;+$

When transiting Jupiter conjuncts natal Mercury, the person is mentally buoyant, exuberant, and optimistic. His mental faculties function efficiently, and he makes accurate judgements and good decisions. The person is balanced in his thinking. He is also confident and sure of himself. He is open to new knowledge, and now is an excellent time for learning, especially religious or philosophical studies. The person is eloquent, his perception is keen, and his abilities with writing, lecturing, and all communications are favored. He does well with advertising, publicity, and legal matters. These approximately five to ten days (in rare cases, sixty days) are a very good period for presenting oneself in a clear, articulate, and favorable manner. The person is diplomatic, tolerant, and understanding of diverse viewpoints.

Organizational matters and detail work are especially favored. The person is clear-headed and perceives issues with both microscopic and broad vision. He can plan his own future appropriately as well as projects outside of his own personal interests. He is peaceful and happy. He maintains grace and poise under pressure. Contacts and negotiations in both social and professional settings are agreeable and harmonious. The person is highly persuasive. It is an excellent time to sign legal documents and contracts.

The person is mentally adventurous and feels tremendous freedom of expression. He may be somewhat impulsive in speech. Travels are fruitful, and the person learns a great deal about foreign ways and cultures in any long distance journeys he takes now. He has pleasant and profitable interactions with teachers, guides, mentors, religious figures, and spiritual gurus. The person does well on tests and exams and is lucky in such matters. He should be careful not to overextend himself in any way, as his mind may be ahead of his body. There is a likelihood of good news arriving during this transit. The person writes many letters, and he may hear from old or long-lost friends. If he works in any area of the communications field: writing, lecturing, speaking, public relations, media, reporting, and so on, the person may receive an important opportunity now.

If Mercury is severely afflicted or in a highly unfavorable condition in the natal birthchart, then Jupiter's transit to Mercury may only expand the inherent difficulties.

$2\!\!\!\!4$

When transiting Jupiter squares or opposes natal Mercury, the person is too expansive in his thinking. He forgets his usual sense of proportion and goes overboard in his inspiration and imagination. There is a danger of making impulsive decisions which are inappropriate and poorly reasoned. The person is too optimistic. He is careless and must try diligently for patience, discipline, and moderation. The person talks too much, and he may waste a good deal of time and energy debating needlessly with others. He exaggerates and should beware of conceit, arrogance, and a brazen attitude. Many individuals undergoing this transit ignore the details and facts of situations because they are sure of their opinions. The person must try to be realistic and recognize the subjectivity of his beliefs. Otherwise life will not go smoothly or well now, and the person will be perceived as sloppy, careless, and imprudent.

The person should be very careful in signing contracts, or he should simply postpone them for these approximately five to ten days (in rare cases, sixty days). Because he feels that everything will be fine, he lacks caution and discretion. He promises more than he can deliver and expects more than he is likely to receive. It is a poor time to make commitments. This period is better used for dreams and visions. The person may let his imagination run wild about large goals and ambitions he would like to achieve in his lifetime. He thinks big, and his viewpoint is enlarged. He should keep a diary to record long-term goals. It is a very good time for devising new inventions and solving problems that require broad, progressive, unfettered thinking. The details and technicalities of such endeavors may be handled later or relegated to others for the time being.

The person may forget things or feel confused. He is mentally lazy and has a tendency to tell fibs or distort information slightly if he feels it serves his purpose. Some individuals feel nervous or mentally restless, depending on the beneficent or afflicted condition of Mercury in the natal birthchart. There is a great deal of mental activity throughout this transit. The person indulges in considerable philosophical thinking, and his thoughts are directed toward freedom. He should try to slow down and be more sensitive to his environment and others. He should listen attentively before blurting out his feelings and opinions. If possible, tests and exams that involve trivial information, many technicalities, or a significant amount of microscopic focus should be postponed. The person must beware of involvement in grand schemes, and he should not take on more activities than he can handle. He needs to work on understanding others fully before drawing impetuous conclusions and taking inappropriate action.

♃

When transiting Jupiter trines or sextiles natal Mercury, the person becomes mentally harmonious. He is optimistic, enthusiastic, and he thinks and communicates well. He is balanced, clear-headed, and effective. Writing, teaching, lecturing, and learning are favored. The person makes the most of whatever information comes his way. His observational abilities increase, and he is therefore able to organize better strategies to fulfill his purposes. The person feels confident, happy, healthy, and at peace. He is aided by a sense of humor and is in no way depressed or negative. Creativity is abundant. The person perceives the overall picture as well the details and particulars involved in the issues at hand. Life goes relatively smoothly during these approximately five to ten days (in rare cases, sixty days). However, the person should try to make the most of his current mental optimism and dexterity because the effects of this transit are quite mild unless acted upon.

The person has excellent business ability. He is diplomatic, spirited, and pleasantly persuasive. He knows what to buy and what to sell, and he is aware of current opportunities. Furthermore, the person is just plain lucky in business deals. It is an exceptionally good time for negotiations, agreements, legal matters, and the signing of contracts. Commitments made now produce the desired results. The person makes very few, if any, wrong decisions during this transit. He scores better than ever on tests and exams. Nature is on his side in scholastic and intellectual pursuits. He can make great advances through advertising and public relations.

Art, music, and all cultural activities bring great pleasure. The person may receive good news and messages. Friendships go well and the person can clear up old problems and misunderstandings easily. He may hear from old friends and acquaintances. The person excels in creative writing, languages, and the deciphering of symbols. He learns new subjects and engages in interesting debates and discussions. The person maintains a sense of poise and grace, and is not troubled by delays or miscommunications. He should, however, guard against laziness caused by excessive idealism.

The transiting trine aspect is significantly more powerful than the transiting sextile. The transiting sextile only represents the opportunity to make the above effects a reality.

When transiting Jupiter conjuncts natal Venus, the person is lucky in love matters. He experiences a joyful state of abundance, and is buoyant, jovial, and enthusiastic. Single individuals may meet a new and significant love partner, while married persons are enthralled by their mate and experience harmony in their marriage. The person feels exceptional warmth and feminine energy. He charms others easily and is protected from accidents, injuries, and negative vibrations. Artistic interests and undertakings are very favored. The person has fine taste, and his aesthetic appreciation increases. He enjoys entertainment, fun, and romance. This is a very delightful transit.

The person may buy or receive beautiful gifts, jewelry, clothing, or pieces of art. He surrounds himself with opulence and plush furnishings. Money matters flourish, and the person may come across positively lucky financial opportunities. Desires of all kinds are easily fulfilled, and the person should take advantage of this fortunate period. He need not censor himself or his ambitions in any major way for these approximately five to ten days (in rare cases, sixty days). The person may now be the center of attention and he enjoys parties, dating, and social gatherings. However, as with all Jupiter transits to benefic planets, there is a possibility of overindulgence in sensual pleasures and diversions, including sweets and other lavish food and drink.

There are gains and benefits through women, including the person's mother. The person is affectionate, amorous, and demonstrative with his mate. He enjoys music, dance, and drama. Certain individuals may go overboard in spending on extravagant comforts. Also, there is no particular depth or profundity to the person's experience unless other features of the birthchart confer them. Nevertheless, this is a fortunate and positive period and may be advantageously used to pursue love, money, romance, and abundance in any form. If Venus is severely afflicted or in a highly unfavorable condition in the natal birthchart, then Jupiter's transit to Venus may only expand the inherent difficulties.

24

When transiting Jupiter squares or opposes natal Venus, the person behaves excessively or compulsively in romance, and is too indulgent in pleasures and comforts. Ambitions are focused on personal entertainment, diversions, and gratification of the senses. The person feels restless and tries to fill the void through sensual pleasure, lustful affection, and by gaining recognition and attention from others. There is a danger of superficial conduct and overindulgence in food and drink, especially sweets. The person longs for love and is too forceful in trying to fulfill his desires. He lacks grace and good timing in love matters, and he may act sentimental or mushy. Discipline, moderation, and prudence are missing.

The person may procrastinate in his responsibilities. He is impulsive or rash in fulfilling his cravings and may spend resources he does not have. The person should beware of inappropriate conduct, laziness, and expecting something for nothing. Some individuals undergoing this transit experience extreme sensitivity to their loved ones. Emotions are abundant and very close to the surface. There may be minor problems or tensions with women in general. The person certainly may attract love affairs at this time, but they are more likely characterized by lust and sensuality than true, long-lasting feelings. The person's judgement is overly influenced by his needs and cravings.

There is a strong desire for beautiful objects and plush surroundings. However, the person's taste is not sound now. He should put off any major aesthetic and artistic decisions until these approximately five to ten days (in extreme cases, sixty days) are over. Individuals who are normally too serious and disciplined in their daily life may now enjoy a well-deserved vacation from their constricted, humdrum existence. Despite the fundamentally negative nature of this transit, there is a good chance that the person will actually enjoy this period due to the two benefic energies involved.

When transiting Jupiter trines or sextiles natal Venus, the person feels happy, pleasant, and lighthearted, particularly in his social and love relationships. It is an excellent time for romance, fun, and entertainment. The person is lucky and may fall in love or meet a new love interest. He enjoys recreation and attends many parties or social gatherings. Financial matters are favored, and business enterprises go smoothly and beneficially. The person appreciates art and has good taste. Individuals involved in music, dance, or drama are especially creative and inventive. The person may receive gifts, presents, and favors.

There is a tendency toward laziness or complacency during these approximately five to ten days (in rare cases, sixty days). Despite the highly favorable nature of this transit, the person should not expect a great deal to occur. The effects of trines and sextiles are benign to begin with, and the combination of two benefics does not generally provoke much action or movement. Still, the person is significantly favored by women and receives benefits and favors from them. Courtship flourishes, and the person feels an overall sense of optimism and abundance. Therefore, he succeeds in most endeavors. He is protected from accident or harm and feels relaxed and friendly. Married life is enjoyable. The person fully enjoys sexual relations as well as other sensual pleasures. It is a good time for obtaining beautiful clothing, fine jewelry, and objects of art.

Travels go well. The person has fun. He is exposed to other cultures and his associations with foreigners prosper. Traditional texts warn not to indulge in excessive food or drink. The transiting trine aspect is significantly more powerful than the transiting sextile. The transiting sextile only represents the opportunity to make the above effects a reality.

♃

When transiting Jupiter conjuncts natal Mars, the person is magnificently energetic. He is bold, confident, and active. Willpower is very strong, and the person stands up for himself. He puts his desires first and gets his way in most endeavors. He is impulsive, takes risks, and plays entirely to win. He is competitive for these approximately five to ten days (in rare cases, sixty days) and especially enjoys sports. The person has great physical energy and endurance. He is adventurous, enthusiastic, and courageous. He must, however, beware of insensitivity toward others. He may overpower others or behave arrogantly or egotistically. The person is assertive and aggressive, and he is not much disposed to compromise.

Business goes well, and the person negotiates skillfully and successfully in his own favor. He works very hard and yet feels little pain or anguish. He is productive and does things in a big way. It is an excellent time to begin new projects, especially those that require bold and inspired action. The person is optimistic and hopeful. Mechanical activity is favored, as are all technical fields such as architecture, drafting, and engineering. The person's libido is active and his sex drive may increase quite dramatically. He has more sexual experiences than usual. His ego expands, and he enjoys showing off. The person is stubborn and does not back down. He focuses on achievement and success in external matters. Introspection and contemplation is minimal. Certain individuals get into trouble because, feeling overconfident, they take unwise risks or behave foolishly. There is danger of overextending oneself during this transit.

The person is ambitious and motivated. He immerses himself fully in his endeavors and feels positive he will win. He may function as a leader and order others around. He is direct and blunt. He fights for causes and does not back down from challenges. His temper may flare occasionally if his desires meet with too much resistance. The person feels no shyness now and he excels at showmanship and any form of theatre.

When transiting Jupiter squares or opposes natal Mars, the person's desires are inflamed, and he responds to life with too much assertiveness and aggression. His ego expands, and he lacks caution, moderation, and restraint. The person's judgement is affected by overpowering desires, and he may behave impulsively and carelessly. These approximately five to ten days (in rare cases, sixty days) are favorable for productivity and success in general, but the person must fully consider the consequences of his actions. He is strongly competitive now and may offend others with his forcefulness and brazenness. The person is fanatical in his convictions and may consciously or unconsciously provoke fights or hard feelings. He directs his attention outward and has little ability for introspection. The person feels courageous and exhibits powerful leadership. He must be careful, though, not to dominate or order others around heartlessly.

The person can make great progress in nearly any area of life during this transit if he is able to maintain equilibrium and focus his energy appropriately (an admittedly complicated task under this astrological influence.) The person engages himself fully in his endeavors and does things in a big way. He commits himself to whatever he tries and does not compromise or give up. There is a danger of conceit and arrogance, and the person should try at least to consider the opinions of those around him. Mechanical ability is enhanced, and the person may do well with architecture, engineering, and drafting, and other tasks that require manual dexterity. However, the person must be careful around machinery and explosives. Accidents are possible because the person is impatient and works too hurriedly. He is completely unafraid of taking risks and may behave carelessly. He must try not to be overconfident, to work too hard, or overextend himself in general.

The person's sex drive is very strong now. He has more sexual experiences than usual and has to restrain himself from forcing unwanted affections on members of the opposite sex. The person is subject to bursts of temper, heat in the body, and a general sense of frustration or irritation. He is overly concerned with winning and tends to show off.

When Jupiter trines or sextiles natal Mars, the person is spirited and highly effective in action. He is confident, assured, and able to function with clear focus and intention. His health is strong, and he feels eager to achieve. He is independent, straightforward, and strong-willed. He fulfills his desires and goals with a minimum of struggle. He enjoys sports and any other competition. He seeks adventure and fun. He feels enthusiasm, optimism, and inner abundance; he is in no way plagued by insecurity or shyness. He maintains his equilibrium and is unafraid of failure. Life works well.

Sexual experiences are favored, and the person attracts the partner of his choice. He is assertive in a nonthreatening way and manages to fulfill his own needs without stepping on others. During these approximately five to ten days (in rare cases, sixty days) there is no danger of conflict, disharmony, or accidents. The person does well with mechanical things. It is an auspicious time to begin business projects or other enterprises. The person is decisive and successful. He takes advantage of new opportunities that may arise and works diligently toward their fruition. His leadership abilities surface now. He is dynamic, powerful, and stimulating or inspiring to those around him. The transiting trine aspect is significantly more powerful than the transiting sextile. The transiting sextile only represents the opportunity to make the above effects a reality.

$$\text{♃}$$

When transiting Jupiter conjuncts natal Jupiter, the person completes a cycle of religious, spiritual, or philosophical understanding and begins a new one. He has finished an eleven- or twelve-year period; he now assimilates what he has learned about faith, God, optimism, trust and abundance. It is a time of renewed hopefulness and idealism. The person experiences prosperity, opportunity, and abundance in the area of life indicated by Jupiter's natal house position. He gets back in touch with major life ambitions, and it is a perfect time to design new plans for a more fulfilling and comfortable life. The person knows himself better and understands his own convictions and ethical beliefs with greater depth, subtlety, and awareness. His decisions and judgements are more sound, practical, and appropriate.

The person may have successful and happy experiences in his religious or spiritual life, especially with gurus, mentors, and teachers of higher knowledge. He may travel to foreign countries or engage in activities promoting foreign cultural affairs. Relationships with foreigners go well, and the person learns about foreign customs and practices. These five to ten days (in rare cases, approximately sixty days) bring good luck, pleasant new opportunities, and feelings of increase or expansion in general. Educational activities are enjoyable, beneficial, and smooth. It is an excellent time for improvements or repairs of any sort. The person has a good deal of patience, and his ability to see the positive side of things is great. He is jovial, content, positive, and hopeful.

Business matters are favored, as are financial transactions. However, the person should beware of expecting too much or behaving extravagantly. He does things in a big way and is in danger of going overboard in his commitments because of his idealism, self-satisfaction, and confidence. This transit does not, of its own, cause a great deal to occur in the person's outer world. Whatever does happen on the outside does so mainly because of the psychological growth going on inside the person. If Jupiter is severely afflicted or in a highly unfavorable condition in the natal birthchart, then transiting Jupiter's conjunction to natal Jupiter may only expand the inherent difficulties.

♃

When transiting Jupiter squares or opposes natal Jupiter, the person is overly expansive, careless, or lackadaisical in his endeavors. He feels great optimism and hopefulness but does not fully consider issues before acting upon them. He expects great results from his undertakings and therefore accepts more opportunities than he can handle. He needs more caution, prudence, and common sense. The person is in danger of overextending himself as well as misplacing his trust or believing the wrong people. He feels very lucky but would be unwise to base decisions on his feelings. Above all, the person should be careful in financial affairs and business propositions. It is very easy to squander resources now. Expenses may be high, and people may take advantage of him because he is gullible.

The person may experience changes or fluctuations in his religious, spiritual, or philosophical beliefs. He may question previously accepted opinions, teachings, and doctrines. He may have more dealings with his mentors, preceptors, or gurus. He may be arrogant or egotistical with them, however, because he believes very strongly in his own opinions. He encounters new offers and proposals and may decide to follow a new direction in life. He takes risks more easily than usual and alters certain courses of action. The person must watch his indulgences. It is possible to behave hedonistically or to go overboard with extravagance and sensual pleasures. This transit is better used for considering one's ultimate dreams than for taking immediate action. The person has poor judgement during these five to ten days (in rare cases, approximately sixty days). The person should try to be practical in his commitments and imaginative about his dreams.

♃

When transiting Jupiter trines or sextiles natal Jupiter, the person feels optimistic, hopeful, and lucky. Life goes smoothly, and the person feels a consistent sense of peace, harmony, and abundance. This transit brings opportunities and potential good fortune, and the person should be alert to put his plans into action and make the most of these five to ten days (in rare cases, approximately sixty days). Otherwise, he may accomplish absolutely nothing, because he is too relaxed and complacent. It is an excellent time for personal growth, self-improvement, and expansion of consciousness.

The person is favored in all dealings with religious teachers, gurus, mentors, and spiritual preceptors. He broadens his perspective and understanding of philosophy and religion. Higher education goes well, and the person may learn interesting information about foreign customs, practices, and cultures.

Business and financial undertakings are successful, and the person is especially prescient. He may gain great profit from gambling and speculation if Jupiter is well-aspected in the natal birthchart. The person feels enthusiastic and expansive, and he may visit other countries. Or he may travel more than usual within his community.

The person is patient, tolerant, and trusting. He is secure. He feels close to God and has faith in the workings of nature. This transit may produce little externally, but the person's effectiveness and success is powerfully aided by his positive attitude and his lack of attachment or arrogance. The transiting trine aspect is significantly more powerful than the transiting sextile. The transiting sextile only represents the opportunity to make the above effects a reality.

When transiting Jupiter conjuncts natal Saturn, the person accepts and embraces his responsibilities, duties, and obligations. He is dependable, patient, and tolerant, and he perceives everything from the broadest possible perspective. It is an excellent time for professional activities, understanding the purpose of his life, and making long-range career plans. The positive or negative effects of this transit depend very much on Saturn's natal position and condition. Saturn must be a strongly beneficial influence in the birthchart for these five to ten days (in rare cases, approximately sixty days) to produce any significantly positive effects. Otherwise, this period mainly brings heightened concentration and discipline in daily chores and responsibilities. However, the person can make progress in real estate and construction, or in broadening his sphere of influence within his craft or occupation.

The person's stature and reputation may rise. He is especially favored by elders, bosses, and those in authority. Confidence expands as the person appreciates everything he has created in the past. The person exhibits wisdom born of experience. He may suddenly act like a leader. His management and organizational skills increase, and he may take a new direction in his vocation. Certain individuals become more committed to their goals, while others suddenly outgrow what they now see as old, restrictive paths. The person is stable and secure, and he is poised to make the most of any business opportunity that comes his way. Success results because of his natural discipline and focus and because the person expands his enterprises in a balanced, wise, and prudent way. Powerful individuals—those who wield great authority and influence—are aided during this period.

The person is moderate and controlled in his actions and ambitions. If Saturn is severely afflicted or in a highly unfavorable condition in the natal birthchart, then Jupiter's transit to Saturn may only expand the inherent difficulties. In this case, the area of life represented by Saturn's natal house placement breaks down and requires attention.

When transiting Jupiter squares or opposes natal Saturn, the person is plagued with restrictions, obstacles in his work, and moral dilemmas. He struggles for balance and gets little support from nature. Normal conditions of daily life suddenly demand immediate, time-consuming attention. It is generally a poor time for business decisions and professional commitments. The person must take care of old, nagging problems that now impede his progress and success. He must confront his predicaments with diligence, discipline, and perseverance. The person's judgement is off, and he cannot rely on his usual wisdom and discrimination. He encounters irritating bureaucracy and minor legal difficulties wherever he turns. For these five to ten days (in rare cases, approximately sixty days) the person's confidence and purpose at work is weakened. He feels confused, and he vacillates between action and inaction—optimism and pessimism. He would love to retreat from his responsibilities and take a nice, long vacation, but circumstances simply do not allow him to.

Despite the negative nature of this transit, the person's problems are not likely to be severe or long lasting. It is simply a period of extra work, pressure, and obligation. Expenses may increase, and the person may encounter delays, hassles, and a lack of freedom. He will need patience and tolerance during this period. Financial matters are not favored, and the person should avoid borrowing or lending if possible. The person has no luck with elders or authority figures, and he may now be held accountable for harmful or unsatisfactory work he has done in the past. His status and reputation may suffer slightly.

In certain cases the person is affected by a moral crisis in personal relationships or other areas of life separate from business and career. He must make compromises and adjust his principles and standards of behavior. He may be overly serious and narrow in his ways, or just the opposite—he may be too passive or lackadaisical. In any case, he may now face the fact that inappropriate ideas about duty and obligation can cause problems in his life.

$\downarrow$

When transiting Jupiter trines or sextiles natal Saturn, the person uses excellent judgement in business dealings and professional affairs. His perspective broadens, and he sees the whole of things rather than only isolated parts. Practical matters are handled properly. The person plans thoroughly, and whatever he constructs now is established on solid ground. He can easily determine what will work and what will not. Therefore, he succeeds at making his dreams a reality. For these five to ten days (in rare cases, approximately sixty days) the person's organizational ability expands. He may decide to branch out in business enterprises or any other career activities.

The person's status and reputation rise, and he is aided by his elders and people in authority. He is responsible and functions with great honesty and integrity. He is stable, controlled, and prudent. He does not waste money or resources now, and he seeks the most efficient, economical way of operating. He thinks in terms of long-range plans and is enthusiastic and confident about enlarging his power and influence. Leadership opportunities may arise. The person is wise and cautious, and he uses common sense. He has a clear sense of direction and does not attempt to avoid paying his dues. He is patient and handles routine, systems, and discipline gracefully. It is a good time for dealings with property and real estate. The person is balanced, stable, and secure. He makes progress in his occupation and is lucky in professional negotiations.

As with all trine aspects, especially those of Jupiter, the person should take action if he is to realize the full benefits indicated. Otherwise, this transit may pass by quite unnoticed. The transiting trine aspect is significantly more powerful than the transiting sextile. The transiting sextile only represents the opportunity to make the above effects a reality.

When transiting Jupiter conjuncts natal Uranus, the person be-haves with great spontaneity, independence, and creativity. He is freed from his usual concern with rules, regulations, and traditions. The person is excited, inventive, and concerned with progress. New begin-nings are likely and the person makes changes instantaneously and without regret. The person's intuition and psychic abilities are especially strong. He may have flashes of insight or genius. He is intent on truth, higher knowledge, and expansion of consciousness. Educational en-deavors are favored, especially those involving astrology, metaphysics, and the occult. Sudden, unexpected opportunities occur, and because the person feels so liberated and flexible, he is able to make the most of them. The person may meet and be strongly affected by spiritual people who are light-years ahead of their time.

The person takes risks. He craves freedom and swiftly breaks away from confining situations. It is an excellent time for problem solving and the deciphering of puzzles or symbols. The person's scientific ability increases dramatically. His perspective broadens, and he sees new possibilities everywhere. He is rebellious and strong-willed. There is a good possibility of exciting long-distance travel which serves to expand the person's awareness of foreign customs and practices. The person is confident in his talents, and he trusts himself. His judgement is quick and sound. He is idealistic, enthusiastic, and optimistic. The house position of Uranus flourishes greatly unless natal Uranus is severely afflicted or in a very unfavorable condition.

The person abhors restraint, routine, and system. He should, however, be careful about gambling and financial speculations. He must also be careful not to behave carelessly or recklessly, which is a distinct possibility now. The person may have sudden luck or financial windfalls. Group activity is favored, especially with humanitarian organizations, spiritual associations, and revolutionary movements. It is an excellent period for personal growth and a good time to end restricting or laborious relationships and put a stop to confining circumstances.

♃

When transiting Jupiter squares or opposes natal Uranus, the person's radical, independent, and rebellious tendencies are awakened. He is creative, adventurous, and spirited but dissatisfied with the status quo. This is therefore a time of great impatience, restlessness, and change. The person may decide to end relationships, jobs, or other affairs with less caution than usual. He is vulnerable to misguided optimism and idealism within himself, and, because he acts so spontaneously, this period may prove hazardous. The person should beware of acting recklessly or taking excessive risk. He is creative and insightful, but he is also stubborn and willful. The person has a lot of nervous tension in his aura. He craves excitement and stimulation. He may attract strange, bizarre, or peculiar circumstances, although they may be minor. The biggest changes and fluctuations occur in the areas of life represented by Uranus' house position.

The person focuses on the future, yet he does not concern himself with his own safety and security. He wants improvement and reform, and he wants it immediately. But he may lack balance, moderation, and follow-through. The person's concentration and judgement will probably be negatively affected during these five to ten days (in rare cases, approximately sixty days). He is annoyed by discipline, rules, regulations, and authority. He expands his knowledge of philosophy, astrology, occult studies, and metaphysics. However, he must be careful not to go overboard or become fanatical about them. There may be sudden, unexpected opportunities, especially those initiated by spiritual, mystical, weird, or eccentric individuals. The person may now have many dealings with people who are highly unorthodox or way ahead of their time. He may have pronounced intuition and psychic ability, but he should beware of overreacting to such phenomena.

The person feels more lucky than he actually is during this transit. He may be better off postponing business deals unless he takes time to consider all the ramifications carefully. The person lives for the moment and is especially concerned with personal freedom. He feels a strong desire to travel, either locally or abroad. He should be careful with anything electrical, including lightning or electrical storms.

$$\text{♃}$$

When transiting Jupiter trines or sextiles natal Uranus, the person meets with sudden, unexpected opportunities. He is astute and receptive, and he uses extraordinarily good judgement. It is an excellent time for making spontaneous changes in his life. The person's perception heightens, and he knows intuitively which actions to take and which ones to avoid. Personal growth occurs more readily than usual. The person may exhibit great objectivity and extreme talent or even genius. He feels free from the restraints of the thoughts and opinions of others. His individuality shines through. He is creative and inventive now. He is inspired, optimistic, and enthusiastic. He craves adventure and excitement.

Minor breakthroughs are likely to occur in certain areas of life represented by Uranus' house position. In addition, the person has accurate perception, and he uses instinctive knowledge. Educational endeavors are highly favored, as the person learns quickly and skillfully. It is an excellent time to engage in anything that is ahead of the times. The person may visit psychics, astrologers, tarot readers, or palmists. He excels in spiritual and metaphysical subjects. Investments, speculations, and business enterprises are generally successful. Ventures involving science, computers, and electronics are especially favored.

The person will be pleased by whatever changes he makes during this transit. New beginnings are likely to prosper. The person may come into contact with fascinating individuals who are spiritual, mystical, free-spirited, or highly progressive. If Uranus is well-aspected natally, then the person encounters extraordinary good luck. He makes new discoveries or he creates ingenious inventions. There may be sudden long-distance travel which proves quite exhilarating. As always with Jupiter's harmonious transits, the person should try to consciously activate the fortunate energies now occurring and make the most of this period. Otherwise, the transit may pass by unnoticed. The transiting trine aspect is significantly more powerful than the transiting sextile. The transiting sextile only represents the opportunity to make the above effects a reality.

♃

When transiting Jupiter conjuncts natal Neptune, the person undergoes an expansion of idealism, imagination, and devotion. It is a time of reverence, inspiration, and awe. The person yearns for perfection, and his thoughts become lofty and sublime. He may turn his energy inward and pursue enlightenment or spiritual liberation. He wants to know God and now sees that it is possible. Meditation, introspection, and contemplation are extremely favored. The person has profound experiences with gurus, mystics, astrologers, and religious figures. His imagination expands dramatically, and he is able to comprehend universal themes and philosophies which normally appear far-fetched. The person daydreams constantly, and he contemplates far-reaching goals and aspirations.

Although this transit is generally a favorable one, there are potential pitfalls. The person loses nearly all objectivity in practical matters. He is guided by his feelings and is too emotional to recognize the consequences of his actions. Transiting Jupiter's conjunction to Neptune does not stimulate the person to act in practical matters. So the person is not likely to make mistakes of his own accord.

He is, however, extraordinarily gullible and susceptible to the opinions of others. He is so generous, empathetic, helpful, and agreeable that he is an easy mark for those who would take advantage of him. He may go overboard in his pursuits. He may fall in love with love. In trying to escape the stifling influence and narrow boundaries of worldly existence, he may indulge in alcohol, drugs, or extreme spiritual techniques. He could also be deceived by fraudulent religious or spiritual figures. And, if Neptune is severely afflicted or in a very unfavorable condition in the natal birthchart, the person may encounter large problems in the areas of life indicated by Neptune's house position.

The person is sympathetic, sensitive, and compassionate. He has a strong desire to help in any way he can. He should, however, be careful about loaning money or possessions. He feels so content and complacent during these five to ten days (in rare cases, approximately sixty days) that he ignores cautionary instincts. He has a tendency to deny or suppress problems or unpleasant thoughts and feelings, which at this time leads to trouble.

It is not a particularly good period for business dealings. Unless the person is normally very lucky, he may do better to postpone major decisions of a practical or professional nature. Spiritual activities are much more likely to prosper than worldly ones. Creativity and self-expression are very strong. If the person is an artist, musician, poet, magician, or photographer, he now experiences an extremely prolific and fruitful phase. His imagination works extremely well.

The person may have many dreams during sleep. Visualization techniques are easy and productive. The person may have mystical or spiritual experiences during which he transcends the boundaries of earthly life. He is, however, subject to disappointment or disillusionment when his consciousness returns to normal. The person is especially kind and tenderhearted now, and his emotions are heightened. Psychic ability is strong. There is some danger of laziness or passivity, and the person must try to be practical and realistic during this transit. It is a very good time for enjoyment of the arts. Visiting the ocean or other bodies of water may also bring pleasure.

$$\text{2\!\!\!+}$$

When transiting Jupiter squares or opposes natal Neptune, the person's judgement becomes confused and he lacks common sense. He loses his sense of balance and proportion, and has trouble distinguishing the real from the unreal. His imagination and fantasy life are active. The person is overly emotional or sentimental, and he is easily fooled. He must beware of being used or falling prey to fraudulent persons. The person feels powerful devotional urges. He may begin to have psychic or spiritual experiences. Unfortunately, he may not be wise and rational enough to put them into their proper perspective. He exaggerates the importance of things and goes overboard in his expectations. He is influenced by wishful thinking. There is a strong possibility of disappointment and disillusionment during these five to ten days (in rare cases, approximately sixty days). The person should beware of religious fervor and spiritual fanaticism.

This transit tends to weaken a person's resolve, self-discipline, and inner strength. The person too easily gives in to negative habit patterns, personal weaknesses, or other character flaws. He may neglect his duties, obligations, and responsibilities. The person may feel an intense desire to escape from the practicalities of the real world. He may indulge in drugs or alcohol, which have an especially negative effect on the body at this time. The person is overly influenced by outside forces. Certain individuals are affected by spoiled foods, potent medicines, or other physical influences. Individuals with delicate health are susceptible to strange, psychosomatic or stress-induced illnesses which are difficult to diagnose. Mentally unstable or psychologically impaired people may now have an extremely difficult or troublesome time.

Because his objectivity is significantly hindered, the person is generally better off if he postpones business dealings. He is not so prudent and discerning now, and he could easily make the wrong move. He is naively inspired and too trusting. He thinks in grandiose terms and may foolishly idealize people he deals with. He is too willing to take a risk.

During this period, the person feels deeply and his thinking expands. With his expanded perception, he enjoys music, drama, film, photography, magic, and the other arts. It is also a good time for meditation and spiritual growth. The person feels generous and wants to help others. But he should try to remain as practical and down-to-earth as possible in his daily activities, watch out for confusion in his thinking, and avoid overzealous mystics and spiritualists.

♃

When transiting Jupiter trines or sextiles natal Neptune, the person's boundaries expand and he becomes spiritually inspired. He is guided by his deepest feelings and may experience sublime perceptions, dreams, and visions. His faith in God or nature increases dramatically during these five to ten days (in rare cases, approximately sixty days). It is a perfect time for meditation, contemplation, and introspection. Activities with mystics, spiritualists, astrologers, occultists, and gurus are favored. The person's religious activities are profound and productive because he feels idealistic and devoted. He is sensitive now and appreciates art and beauty. His artistic abilities and enjoyment of the arts—music, dance, drama, painting, photography, film, and magic—are heightened. The person is very creative, and his work is more subtle and imaginative than usual. The soft transiting aspects of Jupiter to Neptune often produce few concrete events. Most of what occures is internal—emotional and spiritual—in nature.

The person experiences consistent and accurate intuition. He does not mind serving others at this time. He is tenderhearted, sincere, and content with himself. He looks for the best in people, and he easily inspires trust and other fine qualities in others. The person is very relaxed and easygoing now, even to the extent of laziness or complacency. Relationships, however, flourish because the person is concerned with everyone's feelings. He should be careful not to be too idealistic and optimistic in his perceptions of others or he may be used by those others. If Neptune is very well-aspected in the natal birthchart, then the person experiences benefits or unexpected good luck stemming from his previous actions.

The transiting trine aspect is significantly more powerful than the transiting sextile. The transiting sextile only represents the opportunity to make the above effects a reality.

♃

When transiting Jupiter conjuncts natal Pluto, the person experiences a surge of personal power and confidence. He is intense; he concentrates better and focuses his energies more directly. His actions exhibit depth and profundity. The person believes in his talents, and his willpower dramatically increases. It is an excellent time for self-improvement and spiritual growth, as the person becomes acutely conscious of his ability to regenerate himself. Transformation in any area of life is favored but is especially likely to occur in the areas represented by Pluto's natal house position. The person feels strong ambition, drive, and motivation. As a result, he attains success and recognition relatively easily. He makes his presence known with very little effort. His charisma is exceptional and he deals more adeptly and successfully with the public for these five to ten days (in rare cases, approximately sixty days).

The person may exhibit qualities of leadership. His perspective broadens. He takes control of his destiny and is willing to be responsible for nearly all elements of his life. He has more influence and power over others than usual. He must, however, take care not to act too forcefully or to be manipulative with his friends, associates, and family. He may feel a strong desire to get to the ultimate truth of many issues. The person does things in a big way and does whatever is necessary to fulfill his ambitions. His efforts are sincere and productive. In some cases, the person taps dormant inner resources. He may exhibit special or exceptional abilities. He should, however, avoid obsessive or compulsive tendencies.

Healing ability, whether directed toward himself or others, is very strong now. Those who work professionally with metaphysics, occultism, spiritual healing, or psychic phenomenon are aided by this transit. The person feels connected to God and nature, and certain individuals may have powerful spiritual, psychic, or supernatural experiences. He probes things deeply, trusts his instincts, and stands up for himself and his principles. As always with Jupiter transits, this period may promise more than it delivers unless the person consciously acts upon the potential it represents.

When transiting Jupiter squares or opposes natal Pluto, the person feels a strong, occasionally excessive, desire for power, control, and accomplishment. His energy increases, his ego expands, and he believes intensely in his own abilities. Unfortunately, he lacks balance and moderation. Therefore, in his determination to gain influence and authority, he unwittingly arouses the resistance or animosity of those in power. This is hardly an introspective period, but the person would benefit from reflection upon the appropriateness and proportions of his actions. He does things in a grandiose way and loses his perspective. He then becomes embroiled in confrontations, power struggles, and difficult or counter productive situations.

Because his willpower is so strong and he is able to tap deep internal resources now, the person is likely to be victorious in his struggles and successful in his undertakings. But he may lose friends in the process. Relationships suffer from his lack of sensitivity and inability to compromise. Furthermore, the person may try to change or mold others. He experiences extreme vulnerability or emotional volatility in the areas of life represented by Pluto's house position. He may behave fanatically or compulsively in those realms. When he directs his energy toward self-improvement or psychological transformation, he may be ruthless or hard on himself. The person generally overreacts during these five to ten days (in rare cases, sixty days).

Negotiations are difficult. In certain cases, the person attracts events or circumstances in which he himself is dominated, manipulated, or controlled by persons abusing power. More than anything else, the person should try to behave with discretion, moderation, and self-control during this transit. He should maintain faith that in time, with a proper attitude and correct strategy, his goals can be attained without upsetting the balance of nature. Otherwise, he can fulfill his desires, but will pay a heavy price.

♃

When transiting Pluto trines or sextiles natal Pluto, the person's willpower is strong, and he succeeds easily in fulfilling his desires. He is very resourceful, and his focus and concentration are excellent. The person may now direct his attention toward self-improvement, personal transformation, psychological cleansing, and spiritual regeneration. He experiences an increase of psychic ability, intuition, and instinct. He is concerned with spiritual realities and is able to probe issues deeply and seriously. Occult and metaphysical endeavors are favored for the five to ten days (in rare cases, approximately sixty days) of this transit. The person does well in learning or practicing astrology, tarot, palmistry, the reading of omens, and other occult practices. Or he may visit professional psychics and seers.

The person exhibits strong leadership tendencies, and he may suddenly find himself in a position of power or authority. He is more influential and charismatic than usual, and is concerned with the welfare of others. He gains recognition or prominence. Nature supports the person's efforts, and he makes a big impact with little effort.

What occurs during this transit depends largely upon the natal condition of Pluto. The person may awaken to a new reality in the area of life represented by Pluto's house position. If the person is highly evolved and uses his "Plutonian" power to regularly affect the world and those around him, then this period may be important. If, however, the person is not in the habit of taking charge of his destiny and influencing others, then little happens. Neither Jupiter or Pluto are personal planets. It is therefore especially easy for the soft transits of Jupiter to Pluto to pass by unnoticed. The transiting trine aspect is significantly more powerful than the transiting sextile. The transiting sextile only represents the opportunity to make the above effects a reality.

When transiting Saturn conjuncts the natal Sun, the person's soul is tested, and he comes face to face with his level of maturity, strength of character, and willingness to be responsible for himself. This is an extremely important transit, as the person reevaluates everything about himself, especially his direction, goals, and purpose. For some individuals, it is a time of crisis or a career turning point. The person must choose between an easy and comfortable path and the necessary and appropriate direction for his life. He feels heavy internal pressure, and life seems to slow down, as if every moment is all that there is, has been, and will ever be. Thus, the person knows, beyond any doubt, that he must do the right thing or suffer painful and profound consequences. He sees his actions and their results with pristine clarity.

Although this transit is usually frustrating, severe, and demanding, the person matures as a result. Confidence, energy, and vitality may be low, and the person may feel separate from others. But Saturn's conjunction with the all-important Sun ultimately brings integration. The person is compelled to act with integrity and honor, whether he is used to acting that way or not. He is sensitive to everyone in his environment and must make important compromises. He learns to cooperate. But the person feels depressed because he is made blatantly aware of his shortcomings and is called to task by those around him. By the end of this transit, the person has grown in character, depth, and his ability to function responsibly in the world. If he does what he knows to be right, he will command more respect, and his reputation and status will increase.

The person must beware of a negative or self-censoring attitude during this transit. His judgement is affected by a narrow and mundane perspective, and even the most competent and productive person may now feel like a failure. He sees all of his faults and imperfections and is blind to his own virtues and abilities. The person needs patience and perseverance because the nature of Saturn is to delay, deny, and restrict. The person should concern himself with his plans and goals rather than looking for success and achievement in the present. He is simply too affected by psychological censoring mechanisms to create success for himself. If he tries for quick results and gratification, he is unlikely to succeed. The person should work on giving direction to his life and make long-term plans.

The person may have difficulties or frustrations with his father. The father's health and well-being are not favored. However, this is an excellent time for a person to correct any chronic problems with his father and to eliminate any misunderstandings within the relationship. The person may have particularly significant contact with older people, disciplinarians, and people in authority at this time. He may find himself feeling pressured, powerless, and perhaps even resentful toward these individuals, but he nevertheless gains wisdom, insight, growth, and maturity from his associations with them. Saturn's conjunction with the Sun is not a good time for dealings with bosses or government officials. Nature instructs the person about what to work on to perfect himself, and therefore advancement or promotion is rather unlikely now. In certain cases, where the person has been unreasonably denied his due, his status and fortune may rise. But this is a rare occurrence and generally should not be expected.

Health and well-being are crucial issues during this transit, and the person is compelled to correct any weaknesses in his mind or body. He may engage in therapy, counseling, spiritual techniques, or any self-development course which he is attracted to. Growth occurring at this time is deep, real, and lasting because the person cannot hide from the truth about his character, no matter how hard he tries. He sees his ego clearly now, and cannot get away with habitual rationalizations and mental tricks. Furthermore, the person is now willing to work very hard on old, personal issues. Healthwise, the person's heart and lower back are vulnerable. He should avoid stressful situations, get plenty of rest, and engage in exercise which energizes and regulates the heart.

Because the Sun rules men in general, women may have difficulties with their husbands during this transit. Or the husband may have to endure illness, affliction, or suffering.

The person must look deeply into himself and take full responsibility for his own destiny. This means living life with complete accountability for his actions and embracing the notion that he is the creator of every feature of his existence. Otherwise, he will be unhappy, depressed, or miserable during the entirety of this transit.

♄

When transiting Saturn squares or opposes the natal Sun, the person is restricted by outer circumstances, while feeling heavy internal pressure, frustration, and inhibition. It is a tedious time of burdensome responsibilities, testing of character, and hard work. The person exhibits discipline, patience, and perseverance. He has a chance to prove his endurance as never before. Physical energy is at an all-time low and the person must get as much rest as possible. His health is at risk, in many cases as a direct result of a depressed or somber mental outlook.

Ambitions are easily thwarted or delayed, and the person may receive criticism or disapproval. Because everything he tries meets with resistance and opposition, the person begins a long, serious process of self-examination. However, he focuses so directly on flawed or weak aspects of his personality that he loses his perspective. He forgets his strengths and talents, unconsciously censors his own expression and creativity and begins to lose confidence and self-esteem. It is crucial for the person to perceive this transit not as karmic retribution or the wrath of God, but as a period of readjustment and an opportunity to remove himself from inappropriate or harmful circumstances, and to relinquish unhealthy behavioral patterns. It is a time of owning up to one's real desires and letting go of superfluous or life-damaging activities.

Spiritually, Saturn's hard aspects to the Sun are useful for meditation, introspection, contemplation, and of growth of personality. The person excels in anything that requires austerity and discipline. He lets go of outgrown and unnecessary attachments. The person may have difficulties or pressure in his spine, lower back, or heart. It is a good idea to take plenty of calcium, in a healthy form, for the teeth and bones (which are also at risk). The person should try to schedule time for recreation, hobbies, and entertainment with friends in order to ease the perpetual tedium and stress. He is discouraged, tired, and worn-out because he feels that his problems will never end.

Experiences with his elders, bosses, and people in authority are likely to bring problems or frustration. The person is especially called to task for childish or immature behavior, and if he does not stop behaving in a self-centered or egotistic way, he will suffer dearly. The person also experiences obstacles and dilemmas with his father. His father may act strict and severe, or his health may decline. Activities with the government are unfavorable. This is clearly not a time to seek promotions, except in rare cases where the person has, for some strange reason, held himself back from a higher position which he should have accepted earlier. Since the Sun rules men in general, a woman may have difficulties with her husband during this transit.

This period, which lasts approximately two months and may occur up to three times in nine months, brings endings and new beginnings. However, the person should not expect new endeavors to bear fruit for quite some time. The person can make powerful and significant progress through psychotherapy and other techniques. He grows in maturity during this transit, although it may be painful. If he has been attempting something inappropriate or impossible, he now realizes it. He feels inner pressure to "do the right thing." If he has previously been ignoring or suppressing problems, he confronts them now. It is important for him to remain as flexible as possible and open to change. Otherwise, the person's situation deteriorates rapidly, and his serenity is destroyed. This transit occurs every seven years and allows the person to focus attention and reorganize whatever aspects of his life require work. The person must beware of guilt feelings. If the Sun is severely afflicted or in a highly unfavorable condition at birth, then this period may be extremely difficult.

ħ

When transiting Saturn trines or sextiles the natal Sun, the person is purposeful, focused, and efficient. He gains recognition, prominence, or promotions for past professional tasks that were well-executed. The person's organizational and administrative ability increases, and he turns his ideas into reality with little struggle or strain. He understands form and structure better than usual. This transit therefore signifies a period of special accomplishment if the person acts on his impulses. It is an excellent time for long-range career planning. The person is confident and down-to-earth. Business and politics are favored, and the person is successful in his dealings with bosses, people in authority, and powerful people. Activities involving the government go smoothly now.

During these approximately two months (which may occur up to three times in nine months) the person is patient, disciplined, responsible, and tolerant. Because he embraces these higher qualities of life, his life is easy and graceful. He is not plagued by emergencies, confrontations, and crises. If difficult situations arise, the person handles them adeptly and efficiently. He uses his leadership ability. Wisdom, prudence, and discretion are natural features of his character now. The person gains benefits from his father, and their relationship goes well. A woman may receive favors from the men in her life during this transit. The person works hard and makes excellent progress. He is willing to pay his dues without objecting or complaining. He is successful in his undertakings.

The transiting trine aspect is significantly more powerful than the transiting sextile. The transiting sextile only represents the opportunity to make the above effects a reality.

ħ

When transiting Saturn conjuncts the natal Moon, the person feels pressured to focus on his feelings, emotions, and need for security. It is a time of sober introspection and deep personality analysis. The person experiences rejection in some area of life or is denied some important heartfelt desires. He reacts by turning inward and focusing intently on his weaknesses, imperfections, flawed habit patterns, and basic vulnerabilities. During the approximately two months of Saturn's conjunction with the Moon (which may occur up to three times in nine months), the person can gain self-knowledge and achieve inner growth because he is capable of objectively examining his feelings and unconscious motivations. Unfortunately, however, he may also experience pain and sorrow about his mortal, fallible nature. The person too easily loses perspective and is overly hard on himself. He is temporarily self-critical, moody, and hypersensitive. He gives little or no weight to his talents and virtues. Worst of all, he may be unable to accept the love and support of friends, associates, and family members. He feels unlovable, misunderstood, and isolated from the world.

The person's vitality is low, and his excessive fears, worries, and negative attitude may cause sickness. He may have problems with his teeth and bones or ailments involving the stomach, breast, and brain. A woman may experience problems with her menstrual cycle. The person should get plenty of rest, avoid overwork or excessively stressful situations, and take plenty of calcium in a healthy form. (Many nutritionists now consider dairy products harmful, and therefore recommend taking calcium through vitamins or edible seaweed.) The person feels burdened by daily tasks and details. His confidence is low, and he may censor his emotions or delay personal gratification. He feels internal tension, frustration, and pressure. For some, this transit is a depressing, lonely, or unhappy time. Obstacles, dilemmas, or predicaments involving the person's mother may arise suddenly. His mother's health may deteriorate, or she may suffer in some other way. It is a very good time for handling long-standing problems with one's mother and women in general. The person now has the strength and objectivity to deal squarely with issues he has ignored and avoided in the past.

Love relationships or other associations which have lost their potential for fulfillment may end. If the person has been acting out of false hope, he is now forced to face the truth and take action. In general, however, this is more a period of self-reflection, emotional restructuring, and reorganization of the psyche than anything else. The person determines what he needs to be happy. He examines his unconscious behavioral patterns in order to root out obsessions, cravings, addictions, and all forms of emotional dependency. To the extent that the person succeeds at this, he creates a psychologically healthy and liberated future.

The person encounters increased domestic responsibilities. Some individuals now face karmic payback for harmful actions they have inflicted on loved ones in the past. The person feels a strong sense of guilt for any wrongdoings he has knowingly committed. He is more shy than usual, and he should postpone dealings with the public until he feels more optimistic and buoyant. Because the Moon relates to nurturing in early life, children may be especially hurt by experiences during this transit. A great deal of warmth, touch, and emotional support will help children going through this period. The person may postpone important decisions or at least reconsider them in the light of common sense, after this rather gloomy period has passed.

♄

When transiting Saturn squares or opposes the natal Moon, the person undergoes difficult or painful emotional experiences caused by past karma. Domestic problems surface, especially involving his wife, mother, or women in general. The person's vitality diminishes and he feels burdened by his daily chores and duties. He feels more emotionally inhibited and shy than usual. Confidence may reach an all-time low. The person is plagued by guilt (perhaps connected to some current crisis he has unwittingly created) and is uncomfortable trying to fulfill his desires and cravings. Although this transit generally brings on depression, loneliness, and gloom, it is, in most cases, less painful and intense than the conjunction. Because the person concentrates on external problems and relationships more than on his own psyche and inner being, his suffering is not as acute. As with the conjunction, however, the difficulties that arise now do affect his feelings.

The person is plagued by irrational fears stemming from the unconscious mind. He feels inadequate, insecure, or inferior and is in no way aided by others, who may be critical, disparaging, or abusive at this time. The person fears rejection and does not want to take any risks. Because of his restricted and inhibited behavior, he is unlikely to create much joy, happiness, or fulfillment for himself. More than ever, the person needs to schedule periods of recreation and entertainment. He should avoid overwork and stressful situations and try to enjoy hobbies and diversions as much as possible. He should get plenty of rest, as illnesses arise easily due to worry, pessimism, and a negative attitude. He should take calcium in a healthy form for his teeth and bones and guard against ailments involving the stomach, breast, and brain. A woman should also guard against ailments involving her menstrual cycle. As with all Saturn transits, the person is generally better off avoiding salt, hard cheeses, eggs, meat, and other crystallizing or contracting foods. During the approximately two months of Saturn's aspect to the Moon (which may occur up to three times in nine months) he should eat more lightly, favoring vegetables, grains, fruits, and liquids.

Relationships are more difficult than usual, to some extent because the person feels overly insecure and self-doubtful. The person may have problems with women. His wife or mother may become ill or worse, and the person may have to devote energy, care, and attention to her. It is an appropriate time to take responsibility for previous mistakes or wrongdoings. The person has the ability to confront dilemmas normally too distressing to face. Children undergoing this transit may be affected in an especially negative way, since nurturing, warmth, love, and emotional support are conspicuously lacking now. Even if the child gets all the love he needs, he may be temporarily unable to accept emotional support. In certain cases, the person's mother behaves coldly or with great severity. If the Moon is severely afflicted or in a highly unfavorable condition at birth, then this transit is extremely difficult. Certain individuals, especially those who have avoided dealing responsibly with their emotions and childhood hurts, need counseling to help them through psychological dilemmas or crises that occur now. The person should do his best not to isolate himself or withdraw from others. He should especially surround himself with loving, supportive friends, and avoid critical, harsh, or coarse individuals.

This period is not very favorable for business or promotions. Success and progress is delayed or denied, and the person may wish to postpone seeking approval and favors until Saturn has finished making its final aspect (within the eight or nine months Saturn is within orb) to the Moon. Men undergoing this transit may perhaps experience more external dilemmas than a woman would since men are generally less adept at dealing with their feelings and their feminine side. He now reaps the unfortunate results of previous negative actions, especially if he behaved destructively in relationships or has mistreated women in the past. Because the Moon rules women, during this transit a woman may experience more personal anguish or distress, as her instinctive abilities are suddenly obstructed or cut off. Karmic retribution occurring at this time is likely to be extremely precise and specific in nature. The person may feel that God or destiny has entered his life, and there is nothing he can do about it. The person needs patience and perseverance. He must remember the biblical saying, "This too shall pass." At any rate, by the end of this period, the person may learn a good deal about himself, his emotions, and the women in his life.

♄

When transiting Saturn trines or sextiles the natal Moon, the person has good domestic experiences. Family life is smooth, home improvements go well, and the person benefits from his mother, women in general, and women in positions of authority. The person is emotionally balanced, stable, and resilient. He maintains a mature attitude and therefore handles life very effectively at this time. He exhibits excellent common sense and is practical, organized, and disciplined. The person plans and is likely to succeed in his endeavors. He is psychologically healthy, in tune with his feelings and emotions, and makes use of his instincts, impulses, and intuition. Furthermore, he displays depth in his thinking and endurance in his actions. During these approximately two months (which may occur up to three times in nine months), the person is graceful and skilled in the art of living.

Things work for the person now. Relationships are generally favored. The person is objective, and he sees the big picture. He does whatever it takes to make things work. He gleans wisdom from his past experiences and is aware of unconscious desires and motivations. Career and business dealings are favored, especially if they involve the masses in any way. The person is detached in his business dealings; he negotiates wisely and makes accurate and proper decisions. He is unlikely to overpay or be unduly influenced by cravings and passions. He is conservative in behavior and aware of tradition. A child going through this period receives powerful nurturing and support from his mother. Thus, he feels safe, secure, and protected.

The person works diligently and productively. He does not forget his care and compassion for others. He shows his loyalty, devotion, and integrity.

The transiting trine aspect is significantly more powerful than the transiting sextile. The transiting sextile only represents the opportunity to make the above effects a reality.

♄

When transiting Saturn conjuncts natal Mercury, the person becomes serious, thoughtful, and intent upon planning and reorganizing his life. He begins to think very deeply, focusing on important matters. Instead of taking life as it comes, he analyzes his experience objectively. Life seems to slow down while he thinks about it. This is a time to end old, useless, worn-out aspects of his life and to lay the groundwork for a more fulfilling and productive future. The process may be tedious and time-consuming, but the person feels he can no longer stand by and watch his life be influenced by circumstances: external events, habits, personality traits, old choices, and whichever way the wind happens to blow. For the first time in a long while, he recognizes what a profound opportunity life is, and he realizes he must think for himself and decide which direction his life should go. Because thought (or consciousness) is the very basis for action, this is an extremely important transit. Decisions made during this period are likely to have a profound impact for years to come.

Nature demands that the person put his ideas into print and into practice. Some individuals voluntarily sit down and write in their own diaries. Others compose for friends, relatives, and the public. The person feels an almost burdensome responsibility to communicate now, and he weighs his words more carefully than ever. His mind works slowly, with more depth, logic, objectivity, and profundity than usual. However, he is also shy, self-critical, and demands much of himself. He is exacting and overly concerned with failure. At times, he gives too much importance to his communications and cannot say what he really thinks for fear of the repercussions. It is a very good time for persons involved in detail work and all endeavors which involve great precision and accuracy. Research of any kind is favored. Although this transit is not about success and recognition, the person is likely to be effective in his endeavors due to his patience, perseverance, diligent workmanship, and his ability to concentrate.

The person must be careful of nervous ailments. He has a tendency to overwork now and is particularly vulnerable to stress and strain. The lungs, intestines, and nervous system are at risk. Chronic psychosomatic illnesses may flair up or arise for the first time. The person is so serious

186   about life that he needs to schedule plenty of rest and recreation, especially the kind that allows the mind to completely relax. The person's confidence may be somewhat low. He sees his shortcomings before his abilities and may dwell on his failures and deficiencies. He feels unintelligent, and some individuals experience mental blocks.

However, while it is true that the mind works slowly, the person may complete some of his best, most perceptive, penetrating, and comprehensive work ever. The mind is stable and steady, and it is an excellent time to work on self-improvement. The person is contemplative and philosophical, and he thinks about life in a rational and purposeful way. He also handles old problems, projects, and necessary conversations he has been evading for some time.

The person may feel somewhat depressed. He may have difficulties with speech or hearing problems. It is a poor time to give lectures or engage in debates. Machinery breaks down, and the person may have problems with old tape recorders, telephones, radios, and television sets. He is not favored by the press, the intelligentsia, and other highly intellectual individuals. Children going through the transit have a difficult time expressing themselves, especially in the adult world, where they may feel limited ability to communicate. The person must beware of a negative attitude, rigid thinking, and narrow-mindedness. He should also guard against adopting such a practical and disciplined mind-set that he loses his idealism and vision.

It is a good time for planning business or career expansion, but action or major risk-taking should not begin until after Saturn has made its final conjunction to Mercury. Commerce is not at all favored during the approximately two-month period (which may occur up to three times in nine months) when Saturn is conjunct Mercury. The person should be especially careful when signing contracts. He may make binding agreements which are too restrictive and unfavorable in the long run. If the person has been putting off writing a book or some other important literary work, he now feels strongly pressured to begin. If he is a teacher, by hobby or profession, this transit may spur him to action. The person may examine or change his diet. He feels a heaviness of mind and occasionally feels seriously misunderstood. If he is a scientist or works with computers, he may accomplish great things now. If Mercury is severely afflicted or in a highly unfavorable condition in the natal birthchart, then Saturn's transit to Mercury may be extremely rough. In such cases, the person may need professional counseling in order to deal with his insecurities and mental weaknesses.

♄

When transiting Saturn squares or opposes natal Mercury, the person's ideas and convictions are challenged, especially bringing into question the way he has organized his life. It may be a difficult time, as the person's communications unexpectedly meet with resistance, opposition, or protest. The person begins to feel insecure and unsure of himself. Confidence and enthusiasm are low. At the same time, the person is extra sensitive and vulnerable to criticism and censure from others. He is liable to feel misunderstood and suffer mental isolation and alienation. The person's thinking slows to a snail's pace as he focuses microscopically on issues, often neglecting the big picture. There is a danger of stubbornness, narrow thinking, and intellectual rigidity. Still, in the end, the person may benefit greatly from this transit if he is humble enough to reflect upon the mistakes he has made in his thinking or in his speech and responsible enough to take action. Like the conjunction transit of Saturn to Mercury, the person has an opportunity to rethink, restructure, and reorganize his life. However, he may miss his chance if he spends too much time and energy reacting to critical people around him.

The person may have problems with machinery, especially telephones, tape recorders, radios, television sets, typewriters, computers, or any devices that relay information. The person's letters and communications with others may be thwarted or lost, and the same is true of incoming messages. Negotiations may break down and agreements deteriorate. The person should study contracts carefully and reschedule delicate meetings until after the final transit of Saturn to Mercury has passed. Business and commerce are not favored, and it is not a very lucky time in general. The person should put off major decisions involving risk or consequence, as his thinking is too negative or pessimistic and his perspective too narrow. The person may also reap karmic retribution for previous statements, assertions, proposals, ideas, or opinions which were damaging or should not have been made (for whatever reason). Tests, exams, lectures, debates, and speeches should be postponed, if possible. If they cannot, then the person must prepare extremely well and fortify himself against probable mishaps, especially involving faulty microphones and machinery, traffic jams, delays, and all kinds of timing problems.

This transit brings difficulties in other areas as well. The person may be abused, criticized, or verbally attacked by intellectuals, teachers, professors, and the press. He may also have a hard time with siblings and other relatives. He has trouble getting his ideas recognized and is occasionally scared to speak up. Some individuals exhibit poor judgement throughout the entire transit. Travels may be obstructed or thwarted. The person worries more than usual and is bothered by fears and neuroses. He should beware of overworking as this is a stressful time and his health could easily break down. The lungs, intestines, nervous system, and digestive tract are at risk. Psychosomatic illnesses may be caused by tension and anxiety. Persons with asthma, epilepsy, or stress-related ailments must be extra careful. Speech or hearing problems are common. Teachers and writers may have a more difficult time than usual in their work, either because the mind slows down and becomes overly exacting or because others challenge their ideas. In some cases the person is reprimanded for sloppy work he did long ago.

Like the conjunction transit of Saturn to Mercury, the person is very likely to be required to put his ideas, concepts, and plans in writing. He may have to go back and complete unfinished projects. Recreation, especially mental rest, is absolutely crucial now, as the person is unduly serious, somber, or depressed. People who are insecure, weak, fearful, or mentally unstable to begin with may have a terrible time during this transit and should seek support from friends, loved ones, or professional counselors. But although this transit is demanding, it provides a great opportunity to plan new strategies for future accomplishment. However, the person must try his best to remain mentally flexible and to avoid rigid thinking.

When transiting Saturn trines or sextiles natal Mercury, the person is clear-headed, mentally stable, and extremely perceptive. He is practical, objective, and uses good common sense. It is an excellent time for planning, organizing, and putting strategies into action. The person succeeds because of his mental discipline, patience, wisdom, and perseverance. He is realistic and astute, and he evaluates situations correctly. The person has excellent focus and concentration. His thinking is deep and serious, yet he is not somber or depressed. Indeed, the person feels mentally and psychologically healthy during this period and is not bothered by fears, worries, or neuroses. The nervous system is strong and the person is resilient to stress, strain, and overwork. Physical health is hardy.

During the approximately two months of transiting Saturn's trine or sextile to Mercury (which may occur up to three times in nine months), the person's work is likely to be precise, accurate, and very thorough. Anything that requires attention to details is favored and the person does especially well in science, math, engineering, drawing, computer science, or any technical field. Intellectual pursuits are successful, and it is a good time to take tests or exams. The person's ability to communicate is supreme now. He is effective and efficient in teaching, debating, lecturing, and speaking. He uses facts, information, and knowledge to his advantage, and makes few errors or oversights. The person may do some of his best writing. He is able to give form and structure to his ideas and present his proposals in the most practical, sensible light. He understands the art of negotiation and compromise and is therefore able to create agreement and harmony between himself and others. It is a good time for signing contracts and legal agreements.

Business and commerce are favored. The person is confident and secure about himself. He recognizes his abilities as well as his weaknesses. The person may successfully reorganize and restructure his life. The plans that he makes now are established on solid ground. He takes care of old, unfinished projects and paper work, and he may repair damaged or injured relationships with adroit communication. His words and letters are constructive, skillful, and convincing. It is a very good time for all kinds of self-improvement. The person is open to learning, and he is conscientious. He may also be precise, picky, or tend toward perfectionism. He may seek dependable guidance from his elders. Bookkeeping and other tedious technical work requires minimal effort and angst. The person should take advantage of this highly advantageous transit by solving as many predicaments and mysteries as possible. He will not always have such patience, mental dexterity, and concentration as he does now.

The transiting trine aspect is significantly more powerful than the transiting sextile. The transiting sextile only represents the opportunity to make the above effects a reality.

ħ

When transiting Saturn conjuncts natal Venus, the person gets serious and practical about his love life or marriage. He reexamines all of his values, especially those involving his primary love relationship. He sees things more objectively than usual and during this rare period, has the discipline and fortitude to either commit wholeheartedly to his partner or bring matters to a close. The person feels very sensitive and vulnerable and cannot tolerate abuse or lack of warmth and emotional support. He feels pressure from inside to admit to himself that he deserves to receive enough nourishment from his mate. The person is suddenly affected by a powerful sense of fairness and justice. He may act coldly or severely in order to achieve emotional equity. This transit may test the person's marriage.

Emotional experiences during this transit are often karmic. The person reaps rewards or punishment for his actions in previous lifetimes. He may solidify a relationship that will bring happiness and contentment. Or he may find himself terribly victimized by his mate for no apparent reason other than his poor choice of partners. Either way, he feels the hand of fate reaching into his life.

Generally speaking, this approximately two-month period (which may occur up to three times in nine months) is not a cheerful one. The sweetness of life is toned down, and heartaches are typical. The person is acutely aware of everything that is missing from his life. His actions are based upon feelings of scarcity and shortage rather than of contentment and abundance. In extreme cases the person feels cheated, bitter, or envious. Individuals who live their lives perpetually waiting for love to magically appear at their door, constantly complaining about rotten romantic luck, can expect a profoundly lonely period now. Such individuals should take this opportunity to directly confront the fallacy of their thinking. If the person cannot gather the courage and determination to create a loving relationship and happiness for himself, then he should seek professional guidance and counseling now. If he pursues self-improvement techniques at this time, they will have a deep and lasting effect for years to come.

The person's social life may suffer. He is more shy, serious, or unconsciously withdrawn than usual. He may be remote, reserved, and distant without knowing it. He may experience sexual inhibition or dysfunction. The person may be temporarily impotent, frigid, or romantically cold. Spiritual seekers may choose celibacy now and have a very easy time of it while this period lasts. Healthwise, there is a danger of prostate or reproductive ailments. Women should visit their gynecologists during this transit. There may also be illnesses involving the kidneys, throat, or thyroid gland. Some individuals develop acne or skin problems. The person feels a need for monetary security. However, this is a better time for financial planning and consolidation than for earning wealth. The person should not take business or financial risks until Saturn completes its final transit to Venus. All kinds of desires are hard, often impossible, to fulfill.

The person may have difficulties with women, including his mother. He may become involved with someone much older, or with a successful person in a position of authority, or an ascetic, austere individual. If the person is a professional artist, he may create an important work. He is especially adept at bringing form and structure to his creative ideas and inspirations now. The person may buy and sell luxury items or art objects. He may feel homely, unattractive, or unlovable during this transit. If he is vain about his looks or attached to his appearance, he suffers worse. If Venus is heavily afflicted or in a highly unfavorable condition in the natal birthchart, then this period is likely to bring pain or sadness. No matter what occurs, though, the person has an excellent chance to objectively examine all of his values and consciously choose what he wants in his love life and what he doesn't. It is the perfect time to work on relationship issues and come to real solutions, compromises, and settlements.

♄

When transiting Saturn squares or opposes natal Venus, the person experiences troubles or complications in his primary love relationship. Important issues and concerns, which have kept him from fulfilling his desire for romance and which have previously been repressed or ignored, may now surface with power and intensity. The person is called to task by his lover or spouse for any destructive or life-damaging behavior he has perpetrated within their relationship. Much that happens now is the result of past karma, and the person may be paying back love debts from past lifetimes. The opposition transit is especially specific in delivering repayment. In other words, the person now receives bad treatment from the exact same person he previously injured in a past life. Naturally, the person feels unfairly treated or victimized if he has no idea why he is suddenly being abused. It is also possible that the person receives shabby treatment from his partner because he lacks self-respect and has chosen his mate unwisely. In such cases, the person clearly realizes that he needs to work on his psyche before he will ever create a fulfilling and loving relationship.

The person's love relationship may end. In some cases the person's mate leaves suddenly. In other cases, the person realizes that love and passion have long since disappeared from the relationship and all that is left is a formal bond. The person is objective enough to understand that he is being guided by circumstances to face the truth in his love life. Even with the hard transits of Saturn to Venus (the square and opposition) the person has the discipline and resolve to end a worn-out relationship. The person's social life suffers. He feels lonely, more shy, distant, or withdrawn than usual and is extremely sensitive and vulnerable. He is easily hurt. His luck in meeting new lovers during this approximately two-month period (which may occur up to three times within nine months) is poor. He is attracted to partners who are unavailable, selfish, cold, or who simply use him for their own personal gain. Though the person may feel unloved and emotionally needy, he is wise to take a back seat in the area of romance at this time. If Venus is severely afflicted or in a highly unfavorable condition in the natal birthchart, then this transit can be devastating.

Like the conjunction transit, the person is particularly aware of the lack of happiness and abundance in his life. He finds it almost impossible to fulfill heartfelt desires, whether big or small. He may suffer from reproductive ailments, genital infections, prostate problems, and kidney, throat, or thyroid defects. He is affected by sexual coldness or dysfunction and may be subject to bouts of impotence or frigidity. He has difficulty relating to women, including his mother. Creativity is not favored, and some professional artists may now find their inspiration blocked. It is an unfortunate time for earning wealth or taking any kind of financial risk. The person may lose or break art objects or luxury items. Depression, melancholy, or somber moods occur intermittently now for obvious reasons.

ħ

When transiting Saturn trines or sextiles natal Venus, the person is happy and secure in his love life. His primary relationship is stable and balanced, and he takes personal responsibility for creating his own love and happiness. He is sincere, well-behaved, and very concerned with justice and fair play. The person is poised and graceful. He is lucky in his financial matters. He may receive a bonus or some unexpected good fortune. He benefits from elders and authority figures. It is a lucky time in general, but especially so in love.

The person is confident and sure about fulfilling his desires. He is emotionally stable. He is practical about love matters and is unaffected by romantic fantasy. He is well-disciplined and he exercises self-control. His social life goes smoothly. The person may solidify a love relationship about which he was previously undecided. He may suddenly enter a romance with an older person, an authority figure, or an ascetic individual. In certain cases, the person receives significant benefits, favors, gifts, or monetary rewards from his lover as a direct result of positive actions in their relationship during a previous lifetime.

The person enjoys art and entertainment during this transit. Professional artists and musicians have an easy time making their visions a reality. They bring excellent form and structure to their work, and create beautiful, enduring pieces of art. The person appreciates beauty within the traditions and conventions of his culture. It is a favorable period for redecorating one's home or for selling beautiful, artistic, or luxurious articles.

The transiting trine aspect is significantly more powerful than the transiting sextile. The transiting sextile only represents the opportunity to make the above effects a reality.

When transiting Saturn conjuncts natal Mars, the person's assertiveness and desires are put to the test. The person feels more determined and persistent than usual but, paradoxically, his actions meet with resistance. No matter how hard he tries or how disciplined he is, he feels he is spinning his wheels. During this transit, the person must learn the most efficient and productive use of his energy. He must also take responsibility for the times when he places his personal desires over those of other people. The person becomes very serious about achieving his goals during this approximately two-month period (which may occur up to three times in nine months). He is likely to work intensely and with great diligence and precision. Unfortunately, he may get sick as his body strains against nature's continuing resistance.

It is generally a very frustrating time, and the person should take life as it comes. He should try, as best as possible, to maintain distance, objectivity, and detachment from his urges and cravings, strong as they may be. This transit may be difficult on the ego because the person suddenly finds he has a hard time fulfilling his personal desires by his own effort. He notices his willpower is irrelevant now, and he is therefore drawn to reconsider his strength, fortitude, and ability to succeed. The longer this process continues and the more blocked the person feels, the more indecisive and hesitant he may become. However, by the time this transit has ended, the person has learned to correct offensive behavior, emotions, and personality traits such as aggression, anger, hostility, intrusiveness, and selfishness. And, once his efforts begin to produce noticeable results again, his confidence and composure returns. Thus, in the end, he is both psychologically healthier and more effective in action. He is more discerning in his approach, and his strategies for winning are more subtle, wise, and prudent.

The person may experience sexual dilemmas. Some individuals are less virile or stimulated and may experience bouts of impotence. Others may notice increased sexual desire. The specific lessons each person needs to learn about sexuality determine which response he has. And the person will be guided, if not forced, to confront the use of his procreative energy and potency. Sexually insecure men, especially macho or homophobic types who boast about their conquests and use them to prove their manhood, are in for trouble. Their confidence may be shaken, **197** and they are suddenly in a crisis.

The person may experience problems at work with bosses, especially pushy, domineering types. He may also be given a heavy workload. He may have trouble in competition. Although professional athletes may give their best performances ever, average people may be better off postponing sports events, if winning is terribly important to them. The person may have accidents or mishaps. In deep frustration over his obstructed efforts, the person occasionally uses too much force, thereby smashing or breaking things in his way. In certain cases, violence or accidents occur because the person was abusive in past lives. In any case, he must get plenty of rest and recreation. Anti-stress vitamins will help. Individuals who are by nature very restrained may find this transit extremely irritating, as it exacerbates their already timid disposition and tendency to feel restricted.

♄

When transiting Saturn squares or opposes natal Mars, the person's power is thwarted. His actions meet with resistance and he feels frustrated, restricted, and blocked. He is constantly challenged by others. He is unable to fulfill desires easily and the more he tries to achieve goals and ambitions the more futile they seem. Rather than giving up, however, he gracelessly pushes harder. He is subject to false starts, imbalanced energy, and misguided aggression. Because he uses excessive force to try to overcome his unsuccessful efforts, he may antagonize others and start fights or arguments. Worse than this, he may cause accidents and mishaps. During this approximately two-month period (which may occur up to three times in nine months) the person should be very careful with machinery, appliances, tools, automobiles, and other mechanical devices. It is an especially dangerous time to handle guns, weapons, or any form of artillery.

The person is subject to fits of anger. Wherever he places his attention, nature seems to place barriers in front of him. Furthermore, his ego is constantly being bruised as his desires clash with the desires of others. The person needs to get plenty of rest and recreation, and take anti-stress vitamins to combat this tension-filled period. His blood pressure may rise, and he may suffer from blood-related illnesses. He may have rashes, boils, eruptions, and inflammations. His sex life will not be great. The person may find himself impotent, nonorgasmic, or just plain uninterested in sex. It is a poor time for flirting or for romantic conquests.

The person should exercise as much patience and tolerance as he possibly can during this transit. Selfishness is a waste of time and produces a special kind of suffering. The person should do his best to compromise with others. He should take life one day at a time. The person has trouble making decisions, does poorly in competition, and he may be overburdened by responsibility and hard work. He may experience negative emotions normally foreign to him. Many individuals feel frustrated, antagonistic, bitter, or irritable. The person's timing is off; he experiences continual delays, and he has a hard time finding direction. He loses perspective about what he deserves and what he does not, and becomes confused about aggression. He cannot determine when to advance and when to withdraw. He may have trouble with police officers or military people. The person may be harassed by soldiers or other kinds of fighters. Business is not much favored, and the person should avoid important negotiations. He is not in a winning frame of mind, and no matter how he presents his terms the other party is unlikely to concede. By the time this transit ends the person may be tired, but he may have also learned important lessons about aggression, assertiveness, dominance, and the nature and use of personal power.

When transiting Saturn trines or sextiles natal Mars, the person is efficient in action. He is constructive, and he directs his energy wisely. He understands cause and effect exceptionally well. The person fulfills his ambitions without harming anyone in the process. He controls his temper. He experiences ease and grace in life because he is so clearly focused. The person defeats his enemies easily now because of his perseverance and patience. He may suddenly assume a leadership role for reasons unrelated to ego gratification. The person feels energetic and enterprising. He is successful and does not procrastinate. He pays his dues without complaint. The person does well in architecture, drafting, and other technical fields in which he uses his hands. It is an excellent time for hard work and tasks requiring precision and attention to detail. The person makes the best use of tools, machinery, and equipment at his disposal.

The person is controlled yet unafraid to take a risk. His willpower serves him well. He exhibits courage no matter how difficult the circumstances. He is practical and pioneering and has a winning, "can-do" attitude. Sexual experiences go during this approximately two-month period (which may occur up to three times in nine months). The person is more virile than usual, and he has exceptional sexual endurance. He is victorious in competitive events and sports contests. He is resilient to pressure, stress, and strain. The person now may now feel strong direction and purpose. Health problems are unlikely, as are accidents and mishaps. The person gets along with or receives benefits from bosses, commanders, police officers, military people, and fighters.

The transiting trine aspect is significantly more powerful than the transiting sextile. The transiting sextile only represents the opportunity to make the above effects a reality.

ħ

When transiting Saturn conjuncts natal Jupiter, the person's luck runs out and his optimism and buoyancy are dampened. Suddenly the person recognizes the barriers to the fulfillment of his life's dreams. He becomes more practical about realizing long-term goals and recognizes that he must plan and work to make his dreams a reality. This is a time when the person realizes that it is his responsibility to take concrete steps to achieve his long-term objectives. He becomes aware of the effect of tradition and custom upon his life's goals, and he works with patience and tolerance to design his strategy accordingly. Most importantly, the person must examine his life philosophy seriously, scrutinizing his values, morals, and ethics. The decisions and commitments made during this approximately two-month period (which may occur up to three times in nine months) affect his life for many years to come. He should not take this transit lightly.

Opportunities seem limited to the person, but openings that do occur are real, significant, and enduring. And the person is likely to make the most of them. He may become very serious about his religious and philosophical convictions. He makes resolutions and commitments in these areas. If he is disposed toward a spiritual or ascetic life, he may now discover his purpose. This transit allows the person to step back from his subjective experience and analyze life from a greater, more philosophical viewpoint. With this broad perspective, he is able to distinguish between momentary desires and long-term fulfillment. The person exercises wise judgement. He makes important decisions or commitments involving college or other institutions of higher learning. He may have temporary but disturbing difficulties with his teachers or the school he attends. He may have karmic experiences with gurus, educators, or spiritual guides. The person suddenly becomes realistic about teachers and mentors that he normally idealizes. As he sees their flaws, shortcomings, and mortal traits, teachers and mentors may now lose their appeal.

The person feels restricted and perhaps frustrated because his usual sense of prosperity and abundance temporarily disappears. During this entire transit, the person gets to reflect on his luck. Some individuals, whose luck is very poor to begin with, may feel especially bitter or resentful now. Changes in relationships, work, career, or any area of life

202   are possible as the person modifies his beliefs. He experiences financial limitations and may feel impatient and frustrated with his present state. However, he is able to overcome restrictions because of strong perseverance and determination. Healthwise, the person's liver comes under attack and allergies may therefore flare up. The person should avoid speculation and gambling now. In business, he does well as a buyer but not as a seller. He stands his ground and does not overpay, but he does not have the optimism it requires to convince others to take a risk.

Anything progressive or expansive is, for the time being, curtailed. Persons considering a career in philosophy, law, or politics are now able to make a proper choice. The person is serious, he has a strong sense of purpose, and he functions with wisdom, nobility, and reverence.

$$\hbar$$

When transiting Saturn squares or opposes natal Jupiter, the person's luck is curtailed. The person has few opportunities and loses his sense of abundance and optimism. He is forced to deal with restricted, tedious, or confining circumstances. He accepts his new responsibilities and diligently tries his best. But as time passes, he feels frustrated, impatient, and dispirited. Above all, he longs for his usual freedom. This is a very poor time for business and finance because the person has little genuine optimism or enthusiasm. He has trouble selling goods or ideas. He focuses on long-range dreams and is aware of the barriers to his success in the present. He uses this period to lay the groundwork for future accomplishment. Progress and expansion go slow or are simply postponed for the time being. The person cannot fulfill his ambitions, especially those involving money, luxuries, and personal comforts.

The person may find himself in a moral crisis. Others question his honesty and integrity now due to previous indiscretions when he lied or behaved fraudulently. He has problems with religious teachers, spiritual figures, and college professors. He may suffer because of painful incidents involving his schooling. The person now views mentors and teachers differently, especially those whom he previously idolized. He is more serious and objective about them and is less likely to overlook their flaws. Based upon his present difficulties to realize major life goals, he makes changes in his world view and philosophy of life. He scrutinizes past judgements in light of his current circumstances and psychology. He pragmatically contemplates future plans and strategies for gaining happiness.

The person is somber now, and he does not fare well with benefactors and philanthropists. He is laden with monotonous, routine chores and assignments and needs to schedule recreation to take his mind off the tedium of his existence. Otherwise he forgets that life is fun. The person should beware of allergies and liver problems. In certain cases, he has legal difficulties or problems with attorneys. If he has been living with a very negative or life-damaging philosophy, the person is now liable to suffer the consequences of his thinking. When he realizes his mistake, he may suddenly feel very sad about all the time he has wasted pursuing an inappropriate path and ignoring his true values.

When transiting Saturn trines or sextiles natal Jupiter, the person becomes especially comfortable with his philosophy of life and constructively works on long-range goals and ambitions. He exercises good judgement and makes steady progress in his endeavors. He constructs good strategies and he succeeds in his investments and speculations. Business matters go well as the person instinctively knows how and what to buy and sell. His financial situation improves, and, if necessary, he can obtain loans and grants from benefactors, elders, and people in authority. The person encounters opportunities which, although conservative, are practical and long-lasting. He does especially well with improvement and development projects.

Throughout the entire two-month transit (which may occur up to three times in nine months), the person exhibits the high values of human life. He acts with honesty, integrity, discipline, and responsibility. He is aware of religious and spiritual values. All activities involving knowledge are favored. The person has excellent experiences with teachers, mentors, gurus, and religious people. He is favored at school and may receive awards or benefits from his college or university. The person may coordinate activities, seminars, or workshops for his professors or spiritual guides. He may have important breakthroughs in the intellectual understanding of his religion or philosophy. His perspective broadens and his wisdom deepens.

The person maintains a good reputation now. He is favored by elders, bosses, and other people in authority. He is content with his duties and responsibilities and is not overly burdened with work. He is optimistic and hopeful in a calm and tranquil way. He benefits from travel, especially journeys specifically related to business or other important purposes. The person's timing is excellent. He makes good use of opportunities. He is discriminating and not easily fooled. Legal matters go well for him.

The transiting trine aspect is significantly more powerful than the transiting sextile. The transiting sextile only represents the opportunity to make the above effects a reality.

♄

When transiting Saturn conjuncts natal Saturn, the person experiences one of the most intense maturing influences of his life. He is guided, and in some cases forced, by circumstances or his own psyche to relinquish anything in his life that does not support his life goals and purpose. The person prioritizes objectives and activities so he can make the best use of abilities for the next twenty-nine-and-a-half years. This transit is known as the "Saturn return," which is in effect for the approximately two-and-a-half years it takes for Saturn to pass through the sign of its natal house position. The period generally occurs from age twenty-nine until thirty-one-and-a-half and then again from age fifty-eight until sixty-and-a-half. The person is deeply affected in nearly every aspect of his being. He feels pressured to act with extreme integrity, responsibility, and accountability.

The first Saturn return, at age twenty-nine, is perhaps the most crucial because it marks the end of childhood. The person comes to see that much of his prior experience was really investigation, experimentation, and preparation for the things he will accomplish in life. Choices now carry great significance. The person constantly contemplates his purpose on earth. Whether he obtains definitive answers depends upon the natal birthchart and many other factors. But one thing is certain—during this period he becomes clear about what activities and directions are inappropriate to his life. Repressive, unhealthy, and unsuitable conditions that the person has lived with for years suddenly surface in order to be handled. The person feels like God or nature reaches directly into his affairs. Big changes occur that seem to be out of his control. Although it may be disconcerting and painful, nature is clearing away unnecessary baggage paving the way for a more vital, powerful, and fulfilling future.

Paradoxically, in the midst of this karmic phase, the person experiences extraordinary free will to consciously direct his life. If he is ever to distinguish the difference between what he wants during his stay on earth and that which others would have him do, it is now. If the person chooses and commits himself to his choice, based upon intuition, self-knowledge, and heartfelt desire, then future contentment and serenity is assured. The person doesn't necessarily experience overall bliss or

206   happiness during this period, but he does feel freedom within his chosen vocation. If, however, he resists his own nature and his desires, then he will suffer tremendously not only during this transit, but also for the next twenty-nine years when he remains frustrated, discouraged, and miserable that he did not attempt to realize his potential. Although he will have another opportunity to make proper choices again at approximately the age of fifty-eight, he may be too old by then. Generally the second Saturn return is either a time to achieve a higher status in life or to let go of the grip on one's individual mission in order to enjoy the things appropriate to the concluding years of life, such as travel, spirituality, recreation, retirement, and so on.

During the two-month period of transiting Saturn's conjunction to natal Saturn (which may occur up to three times in nine months), the person feels intense pressure, as if life has slowed down to a standstill. This sense of urgency is nature's way of handling laziness, procrastination, and attachment to comfort. Because the person feels that his psyche will nag him forever unless he pursues his proper life path, he is finally moved to action. This period is almost always stressful, and the person should get plenty of rest and recreation. He should take calcium, in a healthy form, to strengthen the teeth and bones, which are now very sensitive. The person may need to have the fillings in his teeth changed.

This transit brings endings and new beginnings. The person may leave an unsatisfactory marriage, an unfulfilling career, and he may end friendships which are based on falsehood. He is sensitive to his surroundings, and he knows that now is the time to end unworkable situations. He thinks in terms of long-range security and stability. Unless it fits his nature, he can no longer tolerate open-ended contracts and spontaneous, changeable arrangements. He may have difficulties and need to be extremely responsible in the areas associated with the house position of natal Saturn. Generally, the person works very hard during these two-and-a-half years and is given much responsibility. He is objective and practical in his self-analysis. He may realize he is under-trained for what he wants to achieve in life and decide to return to school or a professional training program. Or he may realize that he needs higher credentials simply to make him feel more confident.

For many, these two-and-a-half years are a time of crisis. However, much depends on whether the person's prior existence was consistent with his ultimate purpose in life. Above all, the person should let go of aspects of life which are now falling away. And he should summon as much courage as possible to make the necessary choices and commitments that will assure his operating in the appropriate field for the next twenty-nine-and-a-half years.

Transits of the West—Dasas of the East

When transiting Saturn squares or opposes natal Saturn, the person experiences serious career difficulties or professional adversity, forcing him to question or reexamine the validity of his chosen life's path. Unusual circumstances arise in the person's vocation wherein he receives painful criticism causing his confidence and inner security to be shaken. He is emotionally affected by karmic situations in which he reaps the consequences of negative actions related to his past performance. Even more upsetting, he may be reprimanded, censured, or denounced for sound, praiseworthy work he has executed in areas in which he is suited. The person feels frustrated and unappreciated and begins to wonder whether he really fits in his present environment and whether he wants to remain in his current occupation. He becomes serious, introspective, and contemplative about his current direction. As with most Saturn transits, the person is troubled by worries, fears, and tension. However, his main concern is to determine whether he is on the right track in both selecting and carrying out his primary mission.

Saturn either squares, opposes, or conjuncts natal Saturn approximately every seven years. Each occurrence is a critical phase in the person's evolutionary process. He gains greater understanding and wisdom about his calling, and in the final analysis improves his efficiency and management skills in this important area. The person feels internal pressure to change his direction or to end activities that are no longer relevant. He thinks about long-term security and stability and is unconcerned with superficial elements and mundane details. The person may be burdened with responsibility now. He must decide how much duty and obligation he wants to carry. He may feel restricted by tedious work, causing depression or moodiness.

The person should get plenty of rest and recreation and take calcium for the teeth and bones. He may have problems with his father and other authority figures. He lacks a sense of optimism now and therefore has trouble fulfilling desires. Business and money matters are not much favored, and it is difficult to progress or expand. This period obviously requires a good deal of patience and tolerance. Even if the person does not make a major shift in his career or life mission during this transit, he does learn extremely valuable lessons—lessons he would never absorb without some of the anguish this period brings.

♄

When transiting Saturn trines or sextiles natal Saturn, the person is successful in his career and long-term strategies. He is well aligned with his calling or life's mission. He makes steady progress and advancement and may even be promoted due to his wisdom and experience. The person acts conservatively and accomplishes a great deal because he takes full advantage of his past successes and accomplishments. He successfully implements plans and ideas he has been laboring over for some time. He is persevering, diligent, and sure of himself. Professional confidence may be at an all-time high.

The person functions with utmost integrity, honesty, and responsibility during these approximately two-and-a-half months (which may occur up to three times in nine months). He focuses on long-range goals and ambitions and is dedicated to securing stability for himself. He is poised for leadership, and he benefits from older people, authority figures, and his own father. He finishes what he starts. Well-thought-out risks the person takes now are likely to succeed. The person is practical, down-to-earth, and well-organized. He knows his objectives and duties, and he does not procrastinate. He is in control of his destiny. His purchasing ability is enhanced, and business affairs are favored. He drives a hard bargain and is not swayed by emotions. Legal contracts signed at this time work in the person's favor for many years to come. The person rises in status and position due to consistent and industrious efforts in his past. He is objective in analysis and perceptive about his life's purpose.

The transiting trine aspect is significantly more powerful than the transiting sextile. The transiting sextile only represents the opportunity to make the above effects a reality.

When transiting Saturn conjuncts natal Uranus, the person is compelled to take full responsibility for his deepest individualistic tendencies. His originality and creativity are put to the test. The person is pressured, by outside forces or by his own psyche, to turn his inspirations, inventions, and innovations into reality. Inner tension mounts as the person tries to respond to life honestly and individualistically without offending nature, the immediate environment, and the powers that be. The person feels intensely restricted, but not due to any specific cause. Rather, he feels general frustration about his lack of ability to be true to himself. The person must suddenly confront his willingness to act on his own instincts. During this transit, the person is pressured to begin living without making compromises. What makes this period so potentially volatile and so different from Saturn's transit of any of the personal planets, is that the person is not analyzing himself or processing new ideas. Rather, he feels compelled to act on who he *really* is, what he *really* wants, and what he *really* experiences.

Radical changes are possible because the person can no longer tolerate the frustration he feels when he ignores his own spirit. If he has previously withheld his creativity, he now feels a profound lack of the freedom and joy that makes life worthwhile. The person may walk away from traditions or conventions that are boring and routine to him now. He consciously chooses a more innovative, imaginative, and progressive lifestyle. The person grapples with whether to follow society's prescriptions for happiness or his own. He becomes aware of his preoccupation with the past and the future and finds his attachment to them disturbing. He makes a conscious decision to try to live in the moment and experience life as it is, rather than as he or others interpret it. In shifting his attention from conceptual to experiential, and from the past or future to the present, the person makes spiritual progress. The more able he is to live in the present, the more liberated, graceful, and fulfilling his future will be.

The person is reprimanded for previous behavior that was rebellious, egocentric, irresponsible, or obstinate. He should take anti-stress vitamins to counter this period of restlessness, impatience, and potential anxiety. Otherwise he may become ill under the strain. If the person has ideas for inventions which could improve the quality of life, he is now moved to take action. He may be required, in his daily job, to handle tasks involving math, science, technology, or intense research. The person may now become serious about psychic abilities or an interest in the occult that he has ignored in the past. He is challenged to express his creativity and originality. If the person handles this transit well, he releases a great deal of stored inner tension and simultaneously transforms the old, worn-out lifestyle which caused his life to be become stress-filled in the first place. It is time for the person to gain independence, cultivate his genius, and act on his instincts, even if they fly in the face of reason. This is obviously a very important transit.

♄

When transiting Saturn squares or opposes natal Uranus, the person's freedom and independence are thwarted. He encounters situations which conflict with his intentions, and he is unable to turn matters to his favor. The person comes up against authority and people in control who are stubborn and unyielding. He feels stuck between a rock and a hard place. This transit often brings great tension, frustration, and struggle. The person should seek to maintain detachment and cultivate a nonresistent approach to life. The harder he tries to change his situation, the more resistance he encounters. As a result, the person is subject to fits of rage. Many individuals become so frustrated by their inability to control or even slightly alter their aggravating circumstances that they simply throw a tantrum and quit. This transit must be handled with patience, tolerance, humility, and a genuine appreciation for the workings of nature. The person's current dilemmas may defy logic. There is a good reason, however, for his unsolvable dilemma. The person is experiencing a test of his independence that can only be passed by understanding the true nature of freedom. Freedom is a state of being, completely independent of circumstances. The person must therefore retain faith in his inner experience of freedom no matter what may happen on the outside. There is no other way. If the person is still bent on winning, his best strategy is to consider the ancient Jewish proverb: "If there are only two options available, choose the third." A sense of humor is also helpful now.

The person may operate with frenetic or erratic energy. He gets into trouble for behavior that is willful, stubborn, or egocentric. He wants change, and he wants it now. Unfortunately, the person feels burdened and imprisoned, as if he is at the mercy of others. He is especially rebellious and defiant towards the establishment, government officials, and authority figures. The person may be given heavy responsibility at work involving scientific, mathematical, or technological matters. He is challenged to follow his own instincts despite expectations from employers to follow traditional procedures. His integrity is tested by adverse circumstances. This period brings restlessness, impatience, and anxiety. The person should get plenty of rest and recreation, and take anti-stress vitamins to remain healthy. He is negatively affected by boring, routine chores and obligations. When he tries to pursue a more original, imaginative, and progressive path, however, he encounters delays and obstructions. He experiences setbacks in any inventions or innovations he is working on.

It is an unfavorable time to pursue astrology or study occult sciences. Astrologers and occultists may find their efforts hindered, opposed, or ridiculed. The person may experience serious career problems or difficulties in relationships if he loses spontaneity, creativity, and aliveness in these areas. In some cases, the person decides to cut his losses and move on. But if he does, he should try his best not to behave impetuously and recklessly—a typical response during this potentially frustrating transit.

When transiting Saturn trines or sextiles natal Uranus, the person carries out progressive plans and innovative action. He uses traditional, conservative methods in order to accomplish imaginative and exciting change. He expands his business affairs as as personal projects. The time for his experimental proposals to succeed has arrived. The person brings the necessary discipline to make his endeavors succeed. He is open to new ideas, and he is unaffected by society's notions of what is possible and what isn't. He meets with sudden opportunities and is ready to change. This is a very good period to make improvements in almost any area. Activities involving science, math, technology, and research are especially favored.

The person does well with spiritual or occult knowledge. Astrologers, psychics, and occultists make progress in their work and advance their reputations. The person is very intuitive, and he follows his instincts. He is creative, original, and inspired in his approach. He is experimental in a conservative, moderate way and has a good feel for what will work and will not. He trusts his imagination and his skills. He makes quick, effective changes and improvements in his surroundings. It is an ideal time to reform systems, structures, and organizations. The person functions in the present and is unconcerned with the past and the future. He now has the chance to successfully implement plans he postponed in the past because they were too innovative.

The transiting trine aspect is significantly more powerful than the transiting sextile. The transiting sextile only represents the opportunity to make the above effects a reality.

ħ

When transiting Saturn conjuncts natal Neptune, the person's idealistic tendencies and utopian visions are dampened, and in some cases, obliterated. Circumstances arise that pressure the person to confront the harsh realities of human existence and to relinquish or modify his beliefs about perfection and utopia. The person now learns lessons from the hard knocks of life. He experiences disappointment as he discovers that certain things he always hoped were possible are, in fact, not. This results in discouragement, disillusionment, and sorrow. The person begins to see reality differently. Karmic (or fated) experiences demonstrate truths which he cannot deny. Because of this, he can no longer follow his own beliefs because they appeal to his feelings. The person recognizes that delusions and fantasies impair his effectiveness and retard his fulfillment. The discovery is painful, but the results are important.

It is impossible to predict the specific circumstances that will arise when Saturn conjuncts Neptune. This is because many of Neptune's important significations are abstract (spirituality, devotion, idealism, ecstasy, perfection, utopia, worship, fantasy life, etc.) and experienced differently by each particular person. Therefore, the circumstances that do arise during the transit are perfect ones, karmically, to compel the person to confront any "Neptunian" issues he has. This approximately two-month period (which may occur up to three times in nine months) is for many individuals a time of deep soul searching and potential psychological crisis. The person doubts his discriminative abilities and loses his hope for the future. The transit is characterized by depression, dejection, and disillusionment.

On a more positive note, this transit helps some individuals bring to fruition long-held dreams and visions. If the person aspires to a career in art, spiritualism, metaphysics, or mysticism, then he may now feel the urge to pursue it. He suddenly approaches these matters with maturity, practicality, and wisdom. The person's devotion may be seriously tested. He encounters circumstances which cause him to question deep, long-held spiritual convictions and metaphysical beliefs. By the end of this transit, the person finds out how devoted he really is and how much comfort he can actually rely on from religious truths and other transcendental concepts.

The person matures a great deal now. As he lets go of wishful thinking and misplaced optimism he learns the art of compromise. The person may undergo great difficulties in the areas of life ruled by Neptune's natal house position. He may become enmeshed in confusing, mysterious, or nebulous situations. In some cases, the person going through this transit must deal with irrational fears and phobias. He may also become serious about performing selfless work for the benefit of society. Professional psychics may feel blocked now, and individuals who spend great lengths of time in meditation may feel uninspired.

ħ

When transiting Saturn squares or opposes natal Neptune, the person encounters such grim, bleak, and upsetting circumstances that he suddenly feels life has lost its potential for any beauty, splendor, or magnificence. The person may be challenged or harassed by people who are narrow-minded, petty, unimaginative, and selfish and who present themselves as objective, realistic masters of the real world. Worse than this, because this transit involves nebulous Neptune, the person cannot get to the bottom of his problems to correct them. He is plagued by rumors, scandal, and gossip. Private or embarrassing affairs become public. Under these conditions, the person naturally becomes depressed and discouraged. He loses perspective and convinces himself that the happiness and contentment he has dreamed about is an illusion. The person's idealism, optimism, and especially his faith in virtue is being tested. By the time this transit is over, the person knows exactly how he feels about the harsh realities of life and the potential pettiness of fellow human beings.

During this period, the person experiences a good deal of insecurity and self-doubt. He wonders how he has lived with such serious illusions for so long, and he questions his ability to discriminate. However, the person is more pessimistic than he needs to be. He takes matters personally and feels very vulnerable. It is a poor time for the person to make big decisions and plans. He should take good care of his health so that he does not become ill from stress and negativity. The person lacks inspiration. Some individuals find their imagination working against themselves. More than anything, the person would simply like to walk away from life at this time. Unfortunately, that is entirely impossible because Saturn, as always, demands justice, responsibility, and karmic repayment.

The person may suffer from fraud or deception. He may experience irrational fears which are exacerbated by murky or confusing circumstances. People who practice art, music, religion, metaphysics, mysticism, or spiritualism as a career may have professional difficulties now. Their usual abilities fail, and they may now be criticized or censured for things they did in the past. Drugs and alcohol would almost certainly bring trouble during this transit, and therefore the person should avoid them. Above all, the person should do his best to maintain his perspective and realize that his current experiences exist largely to help him root out delusion, excessive optimism, and unbalanced idealism.

♄

When transiting Saturn trines or sextiles natal Neptune, the person acts on his creative aspirations and turns his dreams and visions into reality. He feels the majesty and magnificence of life. His optimism leads him to pursue utopian, romantic, and exotic endeavors that are dear to his heart. He is enthusiastic about creating an ideal existence, and he believes it is possible to do so. The person succeeds in all activities which focus on the expansive, unbounded, transcendental features of life. It is an excellent time for meditation or any spiritual discipline. The person benefits from metaphysical or occult endeavors. Most importantly, he gains tangible results and genuine evolutionary growth, rather than just subjective feelings of bliss. He has good experiences with religious teachers and spiritual authorities. He may even organize workshops and seminars or establish community centers for his teachers.

If the person is a musician, actor, dramatist, or filmmaker, he does excellent work now. He is inspired, imaginative, and his work is better structured than usual. The same is true for magicians, photographers, and those whose professions involve oil, gas, and the sea. The person may have a strong desire to help others in a significant, lasting way. He may volunteer for charitable or humanitarian efforts. He is in touch with the higher part of his being and is notably compassionate, honest, and well-meaning. His faith in God is solid, and his devotion to his ideals is pronounced. The person sees beyond the pettiness of everyday life and the frailty of human nature. He tries to achieve a balance between his spirituality and his materialistic needs. Certain individuals feel an urge to pursue spiritual disciplines with great diligence during this transit.

The transiting trine aspect is significantly more powerful than the transiting sextile. The transiting sextile only represents the opportunity to make the above effects a reality.

♄

When transiting Saturn conjuncts natal Pluto, the person feels pressured to take responsibility for his evolution, self-improvement, and the transformation of old, outgrown ways. Circumstances demand that the person choose between an easy, comfortable, well-controlled life and a more intense, riskier path that will bring more meaning, excitement, and reward. The time has arrived for the person to commit himself wholeheartedly to what he considers real, important, and lasting. This transit may be difficult in some ways because the person may lose control of long-established, important matters such as money, profession, family, and home life. However, as soon as the person surrenders and follows his true nature, he finds himself psychologically liberated and emotionally fulfilled. The results of this period (which may last from a few weeks up to sixty days and may occur up to three times in nine months) can be magnificent for his spiritual evolution.

The person becomes intensely focused and directed. He is suddenly goal-oriented and very purposeful. He undertakes grand projects and will not be dissuaded now. If the person has religious or spiritual inclinations, he is likely to delve deeply into metaphysics, occultism, or mysticism. He is curious about death, reincarnation, past lives, and the immortality of the soul. He may spend all his waking hours contemplating self-improvement, internal freedom, enlightenment, or final liberation. Because the person feels so strongly about things, he must be careful about behaving fanatically. In his fervor and zeal, he may offend friends, associates, and loved ones.

The person may have to confront issues of control and power. His ability to manipulate people or circumstances may be seriously thwarted. Coercion and force do not work in the person's favor now and may backfire, producing especially adverse effects. The person is concerned, in some cases obsessed, with honesty, integrity, and truth. He feels driven to discover the meaning of existence and to get to the core of his being. He realizes during this transit that he creates everything that happens in his life, and it is his responsibility alone to choose which way to go. The decisions that the person makes now will affect his life for years to come. What he does now determines how much control, authority, and power he will wield in the future. The person should approach situations in the present with great care and consideration. It is an excellent time for meditation, research and analysis, and psychic investigation.

♄

When transiting Saturn squares or opposes natal Pluto, the person's control and ability to transform his circumstances are severely limited. He struggles with predicaments that demand growth and change but are unaffected by his efforts. The person has no choice but to determine how he let matters deteriorate to this point and resolve to immediately change his behavior, so that when his normal powers and abilities return he can once again regain control. The person suddenly has no access to his usual resourcefulness. He feels as if he is fighting an uphill battle in every area he confronts. Self-improvement, self-healing, and any other recuperative or regenerative activities are delayed, restricted, and blocked. Worse than this, the person finds it difficult to involve himself in the higher realities of life. He is unmoved by opportunities relating to the divine, no matter how great, sublime, or sacred the enterprise.

Spiritual disciplines now produce little or no perceptible growth for the person. It is a poor time for psychic investigation, metaphysical studies, and occult experiences. If the person has previously misused his energies in these realms, using occult or spiritual disciplines for negative, life-damaging purposes, he may now reap the consequences. Such negative actions may now backfire, and the person's intentions may be exposed. Individuals who habitually control, manipulate, or dominate others are in for trouble during this transit. For these few weeks up to sixty days (which may occur up to three times in nine months), the person may feel upset, confused, and insecure at his inability to take charge and to maintain authority.

The person may encounter problems with coercive, oppressive, overbearing people. He may find himself enmeshed in critical power struggles in which he has little or no ability to defeat his enemies. This is not a time for victory and conquest. The person should maintain detachment and a broad perspective, especially if he is with obsessed with fulfilling important desires and ambitions. He is likely to face oppressive situations which require very hard work to make negligible progress. In some cases, the person suffers from sexual problems or reproductive ailments.

♄

When transiting Saturn trines or sextiles natal Pluto, the person is effective and successful because of his excellent self-control, willpower, and focus. He is extremely resourceful. He analyzes situations well, and he intuitively understands how to maneuver people and circumstances to work in his favor. He gets what he wants. The person is disciplined, purposeful, and determined now. He works hard and makes major breakthroughs. He is serious, genuine, and true to himself, and he does not play games or beat around the bush. The person is consistent, reliable, and mature. He is likely to fulfill ambitions he has had for many years.

Spiritual matters are favored. The person benefits from any self-development techniques he practices. His regenerative ability is strong, and the personal progress he makes is real and lasting. It is an excellent time for meditation and self-reflection. Anything associated with the occult or metaphysical is also favored. The person comprehends reality better than ever. He is not fooled by glitter and flash or pomp and circumstance. He is in touch with his feelings and instincts, and he therefore functions with strength and confidence.

The person may demonstrate unusual healing ability, which he practices on himself or on others. In some cases, the person enters psychotherapy. If he does, he advances quickly because of his willingness to confront sensitive issues directly and probe deeply into them. Whatever the person does now, he does earnestly and diligently. His concentration is very strong and he is practical and discerning.

The transiting trine aspect is significantly more powerful than the transiting sextile. The transiting sextile only represents the opportunity to make the above effects a reality.

When transiting Uranus conjuncts the natal Sun, the person undergoes dramatic change. He opens up to new interests, paradigms, and realities. He becomes consumed with originality, independence, and individuality. Spiritual and metaphysical endeavors are extremely favored, and the person may now experience one of the greatest transformations or shifts in consciousness of his life. He is freed from his usual boundaries and restrictions. The person is unconcerned with society's values and standards, and he is unaffected by the opinions of others. He follows his own inclinations. The person feels internal freedom. It is a time of great excitement and experimentation.

The person meets many fascinating people now. He constantly encounters new opportunities. He may move to another city, embark on a different career, and end old, stagnant friendships and love relationships.

The person is excited and stimulated. He spontaneously abandons boring routines and rigid habit patterns that he has lived with for many years. He breaks with tradition and does not look back. Some individuals discover powerful leadership abilities as they become champions of personal or political causes. The person is intent upon progress and reform. And he is incredibly innovative and creative in his methods. The person functions instinctively with excellent intuition. He trusts himself implicitly and is decisive and dynamic. He experiences important flashes of insight.

The person must beware of behaving fanatically, irresponsibly, and rebelliously. He may be too willful, stubborn, or self-centered. He may be insensitive to or impatient with bosses and authority figures. His spontaneity and unpredictability may shock or offend others who have come to know him as a more moderate, rational person. The person scatters his energy by engaging in too many new endeavors. Healthwise, the person may experience nervous disorders, spasms, or heart palpitations. He should get plenty of rest or, at least, practice a healthy form of exercise. People with a history of heart problems should take extra care now and follow their doctor's advice.

The person may have problems with his father, who may suddenly act strange or weird. On the positive side, the person's father may take an interest in spiritual or occult subjects. This transit is favorable for the study or practice of astrology, tarot, psychic phenomena, and other esoteric knowledge. It is also favorable for projects involving science, computers, electronics, and revolutionary inventions. The person is now able to act on desires he has repressed or ignored for a long time. He is infatuated with his current interests. Above all, the person should flow with change and avoid resistance to his new and temporary way of functioning. The greatest impact of this period occurs in the areas of life represented by the Sun's house position. Because Uranus takes approximately eighty-four years to complete one cycle of the zodiac, not all individuals will experience this transit. Those that do will be notably different for the rest of their lives.

When transiting Uranus squares or opposes the natal Sun, the person experiences sudden, unpredictable changes that are beyond his control. He encounters peculiar or unconventional people who cause problems for him. The person's task is to adapt as best as possible to the challenges and changes around him. The person is consumed with a desire for independence, and this is the most difficult aspect of this period. The person is restless, impatient, and easily excitable. He does not want to feel tied down. More than anything, he wants to do things his own way. Unfortunately, those around him may not let him. The person becomes extremely bored by tradition, routine, and systems, and he may create problems with bosses and other people in authority. He may suddenly walk away from his career or end long-term relationships. It is very important for the person to behave responsibly. There is a danger of acting impulsively, impractically, and inappropriately. The person is more self-centered and egotistical than usual.

Occult studies are favored. The person feels no limitations, and he is unconcerned with approval. He is open to new paradigms and realities. He may receive important astrological, psychic, or philosophical knowledge. It is an excellent time to experience life from a freer, more detached perspective. The person trusts himself completely. Unfortunately, though, he is stubborn and willful now. He should think carefully before making big decisions and changes. Circumstances will certainly look different after this transit ends and the person will no longer feel so restless, impatient, and rebellious.

The person makes errors because of hasty or abrupt behavior. He is more volatile than usual. Relationships of all kinds may suffer during this period of one to four months (which may occur up three times in nine months). The person is erratic and somewhat agitated. He is subject to spasms and heart palpitations. Individuals with a history of heart ailments must be especially careful now. Because the Sun rules men, a woman going through this transit may have a hard time in her marriage or love life. She feels a lack of control, as if she is at the mercy of her partner's instability or unpredictable actions.

The person may have problems with his father. He does not appre-

224 ciate authority at all now. He is excited about life and wants to experiment and grow. His consciousness expands a good deal even though things are peculiar and erratic. The person has strong intuition and he may have important insights. More than anything, this is a time of change, fluctuation, and unconventional behavior for the purpose of gaining freedom.

When transiting Uranus trines or sextiles the natal Sun, the person meets with exciting new opportunities and beneficial change. He is open and receptive, and he makes rapid progress. The person feels a profound sense of inner freedom. He is unmoved by society's opinions and judgements. He is extremely creative, original, and innovative now. He may experience flashes of inspiration or genius. He trusts his instincts, and he knows intuitively which direction to take. He is more flexible, adaptable, and versatile than usual. He is vibrant and spirited. Because he is trusts his experience, he is successful in his activities.

The person seeks new knowledge and new ways of behaving. His consciousness expands. He recognizes truth immediately and may be initiated into yoga or another spiritual path. He may become interested in astrology, tarot, and other metaphysical disciplines. Activities with science, computers, and electronics are favored. The person is courageous and adventurous. He enjoys things he is normally too conservative or timid to approach. He benefits from men, bosses, and the government. If he tries for leadership now, he is likely to succeed. His luck, in general, is strong now.

The person meets fascinating, unconventional individuals who are ahead of the times. He encounters spiritual, mystical, or metaphysical persons. A woman going through this transit may meet an exciting man who becomes her lover or husband. The person severs old, boring relationships that have long outlived their purpose. He may change jobs, careers, or relationships. If he does, the transition will go smoothly, with a minimum of stress. Social activities are favored. The person is socially desirable now because of his magnetism, ability to express himself, and powerful individuality and integrity.

The transiting trine aspect is significantly more powerful than the transiting sextile. The transiting sextile only represents the opportunity to make the above effects a reality.

When transiting Uranus conjuncts the natal Moon, the person learns new emotional behavior. He operates with greater flexibility and adaptability, and he is more varied in his responses to others. The person discovers that he is free to experience life in any way he likes and that he need not react to people or circumstances in a prescribed manner. He begins to realize that life should be based on his own interpretation of his own experience. He feels tremendous inner freedom. By the time this transit ends, the person will live more skillfully and gracefully, with less tendency to overreact to circumstances, for the rest of his days.

The person is emotionally excited and brimming with life. He expresses himself well, and he asserts his individuality. His ambitions intensify and demand immediate action. The person is spontaneous and impulsive. Unfortunately, he is also moody, changeable, and somewhat self-centered. He craves stimulation and will not be denied adventure and pleasure. He may surprise or shock others by behaving abnormally and breaking out of old emotional habit patterns. He now lives for the moment. The person is affected by subconscious motivations, passionate urges, and psychological complexes which may never have manifested so forcefully before.

The person's domestic life is full of activity and commotion. He considers moving or redecorating his house in a distinctive way. He becomes progressive and experimental in his home life. The person travels a great deal within his community, city, or country. He may change his appearance, style, and image. His imagination is active, and he is especially original and creative. He meets with unexpected excitement. He encounters weird and fascinating persons who are ahead of their time. Because the Moon rules women, the majority of the people he meets are female.

The person may become infatuated with a woman who is independent, exciting, spiritual, and magnetic. The relationship occurs suddenly and transcends normal rules, traditions, and boundaries. The person should maintain a sense of detachment about such a relationship because it may end as quickly as it began, when the Uranus transit to the Moon is over. Furthermore, the women that the person now attracts may be unstable, unpredictable, and irresponsible. The person may experience strange or peculiar times with his mother. Or his mother may become interested in occult, spiritual, and progressive disciplines which promote self-improvement.

The person is especially intuitive, and he recognizes the truth quickly. He receives insight and spiritual or occult knowledge from women. Now is an excellent time for the study of astrology, tarot, yoga, and other esoteric knowledge. It is also a favorable time to deal with science, electronics, and computers. The person's attention span is short and concentration is limited during this period of one to four months (which may occur up to three times in nine months). He is both strong-willed and high-strung. In some cases, his health suffers because of nervous tension and excessive activity. It is very important that the person behave responsibly. Some individuals are so exhilarated about fulfilling their desires that they ignore the feelings of friends or loved ones who may be negatively affected by their actions. The person may be socially desirable because of his vibrancy, sparkle, and liveliness.

When transiting Uranus squares or opposes the natal Moon, the person is subject to fluctuations in close relationships and changes or upsets in his immediate environment. He meets with unpredictable dilemmas that require behavior outside his normal habits. Unfortunately, the person is now affected by moodiness, emotional volatility, and an intense urge for freedom. At a time when he needs great flexibility and self-control to handle crises that arise, he is too attached to his own ideas to deal with them calmly. His cravings for fulfillment increase dramatically, he is overly excitable, and he tolerates no interference (or advice) from others. He does only what he wants, when he wants. Relationships of all kinds suffer.

Because the person feels emotionally separate from friends and loved ones, he does not trust others. He is careless of other people's feelings, and he becomes abnormally upset if things do not go his way. The person's home space is an area of special volatility. The person may suddenly become unhappy, restless, or frustrated about his house or its furnishings. He is impatient; he acts abruptly and is therefore prone to accidents or mishaps at home. He must be very careful with electrical objects or outlets. The person attracts weird, unstable, or unconventional women who pit their wills against his. He may have problems with women who are spiritual, metaphysically-inclined, or highly advanced in some way. He has difficulties with his mother, who may now behave strangely or unpredictably. Or she may be erratic or unstable.

The person must do his best to behave responsibly. He must guard against willfulness, egocentric conduct, and rebelliousness. The person abhors rules, regulations, traditions, and any form of censorship now. He tends toward impatience and intolerance, and his judgement is therefore negatively affected. The person may develop health problems due to tension, nervousness, and hyperactivity. As with all difficult transits to the Moon, both common sense and peace of mind are impaired. A woman going through this transit may have irregularities or difficulties with her menstrual cycle.

The person is interested in progress and self-improvement, as long as it comes quickly and with minimal effort. His intuition is strong. He may gain knowledge through occult or metaphysical subjects. His originality and creativity are very strong during this period of one to four months (which may occur up to three times in nine months). The person may change jobs, friends, and circumstances that have plagued him for a long time.

The person is intense and he requires a great deal of excitement and stimulation. He moves around a lot and makes changes in his lifestyle. He wants to break free of restrictions and routines at any cost. However, he should look carefully at how and why he created them before he abandons them. If the person tries to handle his problems by simply altering the externals of his life, before long he is sure to end up back where he started.

When transiting Uranus trines or sextiles the natal Moon, the person feels vibrant, excited, and emotionally free. He discovers important new interests and hobbies. His social life improves because he is so appealing and charismatic and because he suddenly meets very stimulating people. It is an excellent time for the person to make progress in any area of life. He is perceptive and intuitive. Because the Moon relates to common sense (and is well-aspected now), the person makes accurate judgements. His mind works quickly, and he achieves success by following his instincts. Research and investigative projects go well for the person. He recognizes truth immediately because his emotions do not interfere.

Exciting beneficial changes may occur in the domestic sphere. The person makes home improvements or moves to a new house. He discovers new ways to increase his comfort at home. The person's relationships with women are favored. He meets exciting women who are spirited, independent, advanced, or spiritual. He is appreciated by them and he receives favors or benefits from them. He also has good experiences with his mother during this transit. A new love relationship is quite possible now, especially for a man (because the Moon rules women). As with all fortunate Uranus transits, many sudden, unexpected opportunities occur.

The person benefits from astrologers, psychics, tarot readers, and palmists. He receives accurate information from them and may even begin studying metaphysical subjects. He also does well with science, computers, electronics, and any futuristic enterprises. The person succeeds with inventions and innovations. He is free from his usual boundaries and limitations and is not much affected by the opinions of others.

The person is extremely creative now. He expresses himself well and may demonstrate genius. Unfortunately, he acts so quickly that he may become impatient with others and with the slow pace of daily life. Although this is a good time spiritually, the person has difficulty with meditation or contemplation because of his need for stimulation, freedom, and dynamic action. The person does not appreciate rules,

traditions, or any form of restriction or censorship. He feels annoyed at **231**
having to make even short-term commitments now.

The person is flexible, and he flows with whatever changes occur. Any of his five senses may be heightened during this period of from one to four months (which may occur up to three times in nine months). The areas of life ruled by the Moon's house position flourishes. The person is not bothered by jealousy or ego problems now. He benefits from dealings with the public. Although Uranus and the Moon are not financial indicators, many individuals experience sudden financial windfalls at this time.

The transiting trine aspect is significantly more powerful than the transiting sextile. The transiting sextile only represents the opportunity to make the above effects a reality.

When transiting Uranus conjuncts natal Mercury, the person expands far beyond his usual mental boundaries. His intellect is more active than ever before, and he makes breakthroughs because of independent, advanced thinking. The person continually conceives of new ideas, and he is very open to new interests. Unlike his usual way of functioning, he gives little credence to what society considers possible or impossible. For perhaps the first time, the person is mentally free. He is intellectually unbounded and he is receptive to the concepts of infinity and "all possibilities".

This transit brings a great deal of activity, excitement, and inspiration. The person is exposed to philosophies and ideologies he has never considered before. He may begin to study astrology, metaphysics, or psychic phenomenon. He is intuitive now and sees more to life than what is commonly experienced through the five senses. The person has much communication with others. He is unexpectedly contacted by old friends or relatives, and he meets fascinating people who are ahead of their time. It is an excellent time for writing, teaching, lecturing, or debating. The person should carry a dictaphone or journal with him to record the valuable ideas and impressions which flow so spontaneously. Writers, teachers, and those involved in the media make tremendous progress during this transit of one to four months (which may occur up to three times in nine months).

The person's sensitivity intensifies greatly. He may feel nervous or frenetic and should therefore get plenty of rest and recreation. Sports or hobbies which calm the incessant activity of the mind are especially recommended. The person must beware of stubbornness or arguing with others. His mind works so quickly now and he is so independent in his thinking that he may create minor problems in his everyday relationships. He needs as much patience and tolerance as he can muster. If Mercury is afflicted at birth, the person now becomes rebellious or arrogant in his communications. He may be too direct or blunt in his speech. If Mercury is severely afflicted at birth, he faces a danger of mental imbalance and instability.

The person has innovative and revolutionary ideas now. He engages in metaphysical disciplines or New Age techniques. These may involve seminars, visualization, Zen Buddhism, and any methods which promote enlightenment through non-attachment. The person travels within his community a great deal. He lives for the moment and enjoys being spontaneous. He is extremely curious and energetic, but should watch out not to scatter his attention in too many different directions. He talks a lot, has flashes of psychic insight, and may appear hyperactive. Activities with science, electronics, and computers are favored. The person must remain as flexible as possible during this transit because he may want to reschedule activities as he discovers new possibilities. By the time this transit ends, the person's mind has been expanded, and he is likely to be far less opinionated or narrow in his thinking for the rest of his life.

When transiting Uranus squares or opposes natal Mercury, the person becomes mentally overstimulated. He is stubborn and independent and quickly winds up in quarrels. He comes into contact with unreliable, inconsistent people who cause irritating minor problems in his daily life. This is a terrible time for keeping commitments and honoring contracts because the person is receiving too much stimulation from his environment. Negotiations break down and his daily plans and schedules change constantly. If the person wants stability and balance now, he is in for rough going. The person should take life one day at a time and let go of his need to control the minute details of his life.

The person may experience many breakdowns in communication. His mind works too quickly and he does not listen well. He makes decisions without thinking things through, and his judgement therefore suffers. He is more opinionated than usual and has little patience or tolerance. He has many revolutionary ideas to improve matters, but he wants them implemented immediately. He does not mind bending or breaking rules now. In certain cases, the person makes mistakes at work because he hurries too much. He is hyperactive and harms his relationships and overall effectiveness by speaking bluntly or recklessly to others. The person should direct his intense mental energy toward inventions, innovations, and improvements he can create on his own and postpone dealing with others until this period is over.

He needs a great deal of rest and recreation during the one to four months of this transit (which may occur up to three times in nine months). The person's nerves are on edge, and he is prone to stress-induced illnesses. His hearing and sight are vulnerable. The person may scatter his attention in too many directions now. He may experience insomnia because his mind does not slow down. The person encounters transportation problems or difficulties with his own car. He cannot rely on his normal routine now. He may be required to travel suddenly for business or personal reasons. He may receive unexpected news which disrupts his life.

The person is excitable and impulsive. He investigates new philosophies or attends New Age seminars. He finds astrology, metaphysics, and psychic phenomena fascinating now. He is extremely intuitive and may experience flashes of insight or genius. Writers, teachers, and those in communications professions feel excited by their professional activities. The person has difficulty concentrating, and, unless Saturn is strong in the birthchart, the person has a hard time disciplining his energies. If Mercury is afflicted at birth, the person may now become mentally imbalanced or feel weak, insecure, afraid, or even paranoid.

The person has troubles with neighbors or siblings. He may have difficulties with teachers or schools. He should be careful with electronic devices or anything electrical.

When transiting Uranus trines or sextiles natal Mercury, the person's creativity, brilliance, and inspiration increases. The person is exposed to new ideas, philosophies, and interests. He meets stimulating people and is especially receptive to his environment and any opportunities that arise. He becomes unusually effective in his daily life because his mind functions so clearly and objectively. The person is curious, and he learns at lightning speed. He is vibrant, spirited, and mentally buoyant. He communicates with friends or relatives he has not heard from in a long time.

This is an excellent period for writers, teachers, and lecturers. Any kind of communication is favored. The person finds the perfect words to express himself. He is especially good at public relations or advertising. He is imaginative and resourceful, and he solves puzzles or problems effortlessly now. The person makes discoveries or creates new inventions which speed up work-related tasks or laborious activities within his daily life. He focuses on how to process data and disseminate information. He alters his routines to create more freedom and spontaneity. During the one to four months of this transit (which may occur up to three times in nine months), the person is unlikely to get bogged down or overwhelmed by circumstances and surroundings.

The person may travel a great deal now. He may get a new car, boat, or other vehicle. He keeps busy and gets along with neighbors and siblings. He may purchase a new tape recorder, computer, stereo, word processor, or any equipment that makes his life more flexible and enjoyable. The person is receptive to astrology, metaphysics, and occult subjects. He is very intuitive now and much less affected by convention or dogma. He makes gains in scientific endeavors. It is a good time for negotiating agreements and signing contracts. The person sees all points of view.

The transiting trine aspect is significantly more powerful than the transiting sextile. The transiting sextile only represents the opportunity to make the above effects a reality.

When transiting Uranus conjuncts natal Venus, the person is excited about romance and art. He is extremely influenced by his passions and desires, and he experiences sudden intense infatuations. The person may have an intense love affair, but he should use discrimination and common sense. Relationships occurring during this transit are exciting and invigorating but they may end as quickly and explosively as they began. This period is characterized by sudden beginnings and endings of relationships. The person is independent and strong-willed in his approach to his love life. He follows his instincts and inclinations. If he has been considering a separation or divorce, he now takes decisive action. The person is spontaneous and fully involved in his dealings with his spouse or lover. He does not suppress his desires or ignore his needs. He does whatever it takes to infuse excitement and passion into his primary relationship. In extreme cases, where the person does not get enough love from his partner, he seeks it outside his marriage and feels little or no regret.

The person is experimental sexually and in all aspects of love. He feels liberated from traditional restrictions and is remarkably unconcerned with the opinions of others. He is now attracted to lovers who are unconventional, advanced, freethinking, mystical, or spiritual. He may become involved with someone who is very different from himself in age, background, philosophy, race or religion. If Venus is afflicted at birth, then the person attracts a lover who is unpredictable or unstable. Or his existing partner may suddenly behave irresponsibly and inappropriately.

The person grows appreciative of beauty. He is more original, creative, and self-expressive than usual. He excels in activities involving art, music, dance, drama, and any form of entertainment. The person is intuitive and may produce inspired or progressive artwork. His social life improves because of his increased magnetism, sparkle, and vibrancy. He may receive unexpected money, gifts, or favors. He purchases radiant jewelry, unique clothing, or distinctive accessories to enhance his attractiveness and sexual desirability.

The person must beware of egocentric behavior now. He is too concerned with his own pleasure, and in his intense desire for freedom and independence in love, he may be insensitive to the feelings of his family. He may fall in love at first sight, but he must be careful of actions he will later regret. In his existing relationship, it is an excellent time for the person to honestly discuss problems which have bothered him for a long time. The person is suddenly able to analyze his situation with detachment, objectivity, and clarity. Therefore, he can make much progress to affect his happiness in relationships for the rest of his life.

Once this transit ends, the person's love life will never be quite the same again. The person realizes that the nature of life is love and that affections exist to be given and received freely and unconditionally. He is clear that love is always a choice. But, paradoxically, he also experiences a sense of fate about his past and present love relationships. Because Venus rules women, the person's mother may behave strangely, or she may begin to investigate mystical or spiritual subjects. Also, the person comes into contact with many women who are magnetic, stimulating, independent, strange, or ahead of their time.

When transiting Uranus squares or opposes natal Venus, the person experiences sudden, unexpected fluctuations in his primary relationship. He begins to feel restless or bored, and his cravings for passion and pleasure dramatically intensify. The person wants freedom and excitement in his love life. He is sexually excited and in no mood to compromise or deny himself. He becomes highly impulsive and experimental, as non-conformist tendencies arise. The person may feel rebellious and decide to break traditional social rules for fun.

The person feels very independent, and he may be uncooperative or insensitive to other people's feelings. If the person has been living in an unhealthy, unfulfilling, or incompatible relationship, it may suddenly come to an end. It is typical to experience abrupt beginnings and endings of relationships during this transit. If, however, the person's love relationship is strong and solid, then there simply will be more ups and downs or negotiations with his partner.

The person is romantically and artistically aroused. He meets persons of the opposite sex who are fascinating, individualistic, spiritual metaphysical, or ahead of the times. The person's desires are extremely intense now. His affections and infatuations may be overwhelming. He needs caution and prudence because relationships at this time are likely to be unstable, impractical, and short-lived. Furthermore, the new partner may be highly unpredictable, erratic, or volatile. In extreme cases, the partner is just plain crazy. At any rate, this is a time of experimentation and enlivenment, not commitment and responsibility. Many people going through this transit find themselves entering relationships with individuals much younger or older, or of a different religion, race, or background.

The person is highly creative and original. Artistic enterprises may not flow with ease and grace (because squares and oppositions generally create friction), but the person may still do distinctive and innovative artwork now. The person is intuitive during the one to four months of this transit (which may occur up to three times in nine months). He is receptive to astrology and occult subjects. He may, however, encounter delays or obstructions in these realms. The person experiences financial fluctuations and he takes more monetary risks than usual.

It is important for the person to behave responsibly and be willing to compromise. He must avoid rigid, inflexible attitudes about fulfilling his desires. He may be somewhat egocentric and high-strung. And he faces the danger of becoming involved in inappropriate love affairs. In certain cases, especially where Venus is afflicted in the natal birthchart, the person is victimized by his mate. He is surprised by his spouse, who suddenly becomes weird, inconsistent, and unreliable. Or the spouse may demand a divorce or openly indulge in an extramarital affair. If a separation occurs during this transit, it is likely to be difficult, painful, and volatile. It is a good time for dealing with difficulties in relationships, however, because the person is willing to confront issues directly rather than deny and suppress his feelings.

When transiting Uranus trines or sextiles natal Venus, the person attracts attention from members of the opposite sex. He has an effervescent quality about him which is extremely alluring. The person experiences a period of romance, flirtation, fun, and social pleasure. He is artistically motivated and emotionally vibrant. He is happy to be alive. If the person is single, he now stands a good chance of meeting a new love. He is open, receptive, and completely in touch with the free-flowing nature of love. He seeks to enjoy—not to possess or control.

The person is experimental now. He socializes with individuals who are highly independent, advanced, spiritual, or freethinking. He may become fascinated with people who are much older or younger than himself. Love relationships that begin during this transit are favored. They are characterized by freedom, openness, excitement, and self-expression on the part of both partners. The person enjoys amusements and entertainment more than usual. He lives for the moment and expects the best. He senses that any of his desires, no matter how big, could be fulfilled at any time.

The person is very creative and original. If he is an artist, he does some of his finest, most inspired artwork now. The person's finances increase, and the person obtains gifts, comforts, jewelry, and pieces of fine art. He is favored by others and appreciated for his infectious enthusiasm and lighthearted manner. He may enjoy brief but exhilarating sexual encounters that occur quite unexpectedly. The person gets along well with his mother and other women. It is a good period for confronting problems in the person's existing relationship. The person is objective, open, and emotionally trusting and can therefore handle matters normally too painful or delicate to face.

The transiting trine aspect is significantly more powerful than the transiting sextile. The transiting sextile only represents the opportunity to make the above effects a reality.

When transiting Uranus conjuncts natal Mars, the person is charged with erratic or fluctuating energy. He is forceful, aggressive, and likely to have more drive and intensity than he can control. The person feels compelled to fulfill every personal ambition and desire the instant it arises. He is spontaneous, impulsive, and potentially rash. Restlessness and impatience are a problem, and the person may be unpredictable or frenetic. This transit often brings accidents, fights or other mishaps because of the person's inappropriate or abrupt behavior. The person may react more competitively than necessary.

It is important for the person to realize that despite the strenuousness of this period, this transit serves to obliterate unjustifiable or unsuitable ambitions and to infuse fresh spirit, vigor, and vibrancy into the person's desires. The person is going through a phase characterized by cravings that, in the long run, help to teach him to recognize his own desires. On the surface, it may seem that all desires are genuine, but the rigors and demands of human life, the conflicting requirements of family and friends, and the values and standards of society can affect the person's psychology so that it is possible for him to become disconnected from his own real passions and appetites.

Now, however, as the person gets an intense dose of his own cravings for a period of one to four months (which may occur up to three times in nine months), he sees that he is in charge, that his ego exists for a positive purpose, and that it is fun, healthy, and even thrilling to put his desires above the desires of others. The person is now capable of altering plans, improving strategies, and making significant progress toward major goals. On the very positive side, this transit is stimulating, enlivening, and invigorating. The person is in touch with his wants and needs.

The person is aggressive, and he pursues pleasure. His sex drive becomes very strong. Relationships of all kinds are susceptible to difficulties because the person is very concerned with winning. There is a tendency to be blunt, abrupt, and insensitive. Above all, the person must refrain from fighting or forcing his will on others.

The person feels restless and anxious. He may produce shoddy work or make mistakes because he is hasty and reckless. He should beware of carelessness and be cautious when driving. The person should avoid using dangerous machinery, guns, and explosives now. He should practice sports, karate, tai chi, yoga, or any physical exercise which helps regulate his energy flow. The person is under more stress than usual. Rest and recreation are important as the person is susceptible to illnesses. Big changes, complications, or problems in the areas of life ruled by Mars' natal house position will probably occur. If Mars is afflicted or in an unfavorable condition in the natal birthchart, then the negative affects of this period are magnified.

The person is independent, uncompromising, and will not be dissuaded from his path. He may be volatile and willful. He becomes angry or frustrated if his plans are thwarted in any way. The person exhibits courage, but he must avoid rash actions and unnecessary risks. Unexpected mishaps and violence occur all too easily during this transit. The person meets individuals who may prove disruptive, disorderly, and very competitive.

The person feel rebellious and may suddenly commit himself to revolution or drastic change. He is determined and is unconcerned with the nature or size of obstacles before him. The more adventure and risk his task requires, the more excited and enthusiastic he may be.

The combination of Mars and Uranus energy is explosive. In order to predict the effects of this transit, it is especially crucial to note the natal condition of Mars as well as the relationship between Mars and Uranus at birth. Some people will act wild, foolhardy, and rash. Other individuals simply feel agitated, frenetic, and scattered. In some fortunate instances, the person exhibits great creativity and brilliance (especially in science or electronics) and discovers powerful untapped energies within himself.

When transiting Uranus squares or opposes natal Mars, the person is prone to upsets, mishaps, arguments, and accidents. The person is too excitable and impulsive, and he easily loses perspective. He is driven by his ego and his desires. This transit brings assertiveness, tension, frustration, and misuse of energy. The person wants his way, and he does not consider the consequences of his actions. As a result, he provokes arguments and confrontations. He should engage in sports, yoga, breathing techniques, Tai Chi, martial arts, or any physical discipline which can help him properly direct his physical energy.

The person is restless and impatient and therefore does not function with his usual efficiency. Furthermore, he is obstinate and daring. Rather than accepting defeat or temporary setbacks when they occur, he attempts to force the situation. His concentration is impaired, and he tries to focus in too many directions at once. The person should avoid using dangerous machinery and guns. He must be careful when driving. He lacks discretion and makes hasty or even rash decisions. When things do not go as planned, the person gets very angry. He feels that winning and fulfilling his desires are the highest priority. He also believes his freedom and independence are of supreme importance. Naturally, relationships of all kind suffer.

The person must take good care of his health now or he may become ill because of the nervousness, stress, and strain accompanying this transit. He may have trouble with his competitors. He may come into contact with volatile or, in extreme cases, violent individuals. During this period of between one to four months (which can occur up to three times in nine months), it is advisable to adopt a nonresistant attitude as much as possible and to withdraw from menacing people and dangerous circumstances.

The person is sexually aroused. He may enter into sexual relationships in which he is far more experimental and adventurous than usual.

The person may make big changes in his previous goals, plans, and strategies. If he can control his impulsiveness and willfulness and properly direct his intense energy now, he will make excellent progress.

The relationship between Mars and Uranus at birth is of extreme importance in predicting the effects of this period. Naturally, the areas of life governed by Mars' natal house are likely to undergo the greatest changes and complications.

When transiting Uranus trines or sextiles natal Mars, the person quickly achieves basic goals and ambitions and forges ahead with innovative plans and strategies. He is excited, energetic, and spontaneous. He follows his impulses and takes whatever risks are necessary. The person is creative and resourceful and completely in touch with his desires. It is an excellent time for problem solving. The person is experimental in his approach yet practical in his efforts. He is determined and overcomes obstacles with ease. His willpower serves him very well.

The person may exhibit leadership qualities now. He is confident and does not back down from challenges or difficult situations. He is dynamic and direct with others, and he stands up for his beliefs and principles. The person excels in working with machinery, electronics, and scientific projects. He is more original, inventive, and flexible than usual during this period of one to four months (which may occur up to three times in nine months).

The person's sex drive may increase. The person is sexually aroused and he may engage in relationships which are exciting, passionate, experimental, and based upon pure lust. The person may suddenly become refreshingly wild or uninhibited. He is assertive and aggressive in a graceful or charming way, and he succeeds in his flirtations.

Despite the positive nature of this transit, the person may be impatient or restless now, especially if Mars is afflicted in the natal birthchart. The person should be careful when driving his car and when handling dangerous machinery. He may try to progress too quickly in his undertakings and thereby create accidents or mishaps. He is generally quite alert and efficient but may at times be overly concerned with his freedom and independence.

The transiting trine aspect is significantly more powerful than the transiting sextile. The transiting sextile only represents the opportunity to make the above effects a reality.

When transiting Uranus conjuncts natal Jupiter, the person awakens to new perspectives, opportunities, and possibilities. He experiences the incredible freedom that human life offers and deeply appreciates truth and liberty. The person feels extreme optimism as he sees choices and options everywhere. In recognizing his free will, the person feels a new lease on life. He knows he is completely free to make his own decisions based on his personal philosophy and convictions. Along with this comes a genuine sense of power, authority, and autonomy.

In many cases, this period brings instant progress. Some major new opportunity falls directly into the person's lap. The opportunity may bring large financial rewards, career promotion, or any major positive change. The person is exposed to new religions, philosophies, and ideologies. He meets people who embody advanced or distinctive viewpoints and he begins to consider the validity of their beliefs. The person renews his search for meaning, and he has many insights. He may engage in fascinating adventures, crusades, and quests. During this period of one to four months (which may occur up to three times in nine months), the person may travel to foreign countries.

The person is very open-minded now. He lets go of rigid attitudes, skeptical opinions, and negative ideas brought on by the tedium of daily life and by past misfortune or previous lack of opportunity. He experiences strong intuition that aids him in making remarkably quick, accurate judgements. The person may profit greatly through his creativity, originality, or personal genius. He is inspired and idealistic. He expects good things to happen and is unafraid to take risks.

Education of all kinds is favored. The person does especially well in metaphysics, mysticism, astrology, tarot, and other esoteric subjects. He also succeeds in religious studies. In some cases, the person profits from investments initiated in the past. He may have a tendency toward restlessness or impatience. The person feels on the verge of improving his situation, and if the desired changes do not occur immediately he becomes frustrated. He is concerned with future success, which he knows depends upon current progress. The person may become interested

248 in humanitarian efforts. He wants to advance the cause of truth and improve society's understanding and handling of justice.

If Jupiter is afflicted at birth, the person must beware of engaging in excessive or indulgent behavior. He may also be tactless and blunt.

When transiting Uranus squares or opposes natal Jupiter, the person craves freedom, adventure, and new experiences, but unfortunately he lacks moderation and good judgement. He feels so motivated to make progress that he doesn't take time to analyze a situation before acting upon it. The person takes big risks at a time when his luck is most unpredictable. He is both overzealous and naively optimistic. He lacks discipline, ignores his responsibilities, and is too indulgent in pleasures.

His finances may fluctuate wildly. The person must therefore use great caution and common sense while this transit is going on. He should not gamble or speculate. The person is an easy mark for con artists because he lacks discretion and practicality, and he is temporarily gullible. He should avoid get-rich-quick schemes.

The person feels restless. He wants to break free of monotonous circumstances that restrict him. He may alter his lifestyle in unexpected ways, and his luck may change dramatically for no apparent reason. The person gains understanding about truth and justice. Through meetings with foreigners or individuals promoting new ideas, the person changes certain long-held opinions and philosophies. He may, however, have difficulties with mentors and religious teachers. Educational matters are not favored, and the person may suffer because of his school.

When this transit begins, the person feels that anything is possible. By the time it ends, he is clear that "anything" can easily mean negative as well as positive. The person is surprised by missed opportunities or sudden quirks of fate which reduce his fortune. He may be required to travel long distances on very short notice, and he may experience fascinating or strange occurrences while doing so.

Although this transit is generally stressful because it brings sudden and unpredictable events, the person gains a broader perspective by the end of the period. He is also apt to enjoy the excitement and exhilaration of it, no matter what the outcome.

When transiting Uranus trines or sextiles natal Jupiter, the person experiences religious and philosophical breakthroughs as well as good fortune and unexpected opportunities. He is optimistic, exuberant, and open to all kinds of new ideas. He feels liberated, and he knows that anything is possible. Because of his positive attitude and spontaneous ways, the person is lucky, successful, and favored by others. He has a strong chance of gaining sudden recognition, financial abundance, or both. It is a happy time in which progress comes swiftly, and the person is happy to be alive.

The person comes in contact with new knowledge that excites him. He benefits from astrologers, psychics, metaphysicians, and religious teachers and may discover important truths of life from them. The person gains fresh and deeper understanding of the philosophies he has lived with all his life. He is more creative and original in his thinking than usual during the one to four months of this transit (which may occur up to three times in nine months).

This transit brings many fascinating, positive, and expansive experiences. Educational matters go well. The person is alert and intuitive and he learns very quickly. He is thrilled about knowledge. He may receive awards or grants from colleges or universities. He may suddenly decide to travel to foreign countries for educational purposes. Or he may receive a wonderful opportunity to work or vacation in a far-off land. The person has a strong sense of fun, adventure, and freedom, and he is willing to take risks. He wants to learn everything he can about life and the different cultures of the world, and he benefits from his associations with foreigners.

The person values his individuality and the individuality of others. He spontaneously exhibits his talents and genius. And he makes new discoveries constantly. The person should flow with the changes that occur and enjoy the variety and excitement while it lasts. Scientific endeavors and humanitarian efforts are favored. The person has a very strong urge to uncover the truth and to share his knowledge in any way that can uplift society. He craves freedom not just for himself but for everyone else. He is very concerned with fairness, equality, and justice.

The transiting trine aspect is significantly more powerful than the transiting sextile. The transiting sextile only represents the opportunity to make the above effects a reality.

When transiting Uranus conjuncts natal Saturn, the foundations of a person's life go through radical upheaval. The person experiences disruptions within his immediate environment and should adopt an attitude of flexibility, adaptability, and patience. The purpose of this transit is to free the person from restrictions and burdens he bears out of habit, complacency, and a sense of duty. Nature is paving the way for the person to create new, more vital, and appropriate directions. Although this period is often painful because of its instability, disarray, strain, and tension, the person makes great progress as he lets go of the old and begins to consciously design his future. He also grows tremendously by dropping worn-out habits and routines that now appear obviously ineffective.

The person may be confronted or challenged by people in authority about his work or behavior. He suddenly becomes aware of the needs of his elders and begins to see matters from their perspective. The person gains insights into earthly reality and cause and effect. By the end of this transit, he views tradition and convention differently.

The person may experience serious disruptions within his career. He may experience shocking changes or unexpected events which affect his deepest reality. Important affairs which have been the basis for security, confidence, safety, and stability may now be obliterated in one quick stroke. If the person is accustomed to sitting back and taking little or no risk, he may now be in for a rather hair-raising period. This transit requires that the person have faith in nature and the unknowable future. The person must flow with the changes coming his way.

In certain cases, the person has troubles with his father, who may become strange, weird, unstable, or interested in metaphysical subjects. If the father is very old or in failing health, this transit does not help matters. Dramatic fluctuations may occur involving land or buildings belonging to the person. During the one to four months of this period (which may occur up to three times in nine months), the person should try to derive security and strength from his internal resources. This is clearly a time of flux and transition, not accomplishment and fulfillment. The person learns invaluable lessons from his clashes with his elders and with those in authority, and he struggles valiantly to achieve balance between experimental and conservative approaches.

When transiting Uranus squares or opposes natal Saturn, the person experiences environmental disturbances, career disruptions, and unexpected crises which affect the basis of his confidence and security. It is a time of abrupt change and unexpected fluctuation in areas of life that are normally stable and constant. The person feels tense and frustrated about his precarious situation and lack of control over circumstances. He undergoes a testing of his everyday routines, habit patterns, and operating methods. Fundamental procedures and comfortable life strategies which have served the person well suddenly crumble for no apparent reason. The person has trouble with older people and those in authority who demand that he function more efficiently, creatively, and productively. Life may feel especially unfair and random because the person cannot see how he has in any way caused the problems he is suddenly forced to confront. The person must try for flexibility, adaptability, and as much patience as he can muster.

Because Uranian energy is so incongruous with and contrary to that of Saturn, there is almost no difference between the conjunction transit of Uranus-Saturn and the Uranus-Saturn square and opposition transits. (See "Transiting Uranus Conjunct Natal Saturn") All combinations generally produce disruption, upheaval, and chaos, which weaken the person's confidence and grasp of reality. The main distinction, in most cases, is that the conjunction transit produces more intense and noticeably difficult effects than the squares and oppositions. However, when the square and opposition transits of Uranus to Saturn do generate significant results, the person has a much harder time flowing with the changes. He has trouble gaining any objectivity or detachment and therefore is less effective in handling the restructuring process that is taking place. The person resists giving up old routines and behavioral patterns, which are his current source of distress.

The person may change his job or career. His status and reputation may fluctuate wildly, and he may have clashes with his superiors. He may have serious career obstructions or other problems at work, and the person considers changing professions. During the one to four months of this transit (which may occur up to three times in nine months), the person experiences tension and strain which may cause depression or

254 health problems. His teeth and bones may come under attack, and the person should take plenty of calcium in a healthy form (certain dietary authorities consider dairy products unhealthy) and get plenty of rest and recreation. Whatever happens now, the person must try his best to progress with creativity and to infuse spirit, vigor, and imagination into the methodical and conventional areas of life suddenly in question.

When transiting Uranus trines or sextiles natal Saturn, the person brings originality, freshness, vigor, and spirit to his worldly goals and ambitions. He makes rapid progress in business and career because of his open-mindedness, flexibility, and willingness to take risks. He is stable, confident, and secure and therefore welcomes changes and new opportunities that unexpectedly arise. The person uses his intuition to develop practical and effective methods and procedures. He combines imagination and creativity with the wisdom and experience he has accumulated throughout his life.

The person's leadership ability surfaces, and he may suddenly receive promotions now. He is successful and efficient during this transit. He comes up with brilliant plans and innovative solutions. He knows how to deal well with persons in power. His organizational skills increase. The person feels freedom in the midst of his activities, which he performs with discipline and responsibility.

It is an excellent period to seek a new job or higher position. The person is favored by his elders and people in authority. He impresses others with the way he combines prudence and discretion with originality, ingenuity, and inventiveness. He maintains his individuality within the boundaries of the establishment. The person commands authority without being egotistical or using oppressive tactics. He is clear about his intentions and commitments, and he therefore realizes his objectives quickly and gracefully without offending others.

The transiting trine is significantly more powerful than the sextile. The transiting sextile only represents the opportunity to make the above effects a reality.

When transiting Uranus conjuncts natal Uranus, the person awakens to an innocent, spiritual awareness of himself as a free cosmic being of the universe, separate from earthly affairs and material considerations. At the age of approximately eighty-four, the person has completed one life cycle of Uranus. During the one to four months of this transit (which may occur up to three times in four months) in the twilight of his life, he becomes as uncomplicated as a child. The person has brilliant flashes of insight into the truths of life and the nature of human existence. He realizes that he has been incarnated on earth for the growth of his soul. Therefore, he now relinquishes personal attachments and activities that have diverted his attention from spiritual progress his entire life and begins to enjoy the bliss of being. He is content "to be" rather than "to do."

As with all Uranian transits, the person feels independent, individualistic, original, and creative. He is more spirited, vibrant, and alive than usual. He undergoes changes and may end relationships or activities which no longer make him feel vital. It is an excellent time for astrological or occult studies and mystical disciplines. Spiritual disciples can expect a period of remarkable progress and wonderful inner experiences. The person has excellent intuition and many psychic experiences or prophetic moments. By the end of this transit, the person has awakened to a higher reality of life, and his attitude is more detached, dispassionate, and genuinely spiritual for the rest of his life.

It is possible to experience this transit during infancy if Uranus goes retrograde shortly after birth. In addition to the temporary fluctuating or erratic circumstances likely to occur, the person may behave in a more "Uranian" way for the rest of his days because he is affected by Uranus so early in life. Therefore he might be more independent, unpredictable, original, inventive, and progressive. He might also be interested in enlightenment.

When transiting Uranus squares natal Uranus, the person becomes strongly independent, individualistic, and objective, and he experiences major life changes. This transit occurs around the age of twenty or twenty-one and again between sixty-one and sixty-three. The effects of the earlier and later transit are somewhat different. Twenty-year-olds going through the transit experience a sudden and intense emergence of independence and autonomy. It is a time of rebelliousness wherein the person separates himself from his elders, and people in authority. The person suffers disturbing, unforeseen, difficulties caused by previous blind acceptance of the policies and procedures of the establishment. During this transit, he learns that he must rely on his own judgement or his success and happiness will rest outside of his control. He awakens to the fact that although his behavior seemed perfectly appropriate and was appreciated by everyone, he was abdicating personal responsibility in the past. He did not doubt, he did not investigate, he did not question, and now he pays the price. Some adolescents, feeling quite duped and mislead, reject nearly everything traditional, conventional, or in any way connected to their elders. In any case, the person experiences one of the most important maturing processes of his life.

When this transit occurs later in life, between the ages of sixty and sixty-three, the person undergoes sudden endings and new beginnings. He is challenged to confront aspects of his life which are no longer vital, stimulating, and productive. Anything stagnant in the person's life becomes glaringly obvious. He relinquishes old ways of functioning and becomes more progressive and innovative. He breaks away from friends, associates, and lovers who no longer make him feel happy and alive. The person asserts his individuality and stops participating with groups and organizations whose principles do not correspond to his. The person may move to another city and decide to start over in a completely new job or profession. Certain individuals now decide to retire.

Regardless of the person's age during this transit, he craves excitement. He is impatient and restless and may suddenly enjoy socializing with youthful, spirited, and progressive individuals. The person is open to new ideas and philosophies and is particularly interested in finding the truth. He may begin studying astrology, tarot, metaphysics, or any

258   occult science. He is original, inventive, and creative now. He lets go of the past and looks toward the future, taking whatever course provides the most freedom. The person sees things for himself now and generally disregards the influence of others.

When transiting Uranus opposes natal Uranus the person feels an urgent need to rejuvenate and revitalize his life. This is a time of impatience and agitation with the routine, mundane, and monotonous nature of human existence. The person realizes that he can no longer endure stagnant rituals and the ruts he finds himself in. The transit occurs near the age of forty or forty-two and comes as a crossroads or midlife crisis for those individuals whose lives have been too sedentary, inert, and lifeless. The person realizes that half of his life is over. He is confronted with the reality that no matter how successful he has been or how much he has achieved, he has given up all kinds of joys by choosing one path over another. Although the person is sad about this, he may also feel excited about his new-found realization and the opportunity to take command of his future.

The person will go through healthy change, radical transformation, or tremendous disruption, depending on his overall maturity and how skilled he has been in the art of living during all the preceding years. If he has lived to satisfy everyone but himself in the past, he now has to endure the reaction of those around him as he shatters their misconceptions about him. The person now has infinite free will to change his mind, reverse his course, and steer his life in the direction of his choice. He considers changing jobs, his career, his primary love relationship, and even his basic lifestyle at this time. He may associate with youthful and extremely liberated friends. And he may venture into areas which break society's rules and conventions.

In short, the person does whatever it takes to bring spirit and vigor into his life. He creates himself anew, with little regard for what others will think. If he is especially conservative and traditional by nature, and thus unable to access his own Uranian traits, he now attracts an important friend or lover who is highly independent, vibrant, and free-thinking. In such cases, the person's existence is powerfully and permanently altered by the relationship.

Aside from the intense feelings of stimulation, excitement, urgency, and opportunity, the person suddenly gains freedom, independence, and individuality. In doing so, he experiences a new detachment and objectivity. He may have never seen the significance of these traits so clearly, or known how capable he was of creating them. For many, the awakening is refreshing. The person may open up to knowledge that is far ahead of the times. He may indulge in occult or astrological studies. He gains flexibility, loosens his grip on constricting, oppressive philosophies, and eliminates outgrown patterns and attitudes. This transit lasts approximately one year, and the person must be careful to see this period for what it is—a time of experimentation, change, restructuring, and reorganization. Stability and security are not much favored. Therefore, many of the projects the person now engages in are not long-lasting, and the relationships he has now may not endure. Thus, the person may appear unstable, unpredictable, and erratic. He experiences inner turmoil and mental unrest, breaks old ties, and contemplates his path in life.

When transiting Uranus trines or sextiles natal Uranus, the person suddenly experiences opportunities for growth and progress, especially in the realms of life ruled by Uranus' natal house position. The person encounters new ideas and philosophies which are intensely stimulating. He feels a strong sense of independence and decides to divorce himself from old ways of doing things which he blindly accepted from his elders, authority figures, and the establishment. The person now thinks for himself and gracefully makes changes in his life, without rebelliousness or defiance. It is an excellent time for self-development. The person is exposed to new spiritual techniques which bring rapid evolutionary advancement.

Occult studies are favored. The person takes an interest in astrology, yoga, tarot, and other metaphysical subjects. He is extremely intuitive now and may have important flashes of insight during the one to four months of this transit (which may occur up to three times in nine months). He succeeds in scientific studies and in dealings with computers, electronics, aviation, and technologies which are advanced or ahead of the times.

Many relationships may begin, and many may end smoothly and spontaneously, without animosity or resentment. The person is attracted to individuals who are exciting, fascinating, progressive, and spiritually evolved. He may suddenly associate with people very different from himself in age, race, religion, or background. The person is interested in truth and freedom during this transit. He is alert, aroused, and inspired. He may travel a great deal and have fascinating experiences while doing so. The person is especially creative and innovative now. He lives in the moment, unaffected by other people's opinions and judgements. He may have strong urges to help humanity or a strong sense of social responsibility.

The transiting trine aspect is significantly more powerful than the transiting sextile. The transiting sextile only represents the opportunity to make the above effects a reality.

When transiting Uranus conjuncts natal Neptune, the person awakens to dreams of utopia and has visions of sublime realities beyond the realm of the five senses. He becomes interested in spiritual matters and aware of the transcendental side of life. His intuition and feelings are very strong now. He becomes interested in higher consciousness and, perhaps for the first time, sees the possibility of merging with the divine. His heart is profoundly receptive and trusting, and he tends toward surrender and devotion. For many, this transit brings an intense and significant initiation into spiritual life which affects the person forever.

The person learns that anything is possible. He may have strong psychic experiences or be seriously influenced by astrology, tarot, palmistry, or any of the occult arts. The person is exposed to religious or spiritual movements that promote humanitarian ideals and goals. He suddenly envisions a world of peace and harmony and wants to help make his vision a reality. He welcomes the opportunity to serve others. The person realizes how insignificant his personal desires are, and he concerns himself with broader, more far-reaching issues. He focuses more and more on the universal and the infinite. The person is deeply inspired, especially in the areas of life ruled by Neptune's natal house position.

If the person is destined for a life in the arts, he now awakens to it. His artistic energy is stronger than ever and the person appreciates beauty and refinement much more than before. He is creative, expressive, and powerfully imaginative. His thoughts and actions emanate directly from his heart. Painters, musicians, actors, and poets may do some of their most inspired and passionate work during the one to four months of this transit (which may occur up to three times in nine months). It is a wonderful time for magicians, photographers, and filmmakers.

The person may feel discontented with his everyday existence and experience a strong urge to escape worldly matters, especially if Neptune is afflicted. Therefore, it is important to avoid alcohol and drugs, which would be especially detrimental now. The person should instead direct his energies toward metaphysical subjects and spiritual disciplines that will fulfill his desire for a greater, more expansive experience of life without negative repercussions. In the area of health, the person is more **263** vulnerable than usual to stress-induced illnesses and to ailments caused by spoiled foods, toxins, and poisons.

The person has intense or prophetic dreams during sleep and may even have astral or out-of-body experiences. He may have accurate visions of the future. By the end of this transit, the person is aware of his highest ideals for human existence.

When transiting Uranus squares or opposes natal Neptune, the person is subject to illusion, deception, and disorientation predominantly in the areas of life ruled by Neptune's house position. The person is especially sensitive, and his stability and firmness may be seriously tested. For many, this is a time of emotional imbalance, although much depends on Neptune's condition at birth. If Neptune is well-aspected, the person's idealistic tendencies are stimulated, and he has flashes of intuition and mystical experiences. If Neptune is afflicted, this transit is stressful and brings nervousness, confusion, and many fears. The person should try to get plenty of rest, eat well, and avoid strenuous schedules and demanding situations for the time being. Decision making should be postponed until the person is more confident and clear-headed.

The person may experience extreme disappointment and disillusionment. He is too trusting and gullible and does not realize it until it is too late. He is guided by his heart now, not his mind. Therefore, objectivity and detachment are lacking. The person strives for utopian ideals and romantic, perhaps unrealistic, visions. He is less emotionally grounded and spiritually centered than usual. And he may feel quite discouraged or despondent when he is suddenly brought down to earth by harsh reality. The person is easily overshadowed by circumstances.

Some people become discontented with daily life and want to escape through drugs, alcohol, or mysticism. Spiritual endeavors are preferable, but the person should avoid any extremes even in this area. He is subject to fraud and deception and may be exploited before he knows what has occurred. The person's subconscious is very active. He may dream vividly and abundantly and have prophetic visions.

The person is inspired and excited. He is creative and very imaginative. His artistic expression is innovative and original. Singers, poets, photographers, and filmmakers may do excellent work now even though their lives may be shaky and precarious. Individuals who are unstable under normal conditions may find this transit extremely upsetting. Such persons may be disturbed by hallucinations and delusional thinking. Illnesses occurring now are generally brought on by nervousness and stress, as well as by spoiled foods, toxins, and poisons.

When transiting Uranus trines or sextiles natal Neptune, the person's consciousness expands and he has mystical or spiritual experiences and perhaps even a glimpse of enlightenment. It is an excellent time for meditation, yoga, spiritual disciplines, and the study of mysticism. The person is open to realities beyond those perceived by the five senses. He is especially intuitive now and may have psychic visions or prophetic dreams. He is open to the possibilities of reincarnation, astral travel, and all matters that pertain to the spirit and soul. His devotion suddenly increases dramatically and his faith is unshakable. His appreciation and enjoyment of religion stems from his experience of God rather than a mere intellectual understanding.

The person is empathetic and compassionate. He feels in tune with all of life. He wants to help everyone he can. He is idealistic, and he focuses on his visions for a peaceful world where everyone is happy and successful. The person may now involve himself in movements and organizations dedicated to utopian aims. His imagination is extremely fertile during the one to four months of this transit (which may occur up to three times in nine months). All artistic endeavors are favored, and if the person is a professional actor, musician, filmmaker, or photographer, he now enjoys one of his most prolific and creative periods. This is an excellent transit for those interested in magic, fantasy, and the art of illusion.

The person's subconscious mind may be active. He may gain insights into his personality and psyche which were never before available. He is open, receptive, trusting, and fascinated by new ideas and philosophies. He may delve into occult or metaphysical subjects such as astrology, tarot, and palmistry. The person suddenly has a great deal of hope that he will realize his personal dreams in this lifetime. Many things which previously appeared doubtful now seem possible. The transiting trine aspect is significantly more powerful than the transiting sextile. The transiting sextile only represents the opportunity to make the above effects a reality.

When transiting Uranus conjuncts natal Pluto, the person experiences radical change and upheaval in vulnerable and sensitive areas of his life, (as signified by Pluto's natal house position). Most importantly, his desires become phenomenally intense, and he becomes aware of incredibly strong willpower and raw potential he may have never recognized. The person also becomes aware of his concerns for progress and improvement in realms that touch him deeply. He is anxious to have his life make a difference in the world, and he wants to take action immediately. This extremely potent transit, which generally only happens once in a person's life, occurs at different ages for each generation of souls. The effects are therefore quite dependent on how old the person is when this transit occurs. A person experiencing this transit during adulthood may get more meaningful results, materially and spiritually, than a young child or retired person.

The person grows concerned about social matters and the welfare of others. He is passionate about issues now and feels capable of creating his own destiny and influencing others. He becomes involved in revolutionary reform. The person is ready to create positive change, and he is determined, decisive, and unyielding. He may even behave compulsively and be unwilling to compromise or listen to reason. He wants to see significant results, and fast. The person uses his intensity, power, authority, and control more easily than ever. Because he has a big impact on others and life in general now, he must consider his actions carefully. Repercussions for misbehaving can be devastating.

This period of one to four months (which may occur up to three times in nine months) may bring sudden changes in volatile and sensitive areas of the person's life. Above all, the person must flow with the changes and let go of anything coming to an end. If he tries to hold on, he will experience tension, struggle, and potential health problems.

The person's interest in spiritual matters increases and he may have dramatic mystical experiences. He may feel both psychic and telepathic. He opens up to realities beyond those of the five senses. It is an excellent time for the study of astrology, yoga, and metaphysical subjects. The person makes tremendous evolutionary advancement. Most significant of all, he awakens to the fact that he controls not only his life but also what happens around him. Thus, he begins to realize the scope of his creative power in the universe.

When transiting Uranus squares or opposes natal Pluto, the person undergoes sudden uncontrollable disruptions and changes in his life. It is time for obsolete features of his life to come to an end. Unfortunately, in this period of upheaval and tumult the person is likely to strongly resist the evolutionary changes that are happening. The person may have the worst possible reaction, becoming willful, demanding, and controlling. An attitude of surrender and humility would make life easier during this transit. Otherwise the person will have a great deal of stress, tension, and potential health problems. In any case, no matter how hard the person tries, he cannot overpower the forces of nature and will not get his way when Uranus and Pluto are at work. He has lessons to learn, and important restructuring of his life must take place. Difficult or demanding circumstances arise, and he must deal with them appropriately, whether he likes it or not.

During the one to four months of this transit (which may occur up to three times in nine months), the person's mystical and spiritual nature may be awakened. He may have psychic experiences and feel tremendous creative and regenerative power. Although the person has disagreements or troubles with spiritual leaders and instructors because of his willfulness and rebelliousness, he can grow spiritually during this period. He confronts (out of necessity, not choice) intense desires, emotional attachments, manipulative behavioral patterns, and unconscious motivations. By using all of his spiritual resources, he goes to work and improves his psychological health and emotional balance.

The person must beware of compulsive behavior and a tendency to dominate. He must also guard against stubbornness, which would be especially detrimental now. Although he feels very vulnerable and sensitive while important long-term changes are taking place, he is wise to remain open to the advice of friends and loved ones. It is a wonderful time to engage in therapy, self-development work, and spiritual techniques. The person is capable of making deep and long-lasting progress more quickly than before. His regenerative power is acute and he is able to live completely in the moment. If the person takes advantage of this rare combination of abilities, he will recognize and eliminate anything negative in his life. As a result, he will experience profound growth that will change him forever.

When transiting Uranus trines or sextiles natal Pluto, the person makes sudden spiritual progress. His consciousness expands, and he concerns himself with self-improvement. He tries to correct character flaws and personal defects that limit his freedom and destroy his ability to flow with nature. He becomes serious and contemplative, delving deeply into his experience. He wants to understand the mysteries of life and the true workings of the universe. The person benefits from the study of astrology, metaphysics, yoga, and mysticism. More than anything, he wants his life to make a difference.

The person acts with great intensity and willpower. He is intuitive and yet very controlled. His actions spring from deep within his being. Because he is so resourceful and able to focus sharply during this transit, he can succeed almost anywhere he places his attention. He is motivated, determined, and clear about his intentions. He may have an urge to help humanity during the one to four months of this transit (which can occur up to three times in four months). The person has great creativity and regenerative ability now. He sees opportunities to contribute his ideas and talent everywhere he looks. He is vibrant and present, and he feels his power. He is completely aware that only he creates his destiny.

The person is purposeful, yet he remains objective, impartial, and appropriately detached. As with all beneficial transits involving Uranus or Pluto, it is an excellent time for therapy and the practice of spiritual techniques. He will enjoy great progress and benefit in the realms of life ruled by Pluto's natal house position. The person may have powerful mystical or psychic experiences.

The transiting trine aspect is significantly more powerful than the transiting sextile. The transiting sextile only represents the opportunity to make the above effects a reality.

When transiting Neptune conjuncts the natal Sun, the person subtly yet profoundly tunes in to his heart and his feelings. His consciousness expands, boundaries fall away, and the person's perception becomes subtle and refined. Reality changes dramatically, and the person is more aware of spiritual matters than anything earthly. He is extremely sensitive and vulnerable now. He is receptive to forces which transcend the five senses. The person feels little separation from nature, the universe, and God. This is one of the best times ever for meditation, contemplation, and spiritual experiences.

The person feels selfless and devoted. He is more capable of humility and surrender than at any time of his life. His faith in God is unshakable. If he turns within, he finds peace and bliss in his heart, and he experiences the immortality of his soul. During the two to four months of this transit (which may occur up to four times in two years), the person is willing to make sacrifices. He wants to bring harmony to others and help in any way he can. He feels love for everyone and relinquishes his own cravings and desires. For all practical purposes, his ego seems to temporarily disappear. He is compassionate, altruistic, and inspired.

The person appreciates the beauty and splendor of life. He has romantic, even utopian, visions. He has tremendous artistic ability and aesthetic appreciation now. The person is creative and imaginative. This is a wonderful time for anyone involved in art, music, drama, photography, and filmmaking. It is also splendid for poets, magicians, mystics, and spiritualists. The person may become interested in astrology, yoga, metaphysics, and natural healing techniques. He has strong intuition and may have prophetic dreams, important revelations, and dramatic psychic experiences.

On the negative side, this transit can bring serious problems, especially if the person abuses drugs or alcohol or if he is typically prone to delusion and self-deception. Even a normally objective person may lose his detachment and behave impractically, prompted by the strong feelings of his heart. He may lack common sense and feel quite dreamy. He is an easy mark for people who practice deception and betrayal. He does not see practical matters clearly, and he must be very careful not to let his feelings of peace and euphoria influence business dealings, relationships, and negotiations where he needs to firmly stand his ground.

If Neptune and the Sun are in an afflicted relationship at birth, the person may experience a serious identity crisis. His confidence is low, and he may feel a general lack of power, authority, and control. He may also have a strong urge to escape from the world. It is very important to avoid drugs, alcohol, and any unnatural substances during this transit. The person is very sensitive—spiritually, psychically, and physically— and ingesting foreign substances causes particularly damaging effects now. The person should avoid tense and stressful conditions. He should also get plenty of rest, eat well, and consider taking vitamin supplements. Many people become tired or under the weather quite easily when Neptune transits the Sun. If the person gets sick, he has a hard time diagnosing the illness and recovers much more slowly than usual.

The person may be somewhat moody or confused now. Because he is so idealistic and impressionable, he is subject to serious disappointment. For instance, he may let his imagination run away, expect too much from his father, and feel let down. Because the Sun rules men, a woman going through this transit has to be especially careful of illusion and deception in her romantic involvements with men.

If the person is committed to enlightenment or higher consciousness when this period begins, he may now have some of his most sublime, ecstatic spiritual experiences. His devotion to God and his personal Guru produces intense joy and happiness. By the end of this transit, the person is more aware of his own infinite nature.

When transiting Neptune squares or opposes the natal Sun, the person becomes unduly sensitive, vulnerable, and moody. His confidence, direction, and certainty become weak, and he often vacillates. Worse than this, he completely loses perspective. He distorts current problems and past failures way out of proportion. The person's judgement is faulty, and he lacks objectivity, detachment, and common sense. This transit often brings feelings of profound disappointment, discouragement, and disillusionment. The person suffers acutely over unfulfilled hopes and everything that has gone wrong in his life. He feels like a victim and temporarily loses his optimism, idealism, enthusiasm, and inspiration. More than anything, he would like to escape from the world and all his mundane responsibilities. He is disappointed with the results of his efforts, and life seems unfair, unreasonable, and just too hard.

The person is likely to feel tired now. He should take especially good care of himself. He needs to have a great deal of rest, eat very well (including perhaps taking vitamin supplements), and enjoy exercise and outdoor activities. He should socialize more than usual in order to avoid depression, isolation, loneliness, and self-indulgence. He should also surround himself with supportive friends and family who appreciate him and will remind him that his life is worthwhile.

The person feels the stress and harshness of life more than usual. He must avoid taking drugs, alcohol, and foreign substances into his body. He is in a highly susceptible and impressionable state, and such things would harm him physically and exacerbate his confusion and uncertainty. The person has to guard against being deceived by men, government officials, and persons in authority. He may suddenly have problems with his father, who is subject to instability, weakness, and illness. A woman going through this transit must beware of illusion and deception with the men in her life. Also, her husband may experience strange and peculiar difficulties now.

The person is very intuitive now. He may have an intense urge to pursue meditation, contemplation, and other self-development techniques. Such activities may produce powerful mystical or spiritual experiences, but they do not help the person with his current feelings of inadequacy and lack of purpose. Furthermore, any techniques of introspection he practices now may increase his laziness and self-indulgence in his emotional and psychological predicaments. It is a favorable period, though, for the study of astrology, yoga, tarot, metaphysics, and other esoteric sciences, as long as the person does not become compulsive about these pursuits.

During the approximately two-year period when Neptune repeatedly squares or opposes the Sun, the person learns to question whether he can satisfy his ego through accomplishment and achievement. When he realizes that nothing in the relative world will satisfy his ego, the person can begin to gain some perspective and detachment about the higher values of life and his own purpose in the scheme of things. It is, however, a rather poor time to launch new ventures. The person is engaged in an important evolutionary process during which his attention must be focused on his internal, psychological, emotional, and spiritual workings.

The person should be very careful in business dealings. Major decisions may be better postponed until the person is more stable, secure, and sure of himself.

When transiting Neptune trines or sextiles the natal Sun, the person tunes in to higher, more spiritual realities, and he reestablishes a connection between his outer life and his immortal soul. His consciousness expands, and the person is suddenly receptive to energies beyond those of the five senses. He becomes interested in yoga, astrology, religion, mysticism, and other metaphysical subjects. He feels great serenity, peace, and bliss. It is an excellent time for meditation, contemplation, seclusion, and introspection. The person feels close to nature and God. He is released from possessiveness, jealousy, and a need to gratify his ego. He feels harmonious and integrated, at one with all. He is completely in touch with his feminine side, or yin energy, which is now his source of strength.

The person enjoys thinking about his goals and aspirations. He is remarkably creative, imaginative, and inspired now. His aesthetic appreciation is heightened, and all artistic endeavors are favored. Individuals who are involved in music, dance, drama, photography, or magic may do some of their best work during the approximately two years during which this transit repeatedly occurs for two to four months at a time. The person is tenderhearted, sympathetic, and compassionate now. He wants to help others and involve himself in humanitarian, altruistic efforts. He is romantic and sensitive, and his values are more emotional and spiritual than usual. He is comfortable with abstractions and theories, no matter how expansive or ethereal.

The person benefits from mystics, spiritualists, and religious people now. He is extraordinarily capable of humility, surrender, and devotion, and he may begin to follow a spiritual path. He also benefits from his father, government officials, and others in authority. The father may even take a greater interest in religion, mysticism, or spiritual life. A woman has happy romantic experiences during this transit. She may be courted by a man who is soft, peaceful, and pious and who may be involved in metaphysics or spiritualism. The person is more intuitive than usual and may have many dreams, even prophetic ones, during sleep. He becomes aware of his unconscious mind and at one with his spirit and soul.

The transiting trine aspect is significantly more powerful than the transiting sextile. The transiting sextile only represents the opportunity to make the above effects a reality.

When transiting Neptune conjuncts the natal Moon, the person loses all emotional boundaries and experiences a sustained period of strong feeling, compassion, and sensitivity. He feels profoundly connected to others. He wants to help in any way he can. He is, however, so sensitive and impressionable that he does not deal well with stress, strain, struggle, and practical affairs. He feels the harshness of life more than usual, and he is easily affected by the opinions and judgements of others. He is also subject to powerful, sometimes overwhelming, moods and feelings.

This is an extremely profound transit which brings significant self-discovery and personal growth through the experience of love. The purpose of feeling is to experience love—not romantic love, but absolute or eternal bliss—the essential nature of the universe. During this approximately two-year period when Neptune repeatedly transits the Moon for two to four months at a time, the person's feelings expand in order to experience the most refined sensations, infinite perceptions, and subtle level of life possible.

Naturally, however, this high state of human experience brings to the surface everything unnatural and unhealthy within the subconscious in order to be processed and purified. Thus, unless he is particularly highly evolved, the person will probably experience a good deal of confusion, internal commotion, and disorientation before he can experience emotional freedom and a refined state of perception. Nevertheless, by the time this period is over, the person has learned much about his emotional needs and make-up. He experiences deep feelings he may have been previously unaware of and discovers which issues touch him most intensely. If the person has been emotionally dishonest or repressed before this transit, then he may find this period especially disturbing, but also extremely valuable to his overall growth and maturity.

The person appreciates beauty, culture, and all of the arts. His imagination is fertile, and he is open to the higher realities of life. He may take an interest in astrology, yoga, metaphysics, or mysticism. He does especially well in dream analysis or any practice dealing with the unconscious mind. The person feels more devotion to God. He may therefore enjoy religion and spiritual teachers greatly now.

Domestic affairs are not much favored. The person may experience strange, unexpected problems with women or his mother. He must be careful of being deceived by the women in his life. In some cases, the wife or mother of the person may suffer deteriorating health. On the positive side, the person's wife or mother may become spiritual, religious, or pious. The person is especially gullible. He is an easy mark for people who may exploit him because his feelings are so strong that he forgets his common sense and discrimination.

The person is somewhat physically delicate and frail. He is more susceptible to illness than usual and should avoid conflict, stress, strain, harsh circumstances, drugs, and alcohol. He should get plenty of rest and guard against eating spoiled foods, chemical additives, and toxic substances. It is one of the best times for extended meditation, contemplation, and seclusion. The person has excellent spiritual experiences and feels united with God and nature. He may, however, feel a strong urge to escape from the world. His instincts and intuition are more accurate than before and he may have prophetic dreams and visions.

His home environment may suddenly deteriorate. The person's house may start to leak oil, gas, or water, and he may have problems with his swimming pool, if he has one. Some individuals get lazy or overly passive during this transit, and some have trouble with their eyes and bodily fluids.

TRANSITING NEPTUNE SQUARES OR OPPOSES THE NATAL MOON

When transiting Neptune squares or opposes the natal Moon, the person becomes overwhelmed by his emotions. He is sensitive to rejection, easily hurt by others, and subject to powerful moods. The person loses his discrimination and objectivity. He blows things out of proportion and may become compulsive or obsessive in his opinions. He feels things acutely and his perception is colored by his emotions. As a result, he may do irrational and foolish things. The person would be wise to seek advice from friends and loved ones about problems and predicaments, simply because he lacks common sense.

The person may experience domestic problems. Home improvements do not go well, and the person's house may suddenly deteriorate. The house may spring leaks of oil, gas, or water. The person may have problems with the women in his life or experience confusion in his marriage. He must be diligent in his communication with women and be alert to being deceived by them. His wife or mother may become strange, weird, unstable, frail, physically ill, or compulsive about spiritual, occult, or metaphysical matters. Close relationships are especially difficult now because the person is so sensitive, emotionally insecure, and easily thrown off balance. He takes everything personally and misunderstands his partner. He should try, as best as possible, to consider the other person's point of view. Also, the person is seriously influenced by his unconscious mind. Thus, he may be trying to fulfill important needs that his rational mind does not even perceive, much less understand. During this transit, the person is guided by his heart, not his mind.

The person's energy and vitality may weaken. He is sensitive to stress and strain and should avoid conflict and harsh conditions. He responds to difficulties by turning inward and feeling sad or depressed. As this transit progresses, the person may feel like escaping from the world completely. However, this is generally not a favorable course. It is healthier and wiser for the person to surround himself with friends and family who are supportive and loving. Above all, the person must not turn to drugs or alcohol now. He is very sensitive to foreign substances entering his body. The person must beware of poisons and spoiled foods. He may have health problems with bodily fluids and the eyes. Rest, proper diet, moderate exercise, and vitamin supplements are strongly **277** recommended during the two years when transiting Neptune repeatedly squares or opposes the Moon for two to four months at a time.

The person is intuitive and psychic now, but he may have a tendency to distort the meaning of information he gains this way. He is drawn to mysticism and occult or spiritual subjects. However, now such endeavors may cause more harm than good because of the person's lack of discrimination and clarity. Some individuals become lazy or passive during this transit, and some individuals go through painful experiences of loss or the death of loved ones, causing prolonged periods of grief. The person daydreams a lot and may have difficulty concentrating. His imagination is fertile, and he may do especially well in artistic undertakings. It is, however, a generally poor time for dealings with the public and for launching new ventures.

If the Moon is seriously afflicted in the natal chart or the person is emotionally unstable to begin with, then this transit can be quite difficult. The person could now be subject to hallucinations, psychotic episodes, mental illness, or nervous breakdowns.

When transiting Neptune trines or sextiles the natal Moon, the person feels peaceful, content, and spiritually integrated. He enjoys emotional harmony and feels at one with all of nature. The person is sensitive, compassionate, empathetic, warm, and loving. Relationships are smooth and domestic life is especially favored. The person gets along very well with his wife, mother, and the women around him. He meets women who are soft, spiritual, and tenderhearted. A man going through this transit has good experiences in his love life.

The person appreciates beauty and culture. He may upgrade his home with beautiful furnishings or works of art. He is inspired and idealistic. His imagination is fertile. He wants happiness for all and is committed to helping in any way he can. If the person is an artist or musician by hobby or profession, he does some of his most extraordinary, subtle, and sublime work. He is guided by his heart, not his mind.

The person is open and receptive. He enjoys spiritual subjects and any practices which help him go beyond the five senses and transcend material life. He benefits from astrology, yoga, metaphysics, and occult arts. He feels devotion and has no trouble surrendering his ego. Religious studies go well, and the person is favored by his spiritual teachers. The person is intuitive and psychic. Furthermore, he has important and accurate insights into his psyche and subconscious.

The person is impressionable. He is very trusting and must guard against being deceived or exploited. He is in a delicate and refined state now and should therefore beware of harsh people, stressful circumstances, and conflict. The transiting trine aspect is significantly more powerful than the transiting sextile. The transiting sextile only represents the opportunity to make the above effects a reality.

When transiting Neptune conjuncts natal Mercury, the person's mind becomes sensitive enough to perceive the unboundedness of existence. The person suddenly becomes open to spiritual philosophies and mystical ideas that transcend the ordinary knowledge derived through the five senses and that explain life from a universal or divine perspective. The person takes an interest in astrology, yoga, metaphysics, religion, psychic phenomenon, and the occult. He may become involved in spiritual practices in pursuit of enlightenment.

Unfortunately, however, this transit is an extremely difficult one for all practical matters. As the mind lets go of its boundaries and restrictions and unites (to whatever extent possible) with the unbounded, the person temporarily loses his ability to focus, concentrate, and make effective use of his ability to think and communicate. His clarity and sharpness suffer dramatically, and he has a hard time organizing anything. He is strongly affected by his feelings and his vivid imagination. The person demonstrates little objectivity. He is gullible and easily taken advantage of. It is a poor time for making decisions and implementing important plans.

During the approximately two years when transiting Neptune conjuncts natal Mercury repeatedly for two to four months at a time, the person may feel confused, disoriented, and bewildered. He does not see things clearly, his thinking may be distorted, and he has trouble with facts and figures. He does not convey his ideas well, and he experiences many misunderstandings and miscommunications. The person should postpone contract negotiations and agreements. He is forgetful, he does not understand everything that is happening, and he neglects to scrutinize the fine print.

The person is absorbed, even preoccupied, with his dreams and visions. His imagination is fertile and his thinking creative. He succeeds in anything involving art, music, poetry, and drama. His senses are heightened, and he loves beauty and culture. If the person is a writer of fiction or fantasy, he is in for one of the best, most prolific periods of his life. It is also an excellent time for those who study or practice magic, filmmaking, and photography.

280
The person may have constant difficulties with machinery, especially telephones, tape recorders, radios, televisions, computers, or any devices that convey information. He may also lose things daily, and he begins to wonder if he is losing his mind. Educational activities are not favored. The person does poorly on tests, fails at giving coherent lectures, and occasionally becomes scattered or spaced out. His judgement is less than accurate, and he makes mistakes because his imagination betrays him. Others may lie to him or fail to receive letters and messages he sends.

The person is extremely intuitive now. He has dramatically accurate psychic power. He feels strong devotion and is inspired to pray. If the person decides to meditate, he has some of his most sublime experiences ever. He may even receive divine guidance. As for his health, his lungs and intestines are at risk. The person feels stress acutely and should avoid harsh circumstances and abrasive people. Business dealings do not go well. Most importantly, the person should stand by his word and keep his commitments, even though it may be difficult during this transit.

When transiting Neptune squares or opposes natal Mercury, the person is misunderstood, communicates poorly, and may be lied to by others. He is subject to chaotic situations, disruptions in his routine, and difficult working conditions. The person's thinking is too subjective, and he does not perceive things clearly or accurately. He is absorbed in his mind and imagination. The person becomes confused easily, and he often exaggerates. His judgement is poor. It is a very bad time to make important decisions. If he must do so, however, he should seek advice from friends and loved ones. Contract negotiations and legal matters should be postponed, if possible. The person is very susceptible to being deceived or used now. Above all, he should guard against get-rich-quick schemes and opportunities which appear too good to be true.

The person becomes fearful, shy, or timid. His confidence, inner strength, and purpose are weakened, and he may tend toward introversion. His nerves are under attack, and he easily takes ill. He should avoid harsh conditions, abrasive people, and conflict. He should also refrain from using alcohol, drugs, or foreign substances.

The person is disorganized and unfocused, and he has trouble with discipline. He readily forgets things and has difficulty keeping his word. This transit is similar to the conjunction transit. However, the transiting square and opposition aspects do not offer such great potential for spiritual expansion and growth. The person may increase his interest in metaphysics and mysticism but he does not experience major break-throughs in consciousness, as he might during the conjunction transit. Also, while he may now have psychic experiences, they may not be so pure, accurate, and potent.

The person has trouble in educational matters. He does not communicate as articulately as usual, and his writings may not accurately convey his intent. He has trouble with machinery, especially tape recorders, radios, televisions, telephones, and other devices that convey information. Letters, messages, and any communications directed to the person may be accidentally delayed or lost. Commerce is not favored and the person must be careful about being cheated or receiving false information in business dealings. The person has trouble recognizing the truth and confronting challenging situations. He would like to ignore any serious problems that arise now. Such a course of action only makes matters worse.

Psychological problems are also possible. The person is affected by his insecurities, and if Mercury is severely afflicted in his natal birthchart, then the person may experience mental instability or a nervous breakdown. Some individuals have problems with their lungs or intestines. The person experiences difficulties when travelling. He is also subject to gossip or rumors. He appreciates music and the arts more than usual, and his interest in astrology, yoga, mysticism, and the occult arts increases. Efforts at meditation and prayer are successful.

When transiting Neptune trines or sextiles natal Mercury, the person's mind expands, his senses become heightened, and his receptivity increases. The person feels soft, peaceful, and harmonious. He is in a refined state of mind and is particularly sensitive to his surroundings. He is more creative, expressive, and inspired than usual. This transit is excellent for artistic endeavors. The person excels in activities involving painting, music, poetry, drama, magic, photography, or filmmaking.

Educational matters are favored, and the person is open to new ideas, especially those which transcend the normal consciousness associated with the five senses. He may be interested in astrology, yoga, metaphysics, and occult arts. The person enjoys religious and spiritual practices. It is one of the best times for prayer and positive affirmations. The person is extremely intuitive. He has many psychic experiences and gains insights into his subconscious mind. He may feel introspective or desirous of seclusion. The person is sensitive to stress and strain and should avoid harsh situations, abrasive people, and conflict. He should avoid drugs, alcohol, and chemicals, which would have especially detrimental effects now.

The person communicates well and accurately. He succeeds especially well with imaginative or fictional writings. The person is compassionate and sympathetic. He is aware of other people's needs and feelings and therefore enjoys smooth relationships. The person wants happiness for all and is willing to help in any way he can. He is innocent, sincere, and expects the best from others. As a result, he leaves himself open to deception, fraud, and exploitation. If he encounters an opportunity that appears too good to be true, he should seek advice from others who may be able to use more common sense than he.

The person is guided by his heart now and tries to spread love wherever he can. He is diplomatic, polite, and charming. He broadens his awareness and makes good spiritual progress.

The transiting trine aspect is significantly more powerful than the transiting sextile. The transiting sextile only represents the opportunity to make the above effects a reality.

When transiting Neptune conjuncts natal Venus, the person experiences the purest, most sublime love. He becomes tender, passionate, caring, exceptionally emotional, and overwhelmed by appreciation of beauty. The person grows sensitive, responsive, and incredibly empathetic with his lover, spouse, or new romantic interest. Unfortunately, he is completely infatuated with love and cannot see his partner objectively. He is naive, impressionable, and as emotionally gullible as could be.

This transit often creates instances of blind love in which the person becomes involved with someone who seems ideal but who is actually unsuitable as a partner and is, in certain cases, downright deceptive. The person is an easy target for exploitation in love matters, because he is so captivated by his partner and has lost his discrimination and common sense. Life may seem more blissful than ever during the two to four month periods when transiting Neptune conjuncts natal Venus (which may occur repeatedly for approximately two years). But when the transit ends, the person may feel used, discouraged, and profoundly disappointed, and his happiness may now seem as if it were an illusion. Therefore, the person should not make life-altering decisions based on romance until this transit has made its last and final conjunction.

Despite the potential risks and hazards to person's love life, the overall results of this transit can be quite splendid. The person experiences phenomenal inspiration and idealism. He feels anything is possible and therefore is encouraged to pursue his dreams and visions. He discovers his ability to feel compassion, empathy, and union with all of God's creation. Whether the effects are long-lasting or not, the person never forgets the ecstasy, elation, and bliss of this time. He now grasps just how much sweetness and joy he can gain from life when he attunes himself fully to beauty, love, compassion, and refinement. The person learns the fine art of living.

As with all Neptune transits, the person becomes soft and gentle and should avoid harsh or stressful situations. He also must avoid drugs, alcohol, and chemicals, which now cause particularly detrimental effects. The person meets women who are soft, cultured, genteel, and extremely delicate. He may become involved with women who are highly religious, devout, spiritual, or mystical. His mother, also, may suddenly develop an interest in metaphysical or spiritual subjects. The person's imagination and creativity increase dramatically. He feels more inspired than ever and succeeds in all matters involving art, music, poetry, drama, filmmaking, and photography. His senses are heightened, and he feels extremely sensual. For some, there is a danger of overindulgence in comforts and pleasures.

The person is remarkably intuitive, except perhaps in recognizing the true nature of his romantic partner. He may have psychic or telepathic experiences. He is drawn to occult and metaphysical subjects, and his devotion to God may grow. He feels discontented with the harsh realities of earthly life and may decide to pursue enlightenment or monkhood. The person wants to help others. He may volunteer for charity work or humanitarian causes. Even in these areas, however, the person should use common sense and avoid going overboard because he is so powerfully affected by his feelings. He should be made aware that his present feelings, although they are intense, will likely prove to be quite temporary.

Some individuals going through this transit indulge in secret or extramarital love affairs. The person is extremely magnetic and alluring to others now, and he scales the heights of love as his lifelong romantic fantasies suddenly seem to materialize. There is a great danger, however, that the person will fall in love with someone less than his equal. In his highly compassionate and selfless state, he may commit himself to someone who is needy, unstable, destitute, spaced out, or who abuses alcohol or drugs. As for his health, the person's throat, kidneys, and reproductive system are under attack.

When transiting Neptune squares or opposes natal Venus, the person experiences confusion, uncertainty, illusion, or deception in his primary love relationship. He is sensitive, vulnerable, and at the mercy of his own feelings. The person feels restless in his soul and desperately wants affection, happiness, and pleasure. In order to fulfill his desires, he abandons his usual discrimination and objectivity in love. Feelings of adoration and infatuation overshadow his normal judgement, and he is in danger of falling for someone who is extremely unsuited to him. In the end he winds up seriously disillusioned. Some going through this transit are confronted with issues about love that they do not wish to face. The person may choose to ignore or deny the truth and take actions which later backfire in a devastating way.

Because his feelings are so strong and his imagination runs wild, the person is easily taken advantage of. He does not see things clearly now and should beware of opportunities which appear too good to be true. He should avoid becoming romantically involved with someone who is married or otherwise unavailable, or with someone who is insecure, needy, or destitute. He should try to be as practical as possible and use his common sense. The person may have troubles with women who are unstable, weird, or strange. He may have dealings with women who are confused or dishonest. His mother may become a source of difficulty, or her health may suddenly deteriorate.

This transit often brings emotional pain and suffering, causing the person to seek a way out of life. Therefore, he is attracted to yoga, meditation, contemplation, and spiritual practices leading directly to enlightenment or final liberation. The person feels powerful devotion and can make excellent spiritual progress now, even though he never feels completely satisfied during this transit. He is intuitive and may have psychic experiences. He may engage in occult or metaphysical studies such as astrology, tarot, and so on.

As with nearly all Neptune transits, the person is physically sensitive and delicate. He must get plenty of rest, eat well, and avoid conflict, friction, and stress. His throat, kidneys, and reproductive system are at risk. Any illnesses that occur now are particularly difficult to diagnose.

During Neptune transits, natural remedies are preferable to drugs, alcohol, and chemicals, which are very damaging now.

The person is creative. He excels in artistic projects, fiction writing, magic, and anything associated with fantasy. It is also a good time for activities in drama, photography, poetry, and music. During this approximately two-year period when transiting Neptune repeatedly conjuncts natal Venus for two to four months at a time, the person must be careful not to overindulge in pleasures as a means of drowning his sorrows.

When transiting Neptune trines or sextiles natal Venus, the person feels peaceful and content, and he sees beauty everywhere. His feminine energies are heightened, his motives are pure, and he behaves with tenderness and compassion. Romance is entirely favored. The person meets a sweetheart who is soft, cultured, delicate, and exquisite. The loved one may also be spiritual, mystical, and extremely devout. Love affairs begun during this transit are characterized by innocence, idealism, and purity. The person has a profound experience of unity with his partner. His relationship feels holy, and he believes that his soul mate has finally arrived. The person loves selflessly and does everything he can to please his partner. He is happy.

The person excels in artistic endeavors, including music, drama, film, photography, and fiction writing. He is inspired, creative, and exceptionally imaginative. He appreciates fantasy and the world of illusion. The person is idealistic and hopeful, and his vision expands. He is open, receptive, and impressionable. His faith and optimism lead to good fortune. Relationships go very well now because the person is so sensitive and aware of the feelings of others. He is warm and affectionate and he gravitates to people and surroundings that are graceful, charming, and refined. His social life flourishes.

The person benefits from women, including his mother. Domestic life goes smoothly. The person may feel extremely charitable. He may volunteer for humanitarian causes. He may also become interested in spiritual matters and the higher realities of life. The person's devotion to God may intensify, and he may wish to escape his mundane existence. If he engages in religious or self-development practices, he is amply rewarded with enjoyable experiences, as well as significant growth.

The transiting trine aspect is significantly more powerful than the transiting sextile. The transiting sextile only represents the opportunity to make the above effects a reality.

When transiting Neptune conjuncts natal Mars, the person's strength, assertiveness, and willpower diminish. His confidence decreases and he loses his determination and persistence. The person's ego seems to disappear or disintegrate. His energy and vitality are low, and he must be careful not to ingest spoiled foods or toxic substances. His body is weak, and he is temporarily quite vulnerable. It is a good time for the person to take iron supplements or anything which strengthens the blood (hard green, leafy vegetables are recommended). Alcohol and drugs are very detrimental now.

During this transit, the person should just try to maintain the status quo. He should not take on extra tasks or assume new responsibilities. It is a terrible time to engage in competition, professionally or otherwise. The person is powerless to defend himself. He fears failure and becomes easily discouraged or depressed. He is inhibited, indecisive, and hesitant. He finds it difficult to put his desires and ambitions above others now.

The person's sex drive becomes significantly lowered. He may experience temporary impotence, lack of virility, or other sexual dysfunction. In some cases, the person becomes engrossed in sexual fantasies. His imagination expands, and he begins to equate eroticism with the divine. He may experiment sexually.

During this transit, the person must be very careful in business dealings. He is not as organized and practical as necessary, and he could be easily deceived. Also, he may be plagued by feelings of insecurity and inferiority.

During the two-to-four-month periods when Neptune directly transits Mars (which may occur repeatedly for approximately two years), surgical operations are dangerous. The surgeon may be negligent or the anesthesia may prove dangerous. The surgery could also cause infection or blood problems. Operations are better postponed, if possible.

Individuals involved in art, music, drama, filmmaking, or photography can make excellent use of this transit. The person's creations are more imaginative, colorful, and visionary than usual. Even though he

290   has an almost impossible time promoting himself, his artistic creativity is heightened. The person may daydream and fantasize constantly. Spiritual and mystical endeavors are favored. The person has good experiences in meditation, and his consciousness transcends ordinary boundaries. It is also a good period for visualization techniques.

When transiting Neptune squares or opposes natal Mars, the person has trouble fulfilling his desires. He is intense and idealistic in his cravings, but he quickly becomes insecure and timid. He then tries to get his way through indirect means and, in certain cases, underhanded methods, both of which fail miserably. The person needs to be candid and straightforward in his dealings with others and hope for the best. Success and accomplishment is, unfortunately, not at all favored during this transit. Most importantly, the person must beware of deception, fraud, trickery, and exploitation from his peers and associates. Women, especially, should guard against sexual violation or assault. They may attract perverted individuals into their surroundings by unconsciously projecting sexual messages.

Romantic dealings now may bring disappointment and depression. The person perceives no restrictions to his desires and therefore cannot distinguish between a fantasy lover and someone who is a real possibility. Because Mars represents sexuality and is now aspected by transiting Neptune, the person begins to have powerful sexual fantasies. He is experimental and may even become interested in sexual perversion. Sexual restraint and caution disappears.

The person may suddenly become frail and tired. His energy is low, and his health is more delicate than usual. His blood weakens, and he must be very careful of allowing poisons, toxins, and any unnatural substances into his body. The person should take iron supplements and eat foods which nourish the blood (especially dark green, leafy vegetables) during the approximately two years when transiting Neptune repeatedly squares or opposes natal Mars for two to four months at a time. He should avoid drugs and alcohol, which are extremely detrimental now. Above all, he should not schedule surgery during this transit. Correct diagnosis is nearly impossible during Neptune transits, and major difficulties with anaesthesia could arise. Also, the person has problems with surgeons due to illusion, deception, incompetence, and negligence now. To make matters worse, because the person's blood is so vulnerable during this period, he is susceptible to infections and has difficulty recuperating.

292   The person has troubles with persons in professions ruled by Mars. He must be very careful in his dealings with policemen, military personnel, and mechanics. He is very easily deceived by dishonest or unscrupulous individuals now. On the positive side, the person is inspired and imaginative. He may create great music, paintings, poetry, or other artistic creations.

When transiting Neptune trines or sextiles natal Mars, the person becomes optimistic and enthusiastic about fulfilling his desires. He works on high-minded dreams and visions and becomes less concerned with mundane matters and practical concerns. He is driven by altruistic motives and humanitarian goals. He is unaffected by his ego, pride, or need for recognition. The person wants to help. It is an excellent time for spiritual work, personally and professionally. The person successfully spreads the message of higher consciousness or nirvana to others. And if he is on the spiritual path, he has excellent experiences in meditation or with other spiritual techniques. Religious endeavors, especially of a ritualistic nature, are very enjoyable now.

Individuals involved in music, drama, poetry, magic, photography, and filmmaking are strongly aided by this transit. The person creates works of art which are colorful, sensuous, and beautiful. The person's intuition is strong, and he does well in business activities because of this. He is sensitive to others and is able to pursue his ambitions without offending anyone. He is assertive in a nonthreatening way, and his life is therefore graceful and refined. The person may attract a sexual partner who is soft, delicate, ethereal, and spiritual. The relationship is joyful, but may be based more on ideals, illusions, and sexual attraction than true compatibility.

During this transit, the person succeeds in planning philanthropic enterprises. His best work is done in private or behind the scenes. He takes care of projects with discretion and diplomacy. He is protected from harshness and discordant conditions. And he is quite confident that his intentions will be fulfilled easily.

The transiting trine aspect is significantly more powerful than the transiting sextile. The transiting sextile only represents the opportunity to make the above effects a reality.

When transiting Neptune conjuncts natal Jupiter, the person becomes powerfully inspired, and he contemplates his ultimate dreams and visions. His remembers his love for humanity, and he wants to do everything he can to promote justice for all. The person's heart softens and he behaves with pure motives. He temporarily relinquishes material concerns and practical considerations in favor of the higher values of life. He becomes deeply absorbed in his beliefs and convictions. It is an excellent time for religious and spiritual activities. The person is more devout than ever. His faith in God increases, and he begins to revere the mystical and sacred aspects of life. In some cases, the person has prophetic dreams or divine revelations. He is profoundly moved by religion, philosophy, and the meaning of existence.

The person has little objectivity because his imagination is so active. He must beware of living in a dream world or he may be quickly exploited. He is generous, sympathetic, and charitable. He expects the best from others and is oblivious to their baser motives. His judgement is poor in practical matters. If Jupiter is afflicted or in a bad relationship with Neptune at birth, then the person encounters deception or fraud at the hands of religious or spiritual teachers. He is also vulnerable to devious or dishonest lawyers.

During the two to four months when transiting Neptune conjuncts natal Jupiter (which may occur up to four times in two years) the person is likely to feel a tremendous urge to speculate or gamble. Such activities are not favored unless Jupiter is very strong and well-aspected in the natal birthchart. Generally, the person must guard against self-indulgence, extravagance, and lack of discipline. He feels extraordinarily lucky now but may incur great losses if he does not exercise discretion and prudence. The person may have problems with bankers, money lenders, or wealthy people who may suddenly behave questionably. He does not benefit from universities and college professors and he may encounter obstacles in obtaining university grants and loans.

The person is in good spirits, but he has to guard against exaggerated idealism. He should avoid get-rich-quick schemes and financial enterprises which appear too good to be true. This transit is very favorable for those individuals who are involved in film, photography, and magic. As for health, the person's liver is sensitive, and allergies may therefore flare up.

Transits of the West—Dasas of the East

When transiting Neptune squares or opposes natal Jupiter, the person is plagued by faulty judgement. He is sentimental and too affected by his feelings. He is overly idealistic, naive, and gullible. He ignores caution, prudence, and discretion and may be attracted to grandiose schemes. He seeks perfection, but he lacks balance and proportion. The person is an easy target for exploitation. Financial matters are not favored, and the person should avoid investments and speculations, especially those which seem too good to be true. He feels lucky and wants to gamble, but his chances of winning are very poor now.

The person sees what he wants to see. Unless he restrains his natural impulses now, he is in for disappointment and disillusionment. He has tremendous devotional urges and may pursue religion, philosophy, or spiritual activities. He must be careful, however, of fraudulent gurus, deceptive spiritualists, and devious or corrupt religious authorities. His judgement in these realms is very weak.

The person may be extravagant and overly indulgent in pleasures. He should try to remain sensible and practical until this transit ends. Because he has a hard time distinguishing the real from the unreal, he should not make big decisions without seeking guidance. He is especially vulnerable in business matters in which he may jump at the chance to make easy money. He falls for hard luck stories and does not suspect that others might be taking advantage of his naiveté and benevolent behavior.

The person may have problems with universities and college professors. He may experience delays or obstacles in obtaining financial aid or scholarships. He is not favored in his dealings with banks or money lenders, and he could have problems with deceitful lawyers. Some individuals going through this transit feel a strong desire to escape from the world. The person may engage in deep meditation or other spiritual practices for the distinct purpose of enlightenment. He should be careful during long-distance travels, where he may encounter strange, unforseen difficulties or bizarre experiences. Or he should simply postpone long voyages until this transit passes.

The person is intuitive now, but he may also have weird or mysterious dreams and visions. As for his health, a weak liver could give rise to allergies and other related illnesses.

When transiting Neptune trines or sextiles natal Jupiter, the person feels strong religious and spiritual urges, and he becomes acutely aware of his divine nature. His attention shifts to the higher values of life, and he appreciates the great opportunity life has given him. Meditation, contemplation, and self-reflection are all extremely favored now. The person benefits greatly from spiritual gurus, religious teachers, and mystical movements. He is also favored by college professors and institutions of higher learning. Life goes smoothly and gracefully because of the person's heartfelt optimism, enthusiasm, and positive attitude. He has a profound sense of abundance and prosperity, and therefore he fulfills his wishes and desires effortlessly.

The person is kind, tenderhearted, and compassionate now. His charitable tendencies increase, and he wants justice and fairness for all. The person is happy and cheerful, and he is supremely confident that all will be well in the end. Financial matters are favored. The person succeeds in his dealings with banks, money lenders, and wealthy people. He makes money through investments and speculations. The person may travel to far-off lands and learn a great deal about other cultures and civilizations. He wants to learn all he can and expand his knowledge of the world and the universe. He gains sublime joy from studying philosophy and religion now.

The person is inspired and imaginative. He maintains humility and openness and has great reverence for God. He respects the path to enlightenment and does not look for short cuts. The person's motives are pure, and his aesthetic sensitivity is heightened. He enjoys beautiful objects, works of art, and anything that makes life more pleasant and comfortable.

The transiting trine aspect is significantly more powerful than the transiting sextile. The transiting sextile only represents the opportunity to make the above effects a reality.

When transiting Neptune conjuncts natal Saturn, the person experiences a stressful period during which old perceptions of reality erode and worn-out structures of his life crumble. The person's business may disintegrate, his career may end, and certain basic externals of his life may suddenly collapse. The person finds that he can no longer rely on the foundations upon which he has based his existence. Even more disconcerting, his convictions, beliefs, and everything important to him are proved inconsequential by the uncontrollable circumstances that are destroying his past attainments and accomplishments. It is impossible to predict exactly which areas of the person's life will be most affected. But whatever constitutes the basis of his reality now dissolves in order to help the person grow.

The purpose of this transit, on the mundane level, is to force the person to move on to new realms of life because his old reality has outlived its usefulness. An individual who is concerned with his personal growth confronts the ever-changing nature of existence during this transit and realizes that realities are different in different states of consciousness. When the person analyzes the reason behind the profound changes of his external circumstances, he begins to realize that his inner being has slowly been transformed. As he considers the matter carefully and honestly, he realizes that his ambitions are no longer what they were. His motivations coming from within—from the soul, psyche, or spirit—have changed, and, consequently, important features of his life have broken down.

For many, this approximately two-year period when transiting Neptune repeatedly conjuncts natal Saturn for two to four months at a time is difficult. The person feels insecure, vulnerable, and unprotected. He is confused, disoriented, and anxious. Many of his resources are gone, he has little control, and he has lost his authority over others. Worse than this, he has no access to his usual wisdom. He feels his current problems are caused by his past experience. Had he not undertaken the course of action chosen long ago, he feels, he would not be in his current precarious situation. The person should take particularly good care of himself. He is under great stress, whether he realizes it or not, and should eat well and get plenty of rest. His best strategy is to let go of attachments to the form and structure of his life and try to flow with nature. He should follow his heart, his instincts, and his intuition and above all, avoid making decisions based upon what is most reasonable, conservative, and appears like the right thing to do. The person's task is to act in accordance with his feelings and his nature, whatever that happens to be. He may have to endure a temporary but necessary period of uncertainty and adjustment before moving forward. Or he may have to embark upon a path that, though relevant now, seems frivolous from his previous perspective. The important thing is for the person to be true to himself and pursue the most honest, heartfelt desires that he can.

The person has troubles in the areas of life ruled by Saturn's natal position. He is forced to acknowledge his flaws, and he may suffer a great loss of reputation and prestige. Activities begun during this transit flounder, intensifying the person's discouragement and depression. Business activities are not at all favored. The person has problems with real estate and building projects. He gets no help from old, wise persons or those in authority. He should surround himself with loving, supportive individuals throughout this entire period and avoid negative or pessimistic people who add to his fears and gloom. As for his health, the teeth and bones are vulnerable, and the person should therefore take calcium in a healthy form. Individuals with arthritis may experience more discomfort than usual. The person is susceptible to strange illnesses that may be difficult to properly diagnose.

When transiting Uranus squares or opposes natal Saturn, the person feels insecure and vulnerable as he loses his sense of control and authority. He undergoes strange problems in his business and career that he does not completely understand and therefore cannot correct. He is subject to deception or fraud in his professional life. Worse than all this, the foundations of the person's material existence may begin to crumble. Projects he has immersed himself in collapse or exhibit major flaws. The person is challenged to confront defects and imperfections in the form and structure of his life. He feels as if his reality is under attack as fundamental components of his existence suddenly become undependable and obsolete. This period is, for obvious reasons, very stressful.

The person loses confidence. Because he cannot rely on his usual resources, he feels weak and unprotected. He has doubts about his own character, honesty, and integrity. The harder the person's world is struck—that is, the more his creations and accomplishments disintegrate—the more fearful he becomes for his future and his sanity. The person may feel confused, disoriented, and discouraged. He is thrown off balance by current circumstances and he lacks perspective. His greatest assets now are his loving, supportive friends and relatives, whose advice and assistance he should enlist. He does not, however, benefit much from authority figures, elders, and confirmed wise persons.

This transit is much like transiting Neptune conjunct natal Saturn, though generally less intense and transforming. During the conjunction transit, the person makes major, even drastic, changes in his goals and direction in life. During the square and opposition transits, the person's problems are less profound and encompassing, though still disturbing. The person makes changes, but he rarely has to embark on a brand new career or life path.

As for his health, his teeth and bones are vulnerable, and individuals with arthritis may have more complaints than usual. The person should try to maintain as positive an attitude as possible, get plenty of rest, and eat well. He should also take calcium supplements in a healthy form. As with all Neptune hard transits, the person may experience weird health problems which are hard to diagnose.

When transiting Neptune trines or sextiles natal Saturn, the person applies his common sense and idealism to his professional life. He understands cause and effect and uses this knowledge to make his career dreams come true. His status increases and his reputation flourishes. The person looks for opportunities to be more imaginative and creative in his practical endeavors. He is well disciplined and acts with moderation and restraint. In addition, he is quick to use his intuitive abilities in order to succeed. He shows sensitivity and compassion toward others while fulfilling his own goals and ambitions. His intentions are magnanimous and humane. This is a fine period of advancement for those in occult or metaphysical professions. It is also favorable for artists, musicians, dramatists, photographers, and filmmakers, who now have an easy time making their visions a reality.

The person feels in control of his life and knows instinctively what path to pursue. He is composed, balanced, and stable. Because he is in touch with both his idealistic and practical sides, he has excellent perspective and exercises good judgement. He works hard and does not complain. He exhibits honesty, integrity, humility, and responsibility. His timing is good, and his career prospers because of this. The more success the person gains, the broader his vision becomes. It is a good time for the person to plan far into his future. His priorities are balanced. He is able to bring beauty and splendor into his career.

The transiting trine aspect is significantly more powerful than the transiting sextile. The transiting sextile only represents the opportunity to make the above effects a reality.

TRANSITING NEPTUNE CONJUNCTS NATAL URANUS

This transit occurs extremely late in life for anyone born in this century.

When transiting Neptune squares or opposes natal Uranus, the person has a difficult time maintaining his independence and asserting his individuality. His perception of reality fluctuates, and the person feels confused and disoriented. The person may have many mystical, psychic, and celestial experiences, and he has a much easier time of this spiritual transit if he understands higher states of consciousness. The areas of life ruled by Uranus' natal house position are negatively affected by this transit and they exhibit a great deal of instability. The person loses his poise and confidence and becomes very insecure. In extreme cases, he may even fear for his sanity.

The person is extremely intuitive now. He is open to all kinds of different viewpoints and realities. He may be extraordinarily idealistic and inspired, but this period is not good for practical matters. The person should postpone all major decisions and commitments, except perhaps those which concern spiritual growth, expansion of consciousness, or the pursuit of metaphysical, religious, or devotional studies. Even in these, however, the person cannot be particularly balanced because he is uncertain of his preferences. He loses touch with his individuality, independence, and personal desires—the significations of Uranus that are temporarily eroded during this transit.

The person sees more options in his life than before. His imagination and creativity are heightened. He loses his grasp of physical reality but begins to understand abstractions and philosophies that were previously beyond his scope. The person may alter his lifestyle in favor of spiritual growth. He feels isolated and peculiar, but he now has an excellent chance of confronting the ever-changing nature of reality.

When transiting Neptune trines or sextiles natal Uranus, the person is inspired by the possibility of achieving greater independence and individuality. He trusts his instincts and sets out to work on lofty dreams and visions. He is powerfully imaginative, creative, and progressive. The person's consciousness expands to include higher realities, and he loosens his grip on boundaries that would ordinarily retard his resourcefulness, ingenuity, and inventiveness. He advances toward his goals with optimism and enthusiasm.

Spiritual, mystical, and metaphysical endeavors are highly favored now. The person has experiences of heightened awareness. His intuition is very strong, and he has intuitive flashes and prophetic visions. It is one of the best times to study astrology, tarot, yoga, and the occult arts. The person also does well with science, aviation, computers, electronics, and any pursuits that are progressive. The person is inspired about new ideas and alternative lifestyles. He delves into foreign religions and exotic philosophies. He is excited about discovering truths of life and he wants to use his findings to help humanity. He sees opportunities to realize his aspirations, and he is favored by his friends and the groups he participates with.

The transiting trine aspect is significantly more powerful than the transiting sextile. The transiting sextile only represents the opportunity to make the above effects a reality.

TRANSITING NEPTUNE CONJUNCTS NATAL NEPTUNE

This transit does not occur in the normal span of a lifetime.

When transiting Neptune squares natal Neptune, the person becomes discouraged about his failure to realize his dreams. Approximately half of his life has passed (the transit occurs between the ages of forty and forty-two), and he suddenly realizes that certain ideals he has maintained since childhood are unrealistic, foolish, and unattainable. The person questions his fundamental beliefs and discovers that much of what he assumed possible was really wishful thinking. The person becomes depressed and begins to consider what changes he must make. He must be very careful, however, because his imagination is extremely active, and he is likely to delude himself.

The person loses objectivity and detachment. He even goes overboard in discouragement about unrealized ideals (which may be still attainable). He is impractical, and may therefore be better off postponing important plans. Major decisions are inappropriate now, especially if the person feels inspired by some new, seemingly invincible scheme. Business matters are not favored, and the person is easily deceived because of his excessive optimism and enthusiasm. His worst problem, aside from overcoming his depression about failed ideals, is deluding himself about his future. He should seek advice from friends and loved ones.

The more idealistic, naive, and romantic the person was in his thinking before this transit, the more he is likely to make imprudent or rash decisions now. Rather than making needed adjustments to his aspirations, he may feel so hurt that he wants to cut off everything from his past and start over anew. Such a reaction is excessive and will prove unwise.

The person may experience difficulties or upsets in his religious life. He may be confused about religion, disappointed in his spiritual growth, and disillusioned with gurus and mentors he used to idolize. He may question the existence of God or enlightenment, especially if he has been working long and hard to directly experience them and has not yet succeeded. It is a good time for meditation. The person is not limited by his usual boundaries and restrictions. He is intuitive and may enjoy activities involving astrology, metaphysics, and the occult. He may feel rather charitable and benevolent. The person should eat well and get

304   plenty of rest and recreation. He comes under considerable psychological stress if he has wasted his energy and commitment on erroneous or unattainable ideals. He may develop psychosomatic illnesses which are hard to diagnose and even harder to cure, except through natural means. The areas of life ruled by Neptune's natal house position are temporarily impaired.

TRANSITING NEPTUNE OPPOSES NATAL NEPTUNE

This transit occurs around the age of eighty to eighty-four and brings change, confusion, and an examination of ideals. The person reflects upon the goals he has pursued in his life and learns lessons about them.

When transiting Neptune trines or sextiles natal Neptune, the person's inspiration and idealism increase, especially in the areas of life ruled by Neptune's natal house position. The person's consciousness expands, and he is receptive to realities that transcend the five senses. He may take an interest in astrology, metaphysics, and the occult. Or he may begin to practice meditation. Religious endeavors are favored and the person feels very devout. He may have mystical experiences and a great deal of intuition. He is more sensitive and vulnerable than usual.

The person is less affected by personal desires than usual. He feels strongly connected to other people and all of nature. He is compassionate and charitable and may volunteer for humanitarian work. If the person is an artist by hobby or profession, he makes good progress now. This transit is also favorable for working with photography, filmmaking, magic, music, drama, oil, gas, and oceanography. The person is imaginative and inspired. His perspective broadens. This trine transit occurs around the ages of fifty-four to fifty-six and may signify a time when the person begins to seriously hunger for enlightenment.

The transiting trine aspect is significantly more powerful than the transiting sextile. The transiting sextile only represents the opportunity to make the above effects a reality.

TRANSITING NEPTUNE CONJUNCTS NATAL PLUTO

This transit has not yet occurred to anyone born in the twentieth century.

When transiting Uranus squares or opposes natal Pluto, the person is subject to unexpected, peculiar problems which undermine his power. The person's emotional well-being is disturbed and he feels insecure, unstable, and especially ineffective. He can't summon up his usual resources and suddenly believes his potential has disappeared. It is impossible to predict what will occur during this transit except to say that the areas of life ruled by Pluto's natal house position are likely to become confusing and disorienting. These are areas in which the person already feels raw, vulnerable, and sensitive.

The person becomes confused in areas of life that strike him to the core and which he desperately struggles to control. The person's health may suffer due to the constant frustration and stress he feels at his instability, psychological confusion, and lack of control. He is now compelled to search within to find solutions that can provide strength, stability, and assurance. The person may go for psychotherapy or some form of holistic healing so he can affect subconscious motivations and suppressed emotions.

The person may have dramatic psychic, mystical, or supernatural experiences. He is open to realities beyond those known to the five senses. He may visit astrologers, metaphysicians, psychics, and so on. Or he may study occult subjects on his own. Professional healers, astrologers, mystics, and spiritualists going through this transit may have tremendous insights and exciting personal experiences, but their power to help others is greatly reduced. Such individuals might consider a sabbatical for the approximately two years when transiting Neptune squares or opposes natal Pluto repeatedly for two to four months at a time.

When transiting Neptune trines or sextiles natal Pluto, the person becomes inspired about his potential, power, and ability to influence the world. He is interested in the welfare of humankind and wants to make a difference in the lives of others. His healing ability increases, and the person becomes altruistic and caring. He begins to have spiritual insights and realizes that he is the creator of his destiny. Along with this awareness comes the desire to take responsibility not only for himself but for everyone and everything he comes into contact with. This transit is very subtle, but it can give the person profound power if he is evolved enough and wise enough to integrate the spiritual lessons he learns now.

The person takes an interest in yoga, metaphysics, astrology, and the occult arts. It is an excellent time for the practice of meditation, mysticism, and all evolutionary techniques. The person benefits from psychics, palmists, and highly evolved souls. He wants to understand his subconscious mind and his deepest motivations. If he engages in psychotherapy now, he gains quick results and benefits greatly. His consciousness expands and his intuition increases dramatically. He may have remarkable psychic experiences and prophetic visions. The person is receptive to philosophies and experiences beyond the realm of the five senses. He is creative and imaginative and longs for self-improvement and the progress of his soul. He feels sure of his talents and his abilities and has a strong sense of authority. He may become fascinated by the concept of reincarnation.

The transiting trine aspect is significantly more powerful than the transiting sextile. The transiting sextile only represents the opportunity to make the above effects a reality.

P

When transiting Pluto conjuncts the natal Sun, the person undergoes an intense transformation of his behavior and lifestyle. Sudden fateful events and circumstances expand his consciousness, and he experiences phenomenal personal development and evolution. Both his spirit and willpower are regenerated, causing the person to emerge freer, more energetic, and purposeful. The person delves into the core of his being, gaining self-knowledge, self-mastery, and a clear and compelling sense of direction. This is a time of deep psychological cleansing that releases tremendous vitality, intensity, and passion into the person's life. By the end of this transit, the person can be entirely remade. His health (physically, emotionally, mentally, and spiritually) may improve beyond what he ever considered possible.

The person endures a major crisis which forces him to deal with his life honestly and to relinquish unhealthy attitudes. Thus, many obstacles which have retarded his spiritual evolution are annihilated. It is impossible to predict the specific areas of life that will be affected, but no matter what happens, the person will almost certainly experience a significant ending and a new beginning, in some realm which touches him intimately. His father (or another loved one) may become ill or die, his marriage may suddenly break apart, his business may disintegrate, he may awaken to a mystical or spiritual state of consciousness, or he may encounter any other life-altering event.

Most importantly, the person has to let go of personal attachments, materially as well as behaviorally, and flow with the changes. He must adopt a spiritual (holistic or all-encompassing), non-resistent approach to life which honors the ever-changing nature of the universe. If he does not, he will endure intense suffering, and the experience will not abate until he surrenders control. The only way the person can live gracefully now is by accepting and adhering to the natural laws of life. The more consciously the person complies, the quicker and more profound is his growth toward perfection.

Pluto, more than any other planet, brings a person into contact with his power and potential. When the Sun, the ruler of the spirit and soul, is affected by such an influence, the person recognizes his talents, creative power, and purpose in life. The person's ego expands and his leadership ability surfaces; directly before him lies the possibility of taking responsibility for his life. He becomes aware that the circumstances of his life are his own creation. The person is now capable of his greatest self-expression, and he has a chance of lasting enlightenment. However, the person must act on his instincts, impulses, and desires or he misses this incredible opportunity.

Unfortunately, many people going through this several-year transit (depending on the zodiac sign Pluto is transiting) feel as if something monumental is about to happen at any moment and never take action. During Pluto transits, it is absolutely crucial for the person to act. At no other time in his life will he be so resourceful, with such enormous potential for accomplishment, mastery, control, and authority. At no other time will his "walls" and defenses recede so much that he can experience life as it really is rather than how he interprets it.

The person is directed and focused. Wherever he concentrates his energies, he is likely to succeed. He is in touch with his desires and may even choose a new career or life path. He gives up worn-out habits and lifestyles. Because he is so much more aware of his true nature, he can no longer deny his inclinations no matter how unconventional or idiosyncratic they may be. The person may have dramatic mystical experiences, and he is drawn to yoga, astrology, meditation, metaphysics, and the occult. He may also enjoy instances of astral travel, psychic perception, and memories of past lives. He is extremely concerned with the welfare of others and may decide to volunteer for charitable causes or humanitarian efforts. The person may now become a charismatic and effective spiritual leader. Because he is completely "present" while this transit is going on, he has tremendous ability to affect others and act as a catalyst for growth and evolution. His healing abilities are also pronounced.

This is one of the best times to go for psychotherapy and self-development techniques. Growth is immediate and profound. The person also gets excellent results from affirmations and positive thinking. His sex drive increases, and he is dynamic and magnetic. He desires fame and recognition now, and chances are good that he will receive it if he is willing to pay his dues. The person has intense or disruptive experiences with his father, who may fall ill or, if he is very old, may die. It is also possible that his father may become interested in spiritual activities.

A woman experiencing this transit may meet a man who is powerful, intense, domineering, spiritual, or "driven." If she is already married when the transit occurs, her husband may begin to exhibit these characteristics. If the Sun is afflicted at birth, or is in a bad natal relationship with Pluto, the person may have problems, probably power struggles, with manipulative or oppressive men, government workers, or people in authority.

Despite his current passion and fervor, the person should try to maintain balance and guard against compulsive or obsessive behavior. If he handles this period of his life properly, without interfering in the change and evolution now taking its course, he will live the rest of his days more powerfully and with significantly greater success, health, and happiness.

℞

When transiting Pluto squares or opposes the natal Sun, the person experiences crises revolving around ambition, desire, and misuse of power. He is too attached to his own agenda, and he tries to force circumstances and other people in order to get his way. The person is aggressive, stubborn, and overly persistent. He winds up in tremendous and painful power struggles. Relationships go poorly now, and if the person does not adopt an attitude of compromise and surrender, he loses friends or does irreparable damage to relationships. He is willful and egotistical, and instead of flowing with nature he resists at every turn. He is intense in his cravings and feels no detachment at a time when he needs it most. For this reason he is graceless and inefficient in dealing with life.

The person has trouble with arrogant bosses and those in authority. He suffers on account of his father, who may begin to act domineering, pushy, and manipulative. Or the father's health may decline. Because the Sun rules men, a woman going through this transit may experience major problems with her husband or lover. The person is likely to engage in confrontations, skirmishes, and fights more frequently than ever before. He should avoid dangerous or ruthless people who could cause him physical harm. He feels more sensitive and vulnerable than usual and may suddenly become jealous and possessive. He should guard against obsessive, compulsive, and controlling behavior and let go of his fierce attachments.

It is a good time to practice self-improvement techniques. Transformation does not come without pain and struggle now, but whatever changes the person makes are profound and lasting. The person is resourceful and has access to great potential. He may engage in psychotherapy or spiritual endeavors. He may be attracted to yoga, astrology, metaphysics, and occult arts. The person has strong charisma, and his leadership energies increase. He must, however, avoid the dictatorial tendencies that surface now. The person's sex drive is strong, and his passions are acute. In some cases, the person suffers a major loss in his life. He feels victimized, but he must embrace his current situation without bitterness and with respect for the ever-changing nature of existence. During this several, year period (depending on the zodiac sign Pluto transits), the person must try for flexibility, humility, and a willingness to flow with the current changes.

P

When transiting Pluto trines or sextiles the natal Sun, the person manifests his personal power and potential. He feels a psychological or internal integration and is completely in touch with his abilities and talents. He is strong and confident. This is one of the best times for growth, development, and self-improvement. The person's regenerative energies are strong; he is able to heal himself and others. He improves existing conditions in business, friendships, his love life, and any area upon which he places his attention. He is centered, focused, and directed. He feels a sense of purpose.

The person becomes magnetic, charismatic, and intense. He exhibits leadership traits. He is extremely resourceful and creates his own opportunities. He succeeds gracefully. The person benefits from men. He gets along well with his father, who may now become powerful, successful, or interested in spirituality or self-improvement. A woman going through this transit meets suitors who are dynamic, intense, commanding, famous, or "driven." The person has good experiences with bosses and those in authority. Business is favored, as are most endeavors the person undertakes.

The person feels a need to get to the core of existence. He is attracted to astrology, yoga, metaphysics, the occult, and spiritual practices. His consciousness expands, and he is receptive to realities beyond the five senses. He is intuitive and psychic during the several years (depending on the zodiac sign Pluto transits) of this transit. His sexual energy is very strong. The person is masculine and virile, though also sensitive and open. His willpower is remarkable, and he is pioneering and persistent. He can overcome great odds, and he should take advantage of this period when success is so greatly assured.

The transiting trine aspect is significantly more powerful than the transiting sextile. The transiting sextile only represents the opportunity to make the above effects a reality.

P

When transiting Pluto conjuncts the natal Moon, the person experiences the deepest, most intense emotions of his life. He suffers major loss, pain, or separation that acts as a catalyst for profound psychological growth and transformation. The person's desires are purified and his emotional attachments purged. His feelings during this transit are raw, intense, and directly on the surface of consciousness. As he confronts his intimate needs, drives, and motivations daily for the several of years this transit (depending on the zodiac sign Pluto transits), he changes his entire personality, psychology, temperament, and habit patterns. If the person deals courageously, consciously, and responsibly with the evolutionary and transformative process at hand, he will improve every facet of his emotional health: his flexibility, resilience, adaptability, and ability to respond instinctively and spontaneously. When the transit ends, he will no longer be as emotionally reactive as before.

This transit and the process it generates is, however, an extremely delicate and demanding one. The person constantly endures emotional death-and-rebirth experiences that make him feel insecure and unstable. The person recognizes unhealthy behavior and attitudes that need changing through crises that arise. He has to face powerful fears, complexes, and anxieties coming from deep within his subconscious, stemming from childhood and infancy, or he will suffer ever-increasing emotional and psychological pain. He must be willing to relinquish control and release old ties at a time when he has difficulty doing so. His feelings are deeper and more intense than ever before, and he shows little neutrality, objectivity, and impartiality.

As with all major Pluto transits, the person may be attracted to metaphysics, mysticism, yoga, and spiritual studies. He wants to get to the core of his existence and understand the workings of nature. His intuition and psychic tendencies increase. He is more sensitive, receptive, and empathetic than ever. He may have mystical experiences as well as important insights into his psychology and behavior. Self-improvement efforts and spiritual practices produce immediate and dramatic results for the person. He benefits tremendously from meditation, introspection, and positive thinking. It is an excellent time to engage in analysis or psychotherapy. The person's ability to transform himself is supreme. So is his creative ability. He is especially successful with affirmations now because his thoughts are imbued with feeling.

The person's maternal energy expands and he is suddenly very nurturing. He may exhibit powerful healing ability. He is concerned with universal welfare and he contributes greatly by his warmth, caring, and heartfelt connection to others. He feels an affinity with the entire human race and may be consumed with a desire to merge with loved ones.

The person has intense experiences with women. He meets women who are passionate, powerful, spiritual, and highly evolved. He may also encounter problems with women who are domineering, manipulative, and "driven." In his dealings with them, he should beware of power struggles and consider adopting a benign and nonresistent attitude until this transit ends. Above all, he must avoid compulsive or obsessive behavior stemming from emotional upheaval, undue sentimentality, and oversensitivity.

The person may confront important unresolved issues with his mother during this transit. His mother may become interested in evolution and spiritual practices. She may also, however, become overbearing or bossy. If the person's mother is old or in failing health, her condition may dramatically worsen. During transiting Pluto's conjunctions to the Sun or Moon, the person's father (the Sun) or mother (the Moon) may develop cancer and die. This only occurs, however, when many other astrological factors confer, and therefore the reader should not become alarmed about facing this transit.

The person experiences changes in his domestic sphere. He may move to another house that provides greater security and happiness. Or he may significantly improve his existing house. The person may have flooding or water problems. If the person has an interest in farming or archeology, he can make tremendous progress in these realms. As for his health, the person's stomach, breast, and brain are vulnerable. Women during this transit may have menstrual fluctuations or oddities. The person senses how to deal effectively and powerfully with the public now, a skill that helps him gain fame and recognition.

As a result of this transit, the person learns how to function in a more emotionally balanced, moderate, and objective way. He gains insights into his sensitivities, vulnerabilities, motivations, and inner workings, and this frees him emotionally and psychologically.

P

When transiting Pluto squares or opposes the natal Moon, the person suffers emotionally. He is moody, sensitive, and vulnerable. He is too attached to his feelings and may become possessive and jealous. Unhealthy behavioral patterns surface that need to be confronted, healed, and purged. The person is deeply affected by childhood memories, psychological complexes, and subconscious motivations. Therefore, it is a good time for psychotherapy or any technique that helps the person become more emotionally flexible and open. If he seeks growth now, he is rewarded by profound and lasting progress. Such work is anything but easy because the person is hypersensitive, touchy, and emotionally volatile.

The person is likely to experience major disturbances with his family. He may have problems with his mother, whose health may decline or who may become domineering, manipulative, and bossy. He must beware of confrontations and power struggles with intense, controlling women. A man may have marital problems or discord in his love life during this transit. The person should get plenty of rest and recreation because he is under stress, whether he knows it or not. He must deal squarely with his feelings now or he may develop ulcers or digestive problems. Other health risks include problems with the breast, brain, and (for a woman) menstrual cycle.

The person is intuitive now and may be attracted to yoga, metaphysics, occult arts, or any practice which helps him understand the workings of creation. Activities with the public may bring problems. The person feels restless or agitated. He feels his desires keenly and must beware of compulsive, obsessive, or childish behavior. In extreme cases, the person undergoes intense transformation. He may lose something or someone dear to him, causing severe pain. If this occurs, he must learn to experience, rather than resist, his grief and flow with nature.

P

When transiting Pluto trines or sextiles the natal Moon, the person improves his domestic life and confronts personal problems he normally represses. He feels secure and he gets along well with his family, especially the women in his life. He works on unhealthy habits and psychological weaknesses. The person is emotionally balanced, and current endeavors go well because of this. He is more flexible and resilient than usual. He is resourceful and he focuses on self-improvement. It is an excellent time for therapy or practicing spiritual techniques. The person is drawn to yoga, astrology, metaphysics, and the occult. He makes rapid progress now, and his consciousness expands dramatically.

The person benefits from his mother. His mother may become interested in spiritual matters. He meets women who are powerful, intense, famous, spiritual, or "driven." He operates instinctively and has powerful psychic experiences. The person succeeds in his dealings with the public. He has good results with land, real estate, and home improvements. The person's healing ability increases, he feels protective of others, and he wants to help. It is a wonderful time for those involved in the healing arts. The person has more emotional depth than usual. He does well with affirmations because his thoughts are imbued with feeling.

As with most Pluto transits to personal planets, the person feels an urge to understand himself and the workings of the universe. He gains psychological insights easily because he has access to his subconscious. Also, he is particularly sensitive and receptive. Relationships go smoothly, and the person feels inner well-being. He is confident that he can handle any emotional or psychological problem that might surface.

The transiting trine aspect is significantly more powerful than the transiting sextile. The transiting sextile only represents the opportunity to make the above effects a reality.

P

When transiting Pluto conjuncts natal Mercury, the person's intellectual powers and communicative abilities intensify dramatically. Concentration and focus are intense, and the person delves more deeply into ideas than he ever has. His reasoning ability becomes strong, and he excels at problem solving. The person is resourceful, and he has access to the entire range of his consciousness, even his subconscious mind. He is relentless in his search for information and answers to lifelong, core issues. He now becomes interested in the mysteries of life and may investigate astrology, mysticism, metaphysics, the occult, or other progressive, all-encompassing philosophies.

The person communicates more powerfully than ever before. His speech influences others, and he should think carefully before speaking because his words will not be forgotten. Even his thoughts carry tremendous psychic (or telepathic) power. The person's creative self-expression is at an all-time high. He speaks powerfully and uses words to express his exact meaning. If he is involved in writing or any related profession, then he now produces the deepest, most powerful and profound work of his lifetime. Educational matters of all kind are also favored. It is an excellent time for affirmations, positive thinking, and creative visualization. However, because his thoughts carry power, the person must beware of negative thinking or critical attitudes toward others. The amount of energy behind the person's thoughts is so intense that wherever he focuses his consciousness, the effects will be great. Stubbornness or fixed thinking can bring devastating effects if the person's ideas are wrong.

The person benefits tremendously from psychotherapy or analysis. If he seeks better mental health and is open-minded with his therapist or guide, he will gain the deepest, most profound insights and self-understanding possible. It is an excellent time to study or investigate the field of psychology. Meditation is another avenue of self-development that produces especially significant results during the several years of this transit (depending upon which zodiac sign Pluto transits). Because the person's ability to concentrate and his perfectionist tendencies are so intense, any techniques that help him transcend the surface of his mind are extremely effective.

In order to take full advantage of the remarkable opportunity this transit brings, it is crucial for the person to consciously choose where he wishes to focus his energies. Most people see major transits to Mercury as somewhat less substantial and meaningful than major transits to other personal planets (Sun, Moon, and Venus). They may not appreciate the role the mind plays in producing the ultimate state of human life, enlightenment. Because the eternal bliss of final liberation occurs through the refinement and purification of both the mind and nervous system (which Mercury rules), the person should take full advantage of transits to Mercury. Pluto's conjunction to Mercury provides the longest, most sustained opportunity for growth of consciousness of all transits.

Unfortunately, the significance of this transit has been ignored because 1) society is just now beginning to awaken to spiritual realities and 2) unlike most Pluto transits to personal planets, the person is not in a state of pain and is therefore not compelled to focus on growth or self-development. Unlike Pluto's transits to all the other planets, the person is absolutely free to direct his consciousness wherever he wishes. If he is spiritually inclined at all, the person should consider seriously whether to use his mental power, perception, and dexterity for worldly accomplishment or spiritual growth. As a renowned Indian yogi once proclaimed, "To get a human body without gaining enlightenment is like selling a diamond for the price of spinach."

The person excels in science, languages, and the deciphering of puzzles now. He is psychic and highly intuitive. The person must guard against power struggles, whether mental, verbal, or written. He must also avoid trying to overpower or dominate others with his opinions. As for his health, his lungs, intestines, and nervous system are vulnerable. If Mercury is badly afflicted at birth or in a detrimental relationship with Pluto natally, the person may suffer nervous disorders or speech problems.

P

When transiting Pluto squares or opposes natal Mercury, the person becomes emotionally attached to his thinking and loses objectivity about his ideas. He becomes opinionated and dogmatic and winds up in arguments and intellectual power struggles. He is stubborn and needs to learn how to compromise. Relationships go poorly now because the person lacks sensitivity and tact. He tries to manipulate or overpower others with his communications. He criticizes people too readily. Meanwhile, he is more sensitive to criticism than anyone. He is touchy, irritable, and nervous. When Mercury is heavily afflicted in the natal birthchart, the person has mental problems or, in a worst-case scenario, a nervous breakdown. Rest and recreation are extremely important now, and the person should guard against stress and overwork. He should avoid discordant surroundings and any conditions that jar his senses.

Existing worries, problems, and phobias intensify, and the person may suddenly find himself in an unexpected crisis. No matter how hard he tries to explain himself, he feels isolated and misunderstood. Because he cannot separate his ego from his thinking, he is less effective than usual in almost all areas. He has problems with educators, writers, and the press. He must be careful not to accept bad advice. The person should postpone negotiations and signing contracts, if possible. His ideas are challenged by others who are offended by his emphatic presentation. His lungs, intestines, and nervous system are at risk.

The person may have problems during short journeys. He experiences delays, mishaps, and unexpected scheduling problems. He should avoid traveling to risky areas and any unsettled places that might exacerbate his sensitivity and irritability. He has more problems with machinery than usual, especially with televisions, radios, tape recorders, telephones, typewriters, and so on. The person may delve into subjects which provide answers to the mysteries of life. He is attracted to metaphysics, astrology, and the occult. He also looks for solutions to long-standing dilemmas within his life.

This transit is more difficult for individuals involved in a communications career. Writers, teachers, and journalists may do some of their deepest, most intense work now, but may have difficulty getting their work recognized and accepted during the several years (depending on the zodiac sign Pluto transits) of this transit. The person must beware of embracing fanatical ideas, using incorrect information, and behaving self-righteously. Humility, openness, and regard for the viewpoints of others are essential to survive this period without struggle and suffering.

℘

When transiting Pluto trines or sextiles natal Mercury, the person's mental faculties and communication abilities increase, intensify, and deepen. The person's thinking becomes more subtle and his mind more penetrating. He excels at investigation and analysis. He is like a detective who does not miss a trick. The person is very persuasive. He uses words to great advantage and says exactly what he means. This is an excellent time for writers, educators, journalists, and anyone involved in communication. It is also a wonderful time to engage in negotiations and sign contracts.

The person is extremely thorough during this transit. He can solve all kinds of problems and create solutions to complex predicaments. If the person has procrastinated about important mental pursuits, such as literary works, research projects, or lecture tours, because of the effort involved, he may now achieve his goals with minimal struggle.

The person becomes curious and excited about new ideas and philosophies, especially those which explain the mysteries of life. He is drawn to astrology, yoga, metaphysics, and the occult. He is focused and unrelenting in his search for truth. Because Mercury, which rules the nervous system, is so well-aspected now, the person feels stable, secure, and confident. He is not bothered by fears and does not try to repress psychological dilemmas. Instead, he looks for insights into himself and his behavior. He is open and receptive, and his reasoning powers are acute. He is keen and sharp, and he probes the depths of subjects effortlessly.

The person benefits from teachers, intellectuals, and the press. If he attempts meditation, contemplation, or any mental technique for evolution, he attains the highest results. Affirmations and positive thinking bring the person quick results. In order to use this transit to the best advantage, the person should use this time to plan his future. In addition to having remarkably acute perception, he also exhibits broad, holistic thinking. He may never again see things so clearly and profoundly for such an extended time. The transiting trine aspect is significantly more powerful than the transiting sextile. The transiting sextile only represents the opportunity to make the above effects a reality.

P

When transiting Pluto conjuncts natal Venus, the person learns the greatest love lessons of his life. If he is single, he becomes involved in an extremely potent and fateful relationship that changes his life forever. If he is married, repressed problems surface in order to be dealt with. Circumstances conspire to teach the person how to love selflessly, generously, and unconditionally. Such behavior, however, does not come effortlessly. The person has trouble maintaining any detachment or objectivity in his love life. He is consumed with passion. His sexual feelings run deeper than ever before, and he wants both to possess and merge with his lover.

However, as with all major Pluto transits, control does not lie in the person's hands. Emotional or psychological complexes that keep the person from fulfilling his desires surface so that he can analyze and eliminate them. The person discovers his real motives in love from his mate's response. His lover will not tolerate a relationship based on need or self-gratification. If he does not allow his partner enough freedom, his partner will leave. The person must embrace the lessons he learns now, even though the process may be painful. He must respond appropriately to the situation at hand and give up any character flaws that stand in the way of healthy behavior. An attitude of humility and surrender is crucial to the person's well-being now. Otherwise, he torments himself terribly by resisting the force of nature guiding him towards more happiness. On the other hand, if the person handles the lessons maturely and responsibly, his emotional and psychological health will improve tremendously, and he will enjoy much greater freedom and happiness in love from then on.

The person falls in love with someone who is powerful, intense, passionate, and "driven." Or, the loved one could be compulsive, obsessive, famous, or highly spiritual. In certain cases, especially where Venus is seriously afflicted or in a bad relationship with Pluto at birth, the person attracts someone who is aggressive, domineering, bossy, or has criminal tendencies. Relationships during this period are characterized by extreme physical attraction, and they feel predestined and important. The person may find himself being paid back by his lover for things he did in a past life. Such payback may be positive, negative, or a combination of both.

During this transit, which may last several years depending on the zodiac sign Pluto transits, the person has some of the most intense sexual experiences of his life. His sexuality and procreative powers intensify, and he feels erotic and aroused. He has an urge to probe the mysteries of love and sex. He is experimental and may break society's sexual rules and standards. He pursues beauty, sensuality, pleasure, and lust. He also appreciates culture and refinement, and if the person is an artist, he now produces some of his greatest, most moving works of art.

Despite the difficulties of this transit, the person may enjoy a sublimely pure and wonderfully profound experience of universal love. During the moments when he is able to forget his own selfish needs, he soars to the heights of devotion. He even discovers what it means to love without any boundaries. He discovers not just unconditional love but love that flows so unceasingly that the person loses awareness of who does the loving and who is being loved. The person's love is so complete that it flows right back to him, producing an experience of spiritual unity or oneness with the universe. In rare cases, the person experiences a glimpse, or more, of enlightenment—ultimate liberation, God consciousness, or nirvana—brought on through development of his heart chakra.

The person becomes particularly attractive to the opposite sex. He is magnetic, alluring, and fascinating. However, he is also very sensitive and vulnerable. Rejection or criticism from lovers is especially painful. Furthermore, the person may suffer because of possessiveness and jealousy. He is likely to question his desirability and lovability. It is an excellent time to engage in therapy or analysis in order to work on intimacy and healthier ways of relating. It is the best time to work on sexual problems such as frigidity or impotency. Traditional astrological texts report that "intrigues" in love are possible, as well as intense financial fluctuations.

The person's throat, kidneys, skin, and reproductive system are vulnerable during this period. Finally, it should be mentioned that this transit could coincide with the death or disappearance of a lover, which would bring phenomenal pain, as well as tremendous growth. But the likelihood of such an occurrence is quite rare and not to be expected.

P

When transiting Pluto squares or opposes natal Venus, the person has difficulties in his love life because of his overly intense passions. The person hungers for intimacy and sexual pleasure, and he chooses partners based upon physical attraction rather than compatibility or friendship. His feelings are strong, and he is in danger of obsessive and compulsive behavior. Love affairs begun now are rarely long-lasting. They are likely to be turbulent and highly erotic. The person is attracted to lovers who are quite different from himself in nature and temperament. These partners may also be intense, powerful, domineering, and manipulative. Or they may be spiritual, famous, or "driven." The person should guard against entering a relationship in which he will be taken advantage of by an overbearing mate.

The person is extraordinarily sensitive and vulnerable now. He feels rejection more acutely than ever before. He has karmic experiences in love and is guided by his current circumstances to confront psychological complexes and unhealthy behavior in his love life. He is fascinated by his lover and may lose his objectivity in the relationship. He is highly attractive to the opposite sex. If the person is married, he has major conflicts with his spouse. He may also feel unduly jealous or possessive of that person. In some cases, the person becomes captivated by someone outside the marriage and engages in an intense extramarital affair, that brings more pain and complication than the person bargained for.

The person's sex drive is stronger than ever. He feels particularly aroused. He is also sexually experimental during the several years (depending on the zodiac sign Pluto transits) of this transit. The person creates powerful and moving works of art but may have difficulty getting the recognition he deserves. If the person is involved in an unfulfilling, lifeless relationship, he may decide to cut his losses and move on. No matter what occurs during this transit, the person has an opportunity to transform his ability to love. The person's throat, kidneys, skin, and reproductive system are under attack. Because Venus is an indicator of money, the person may have financial problems now. He should be wary of speculations and get-rich-quick schemes.

P

When transiting Pluto trines or sextiles natal Venus, the person enjoys the greatest joys and blessings that love has to offer. He creates, either within his existing relationship or in a brand new romance, a bond of loyalty, devotion, respect, deep affection, and profound intimacy. The person may meet a lover whom he has known in a past lifetime and whom he feels destined to be with forever. That person may also be intense, powerful, famous, or highly spiritual. The person is extremely aroused and has wonderful sexual experiences. He is attractive to the opposite sex and has a magnetic, alluring quality about him. He is very receptive to or perhaps psychic with his partner.

The person is sensuous, romantic, creative, and expressive. He appreciates beauty to the fullest. His aesthetic sensibilities are heightened, and he does some of his best artwork now. His current artwork is not only deep and profound, but it is also acknowledged and appreciated. The person is happy. He enjoys the sweetness of life. He goes to more movies, plays, concerts and other forms of entertainment and is thrilled with his experiences. He is popular and his social life goes well. He is favored in financial dealings and may suddenly make a large amount of money. He may receive gifts, beautiful objects, jewelry, comforts, and works of art. Or he may purchase a new wardrobe.

The person does not take love lightly during this several-year period (depending on the zodiac sign Pluto transits). His feelings are deep, and his passions run high. However, he has complete control of his emotions and does not lose his objectivity or balance. The person finds a genuine and sincere partner, and he learns the true meaning of love. His creativity is strong.

The transiting trine aspect is significantly more powerful than the transiting sextile. The transiting sextile only represents the opportunity to make the above effects a reality.

P

When transiting Pluto conjuncts natal Mars, the person gains unlimited energy to accomplish his goals. He suddenly becomes more aggressive in pursuing his own desires. The person is enthusiastic, active, and dynamic; he intends to win. It is an excellent time for competition and sports activities. The person feels strong and healthy. He succeeds at normally difficult or strenuous tasks quickly and painlessly now. He is clear, focused, and purposeful. He moves toward his goals like an arrow to its target.

The person must be careful, however, not to force his will on others. He needs to show sensitivity toward people. Otherwise, he creates resistance in others and may wind up in quarrels or intense power struggles. The person wants his way and may be ruthless in his actions. His temper may flare up more than ever before. Because the person's energy is so unrestrained during this transit, there is a danger of volatility, excessive risk taking, and accidents. No matter how invincible the person feels, he should avoid even remotely dangerous situations. If Mars is afflicted at birth or in a bad natal relationship with Pluto, the person could attract unexpected violence or brutality. Women, especially, should be on guard because sexual harassment or worse is possible during Pluto-Mars transits.

The person is especially courageous now. He is decisive, determined, and persistent. He can triumph over enemies and achieve success with ease. The person suddenly becomes extremely physical, and his masculine energies increase. His sex drive intensifies, and he is more passionate than usual. Men should refrain from harsh or crude behavior during this transit and be careful not to force themselves on women. The person's ego expands. He may behave flamboyantly or act macho.

The person is a powerhouse of energy now and should take advantage of this several-year period (depending on the sign Pluto transits) to the fullest. He can make tremendous gains in his life if he consciously chooses to direct his magnificent strength in a wise and prudent way.

Weak individuals or those with flawed character may resort to crime during this transit.

P

When transiting Pluto squares or opposes natal Mars, the person is obsessed with winning. He does whatever it takes to get his way, occasionally hurting people around him. The person is forceful and potentially ruthless. He lacks discipline, prudence, control, and patience. He is controlled by his ego, and he loses perspective. Naturally, he clashes with others. This is a difficult transit that can bring arguments, accidents, and violence. The person takes risks without thinking and he does not realize he is in danger. He should avoid criminals and hostile persons during the several years (depending on the zodiac sign Pluto transits) of this period.

The person is more physical than usual, and his excess energy quickly leads to trouble. He comes into contact with antagonistic people who may try push him around. His reacts with anger, rage, or fierce competitiveness; however, a wiser tactic would be to adopt an attitude of nonresistance and walk away, if possible. The person's sex drive increases tremendously. He must, however, beware of forcing his attention on uninterested or unwilling partners. Women should be very careful about dating aggressive, persistent men who may abuse them sexually. It is an especially poor time for love relationships. The person or his mate acts willful, harsh, or cruel.

The person craves excitement. He is impulsive and reckless. He should not handle guns, ammunition, and explosives, and he should be very guarded while driving now. His attention is focused outward, and he is therefore unaided by his intuition. He can regulate his energy by engaging in safe exercise or noncompetitive sports on a daily basis. The person should refrain from devious behavior in fulfilling his desires. He must try for discipline and self-control. In extreme cases, the person exhibits criminal tendencies.

P

When transiting Pluto trines or sextiles natal Mars, the person has great energy for realizing his ambitions and fulfilling his desires. He is focused and purposeful. Wherever he places his attention he is likely to succeed. He is determined and persistent. He is also confident and assertive in a graceful way. He feels comfortable putting his desires above those of others, yet he is not driven by ego, conceit, or vanity. During these several years (depending on the zodiac sign Pluto transits), the person has a marvelous opportunity to advance toward major goals with little effort. He is enthusiastic, motivated, and overcomes obstacles by his perseverance.

The person exhibits leadership qualities. He takes charge and directs others in a masterful way. He is courageous and does not back down from a challenge. He pursues his goals and he does not give in to discouragement or despair. He works hard. The person does well in sports and all forms of competition. His mechanical skills increase, and he is able to repair things more easily than usual.

Sexual activities are favored. The person is strong and passionate. He is successful in his flirtations, and he wins many sexual partners because of his powerful charisma and sex appeal. The person is healthy and enjoys exercise now. He may decide to work seriously on his fitness. He has tremendous vigor, vitality, and zest.

The transiting trine aspect is significantly more powerful than the transiting sextile. The transiting sextile only represents the opportunity to make the above effects a reality.

P

When transiting Pluto conjuncts natal Jupiter, the person is successful in his endeavors because of his optimism, enthusiasm, and confidence. He does things in a big way, and his current goals are larger than usual. The person experiences a rebirth or regeneration of his interest in religion. He is consumed with truth and feels compelled to determine the purpose of life. He looks for the best path toward freedom. He analyzes life from the broadest of perspectives and concentrates on planning for a successful and fulfilling future. The person thinks constantly of the values, principles, and morals he must embrace in order to get the most out of his experience. He wants to make a big impact on society with his positive actions.

The person sells his ideas to others easily. He is cheerful and spirited, and he feels extremely lucky. He may have a strong urge to gamble or speculate now. But he should be careful because success in this realm depends largely on the condition of natal Jupiter and the relationship between Pluto and Jupiter in the birthchart. During the several years (depending on the zodiac sign Pluto transits) of this transit, the person must beware of extravagance, excessive behavior, and overindulgence in all areas.

The person searches for higher knowledge. He wants to delve into subjects that explain life from a universal perspective. He is interested in all religions and philosophies, especially foreign ones. He may be drawn to astrology, metaphysics, and the occult. He is looking for the meaning of existence. Some people learn about higher states of consciousness during this transit and decide to practice spiritual techniques in order to gain these states. Or the person may join a spiritual movement or religious order in pursuit of higher evolution. It is an excellent time for self-development and spiritual growth, because the person has tremendous faith and devotion. He perceives order in the universe and feels integrated with nature.

The person may have intense experiences with bankers, money-lenders, and rich people. His finances may dramatically increase or decrease. Business is generally favored because the person functions with a sense of abundance. In some cases, the person gains fame, honor, or great success now.

P

When transiting Pluto squares or opposes natal Jupiter, the person has problems in his religious and spiritual life. He is manipulated or coerced by priests, ministers, rabbis, religious teachers, spiritual leaders, or other pious people. He encounters oppressive individuals who hamper his freedom and attack his credibility. In order to deal with the situation, he is forced to examine his beliefs, values, and morals. Unfortunately, though, he lacks perspective. He blows things out of proportion and makes poor judgements. He is consumed with his own opinions and convictions.

The person craves success, accomplishment, and prosperity. However, he is too expansive, and he fails to pay attention to details. He lacks caution, prudence, and discretion. The person must strive for moderation. He must beware of extravagance and excessive behavior. He is overconfident and arrogant. He feels lucky and prosperous, but he is in danger of major financial losses. The person would be wiser to wait until the transit has completely passed (until Pluto has made its last and final transiting aspect) and then consider how to make money.

The person may have problems with bankers, investors, money-lenders, and rich people. He should be careful with speculations or avoid them altogether now unless natal Jupiter is very well-aspected or Jupiter and Pluto are in a very favorable relationship at birth. The person may also have troubles with professors, teachers, and any university and college personnel he encounters in his higher education. He may have difficulties with lawyers, or the person may intentionally or unintentionally break a law.

It is a poor time to deal with churches and religious institutions. The person should be careful not to go overboard in his spiritual beliefs. He may behave somewhat fanatically or self-righteously. The person's liver is at risk, and he may temporarily suffer from allergies.

P

When transiting Pluto trines or sextiles natal Jupiter, the person gains wealth and success. Obstacles to his freedom and joy suddenly disappear. The person feels lucky, and he functions with a feeling of abundance. He is optimistic, tolerant, and peaceful. Spiritual endeavors are favored. The person may have a special religious experience that fortifies his faith in God. He benefits from priests, ministers, gurus, religious teachers, and other devout persons. He searches for the meaning of life. It is an excellent period to study yoga, metaphysics, mysticism, and all teachings of higher knowledge.

The person may travel to other countries and gain great happiness there. He wants to learn everything he can about different cultures. He gets along well with foreigners and broadens his understanding of humanity through these associations. The person's business enterprises flourish. He is eager to increase his accomplishments and expand his power and influence. He earns large sums of money more easily than usual and is favored by bankers, moneylenders, and wealthy people. He may have financial windfalls or profits from investments and speculations. Unless Jupiter is afflicted or in a bad relationship with Pluto natally, it is a good time for gambling and financial risk taking.

The person receives honors, awards, loans, and grants from colleges. He is happy and successful in his educational endeavors. He exercises good judgement and is mindful of proper values, morals, and principles. He wants to do good deeds and improve society. The person benefits from attorneys and may suddenly take an interest in law.

The transiting trine aspect is significantly more powerful than the transiting sextile. The transiting sextile only represents the opportunity to make the above effects a reality.

P

When transiting Pluto conjuncts natal Saturn, the person endures a long period of burdensome responsibilities, stressful conditions, and unyielding external pressures. He has problems with domineering, manipulative persons in authority, especially in his job. He has intense experiences revolving around career, but instead of flowing with the changes, he resists at every turn. He is obsessed with security, caution, and holding on to his old ways at a time when he needs to let go of everything obsolete. It is time for the person to look ahead toward new responsibilities. He now has the ability to forge new paths in his life that eventually lead to great success and personal growth.

The person is compelled to concentrate on areas of life (corresponding to Saturn's natal position) in which he is handicapped by fears, insecurities, and uncertainties. These areas hold great benefit both spiritually and materially for the person, and he finally makes progress in them. He begins to build a solid base in these normally difficult realms. He is unusually sincere, and his dedication and perseverance are stronger than ever. Commitments made now bring monumental results as the years progress. For this reason, the person must not delay or procrastinate about decisions he knows he must make. Unfortunately, many individuals are so scared of change during this period that they feel paralyzed by what seem to be overpowering circumstances. If the person perpetuates the status quo and tries to hold on to what he believes is comfortable, he suffers hardship, fatigue, mental strain, and health problems. This transit is difficult for most people.

The person must beware of excessive discipline and an overblown sense of responsibility. He may be too austere, conservative, and hard on himself. The person puts up with unacceptable burdens at work and inappropriate demands from superiors. He is hardworking and has more patience than ever before, but he needs to appreciate his own worth. The person has good organizational ability now. He may experience a change of perspective which transforms his major ambitions. His task during this period is to plan long-term goals, design workable strategies, and then go straight to work.

P

When transiting Pluto squares or opposes natal Saturn, the person endures hardship and anxiety, as fundamental structures of his life are destroyed by external forces outside of his control. The person has problems in his professional life that tax his patience, strength, and endurance to the limit. His greatest ambitions are thwarted throughout the several years (depending on the zodiac sign Pluto transits) of this transit, and he may become frustrated and depressed. He feels manipulated by his superiors and burdened by the demands placed upon him. Dealings with people in authority are discouraging if not painful. The person is under pressure to fulfill too many difficult responsibilities. He is overworked.

The person should get plenty or rest and recreation now and try not to take life too seriously. He needs to take calcium supplements in order to strengthen his teeth and bones, which suddenly become vulnerable. Health problems may occur because the person grows fatigued by stress, strain, and worry. People with arthritis are likely to have worse symptoms than usual.

The person is plagued by guilt, an overblown sense of responsibility, and feelings of scarcity. He is hard on himself and should do his best not to censor his self-expression. He should make whatever changes are necessary and research whatever he needs to know in order to accomplish long-range goals. The person is aided by great patience and discipline and can execute painstaking work normally too tedious for him. During all Pluto-Saturn transits, the person resists change and tries to maintain existing conditions even when they are obsolete. If the person does this now, he suffers tremendously. He should look for the positive things that happen when he lets go.

In some cases, the person suddenly has to take care of old or ailing parents or relatives.

P

When transiting Pluto trines or sextiles natal Saturn, the person is highly practical and efficient, and he puts his ideas into practice gracefully. He understands cause and effect better than ever before. The person builds, organizes, and structures the externals of his life to ensure a fulfilling future. He climbs steadily toward his goals and goes a long way toward fulfilling his major ambitions. His wisdom increases, and he analyzes matters from the broadest perspective. The person is patient, austere, and thrifty. He works hard and without complaint no matter how tedious his task. He is persistent, purposeful, and successful.

The person makes significant progress in his self-development by successfully handling difficult areas of life (corresponding to Saturn's natal house position). Normally these areas would paralyze him with fear or cause him to respond with rigid behavior. Now, resourceful and composed, he makes positive changes wherever needed. His career activities are greatly favored, and the person may be promoted to a leadership or administrative position because his wisdom and experience become conspicuous. He exhibits common sense, is humble, responsible, and extremely thorough. He benefits from his elders and those in authority.

The person succeeds in construction or real estate. He creates structures which are sturdy and long-lasting. He does some of his best work ever. His focus and control are masterful, and wherever he places his attention, he obtains profound results.

The transiting trine aspect is significantly more powerful than the transiting sextile. The transiting sextile only represents the opportunity to make the above effects a reality.

P

When transiting Pluto conjuncts natal Uranus, the person becomes consumed with independence and freedom. He encounters a period of major upheaval and has powerful urges to break away from anything that restricts him. He is excited about progress and impatient with convention. The person follows his own beliefs and instincts. He feels separate from the values of society and his elders, and he breaks from tradition with neither deliberation nor regret. In recent times, this transit only occurs during the last thirty years of the twentieth century and approximately the first forty years of the twenty-first century. During the twentieth century, the individuals going through this transit are youngsters and pre-teens. The person's youth is therefore a factor in how this transit is experienced.

The person's perception broadens. He seeks the truth, and because he trusts his own experience so implicitly now, he is not easily fooled. He lives in the moment. He opens up to realities beyond the five senses and may become interested in yoga, metaphysics, astrology, and mysticism. His leadership ability increases, and the person may attract others because of his individualism, determination, and magnetism. The person acts on desires he has had for a long time. He must be careful, however, of defiant, rebellious, and willful behavior.

The person is excited and highly creative. He feels extremely detached and experiments with new ways of behaving. Endeavors involving science, computers, aviation, and progressive technologies are very favored. The person may succeed at creating inventions. He comes into contact with people who are spiritual, mystical, fascinating, and spirited. He meets with sudden, unexpected opportunities. He has intense, possibly disruptive, experiences in the realms of life ruled by Uranus' natal house position. Such experiences affect the person deeply for the rest of his life.

℞

When transiting Pluto squares or opposes natal Uranus, the person undergoes change and upheaval aroused by external or societal forces around him. He experiences sudden endings and new beginnings, and the person must restructure anything in his life that inhibits his independence and individuality. This period brings instability and unpredictable experiences. Therefore flexibility and surrender are crucial. The person feels a strong urge to rebel and to influence others. He must, however, beware of extreme or fanatical behavior. If he does not maintain some balance and moderation, he offends others and winds up losing whatever advantages he may have possessed.

The person is extremely willful now. He experiences major changes in the areas of life ruled by Uranus' natal house position. He is excited and enjoys many new interests. He gains some detachment, which broadens his perspective and helps him to live in the moment. He is experimental, creative, inventive, and innovative. He is also stubborn. Relationships may suffer due to his impatience, erratic behavior, and unwillingness to compromise. He has little respect for tradition, conservative methods, or authority figures. He wants results, and he wants them quickly.

The person seeks the truth. He is open to new ideas and philosophies, and he is attracted to realities beyond the five senses. He becomes interested in metaphysics, astrology, yoga, or mysticism. He meets people who are individualistic, revolutionary, high-spirited, or rebellious. The person may drastically alter his lifestyle now. He does everything he can to ensure a liberated future, but in his fervor, destroys valuable possessions and resources. During the several years of this transit (depending on the zodiac sign Pluto transits), the person is under more stress than usual. He should get plenty of rest, recreation, and enjoyable exercise. He may also benefit from vitamin supplements.

P

When transiting Pluto trines or sextiles natal Uranus, the person experiences a period of exciting change and progress. He improves existing conditions by his creativity, experimentation, and innovation. He feels liberated, and he does things he has always wanted to do. He is active and engages in many new interests. The person is highly intuitive and he acts on his impulses. He is dynamic and expressive. He lives in the moment, he trusts himself implicitly, and he is unaffected by psychological complexes or dilemmas. The person is successful because he is objective and detached. Wherever he places his attention, he progresses.

The person is receptive to higher realities. He benefits tremendously from astrology, yoga, metaphysics, mysticism, and New Age philosophies. He may even have startling spiritual experiences or flashes of insight, genius, or prophetic vision. The person succeeds quickly and easily in science, electronics, computer technology, and anything that is ahead of the times. Everywhere he looks he sees opportunities to break boundaries. He ignores popular opinion and traditional viewpoints. He is original and unconcerned about what others think of him.

The person comes into contact with spiritual persons and highly evolved individuals. He meets people who are independent, fascinating, inspired, and individualistic. The person may join humanitarian groups that promote social freedom, self-development, or higher consciousness. He alters his lifestyle in ways that offer him more options and fewer boundaries.

The transiting trine aspect is significantly more powerful than the transiting sextile. The transiting sextile only represents the opportunity to make the above effects a reality.

P

When transiting Pluto conjuncts natal Neptune, the person's religious and spiritual inclinations intensify, and his perception expands. He becomes aware of the higher realities of life and begins to directly experience the infinity of his soul, the unity of all beings, and the true meaning of heaven or nirvana. The person is extraordinarily sensitive, and he spontaneously gains self-knowledge. He is in tune with nature. He is strikingly clairvoyant now, and he may have prophetic visions. If he has been practicing spiritual techniques to gain enlightenment for a long time, he now reaps the rewards of his efforts and tastes the bliss of higher states of consciousness. He also surrenders completely to the higher forces of the universe and feels a direct link with God. The person sees life differently now; he embraces a new reality. By the end of this transit, he fully comprehends the limitations of ordinary perception and remains forever aware that life is made of far more than meets the eye.

The person is full of love for everyone. During the several years (depending on the zodiac sign Pluto transits) of this transit, the person is the embodiment of compassion. He wants to end the suffering of others and help society in any way he can. He feels great devotion and appreciates every human being's uniqueness. He is tolerant and does not pass judgement on anyone. He lives the golden rule.

Artistic endeavors are favored, and the person is inspired and imaginative. He pursues his dreams and is less concerned with mundane obligations and affairs. He is highly idealistic. If the person happens to fall in love during this period (perhaps because of other astrological indications), he will feel pure ecstasy and euphoria.

The person is attracted to yoga, astrology, metaphysics, and the occult. He may become involved in mysticism and decide to live in an ashram or monastery. He enjoys introspection, meditation, and contemplation more than ever before. He has profound spiritual experiences and may remember past lives or travel on the astral plane. He feels no boundaries or restrictions now. The person may be emotional and moody. He may have a strong urge to escape from the world and should avoid indulging in drugs and alcohol. He meets fascinating people during this transit who are weird, psychic, mediumistic, mystical, devout, and highly religious.

P

When transiting Pluto squares natal Neptune, the person experiences a period of confusion, disorientation, and loss of control. He is at the mercy of outside forces and must do his best to flow with the changes that occur. The person is deeply affected by his subconscious mind, and he has a difficult time determining what is causing certain things to deteriorate so quickly. He may be hurt by gossip or scandal. The person must beware of moodiness and discouragement. More importantly, he must maintain faith and rely on inner strength rather than material possessions and external circumstances.

Today, this transit occurs late in life, between the ages of sixty and seventy. The person may have interesting psychic experiences, and he may take an interest in realities beyond the five senses. He may feel devout and decide to study astrology, yoga, metaphysics, or other mystical subjects. However, he must be careful of deception in these realms. He is likely to have problems with religious, spiritual, and highly devout persons. He should get plenty of rest and eat well as he is vulnerable to strange, hard-to-diagnose illnesses caused by emotional stress. Alcohol and drugs are particularly detrimental during this period.

If the person is an artist, he may produce wonderfully inspired works because his imagination is so fertile.

P

When transiting Pluto sextiles natal Neptune, the person has an opportunity to pursue the higher realities of life. He benefits from yoga, metaphysics, astrology, and meditation. His intuition increases, and he is more sensitive than usual. He thinks about religious, spiritual, and philosophical issues. The person is less concerned with material possessions and worldly affairs and more interested in personal evolution and humanitarian efforts. He may come into contact with mystics, spiritualists, astrologers, and professional psychics.

The person succeeds in artistic pursuits. His imagination is fertile, and he produces profound and moving works of art. He is inspired, and he follows his dreams. He is empathetic, tenderhearted and loving. He wants to help. This transit is an asset to individuals who work with film, photography, magic, oil, gas, and oceanography.

The transiting sextile only represents the opportunity to make the above effects a reality.

TRANSITING PLUTO CONJUNCTS NATAL PLUTO

This transit does not occur in the normal span of a lifetime.

P

When transiting Pluto squares natal Pluto, the person experiences major conflicts that can only be resolved by abandoning detrimental, obsolete behavior. During this period, the person is forced to work on his spiritual evolution and personal growth by confronting unhealthy emotional attachments and psychological fears. The person encounters circumstances that cause him to want desperately to control matters, but he quickly learns that the only way he can have his way is through humility, surrender, and compromise. The person has to learn that all beings are interconnected, and that he only wins if others also win. Therefore, he is now challenged to develop a strategy that is in harmony with the laws of nature and does not exclude or offend others. If the person insists on doing things his way, without concern for repercussions, he will suffer tremendously and his needs will not be met. He must try for flexibility, receptivity, and openness.

The person may experience important endings in his life. But he gains awareness and maturity in the process, and his life is less encumbered by obsessions, compulsions, and inner turmoil in the future. It is a good time to engage in psychotherapy or spiritual techniques. The person delves deeply into all matters. His focus is strong, and he is intense, powerful, and probing. He benefits greatly from spiritual endeavors and activities such as yoga, astrology, metaphysics, and the occult. His regenerative abilities are strong. Wherever he places his attention, he makes great progress.

The person should get plenty of rest, eat well, and exercise. He is under more stress than usual because he is affected by subconscious forces that he ordinarily ignores or represses. He may be disturbed or plagued by health problems until he confronts the inner dilemmas that retard his emotional well-being and growth toward perfection. In addition, his reproductive system may be under attack. It is impossible to predict the exact nature of the person's troubles, but the areas of life ruled by Pluto's natal house position are harmed and upset.

P

When transiting Pluto trines or sextiles natal Pluto, the person makes spiritual progress on the path to perfection. He is interested in self-improvement and evolutionary development. The person lets go of obsolete behavior in favor of new, more enlightened ways. He relinquishes control and maintains an attitude of openness, receptivity, and flexibility. The person is temporarily less attached to material possessions as he turns his attention to higher, more meaningful values. He is concerned with his purpose and direction, and he wants to do all he can for the welfare of others.

The person has tremendous ability to transform himself, and he makes good personal progress. It is an excellent time for psychotherapy and the practice of spiritual techniques. The person benefits from activities with astrology, yoga, metaphysics, and mysticism. He is more intuitive or psychic than usual. His drive, intensity, and willpower are strong, and he exhibits leadership ability. He is successful in his endeavors because he adopts an attitude of responsibility. He is psychologically healthy, and he deals directly with subconscious issues that arise.

The person is very virile, and he may have intense sexual desires. He is honest, creative, and more aware than usual. He alters his lifestyle to better support his life's purpose.

The transiting trine aspect is significantly more powerful than the transiting sextile. The transiting sextile only represents the opportunity to make the above effects a reality.

Part Two
Dasas of the East

THE PURPOSE OF PART TWO

This section on Hindu dasas (pronounced dashas) and bhuktis (pronounced booktees) has two purposes. One is simply to share more information on the subject with those who have read my first text, *Ancient Hindu Astrology for the Modern Western Astrologer,* written nearly eight years ago. The second is to introduce western astrologers to the rich and profound dasa-bhukti technique of Hindu predictive astrology. Astrologers who practice both Hindu and western astrology have a tremendous advantage in their astrological work. I believe that those who read this section will be favorably impressed by the Hindu system.

I wish make it extremely clear to beginners of Hindu astrology, however, that the following pages are presented only to whet the reader's appetite and to give a glimpse of the predictive accuracy that is possible through dasas and bhuktis. If my purpose succeeds and readers want to know more, there are now three or four easily understandable and readily available Hindu astrology books written by Westerners. For more information, see the chapters titled "Reading List" and "Services."

For beginners, the following pages can only serve as an introduction to the benefits of Hindu astrology because it is impossible to gain predictive accuracy through dasas and bhuktis without first understanding natal Hindu astrology. Hindu astrology is an entirely different system from western astrology. Although attaining proficiency in the system is not nearly as difficult as western astrologers believe (if they have read confusing texts by Hindu authors), neither is it a small task. In 1982, when I asked my first Hindu astrology mentor, R. Santhanam, when I could expect to practice Hindu predictive astrology comfortably and well, he accurately replied, "About one year." That forecast was based upon my experience in western astrology.

I also want to make it clear that HINDU ASTROLOGICAL TECHNIQUES MUST NEVER BE MIXED WITH THOSE OF WESTERN ASTROLOGY. Nothing could produce more distorted information than interpreting Hindu dasas and bhuktis on the basis of a western chart. What can be effectively mixed is the knowledge, insight, and wisdom gained separately from the two highly complementary systems. Both Hindu and western astrology are capable of predicting either personality traits or events. But because western culture embraces the doctrine of free will, western astrology is more sophisticated in predicting a person's psychology and personality than in predicting a person's fate. In a culture where individuals like Abe Lincoln and Lyndon Johnson can, by will and perseverance, rise from abject poverty to become presidents how appropriate would a fate-oriented astrology be?

India, on the other hand, is a culture steeped in the philosophy of karma and reincarnation. If a person has done good actions in past lives, then he or she reaps the inevitable benefits in the present life. Furthermore, Indian culture has long embraced a four-tiered caste system comprised of servants, merchants, warriors, and brahmins (priests or intellects). This systems dictates that a person who is born a servant shall die a servant; a person born into the merchant caste shall remain a merchant; and so forth. Therefore, free will is of relatively little value. It is perfectly natural that ancient Hindu astrologers developed an astrology of fate or destiny rather than of personality. Even though Hindu astrologers have some ability to predict personality and behavior, they are better equipped to forecast how many children a woman may have, when one is likely to marry, or if a person will gain riches. Astrologers who use both systems and are careful to maintain the integrity of each separate system, benefit from the wisdom of each culture.

DASAS—PLANETARY PERIODS (in order of occurrence)

The Sun	6 years
The Moon	10 years
Mars	7 years
Rahu	18 years
Jupiter	16 years
Saturn	19 years
Mercury	17 years
Ketu	7 years
Venus	20 years

The dasa system of prediction is one of the greatest features of Hindu astrology. Although transits are also used in Hindu astrology in a slightly different way than western transits, it is the dasas and bhuktis that produce the great predictive accuracy for which Hindu astrology is famous. Dasas and bhuktis are periods and subperiods during which a person's life is affected by, or corresponds to, the attributes and significations of particular planets. The first dasa of a person's life is based upon the position of the Moon in one's natal horoscope. Dasas last from six to twenty years. The longest dasa is that of Venus, and the shortest dasa, the Sun. One may be born at any point during a dasa, and from then on the dasas follow the above order. For example, one may be born in the final six months of a sixteen-year Jupiter dasa after which begins the nineteen-year Saturn dasa, and then the seventeen-year Mercury dasa, and so on. Or, a person may be born in the third year and fifth month of a twenty-year Venus dasa, after which comes the six-year Sun dasa, ten-year Moon dasa, and so on.

Dasas, which show the overall picture of a person's life for such long periods of time, are then broken down into bhuktis, which give more detailed information about shorter intervals within the dasas. As an example, a person may be in a sixteen-year Jupiter dasa which, if Jupiter is powerful and well-aspected in the natal chart, indicates that person will have wonderful gains, benefits, and happiness in the realms of life governed by Jupiter and the houses that Jupiter rules. However, if the person enters a two-year Moon bhukti within the Jupiter dasa and if the Moon is weak, afflicted, and badly aspected, then the person suddenly begins to encounter various problems in the areas of life signified by the Moon and the houses the Moon rules. The good effects of the sixteen-year Jupiter dasa are still in effect, but the person's happiness and benefits cease while he or she endures obstacles or difficulties.

Over forty Hindu dasa systems exist, of which only two are widely accepted as reliable. These two are called the Vimsottari and Asottari (pronounced "vim-sho-tree" and "eh-sho-tree") systems. Because the Vimsottari system is the most consistently accurate, it is the one that is most widely used and the one taught in this book. All dasa examples in this text are calculated according to the Vimsottari method.

According to Hindu philosophy, the normal span of human life would be 120 years in a physically and spiritually healthy world, without the excessive stress, strain, pollution, and mental unrest of present-day life. Appropriately then, the combined duration of all nine dasas totals 120 years. Uranus, Neptune, and Pluto could not be seen in ancient times and are therefore not part of the dasa system. The nine dasas include the seven original planets (including Sun and Moon), Rahu, and Ketu (North Node and South Node). The order of the dasas is as follows: Sun, six years; Moon, ten years; Mars, seven years; Rahu, eighteen years; Jupiter, sixteen years; Saturn, nineteen years; Mercury, seventeen years; Ketu, seven years; Venus, twenty years.

The same scheme exists for the bhuktis, and they also follow a set order. The first bhukti of any dasa is the same as the dasa planet. For example, in a Moon dasa the periods and subperiods run like this: Moon-Moon, Moon-Mars, Moon-Rahu, and so on. In a Sun dasa, they go as follows: Sun-Sun, Sun-Moon, Sun-Mars, Sun-Rahu, and so on.

Calculating a person's dasas and bhuktis is a complicated and time-consuming process and is subject to human error. I therefore recommend either buying a Hindu astrology software program or mailing away to one of the astrological computer services listed in the "Service" chapter at the end of this book. For those who want to know exactly how dasas and bhuktis are calculated, however, I have included instructions in the appendix of this text.

To understand dasas, it is necessary to know some fundamentals of Hindu astrology. First, I will explain the differences between the zodiac used by the Hindus and that used by westerners. On the following pages, I have gone into some detail betweeen the differences in describing the two zodiacs. If some of the material is too technical or difficult to comprehend, do not worry. All that beginners need to know, for now, is that the zodiacs are different and there are easy calculations to transform one's western horoscope into the Hindu one. Most beginners will employ a computer service for this process anyway.

I have addressed the issue of the two zodiacs rigorously because many astrologers today believe that only one zodiac is accurate. Part of the problem may arise because many New Agers consider anything Eastern to be deep, pure, and profound and anything Western to be shallow, superficial, and tainted. Where astrology is concerned, this is a sad mistake. Other astrologers may have hesitated to research another system of astrology on the advice of others. This is as short-sighted as the person who discredits astrology but has never had a professional birthchart interpretation. In a discipline as expansive, mystical, and arcane as astrology, it is important to learn through personal experience rather than intellectual belief. Because so many astrologers lately are drawing conclusions about astrological systems and zodiacs based upon theory rather than practice of those systems, I feel it is important to try to show how two different zodiacs could work equally well.

There is a fundamental difference between the zodiac used in the Hindu system (sidereal) and the one used predominantly in western astrology (tropical). A zodiac is an imaginary circle in the heavens, inside of which the Sun, Moon, and planets travel in their orbits. In order to plot the positions of the heavenly bodies, it is necessary to determine a starting point within the circle. To construct a starting point, it is necessary to establish a reference point, some kind of fixed element to be used as a backdrop to the ever-orbiting planets, the Sun, and the Moon. Herein lies the difference between the two zodiacs. The sidereal zodiac uses as its reference point the positions of "fixed stars"— stationary star clusters which have no motion whatsoever. In other words, the sidereal zodiac is calculated by determining the positions of the planets and the Sun and Moon in relation to a stationary point in the sky, a particular "fixed star" cluster, which is delegated as the first degree of Aries. Aries then becomes the first of twelve 30° zodiac signs (portions of space) making up the 360° zodiac.

The tropical zodiac uses an entirely different, but equally fixed, reference point. For measuring purposes, it uses the equinoxes (the relationship between the Sun and the Earth which creates the four seasons: the Spring Equinox, the Summer Solstice, the Autumnal Equinox, and the Winter Solstice). The starting point of the tropical zodiac, also called the first degree of Aries, is determined by the spring equinox—the first day of spring. Each year when spring arrives, the position of the Sun within the imaginary circle establishes the first degree of Aries. All other planets are then calculated in relation to the Sun. This works well because the Sun moves approximately 360 degrees in one year, the same number of degrees in the zodiac, and because the first day of spring occurs at the exact same time each year (even though our yearly calendar makes it seem to vary by a day or two). Tropical astrology is not based upon a fixed position in the heavens, as is the sidereal zodiac. It is based upon an undeviating, similarly fixed, atmospherical condition called the four seasons—specifically, spring.

For thousands of years there has been confusion and disagreement as to whether both zodiacs are legitimate, and if so, which one is preferable and produces the most accurate results. Astrologers who have studied and practiced both systems, USING THE TROPICAL ZODIAC FOR WESTERN ASTROLOGY AND THE SIDEREAL FOR HINDU ASTROLOGY, almost always conclude that both work because they have experienced accurate results from both. (It is possible that the information gained from tropical or seasonally-based astrology may relate somewhat more to a person's psychology and behavior than events and circumstances.) Unfortunately, most astrologers are not expert in both Hindu and western astrology and have therefore confronted the question of the two zodiacs only from a theoretical perspective.

Unfortunately most people, astrologers and astronomers often included, overlook the fact that the zodiacs are based on different principles and have different reference points for determining the first degree of Aries. Therefore, when the first degree of Aries in the tropical zodiac differs from the first degree of Aries in the sidereal system, it is assumed that one zodiac is incorrect. This is not the case. The problem is exacerbated by the fact that there is a consistent mathematical relationship between the two zodiacs so that the first degree of Aries in the sidereal zodiac is always a perfect mathematical formula away from the first degree of Aries in the tropical zodiac. This can also make it appear that the two zodiacs are based upon the same reference point but that one zodiac has somehow been miscalculated.

The mathematical difference between the two zodiacs—specifically the difference between the first degree of Aries in the tropical zodiac and the first degree of Aries in the sidereal zodiac—is known by Hindu astrologers as the *ayanamsa* (pronounced aya-nam-sha). The *ayanamsa*, though able to be precisely calculated for any single moment, is a moving figure. For example, in 1900 the difference between the first degree of Aries in the tropical zodiac and the first degree of Aries in the sidereal zodiac was twenty-two degrees and twenty-seven minutes. In 1970, the *ayanamsa* was twenty-three degrees and twenty-six minutes—a difference of approximately one degree. This motion of approximately one degree per seventy-two years between zodiac starting points, describes the precession of the equinoxes. The precession of the equinoxes is a perpetual, though extremely slight, tilting of the earth.

In present day, the way astronomers arrive at the starting point of the sidereal zodiac is by using the calculated positions of the tropical zodiac and then taking into account the movement of the precession of the equinoxes. Because the starting points of the zodiacs are always moving apart from each other (within a circle), there are times when the starting points coincide. Therefore, astronomers try to determine exactly what year the first degree of Aries was the same in both zodiacs. From there, they simply begin to subtract approximately one zodiac degree for every seventy-two years and thus arrive at the current sidereal first degree of Aries. There are slight disagreements amongst certain astronomers as to the exact year that the zodiacs coincided. But the Indian government has sanctioned the work of N.C. Lahiri, and it is therefore his *ayanamsa* which is most widely used for astrological purposes. My experience in trying different *ayanamsas* is that Lahiri's *ayanamsa* is the accurate one (There are about three or four popular ones. They produce differences of only two or three zodiac degrees different from Lahiri's). Hindu astrology texts generally offer a few different ones so astrologers are free to choose for themselves.

In trying to come to terms with the two zodiacs, please consider that different techniques often produce the same results. Different spiritual paths lead to the same enlightenment. There is good reason that tropically-based western astrology has endured for thousands of years in the West and sidereally-based Hindu astrology has endured in the East.

THE CHAKRA — THE BIRTHCHART

There are two prevalent Hindu horoscope formats, one that comes from South India and one from North India. The designs have no effect on the results and are simply a matter of tradition. The South Indian method is somewhat more popular in India, and that is the one taught in this book. For those who use the North Indian method, I will include both chart formats of the horoscopes that are analyzed in this text. But, for now, beginners should go by the South Indian method and completely ignore the North Indian chart, which is approached in an entirely different way.

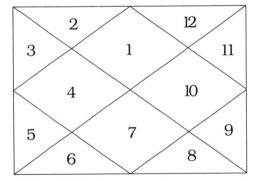

SOUTH INDIAN CHART

NORTH INDIAN CHART

Contrary to the western birthchart, where the houses are fixed (if the chart were a clock, twelve o'clock is the tenth house and nine o'clock is the first house) and signs rotate, in the South Indian chart the signs are fixed and houses rotate. In other words, zodiac signs always fit the same squares (the top left square is always Pisces and the bottom right square **353** is always Virgo) and house numbers rotate. The first house, whichever square it might be, is denoted by a diagonal line within the square. Another difference from western astrology is that the chart flows in a clockwise direction rather than counterclockwise.

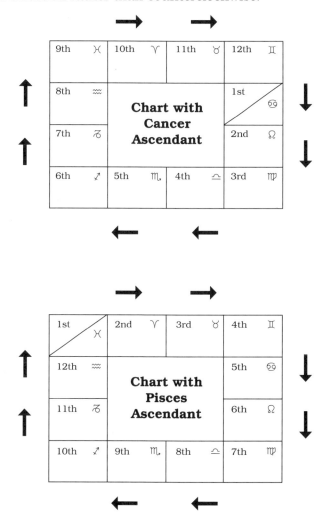

As for the house systems, there are two that are generally used in India. One is older and more traditional and the other is somewhat more contemporary. The older method is the one used in this book. This is the equal house system, meaning that if the first house begins at ten degrees Capricorn, then all other houses begin also at ten degrees (i.e., second house starts at ten degrees Aquarius, third house at ten degrees Pisces, and so on). In the traditional Hindu chart system, the degree of the house

354   cusp is completely irrelevant. This means that although the first house may begin at twenty-five degrees of Scorpio, even a planet in two degrees Scorpio occupies the first house. This differs from western astrology in which all planets in degrees less than the ascendant will occupy the twelfth house. In typical western house systems, the first house may start at the middle of one sign and continue until the middle of the next sign (e.g., from three degrees Leo to three degrees Virgo or from twenty degrees Gemini to twenty degrees Cancer). This does not happen in the traditional Hindu equal house system. (It does occur in the contemporary Hindu chart method, but that is not the method we are using.)

To put it simply, planets in the second SIGN from the ascendant occupy the second house. Planets in the fifth sign from the ascendant occupy the fifth house. The ascendant degree is irrelevant in positioning the planets. (The ascendant degree is not insignificant in other ways—only in terms of determining the other houses.)

DRAWING THE CHART

In order to transform a western birthchart (calculated with tropical zodiac) to a Hindu one (that employs the sidereal zodiac), simply subtract the *ayanamsa*, the figure that accounts for the precession of the equinox or tilting of the earth, from the positions of the ascendant, the planets, and the North and South Nodes. (Uranus, Neptune, and Pluto may be disregarded as these are not used in ancient Hindu astrology.)

The precession of the equinox moves approximately 50 1/4" per year. Given below are some *ayanamsas* during the twentieth century.

LAHIRI AYANAMSAS DURING THIS CENTURY

January 1, 1900	22° 27' 59"	January 1, 1960	23° 17' 54"
January 1, 1910	22° 35' 51"	January 1, 1970	23° 26' 21"
January 1, 1920	22° 44' 43"	January 1, 1980	23° 34' 31"
January 1, 1930	22° 52' 40"	January 1, 1990	23° 43' 14"
January 1, 1940	23° 01' 21"	January 1, 2000	23° 51' 11"
January 1, 1950	23° 09' 34"	January 1, 2010	24° 00' 04"

In order to determine approximate ayanamsas for years in between the ones listed below, use 50 1/4 seconds per year (but remember that the precession moves *approximately* 50 1/4 seconds per year. Therefore, your final calculation for the *ayanamsa* will be close but not exact). As an example birthchart let us use the chart of Richard Nixon.

Birth Data For Richard Nixon
January 9, 1913, 9:35 P.M. P.S.T.
longitude 117 W 49, latitude 33 N 59

Tropical Zodiac Positions

Ascendant	♍	17°24'
Sun	♑	19°24'
Moon	♒	20°08'
Mars	♐	29°45'
Mercury	♑	00°01'
Jupiter	♑	01°40'
Venus	♓	03°29'
Saturn	♉	27°29'
Rahu (N. Node)	♈	07°15'
Ketu (S. Node)	♎	07°15'

The easiest way to proceed is to first reduce the sign degrees of each item to its proper degree within the 360 degree zodiac. Therefore the following table may be helpful.

Aries	0° — 29° 59'
Taurus	30° — 59° 59'
Gemini	60° — 89° 99'
Cancer	90° — 119° 59'
Leo	120° — 149° 59'
Virgo	150° — 179° 59'
Libra	180° — 209° 59'
Scorpio	210° — 239° 59'
Sagittarius	240° — 269° 59'
Capricorn	270° — 299° 59'
Aquarius	300° — 329° 59'
Pisces	330° — 360°

Nixon was born in 1913, three years after the 1910 *ayanamsa* of 22° 35' 51". Therefore, add 50 1/4 seconds for each of these three years

50.25"	22° 35' 51"
x 3	+ 2' 51"
150.75" divided by 60" = 2' 51"	22° 38' 42"

The final figure, 22° 38' 42" is an approximation of the *ayanamsa* (because, as already mentioned, the precession moves *approximately* 50 1/4"). The exact *ayanamsa* was 22° 38' 31". For our purposes, we will simply use 22° 38'.)

The Sun — 19°♑24' = 289° 24' minus 22° 38' = 266° 46' = 26° ♐46'.
The Moon — 20°♒08' = 320° 08' minus 22° 38' = 297° 30' = 27°♑30'.
Rahu (north node) — 07°♈15' (add 360° since 22° 38' cannot be subtracted from 07° 15') = 367° 15' minus 22° 38' = 344° 37' = 14°♓37'.

For those who wish to, there is an easy way to quickly transpose western charts to produce APPROXIMATELY ACCURATE Hindu birthcharts. The technique is a simplified way to make zodiac subtractions and works well for all planets and ascendants except those that occupy twenty-two or twenty-three degrees of a sign. During the entire twentieth century, the *ayanamsa* is approximately twenty-three degrees, so that is the figure to subtract from the ascendant, planets, and the nodes. Subtracting twenty-three degrees from planets located between twenty-four degrees and thirty degrees is simple. Subtracting twenty-three degrees from, say, ten degrees (or any figure below twenty-three degrees) becomes confusing. To make the calculation easy, just add seven degrees to the figure (in this case, add seven to ten), and then subtract a sign. This works because seven and twenty-three equals thirty, the number of degrees in each sign.

For example, the Moon in Richard Nixon's western chart is approximately twenty degrees of Aquarius. Therefore, to find the sidereal position of the Moon, add seven degrees to twenty, and subtract a zodiac sign. The result is twenty-seven degrees of Capricorn. Remember that this is only a quick way to gain an approximate Hindu chart and cannot work for planets occupying a degree near the *ayanamsa* (twenty-two or twenty-three degrees during twentieth century births). The exact figures of such planets as well as the exact *ayanamsa* are necessary in order to determine whether such planets fall in the final degree of one sign or the earliest degree of the next sign.

COMPUTER CHART SERVICES THAT PROVIDE HINDU CHARTS WITH DASA BHUKTIS OR WESTERN CHARTS WITH TRANSITS:

Astro Communications Services Inc.
P.O. Box 34487
San Diego, Calif. 92163-4487
(800) 888-9983

Astrogram
3600 N. Lake Shore Dr.#1817
Chicago, Ill. 60613
(312) 589-6314

There are many factors to consider when analyzing dasas and bhuktis. In fact, there are so many that to list all the subtleties and nuances would be overwhelming to beginners. Normally, one learns dasas after possessing a working knowledge of natal Hindu astrology. Because this section is meant to serve as an introduction to the possibilities and benefits of Hindu predictive astrology, only the most necessary information is presented here. More fundamentals will be presented in the following pages. Thus, the birthchart descriptions that follow will start out as simple as possible and become progressively more complex.

PLANETS ARE BENEFIC OR MALEFIC BY NATURE

BENEFICS — Venus, Jupiter, Mercury, Moon (waxing and bright is much more benefic than waning and dim)

MALEFICS — Mars, Saturn, Rahu, Ketu (North and South Nodes), Sun (Sun is a hot star and burns anything in its way)

Hindu astrology is different from western astrology in that it is more simplistic (not necessarily easier, but more simplistic). Houses are either benefic or malefic. Planets are either good or bad. If a planet is aspected by Venus, Jupiter, or other benefics, it flourishes. Planets aspected by malefics suffer. Unlike western astrology, aspects are not called squares, oppositions, trines, and sextiles, though they may be comprised of the same specifications. Aspects in Hindu astrology are good or bad depending on the planet throwing the aspect. For example, if Venus is opposite Saturn, this is not called an opposition as it is in the western system, and damage is not done to both planets. Venus is harmed because it is aspected by malefic-natured Saturn. On the other hand, Saturn becomes tremendously powerful and well-disposed because it is aspected by benefic Venus.

In analyzing dasas, it is crucial to determine the dasa planet's natal condition. This is done by examining such fundamental birthchart factors as the dasa planet's sign and house placement, the houses it rules, and the aspects it receives (whether benefic or malefic) from other planets. The most common mistake beginners make is expecting wonderful results from a Venus or Jupiter dasa or bhukti simply because these are benefic-natured planets. Or, predicting terrible results from a Saturn, Mars, or Sun dasa or bhukti merely because these planets are malefic by nature. This is not how dasas and bhuktis work. The critical factor is the overall natal condition of the planet involved. For example, if Venus, a wonderful benefic, is "fallen" by sign position (in Virgo), in the eighth house (a *dusthana* or grief-producing house), conjunct with Mars, and aspected by Saturn, the twenty-year Venus dasa for this person would be horrific because Venus in this example is terribly afflicted. So the person's love life would suffer, he or she would have illnesses involving the throat, thyroid, or reproductive system, and serious problems with women. Furthermore, the areas of life signified by the house Venus occupies as well as the houses Venus rules (the houses of Taurus and Libra) would also seriously deteriorate. On top of all this, life in general would be rough, painful, and difficult.

On the other hand, if a person enters a nineteen-year dasa of malefic Saturn but Saturn is very well-disposed, the person could expect good results. For example, if Saturn rules excellent houses (in Hindu astrology, the best houses are the fifth and ninth and the worst are the sixth, eighth, and twelfth), and it is aspected by Jupiter and a full Moon, the person would definitely prosper. The person could expect significant career advances and leadership opportunities, and his or her organizational skills would increase. Also, the significations of Saturn's house position as well as the houses Saturn rules (Capricorn and Aquarius) would flourish. Clearly, the condition of the dasa or bhukti planet is more significant than whether the planet is benefic or malefic by nature.

While the overall condition of the dasa planet indicates the positive or negative effects of the dasa, it is the significations of the dasa planet and the significations of the houses that the dasa planet occupies and rules that reveal the exact areas of life to be affected. For example, Mercury rules education, writing, learning, the mind, the nervous system, and the lungs and intestines, among other things. If one enters Mercury dasa and Mercury is strong and well-disposed, the person may happily return to school and enjoy all kinds of new information and psychological realizations. Life would be enjoyable and the person would succeed because of his or her alertness, mental clarity, and increasing intellectual dexterity. If, however, Mercury is afflicted natally, then in the Mercury dasa the person suffers from nervousness, mental problems, or depression. The person would also have problems in schooling and upsets with teachers, writers, and the press. The person might suddenly develop bronchitis or intestinal problems.

In another example, if the person enters a Venus dasa and Venus is well-placed and well-aspected natally, then the person begins to have happy love relationships, enjoyments with music and drama, and he or she might receive many gifts of art or jewelry. Also, the houses Venus rules would benefit. If, in this case, Venus rules the fifth and tenth houses, the significations of the fifth and tenth houses flourish and the person's fame (tenth house) increases, and the person will have good luck with investments and children (fifth house). It is crucial to analyze the significations of the dasa or bhukti planet and its house position and house rulerships.

♓ ♃	♈ ♂	♉ ♀	♊ ☿
♒ ♄			♋ ☽
♑ ♄			♌ ☉
♐ ♃	♏ ♂	♎ ♀	♍ ☿

In Hindu astrology, rulerships are monumentally important, perhaps more important than planets in houses. Rulerships are the connections each planet makes with the house or houses it owns or "rules." For example, Venus governs Libra and Taurus, and Venus therefore rules the houses occupied by those signs. Mars governs Aries and Scorpio, and therefore Mars rules the houses containing those signs, and so on. Rulerships and planets in houses are the essence of Hindu astrology. Birthchart analysis based upon them produces consistently accurate results. This differs from the western system where rulerships and planets in houses are very important but function so inconsistently that astrologers must search among a multitude of house systems to find one that produces relatively dependable results. (I certainly do not mean to disparage western astrology. It is simply my experience that western rulerships and planets in houses are far less reliable than those in Hindu astrology and that the most profound features of the western system are the sign meanings (Aries, Taurus, Gemini etc.) and the astrological aspects (the squares, trines, oppositions, etc.)

The most common mistake beginners make in trying to analyze dasas and bhuktis is to make predictions about a period based solely on the nature of a planet and the house it occupies while ignoring the houses the dasa or bhukti planet rules—the houses that planet is intrinsically connected to. For example, consider a person who has a Taurus ascendant entering a seven-year Mars dasa. What will be the results if Mars occupies its exaltation sign (Capricorn) in the ninth house and is very well-disposed because it receives beneficial aspects from Jupiter, Venus, or a bright Moon? Of course the person will become temporarily energetic, ambitious, and aggressive, because that is the nature of Mars. The person is likely to travel to far off countries on and off for seven years because Mars occupies the ninth house (travel) and is so well-disposed. The person will gain higher knowledge from gurus and religious teachers during the entire Mars period. And certainly the person's luck may increase dramatically (the ninth house rules luck in Hindu astrology). In addition, however, the person stands a good chance of getting married soon after the dasa begins, or at least sometime within the seven years of Mars dasa (especially during a favorable bhukti). Why? Because Mars rules Scorpio and for a Taurus ascendant birthchart, Scorpio comprises the seventh house, the house of marriage. The person may also have some of the greatest spiritual experiences of his or her life and enjoy "remote foreign countries" such as India, Africa, Israel, etc. because Mars rules the twelfth house (Aries) and the twelfth house governs enlightenment and remote foreign countries, among other things.

Some examples within the lives of famous living people to illustrate the importance of rulerships in dasa prediction are as follows:

1) Al Gore, who has a Cancer ascendant, watched his son get struck by a car during the worst bhukti of a Mars dasa. Mars, in his case, is very afflicted and rules the fifth house, the house of children.

2) Robert De Niro, who has a Gemini ascendant, has enjoyed great fame during Mercury dasa. Mercury occupies the third house in his birthchart (in Hindu astrology the third house rules music, dance, and drama) and is extremely well-aspected, thereby giving great artistic success during the dasa. Fame was forthcoming because Mercury RULES the first house, the ability to be recognized and appreciated.

3) Robert Duval, who has a Pisces ascendant, won his academy award in Jupiter dasa, Saturn bhukti. Saturn occupies the tenth house (career success and fame) and Jupiter RULES the tenth house. Jupiter also rules the first house (ability to be recognized, promoted, and so forth).

Some of the general manifestations likely to occur during dasas and bhuktis of planets ruling the twelve houses are listed on pages 362-368. The same descriptions apply to dasa or bhukti planets occupying these houses. The reason I have not included the term "occupying" in the headings is because beginning astrologers consistently base their dasa analysis on dasa planets in houses, forgetting that rulerships are often more important than planets in houses. It is difficult, however, to make an absolute statement about whether house rulers carry more weight than planets in houses. The best explanation I can make about the issue is that a house ruler is like the structure of a building while planets in a house are like the furnishings. Tom Hopke in *How to Read Your Horoscope* says that house rulers are like landlords while planets in houses are like tenants. In my own practice, I place slightly more importance on house rulers.

Please remember that planets always rule two houses, except for the Sun and Moon, which rule Leo and Cancer, respectively. Therefore, in most cases, dasas or bhuktis involve effects generated by three different houses the two houses a planet rules and the house that planet occupies. For example, if a person with a Scorpio ascendant enters a Jupiter dasa, and Jupiter occupies the ninth house and is very well-aspected, then there are three fundamental benefits that the person gains: the person will probably travel a great deal and enjoy religion, philosophy, and higher knowledge because Jupiter is posited in the ninth house: the person also makes a great deal of money because Jupiter rules the second; and he or she has wonderful experiences with children or investments because Jupiter rules the fifth house.

Western astrologers should bear in mind that while most house meanings are the same in Hindu astrology as they are in the western system, some are very different. Those that differ significantly are marked with an asterisk.

DASA OR BHUKTI RESULTS OF A PLANET RULING THE FIRST HOUSE

IF POWERFUL, WELL-PLACED, AND WELL-ASPECTED:

- fame, recognition, promotions, awards
- good health, general well-being
- improvement of one's appearance (face lifts, nose jobs, etc.)
- support of nature

IF WEAK AND AFFLICTED:

- deterioration of status
- weakening confidence
- poor health, bodily harm (through accidents or otherwise)
- head ailments
- negative reactions from others
- no support of nature

DASA OR BHUKTI RESULTS OF A PLANET RULING THE SECOND HOUSE

IF POWERFUL, WELL-PLACED, AND WELL-ASPECTED:

- financial gains, monetary rewards
- enjoys happy and fruitful family life* (includes marital harmony)
- successful educational pursuits*, writing ability*, teaching ability*
- benefits from lecturing activities*.

IF WEAK AND AFFLICTED:

- money problems, loss of wealth
- Deterioration of family life* (includes marital disharmony)
- educational difficulties*, problems in literary endeavors*
- throat problems, ailments of the right eye.

DASA OR BHUKTI RESULTS OF A PLANET RULING THE THIRD HOUSE

IF POWERFUL, WELL-PLACED, AND WELL-ASPECTED:

- tremendous energy, lots of courage, great adventures
- ability to fulfill daily desires*
- benefits and happiness from brothers and sisters
- success in the fine arts of music dance and drama*
- enjoyment of entertainment*

IF WEAK AND AFFLICTED:

- disturbances and suffering on account of brothers and sisters
- loss of desires and ambitions*, weak energy*, lethargy*
- inability to fulfill daily desires*
- no enjoyment of entertainment*
- problems in artistic endeavors (specifically music, dance, and drama)*

364

- ailments involving arms or lungs, problems with hearing (especially the right ear)

DASA OR BHUKTI RESULTS OF A PLANET RULING THE FOURTH HOUSE

IF POWERFUL, WELL-PLACED, AND WELL-ASPECTED:

- happiness from mother, mother becomes successful
- obtains new home, obtains land
- successfully moves to new city or country
- obtains cars or other conveyances*
- obtains jewelry and all kinds of other comforts* (stereos, computers, televisions, etc.)
- enjoys contentment and happiness*
- success in gaining academic degrees*

IF WEAK AND AFFLICTED:

- problems with mother, mother suffers intensely
- disturbances inside the home, problems with houses
- problems with cars*
- suffers from lack of happiness and contentment*
- difficulty gaining comforts* (jewelry, stereos, televisions, etc.)
- problems in obtaining academic degrees*
- heart ailments*

DASA OR BHUKTI RESULTS OF A PLANET RULING THE FIFTH HOUSE

IF POWERFUL, WELL-PLACED, AND WELL-ASPECTED:

- childbirth, success with children
- financial gains through investments and speculations
- successful endeavors in the arts of painting or crafts
- abundant fun and pleasure, help and benefits from benefactors*
- chanting of mantras*, practicing spiritual techniques*
- mental clarity and power*, mental happiness and optimism*
- kingship or political power*
- comprehension and realization about one's destiny*
- benefits relating specifically to one's *poorvapunya* or past-life credit*

IF WEAK AND AFFLICTED:

- troubles or suffering on account of children

- losses through speculations and investments
- unfavorable endeavors in painting or crafts
- unable to have fun and pleasure
- mental suffering including depression and confusion*
- no desire to practice mantras and spiritual techniques*
- loss of political power*
- miscellaneous problems relating to one's *poorvapunya* or past-life credit or debt* (i.e., the person reaps specific negative effects of bad actions done in past lives)
- confusion about one's destiny*
- stomach ailments*

365

DASA OR BHUKTI RESULTS OF A PLANET RULING THE SIXTH HOUSE

IF POWERFUL, WELL-PLACED, AND WELL-ASPECTED:

- improvement of health, healing ability
- success and happiness at daily job
- overcomes enemies and competitors*

IF WEAK AND AFFLICTED:

- health problems relating to exact nature of planet ruling (or occupying) the sixth house (i.e. Venus = throat, Mars = bloodstream, Jupiter = allergies, and so forth)
- difficulties in daily work
- suffers on account of enemies and competitors*
- charged in court cases*
- various difficulties and obstacles* (for no reason except that the sixth house is a *dusthana* or bad house — this is explained further on)
- intestinal problems

DASA OR BHUKTI RESULTS OF A PLANET RULING THE SEVENTH HOUSE

IF POWERFUL, WELL-PLACED, AND WELL-ASPECTED:

- likelihood of marriage
- happy love relationships
- dealings with the public
- expansion in business*

IF WEAK AND AFFLICTED:

- marital problems or divorce
- unhappiness in love
- few opportunities for marriage
- romantic involvements with unfavorable or unhealthy partners
- ailments involving the genitals
- problems in business

DASA OR BHUKTI RESULTS OF A PLANET RULING THE EIGHTH HOUSE

IF POWERFUL, WELL-PLACED, AND WELL-ASPECTED:

- interest in astrology or psychic phenomena
- visits to astrologers and psychics, interest in occult arts
- increase of intuition
- beneficial spiritual or mystical experiences
- financial gains from "unearned means" (lotteries, wills, legacies, insurance companies and so forth)
- monetary rewards from spouse or other partners

IF WEAK AND AFFLICTED:

- problems with joint finances
- difficulty paying or receiving alimony
- inability to receive money from wills and legacies
- accidents and assorted obstacles* (for no other reason than the fact that the eighth house is a *dusthana* or grief-producing house, as explained further on)
- reproductive ailments

DASA OR BHUKTI RESULTS OF A PLANET RULING THE NINTH HOUSE

IF POWERFUL, WELL-PLACED, AND WELL-ASPECTED:

- enjoys travel to other countries or far away places
- obtains a guru or spiritual teacher
- becomes interested in religion and devotion
- benefits from philosophical and spiritual teachings
- favorable experiences with the father* (for some individuals, the ninth house represents the father—for others the father is seen through the tenth house)
- increase of general luck and fortune*

IF WEAK AND AFFLICTED:

367

- travel plans are cancelled, endures hardships while traveling
- problems with gurus and religious teachers
- deterioration of faith and devotion
- inability to gain higher knowledge
- obtains faulty or erroneous higher knowledge
- problems with father*
- ailments involving the thighs

DASA OR BHUKTI RESULTS OF A PLANET
RULING THE TENTH HOUSE

IF POWERFUL, WELL-PLACED, AND WELL-ASPECTED:

- career expansion, career success
- obtains awards and honors, increasing status and fame
- increasing influence on the world
- performs benevolent acts for society
- benefits from authority figures and government officials
- holy pilgrimages*

IF WEAK AND AFFLICTED:

- career downfall
- professional problems
- confusion about one's dharma (life purpose)
- problems with authority figures and government officials
- ailments involving the knees

DASA OR BHUKTI RESULTS OF A PLANET
RULING THE ELEVENTH HOUSE

IF POWERFUL, WELL-PLACED, AND WELL-ASPECTED:

- financial gains and profits* (including but not limited to side ventures)
- makes new friends, benefits from friends
- engages in group activities, forms his or her own group
- abundant opportunities
- realizes major goals and ambitions
- benefits and successful experiences with eldest sibling*

IF WEAK AND AFFLICTED:

- financial losses* (including but not limited to side ventures)
- loses friends, suffering on account of friends
- problems with groups
- scarce opportunities, missed opportunities
- confusion about one's major goals
- inability to fulfill major goals
- problems or suffering on account of eldest sibling*,
- ailments involving the ankles.

DASA OR BHUKTI RESULTS OF A PLANET RULING THE TWELFTH HOUSE

IF POWERFUL, WELL-PLACED, AND WELL-ASPECTED:

- interest in obtaining enlightenment or final liberation
- spiritual growth, powerful experiences of enlightenment
- enjoyment of meditation
- enjoyable seclusion or confinement in a monastery or ashram
- financial bargains* (the twelfth house rules debts and expenses—the positive side of debts and expenses is bargains)
- travel to remote foreign countries* (for a Westerner, remote countries means places like India, Nepal, Africa, Israel, and so on)
- enjoyment of "bed pleasures*" (positive sexual experiences)

IF WEAK AND AFFLICTED:

- encounters unexpected debts and expenses*
- hard to experience spiritual growth or enlightenment*
- problems with "bed pleasures*" (sexual enjoyment)
- travel plans to remote foreign countries are cancelled*
- problems in remote foreign countries* (for Westerners, this means places like India, Africa, Israel, Nepal and so on)
- confinement in a prison or hospital, disturbances caused by "secret enemies"
- problems on account of thieves and robbers*
- assorted difficulties and problems* (for no other reason than the fact that the twelfth house is a *dusthana* or grief-producing house, as explained further on)
- ailments involving the feet
- problems with hearing and sight* (specifically the left eye and left ear)

GOOD AND BAD PLANETS FOR EACH ASCENDANT BY VIRTUE OF RULERSHIP			
Asc.	Best	Good	Bad
♈	♃	♂☉	♀☿☽♄
♉	♄	☿♂☉	♃☽
♊	♀		♂☉♃♄
♋	♂	♃	☿♀♄
♌	♂	☉	☿♀
♍	♀		☽♂♃
♎	♄	☿♂♀	☽☉♃
♏	☽	☉♂♃	☿♀
♐	☉	♂	☿♀♄
♑	♀	☿♄	♂♃☽
♒	♀	♄♂☉	☽♃
♓	♂	☽	♄☉☿♀

PLANETARY COMBINATIONS FORMING RAJAYOGAS	
♈	☉♃
♉	♄
♊	♀☿
♋	♂
♌	♃♂
♍	♀☿
♎	♄
♏	☉☽
♐	♂♃
♑	♀☿
♒	♂♀
♓	☽♂ or ♃♂

Planets not listed as good or bad for each ascendant
are considered neutral by virtue of their rulership.

In Hindu astrology, planets carry with them a benefic or malefic influence by virtue of the houses that they rule. This is an extremely important principle that affects not only natal chart interpretation but also the effects that planets have during their dasas and bhuktis. Indeed, the positive or negative nature of a planet by virtue of rulership is one of the first conditions used to determine whether a period or subperiod will give good, bad, or mediocre results. Malefic planets (Mars, Saturn, and Sun) when ruling "good houses" become what are called "functional benefics" (or temporal benefics). While retaining their fundamentally harmful nature, functional benefics also carry with them the ability to do good. Benefic planets (Venus, Jupiter, Moon, and Mercury) that rule "bad houses" become "functional malefics," which means they simultaneously cause damage and produce good effects.

The most auspicious houses in a horoscope are the fifth and ninth (the ninth is considered the best house and the fifth comes next). These houses are called *trikonas* or trinal houses, and they bestow enormously beneficial energy wherever their influence is felt. Planets that occupy the fifth or ninth house become strong, powerful, and able to function in their most positive way. For example, if Venus is in the fifth or ninth house, Venus' significations (art, beauty, love, etc.) are strengthened because Venus occupies such a good house. If Mars is in the fifth or ninth house, the significations of Mars (sports, physical energy, mechanical ability, etc.) flourish. Also, the houses that are ruled by planets in the fifth and ninth houses (in the above cases, the houses that Venus and Mars rule) become strong and favored.

More important, planets that rule *trikona* houses carry tremendous positivity and bestow their beneficence onto the houses they occupy and the planets and houses they aspect. (In Hindu astrology, planets actually aspect houses. This is explained in the following chapter, "Aspects.") In other words, if the ruler of the fifth or ninth house occupies the second house (money), then the person's financial conditions are strengthened, even if the ruler of the fifth or ninth house happens to be a malefic (Mars, Saturn, or Sun). Furthermore, the aspects that the fifth house ruler and ninth house ruler throw onto other planets and houses are beneficial, even though the planet throwing the aspect may be malefic, therefore simultaneously throwing some harmful energy.

The business of functional benefics and functional malefics is a basic premise of Hindu astrology, but beginners who are reading about Hindu astrology for the first time should not expect to completely absorb this material now. The purpose of part two of this book (where western astrologers are concerned) is merely to show what is possible through Hindu astrology. If the reader's curiosity is piqued, he or she should obtain a comprehensive introductory text (see "Services"). For now, understand that in Hindu astrology, the best houses in a chart are the fifth and ninth, and the worst houses are the sixth, eighth, and twelfth, which are known as *dusthanas* or grief-producing houses. Of the three

bad houses, the sixth is slightly less bad because it is also known as an **371**
upachaya or growing house (the exact meaning of *upachaya* is "increasing.") This means that although a planet occupying the sixth house is
wrecked, the affairs relating to that planet can gradually improve if the
person works hard on the problems indicated.

In the descriptions of dasas of famous people, the main references
made about rulerships and good and bad houses concern the *trikonas*
(the beneficial trinal houses—five and nine) and *dusthanas* (the grief-
producing houses—six, eight, and twelve). I have also mentioned *kendras*,
the angular houses of a horoscope (one, four, seven, and ten) that render
planets powerful. I have purposely omitted many more complexities lest
the reader wind up in an endless maze of technical material. The ancient
Hindu astrological sages considered many more rules when determining
functional benefics and functional malefics. (For those who are interested, some basic rules are included at the end of this chapter.) For
example, in the case of Gemini ascendant birthcharts, Venus rules the
twelfth house, a *dusthana* or bad house, as well as the fifth house, a
wonderful *trikona*. Further, Saturn for a Gemini ascendant chart rules
the ninth house, the best house of a chart, while also ruling the terrible
eighth house.

Follow the graph on page 369, which presents the conclusions of the
ancient astrological seers, and note that for a Gemini ascendant, Venus
is judged to be the best planet for the chart by virtue of rulership (the best
planet for a chart by virtue of rulership is called the *yogakaraka*, or
union-maker). Notice that Saturn for a Gemini ascendant falls under the
category of bad planets not because it is a malefic by nature, but because
after considering all the intricate, detailed astrological rules and formu-
las, Saturn is deemed to be carrying malefic energy by virtue of the
houses that it rules. In predicting the effects of a dasa, it is important to
note whether the planet is a functional benefic or functional malefic.
Furthermore, if the planet happens to be the *yogakaraka* (the union-
maker or best planet for the ascendant—i.e. Venus for Gemini, Jupiter
for Aries, Saturn for Taurus, and so forth, as noted in the graph on page
369), then the dasa will bring the best results of all (unless that planet
is otherwise extremely afflicted). This point cannot be overemphasized.
Yogakarakas, even when occupying their fallen sign, produce significant
benefits.

Regarding the graph on page 369, planets not listed as good or bad
are neutral by rulership. For example, look at the good and bad planets
for Virgo ascendant. Only four planets out of seven are listed. Three
planets, Sun, Mercury, and Saturn are missing. Thus, these planets are
neutral. This means that the Sun and Saturn, as natural malefics,

simply carry their usual harmful energy with no supplementary positivity or negativity by virtue of house rulerships. Similarly, because Mercury is also considered neutral in this case, it carries only its usual positive energy without any additional positive or negative force. (Technically speaking, Mercury is actually considered a neutral planet by nature, not a benefic. It is considered neither masculine nor feminine and is said to be extremely adaptable, taking on the positive or negative nature of the planets it is aspected by. In practice, however, Mercury only casts good aspects and causes good effects to the houses it occupies. Therefore, even though technically neutral, Mercury behaves in a benefic way. But because it is technically neutral, which makes it the most adaptable of all planets, Mercury's dasas and bhuktis are much more affected by the benefic or malefic aspects Mercury receives. As an example, Richard Nixon's presidency was destroyed during a seventeen-year Mercury dasa that began in November, 1970. Mercury is conjunct in the same degree as malefic Mars, and Nixon was brought down by the press, college students, the intelligencia, tape recordings, and his own lying—all Mercury significations.)

One last point. A special condition called a *rajayoga*, or royal union, occurs when two planets that both rule good houses form a conjunction in one house of a chart. (See the right hand column of the graph on page 369.) (Remember that in Hindu astrology conjunctions and aspects always occur within a thirty-degree orb. In other words, if Mars is two degrees of Leo, and the Sun is twenty-eight degrees of Leo, a conjunction exists.) A *rajayoga* is one of the best astrological indications possible, and the house containing the two *rajayoga* planets flourishes tremendously. The three or four houses ruled by the two planets forming the royal union also prosper. *Rajayogas* and other special planetary unions can be created in a great many different ways. (Ancient Hindu astrological scriptures contain literally thousands of good and bad astrological yogas or unions.) The *rajayogas* that are listed on the far right side of the graph on page 369 are the most fundamental ones based upon rulership conditions.

If a person enters a dasa or bhukti of a planet forming a *rajayoga*, excellent results can be predicted. If the *rajayoga* planet also happens to be afflicted because of some other birthchart factor, then both good and bad effects will occur. Please note that for birthcharts with Taurus, Cancer, and Libra ascendants, an automatic *rajayoga* exists because in these charts, one planet rules two very good houses. For Taurus, Saturn rules the ninth and tenth houses. For Cancer, Mars rules the fifth and tenth houses. And for Libra, Saturn rules the fourth and fifth houses. All of these planets are malefics by nature that rule *kendras* and *trikonas* (angular houses and trinal houses). Never underestimate the power and beneficence of planets involved in *rajayogas*.

ARIES—the Sun and Jupiter, when joined together, cause *rajayoga*

TAURUS—Saturn, which rules houses 9 and 10, alone causes *rajayoga*

GEMINI—Venus and Mercury, when joined together, cause *rajayoga*

CANCER—Mars, which rules houses 5 and 10, alone causes *rajayoga*

LEO—Jupiter and Mars, when joined together, cause *rajayoga*

VIRGO—Venus and Mercury, when joined together, cause *rajayoga*

LIBRA—Saturn, which rules houses 4 and 5, alone causes *rajayoga*

SCORPIO—The Sun and Moon, when joined together, cause *rajayoga*

SAGITTARIUS—Mars and Jupiter, when joined together, cause *rajayoga*

CAPRICORN—Venus and Mercury, when joined together, cause *rajayoga*

AQUARIUS—Venus and Mars, when joined together, cause *rajayoga*

PISCES—Mars and the Moon or Mars and Jupiter, when joined together cause *rajayoga*

SOME RULES WHICH FORM THE RULERSHIP TABLE GIVEN ON PAGE 369

KENDRAS (angular houses)—1st, 4th, 7th, & 10th

- Benefics which rule *kendras* take on negative energy and the ability to do harm.
- Malefics which rule *kendras* take on positive energy and the ability to do good.
- Lords of *kendras* are powerful. Of them, the lord of the 1st is weakest, the lord of the 4th stronger, the lord of the 7th stronger still, and the ruler of the 10th strongest.
- Planets in *kendras* are powerful, and they are prominent influences in a person's life.

TRIKONAS (trinal houses)—5th & 9th

- Any planet ruling a *trikona* is auspicious and carries the most positive energy with it.
- *Trikona* lords are so auspicious that they produce great benefits even when they simultaneously rule evil houses.
- Planets posited in *a trikona* house flourish, as do the houses they rule.
- The Lord of the 5th is not quite as powerful as the lord of the 9th.

Note—Some astrologers consider the ruler of the 1st as a trikona and a kendra lord.

Note—the 10th house is an upachaya house in terms of its nature and behavior, but for lordship purposes it is considered a kendra

- *Upachayas* are growing houses where planets gain in strength throughout a person's life, and conditions indicated by the house can improve in time with effort.
- Any planet ruling an *upachaya* house takes on negative energy, though not of an intense nature, and may cause slight harm.
- Malefics in *upachayas* give excellent results.
- Benefics in *upachayas* give good results and are not particularly enhanced or benefited by the house energy.
- Of the *upachayas*, the 3rd is the weakest and the 11th the strongest.

NEUTRAL HOUSES–the lords of the 2nd, 8th, & 12th

- Give good results if they are conjunct with a benefic planet. (In practice, Indian astrologers do not follow this advice except perhaps for the lord of the 2nd. Practically speaking, the 8th and the 12th destroy all of their associations.)
- Planets posited in the 2nd house are not greatly influenced one way or the other, unless by aspect or sign placement.

DUSTHANAS (evil houses)—6th, 8th, & 12th

- Any planet rulling a *dusthana* carries negative energy with it and causes destruction where it is posited.
- Any planet posited in a *dusthana* is ruined, as are the houses it rules.
- The 6th house and its ruler are the least malefic of the *dusthanas*, especially since the 6th is a growing house where conditions may improve.

MARAKAS (Death-inflicting planets)—the rulers of the 2nd and 7th houses.

- The houses of life are the 8th and the 3rd (the 3rd being the 8th from the 8th). The 12th house is known as the house of loss. The 12th from the 8th house is the 7th; therefore the 7th takes on an evil influence to life. The 12th from the 3rd is the 2nd, and it also becomes destructive. This matter is an extreme subtlety, and concern over *marakas* should be delayed until the astrologer is highly experienced in Hindu astrology. The most obvious effect occurs when both *marakas* are posited in the same house. In such a case there may be an evil effect which is otherwise astrologically undetectable. Most astrologers use the *marakas* to determine the time of death, because many people die in a period or subperiod of a *maraka*. However, this is a very complicated matter, and there must be other strong afflictions to the planet in question for a death to occur. Also, *marakas* are more ominous during old age, when death is most likely. Young and middle aged individuals need not be overly concerned about dasas of *marakas*.

- All planets aspect the seventh house (opposite) from themselves.
- Mars aspects the fourth, seventh, and eighth houses from itself.
- Jupiter aspects the fifth, seventh, and ninth houses from itself.
- Saturn aspects the third, seventh, and tenth houses from itself.
- Any planet occupying a house that is being aspected is also aspected.
- Two planets in the same sign form a conjunction.

Planetary aspects influence both the quality and content of dasas and bhuktis. For example, if a person enters a Moon dasa and the Moon is closely aspected (close by planetary degrees) by Saturn at birth, then during that ten-year period, the person will be more serious, disciplined, and organized because of Saturn's aspect. The period will also be difficult, tedious, and frustrating because Saturn, as a malefic, seriously harms the Moon. If, in this case, the Moon occupies the fifth house, then the problems and frustrations during the dasa center around fifth house significations. There will also be problems relating to the house that the Moon rules, Cancer. As another example, if Mercury occupies the second house and is tightly aspected by benefic Jupiter at birth, the seventeen years of the Mercury period will bring great financial gains or educational benefits (both Mercury and the second house rule education and literary endeavors in Hindu astrology). During this dasa, the person will also feel more interested in God or religion than usual because of Jupiter's intrinsically spiritual nature. The houses that Mercury rules will also flourish because Mercury is so well-aspected.

Astrological aspects in Hindu astrology function somewhat differently than those in the western system. There are no such things as squares, trines, oppositions, sextiles, and so forth. Each planet has certain houses that it aspects and if a planet happens to occupy the house being aspected, then that planet also receives an aspect. The beneficial or harmful nature of an aspect depends on the nature of the planet throwing the aspect. The benefic planets (Moon, Venus, Jupiter, and Mercury) throw positive aspects onto other houses and planets. The malefics (Mars, Sun, and Saturn) cast damaging influences. On top of this, rulership factors must be considered (refer to graph on page 369).

Benefic planets that rule good houses (i.e., the fifth or ninth) throw extra positive energy while malefics that rule good houses throw some good energy, along with their essential harmful forces. Benefic planets that rule *dusthanas* (grief-producing houses) throw malefic energy as well as their natural positive forces.

One of the most significant differences between Hindu aspects and western aspects, a difference that many western astrologers often find hard to grasp in the beginning is that when two planets aspect each other, as they do in conjunctions and seventh house aspects (what western astrologers call oppositions), one planet may benefit tremendously while the other may suffer tremendously. For example, if Venus is conjunct Saturn then Venus is terribly harmed by Saturn's malefic energy. (Degrees are irrelevant in Hindu aspects. Therefore, if Venus is in the same sign as Saturn, a conjunction exists. Of course, however, the tighter the aspect by degree, the more intense the effect.) However, Saturn's condition flourishes because it receives Venus' extremely beneficial energy. As another example, take a case where Jupiter occupies the fourth house while Mars is in the tenth house. Because all planets aspect the seventh house from themselves (their opposite) Jupiter aspects Mars while Mars aspects Jupiter. However, this does not constitute an "opposition" as in western astrology because oppositions in western astrology are difficult or "challenging" for both planets. In Hindu astrology, Jupiter is damaged by receiving Mars' harmful rays, but Mars becomes powerful and very happy because it is aspected by benefic Jupiter. This is the way Hindu astrology aspects work.

Whenever a planet aspects a sign that it rules or the sign of its exaltation or fallen placements, the results are altered for better or worse. For instance, if Jupiter aspects the fourth house and that house happens to be Pisces, the sign that Jupiter rules (in Hindu astrology, ancient rulerships apply because Uranus, Neptune, and Pluto are not used), then the aspect is much more beneficial than usual. If the Moon aspects Taurus, the house of Moon's exaltation sign, then that house is exceptionally strengthened. If Mars throws an aspect onto its fallen sign, Cancer, then the harm to the house of Cancer is far worse than if another house received Mars' ordinary malefic energy. Furthermore, any planet occupying Cancer would also be harmed by the Mars aspect much more than usual.

In the case of malefics aspecting their own or exaltation signs, this matter of "special" aspects is a subtlety requiring practical experience to properly grasp. Certain houses simply cannot fully integrate malefic energy, no matter how much additional benefic energy the malefic planet may carry. Specifically, the houses representing persons are the most sensitive in this matter. These houses are the first (the person himself or herself), the third (all brothers and sisters except the eldest), the fourth (mother), the fifth (children), the seventh (spouse), the ninth and tenth (either of which may signify one's father. In South India, the ninth represents the father because in that part of India the father also functions as the guru, which is a ninth house matter. North Indian astrologers see the father from the tenth house.), and the eleventh house (the eldest sibling, not older but eldest).

Let us first consider the case of a malefic planet aspecting its own house where that house does not signify a person. If Mars aspects the second house and the second house happens to be Aries or Scorpio (Mars' signs), the aspect will cause only good effects for money. However, if Mars aspects the seventh house, the house of marriage, and that house happens to be Aries or Scorpio, there will be good effects regarding the spouse, but there will also be serious damage to the relationship with the spouse. The seventh house is too sensitive an arena for Mars energy. In this case, the spouse would likely be powerful, successful, assertive in a good way, and beautiful (or handsome) or exceptional. However, there would still be arguments or fighting in married life.

As another example, if Saturn aspects the third house and the third house is Capricorn, Aquarius, or Libra (Saturn's own or exaltation signs), then the person might have a younger brother or sister who is Saturnian in a positive way. That sibling might be disciplined, responsible, highly evolved, successful, or an authority in his or her field. But the relationship with the sibling would suffer, and there would be very few siblings (or none) because Saturn bestows its restrictive nature onto the third house. As I state repeatedly throughout this text, positive influence does not cancel negative influence. There are many realms of life where a person experiences some extreme good and some extreme bad. Mixed birthchart influences are the astrological explanation for such conditions.

Most ancient Hindu astrological texts say that Rahu and Ketu, the "shadowy" planets, have no ability to cast aspects. However, there is a school of thought, based upon the writings of the sage Parasara, that holds Rahu and Ketu cast inimical glances onto the fifth and ninth houses from their natal placements. Because I was not instructed in this method and have not fully researched the matter, I do not include these aspects in my birthchart interpretations. I include this information solely for those who wish to further investigate the matter.

The aspects listed above and analyzed in my descriptions of dasas of famous individuals are "full" or 100% aspects, and these are ones used by all practicing Hindu astrologers. There are, however, aspects called three-quarter aspects, one-half aspects, and one-quarter aspects, that beginning astrologers should simply ignore. I will, however, include these aspects for reference purposes.

1) All planets aspect the third and tenth houses from themselves with a one-quarter effect.

2) All planets aspect the fifth and ninth houses from themselves with a one-half effect.

3) All planets aspect the fourth houses from themselves with a three-quarter effect.

Using only the full aspects, which are listed in the beginning of this chapter, let us now consider Lord Rama's chart. Lord Rama was a Hindu avatar who was so great that every planet in his chart except Mercury and Rahu is exalted or in its own sign. Despite Rama's greatness, his father died during his childhood because Saturn aspects the Sun in his chart, and the aspect is a worse one than usual because Saturn throws its harmful energy onto Aries—the sign where Saturn is fallen. Rama's father died, the story goes, of a sudden heart attack after Rama's mother announced that their child was destined to leave home in order to serve God.

LORD RAMA

RASI

9th ♓ ♀	10th ♈ ☉	11th ♉ ☿	12th ♊ ☊
8th ♒			1st ♋ ☽ ♃ Asc.
7th ♑ ♂			2nd ♌
6th ♐ ☋	5th ♏	4th ♎ ♄	3rd ♍

- Moon aspects the seventh house.

- Moon aspects Mars in the seventh house.

- Jupiter aspects the fifth, seventh, and ninth houses. The aspect to the seventh house is not as beneficial as usual because Jupiter aspects Capricorn, its fallen sign.

- Jupiter aspects Mars in the seventh house, aspecting its fallen sign, Capricorn.

NORTH INDIAN

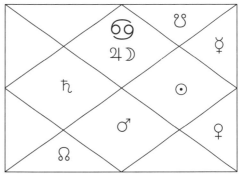

- Jupiter aspects Venus in the ninth house—an excellent aspect because Jupiter aspects its own sign, Pisces.

- Saturn aspects the sixth, tenth, and first houses. The aspect to the tenth house is an especially bad one because Saturn aspects its fallen sign, Aries.

- Saturn aspects Rahu in the sixth house.

- Saturn aspects the Sun in the tenth house—in Saturn's fallen sign, Aries.

- Saturn aspects the Moon and Jupiter in the first house.

- Rahu throws no aspects. (According to sage Parasara, Rahu aspects the tenth, twelfth, and second houses of Rama's chart.)

- Mars aspects the tenth house and the Sun in the tenth, causing some good and some bad because, on the positive side, Mars aspects its own sign, Aries, but on the negative side, malefic Mars throws harmful aspects.

- Mars aspects the first house and the Moon and Jupiter in the first house, aspecting its fallen sign, Cancer.

- Mars aspects the second house.

- Venus aspects the third house, aspecting Virgo, its fallen sign.

- Sun aspects the fourth house and Saturn, aspecting the Sun's fallen sign.

- Mercury aspects the fifth house.

- Ketu throws no aspects. (According to Parasara, Ketu aspects the fourth, sixth, and eighth houses of Rama's chart.)

In Hindu astrology, planetary exaltations and falls work in much the same way as western astrology. However, there are two main differences. First, Mercury is considered exalted in Virgo and fallen in Pisces, whereas western astrology gives the exalted and fallen placement as Aquarius and Leo, respectively. Second, the Hindus have narrowed down the exact degrees of exaltations and falls. They are as follows:

	Exalted		Fallen	
Sun	10°	♈	10°	♎
Moon	03°	♉	03°	♏
Mars	28°	♑	28°	♋
Mercury	15°	♍	15°	♓
Jupiter	05°	♋	05°	♑
Venus	27°	♓	27°	♍
Saturn	20°	♎	20°	♈
Rahu		♍	inconclusive	
Ketu		♍	inconclusive	

Planets approaching their highest degree of exaltation gain in power and reach their peak of strength in their highest exaltation degree. Planets that occupy exaltation sign degrees beyond their highest exaltation function clearly better than average but are no longer exalted. The same is true for fallen planets. Those planets that approach the lowest point of the fall get weaker and more afflicted the closer they get to the most extreme degree of their "fall." If a planet occupies its fallen sign but is beyond the utmost degree of fall, it functions poorly but is no longer technically fallen. It therefore causes less damage than if in a degree preceding its fallen extreme.

Exaltations and falls are extremely important in Hindu astrology, especially if the planet involved is in a degree close to its positive or negative extreme. Dasas or bhuktis of exalted planets are significantly strengthened, and a person's life increases in fortune and benefit during such a planetary period. Likewise, during a dasa or bhukti of a fallen planet, a person may have unending problems until the period ends. As always, rulerships, aspects to planets, and other natal birthchart factors must be taken into consideration.

GEMSTONES, MANTRAS, AND YAGYAS

Because Hindu astrology is so predictive, it would be absurd for the system not to include definitive methods to alleviate karmic difficulties that appear in one's birthchart. After all, what is the point of knowing that a life-threatening dasa-bhukti is ahead if one does not have the means to alter the problem? Hindu astrologers are famous for their *upayes* or antidotes to planetary afflictions. The most common methods that are used are gemstones, mantras, and *yagyas*, which I will briefly describe. The gemstones for the planets are:

Red Ruby is the gem for the Sun
Pearl is the gem for the Moon (moonstone is a secondary stone)
Red Coral is the gem for Mars
Hessonite is the gem for Rahu
Yellow sapphire is the gem for Jupiter (yellow topaz is a secondary stone)
Blue sapphire is the gem for Saturn
Emerald is the gem for Mercury (tourmaline is a secondary stone)
Chrysoberyl is the gem for Ketu
Diamond is the gem for Venus (white sapphire is a secondary stone)

Although ancient astrological seers explained which gemstones are related to which planets, they were unspecific about how to prescribe the gems. Thus, astrologers differ on their use. There are, however, some commonly agreed on viewpoints. The two most traditional recommendations are that a person should wear the gemstone corresponding to his or her birth planet permanently and wear the gemstone corresponding to each dasa temporarily. The birth planet is the planet that rules the ascendant or first house of one's horoscope. For example, a person with a Scorpio ascendant should wear the stone of Mars (red coral) because Mars rules Scorpio. A person with Sagittarius should wear the stone of Jupiter (yellow sapphire) because Jupiter rules Sagittarius. (Westerners beware that these recommendations are ONLY TO BE PRESCRIBED FOR ONE'S HINDU BIRTHCHART CALCULATED BY THE SIDEREAL ZODIAC. Wearing a wrong stone can be harmful and destructive.) By wearing the gemstone of one's birth planet, a person strengthens confidence, self-esteem, support of nature, and the ability to gain recognition. Everyone should wear the gemstone of their birth planet.

Aside from wearing the gem of the birth planet, a person should wear the stone for the current dasa. During the six years of the Sun dasa, wear the stone for the Sun (red ruby). When that period ends, take off the red ruby and replace it with the stone of the next dasa, the Moon (pearl), and so on. The stone that corresponds to the dasa strengthens the dasa planet, causing it to give the best possible effects. If the dasa planet is powerful, well-aspected, and well-placed, wearing the dasa gemstone makes the period even more beneficial. If the dasa planet is weak or afflicted, wearing the dasa gemstone lessens potential damage.

The effects of gemstones are subtle. But they are profound enough for most sensitive individuals to notice a positive difference in their lives. Gemstones can also be worn to strengthen afflicted planets unrelated to one's birth planet or one's dasas. They may also be worn to strengthen beneficial planetary influences, thereby creating even more good fortune for a person. Determining which planets can be strengthened without harming other birthchart features, however, requires expertise in Hindu astrology, and beginners should consult an expert. As mentioned before, wearing the wrong gems causes negative effects. For now, beginners should simply wear the gemstone corresponding to their Hindu birthchart ascendant and the stones corresponding to each dasa.

Gemstones should be natural, of very high quality, and should not be heated, dyed, or chemically altered. The stones should touch the skin, if possible. As a general rule, most astrologers advise wearing stones that are two carats or larger. If this is not possible, one should consider purchasing a slightly smaller gem or a "secondary" stone — a stone that is similar in color and chemical properties to the traditional gem (since the effect of secondary stones are weaker, the size should be increased). Size and quality are crucial. Do not expect an extremely flawed stone or several tiny stones that add up to two or three carats to have a positive effect. This point cannot be overemphasized.

Perhaps the most powerful *upaye* of all is called a *yagya* (also spelled *yagna*). A *yagya* is a religious or spiritual ceremony performed by a Hindu priest in order to alleviate karmic difficulties. It is a kind of offering or sacrifice in which a priest appeals to the planetary beings or the forces of nature (or the gods) for grace and intervention on behalf of the person requesting the *yagya*. During the *yagya*, the priest lights a fire, burns incense, and throws rice and ghee (clarified butter) into the flames. This symbolizes the burning of negative karma from the past so that the person may be relieved of the most intense influences of past destructive actions. During the *yagya*, the priest continuously chants astrological mantras. Astrological mantras are Sanskrit prayers which entreat higher evolutionary beings to remove obstacles in the person's life.

384　　　*Yagyas* are extremely powerful and should be prescribed during a dasa or bhukti that is difficult or life-threatening. *Yagyas* can also be done during good periods to help fulfill heartfelt desires or to remove unrelenting impediments in life. I have had several *yagyas* performed during rough periods and can attest to their force and efficacy. *Yagyas* can be obtained by calling any Hindu temple in the U.S. or India that employs a Hindu priest. (Some temple addresses are given on pages 386 and 387.)

There are many kinds of *yagyas* available. There are *yagyas* for wealth, childbirth, removal of obstacles, family happiness, acquisition of a spouse, and so on. For the purposes of ameliorating a difficult period or subperiod, the *nava graha*, or nine-planet *yagya*, is usually recommended because it is both effective and easily affordable. Most temples (as of this writing) ask for a minimum donation of around $125 or $150 for the two-hour ceremony.

Because a *yagya* is a religious sacrifice (*yagya* literally means sacrifice), the size of donation given to the priest has a definite bearing on the results. One hundred dollars may be a perfect donation for one person while someone wealthy may feel no sacrifice at all by donating that amount. If no real sacrifice is made by the person requesting the *yagya*, the results of the ritual may be meager. It is also important to maintain an attitude of humility and surrender when asking a priest to pray for your well-being.

Another very important point: much of what causes a *yagya* to work is the subtle power of the mantras being chanted. As the priest chants and chants, his consciousness naturally transcends to finer levels of creation. It is on these subtle levels of nature that a person's karma can be altered. Therefore, it is crucial that the priest perform his chanting uninterrupted. Because *yagyas* are performed in the Sanskrit language, Hindu priests will sometimes interrupt the *yagya* in order to explain to a Westerner the symbolism or meaning of what is happening. This can have a weakening effect and should be avoided as much as possible. I therefore recommend asking any questions about the *yagya* before or after the ceremony and explaining to the priest clearly and firmly that there should be no interruptions during the *yagya*. This point cannot be overemphasized.

It is preferable to be present with the priest during the *yagya*, but if this is impossible, a *yagya* can be performed in absentia with fine results. I recommend sending a photograph to the priest, explaining the nature of difficulties you are having or what kind of results you are seeking, and perhaps sitting in meditation or prayer while the *yagya* is performed (even though the *yagya* may take place hundreds or thousands of miles away). Some priests want to know your birthday and birthtime so they can ascertain your birthchart *nakshatra*. (The zodiac is divided into twenty-seven *nakshatras* or "lunar mansions" each consisting of thirteen degrees and twenty minutes. Most computer printouts of Hindu birthcharts give the Moon *nakshatras*.) It is a good idea, though again not crucial, to have the *yagya* performed on the day that relates to the afflicted planet. For example, if the problem concerns the Sun and your Sun is afflicted, then have the *yagya* performed on Sunday. If the problem is with the Moon, have the *yagya* performed on Monday. The rest of the days are as follows: Mars, Tuesday; Mercury, Wednsday; Jupiter, Thursday; Venus, Friday; Saturn, Saturday. Finally, if possible, have the *yagya* performed on a waxing Moon (growing larger) that is also very bright; the brighter the moon the better. However, do not be overly concerned if these conditions cannot all be met. *Yagyas* are powerful enough whenever they are performed.

Another way to heal afflicted planets and difficult dasas and bhuktis is to chant astrological mantras. These are the same mantras that the Hindu priest performing a *yagya* chants, although the priest chants all nine planetary mantras as well as other traditional mantras. Chanting a mantra is something many Westerners may be uncomfortable with, but I have included them in this text for those who are interested. In my astrology practice, I have prescribed astrological mantras for people with afflicted planets and many who have tried chanting them have reported that their lives were dramatically altered for the better. The planetary mantras and their prescribed number of repetitions are given on pages 387-389.

Mantras should be started at an auspicious time. Therefore, begin mantra chanting on a waxing Moon (growing brighter), when the Moon is bright, not dim. Also, begin on the day that relates to the planet being propitiated. For instance, start chanting the Jupiter mantra on a Thursday, begin chanting the Venus mantra on a Friday. These instructions apply ONLY TO THE COMMENCEMENT OF CHANTING. Once you start the chanting, it can be done anytime. The purpose of starting anything at an auspicious time is to assure that you will gain full results. If a person starts the chanting process on a waning Moon that is also very dim, there is a strong chance that the person will stop chanting before completing the full number of mantra repetitions.

It would be wonderful if one could stop everything and chant 23,000 Saturn mantras, for example, in one sitting. However, since this would take about three or four days without sleep, it is fine to chant ten or twenty minutes per day, or however long you desire. The easiest way to count mantra repetitions is with the use of a strand of beads (similar to a rosary). In India, 108 *tulsi* or *rudraksha* beads are strung together along with a protruding bead called the guru bead. As each mantra is chanted, the person moves to another bead until he or she has chanted 108 mantras. Chanting the full circle of beads is called one *mala*, and it is easy to keep track of mantra repetition by keeping track of how many malas you chant over a period of weeks or months.

One final note about prescribing astrological mantras: although mantras are widely available in print in India, it is traditional for them to be given out only by enlightened gurus. There is a widespread belief that any person who prescribes a mantra for someone else becomes forever responsible for that person's evolution. Whether this is really the case or not I cannot say. Therefore, each person must make his or her own decision about the matter. For my part, I believe the injunction about who shall give out mantras belongs to an age that is coming to an end—an age where traditions, rules, and regulations were crucial in order to ensure that the purity of higher knowledge would remain intact. I am also reminded of a wonderful Indian legend about a master and his disciple.

Once upon a time, an enlightened guru gave his disciple a mantra that he declared would bring full enlightenment to anyone who chanted it. The disciple was told in no uncertain terms, however, to keep the mantra secret. But the disciple was as interested in serving others as he was about his own happiness. He therefore questioned his master thoroughly about who could use the mantra and who could not, and the master repeated that the mantra would bring enlightenment to anyone who chanted it. At this point the guru went a step further and warned his disciple that he surely would go to hell forever or endure some such terrible punishment if he told anyone else the mantra. The next day, the guru was astonished to find his disciple on a rooftop shouting this mantra at the top of his lungs to a throng of listeners. When the guru asked the disciple if he had not understood the retribution that awaited him, he replied, "If thousands of people are going to reach full enlightenment and only I will have to bear the punishment, I am certainly willing to pay the price."

TEMPLES WHERE YAGYAS CAN BE OBTAINED:

Sri Shirdi Sai Baba Temple
3744 Old William Penn Highway
Pittsburgh, Pa. 15235
Contact Pandu Malyala

Phone (412) 374-9244 or (412) 823-1296

Hindu Temple of Greater Chicago
P.O. Box 99
12 South 701 Lemont Road
Lemont, Illinois 60439

Phone (708) 972-0300

Or look in the local yellow pages under Temples and Churches.

PRONUNCIATION OF ASTROLOGICAL MANTRAS

Mantra For The Sun — to be chanted 7000 times

PRONUNCIATION

Japa koosooma sankarsham kashya-peeyam mahajuteem, tamoreem sarva pahpagnam pranato smee deevahkaram.

Let us chant the glories of the Sun god, whose beauty rivals that of a flower. I bow down to him, the greatly effulgent son of *Kasyapa*, who is the enemy of darkness and destroyer of all sins.

Mantra For The Moon — to be chanted 11,000 times.

PRONUNCIATION

Dadee shanka tusha-rabam ksheero-darnava sambhavam na-mahmee shasheenam somam samboor mookuta booshanam.

I offer my obeisances to the Moon god, whose complexion resembles curds, the whiteness of conchshells, and snow. He is the ruling deity of the *soma rasa* born from the Ocean of Milk, and he serves as the ornament on top of the head of Lord *Shambhu.*

Mantra For Mars — to be chanted 10,000 times.

PRONUNCIATION

Daranee garbha sambootam vidyut-kahntee sama-prabam koomahram shaktee hastam-cha mangalam prana-mam mya-ham.

I offer my obeisances to *Sri Mangala,* god of the planet Mars, who was born from the womb of the earth goddess. His brilliant effulgence is like that of lightning, and he appears as a youth carrying a spear in his hand.

Mantra For Mercury — to be chanted 4,000 times.

PRONUNCIATION

Preeyangava guleekash yam roopeyna prateemahm budam sowmyam sowmya goono-peytam tam boodam prana-mahm mya-ham.

I bow down to *Buddha*, god of the planet Mercury, whose face is like a fragrant globe of the *pryangu* herb and whose beauty matches that of a lotus flower. He is most gentle, possessing all attractive qualities.

Mantra For Jupiter — to be chanted 19,000 times.

PRONUNCIATION

Deva-nancha rishee-nancha gurum-kanchana shaneebam boodee bootam treelo-keysham tam na-mamee brihas-pateem.

I bow down to *Brihaspati*, god of the planet Jupiter. He is the spiritual master of all the demigods and sages. His complexion is golden, and he is full of intelligence. He is the controlling lord of all three worlds.

Mantra For Venus — to be chanted 16,000 times.

PRONUNCIATION

Heema-kunda mri-nala-bam deyt-yanam para-mam gurum sarva-shastra pravak-taram barga-vam prana-mam mya-ham.

I offer my obeisances to the descendant of *Bhrigu Muni* (i.e. Venus), whose complexion is white like a pond covered with ice. He is the supreme spiritual master of the demoniac enemies of the demigods, and has spoken to them all the revered scriptures.

Mantra For Saturn — to be chanted 23,000 times.

PRONUNCIATION

Nee-lanjana sama-basam ravee-putram yema-grajam chaya-martanda sambootam tam na-mahmee sanee-charam.

I bow down to slow-moving Saturn whose complexion is dark blue like *nilanjana* ointment. The elder brother of Lord *Yamaraja*. he is born from the Sun-god and his wife *Chaya*.

PRONUNCIATION

Arda-kayam maha-viryam chandra ditya veemar-danam seeng-hee-ka garba sambootam tam rahum prana-mam mya-ham.

I offer my obeisances to *Rahu,* born from the womb of *Simheeka,* who has only half a body yet possesses great power, being able to subdue the Sun and the Moon.

Mantra For Ketu — to be chanted 17,000 times.

PRONUNCIATION

Palasha-pushpa-sankasham taraka-grahu masta-kam rowdram row-drat makam goram tam keytoom prana-mam mya-ham.

I offer my obeisances to the violent and fearsome *Ketu,* who is endowed with the potency of Lord Shiva. Resembling in his complexion the flower of a *palasa* plant, he serves as the head of the stars and planets.

RASI

5th ♓	6th ♈	7th ♉	8th ♊
4th ♒ ♃ 10°			9th ♋ ☊ SR 8° ♂ 24°
3rd ♑ ♄ 12° ☋ SR 8°			10th ♌ ☽ 10°
2nd ♐	1st ♏ ☉ 3° ☿ 0° Asc. 24° 35'	12th ♎ ♀ ℞ 22°	11th ♍

VIMSOTTARI

DASA		BHUKTI	
	Mo. Day Year		Mo. Day Year
☉	08-16-1984	♀♃	10-16-1974
		♀♄	06-16-1977
☽	08-16-1990	☉♄	06-22-1987
♂	08-16-2000	☉☿	06-04-1988
☊	08-16-2007	☽☊	01-16-1992
		☽♃	07-16-1993
♃		☽♄	11-16-1994
		☽☿	06-16-1996
♄		☽☋	11-16-1997
		☽♀	06-16-1998
☿			
		♂☊	01-13-2001
☋	11-19-1962	♂♃	02-01-2002
		♂♄	01-07-2003
♀	08-16-1964	♂☿	02-16-2004

NAVAMSA

2nd ☋	3rd ♀ ♄	4th	5th
1st ♂ Asc.			6th ☽ ☿
12th ♃			7th ☉
11th	10th	9th	8th ☊

NORTH INDIAN

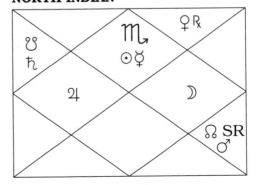

This chart is a good example of two highly successful, career-oriented dasas followed by a difficult dasa. Both the Sun and Moon dasas in this chart relate to the tenth house (career), and both are powerfully aspected by benefics. Jodie Foster has been honored with Academy Award nominations numerous times throughout the Sun and Moon dasas, and she has won twice. The Moon, which is the most important influence in a Hindu chart, occupies the career house. The Sun rules the career house and is placed in the first house (personality, recognition, self-promotion, etc.). This is an excellent combination for a career-oriented life. On top of this, the Sun is aspected very closely by Mercury, a benefic. Therefore, in a Sun dasa (and to a slightly lesser extent, in Sun bhuktis) fame and career success are predictable. The best dasa-bhukti within the six-year period is Sun-Mercury because the Sun receives the benefic energy of Mercury. The Sun-Mercury dasa-bhukti started in 1988, and Foster's prominence increased dramatically when she won her first academy award for her film performance in *The Accused.*

Foster's Moon dasa began on August 16, 1990, and runs until August 16, 2000. It is an excellent period because the Moon occupies the tenth house (career) and is aspected within one degree by benefic Jupiter. The Moon is further strengthened by its rulership of the ninth house of this chart. In Hindu astrology, the best houses of a chart are the ninth and fifth. Planets ruling these houses carry beneficial energy and bestow their great beneficence on the houses they occupy and the planets and houses they aspect. The fundamental meaning of the Moon in the tenth house is successful dealings with the public, fame, performing in the limelight, and so on. Therefore, the Moon dasa is wonderful for career achievement. Jodie Foster received her second oscar in 1992, early on in her Moon dasa for her work in *The Silence Of The Lambs.* The award was given during her Moon dasa, Rahu bhukti. Rahu, known as the North Node in western astrology, represents insatiable cravings and desires for worldly power, achievement, and accomplishment. It signifies everything materialistic and earthy, and it is extremely common for public figures to increase in prominence during Rahu periods and subperiods. In Jodie Foster's chart, Rahu's placement in a very good house (the ninth), and, more importantly, Rahu's "stationary retrograde" position (in which a planet comes to a complete halt before beginning to move backwards) on the day of Foster's birth are significant. There is almost no stronger planetary condition than that of a planet stopped dead in its tracks while the rest of the planets continue in their motion. (Planets never actually stop moving or turn retrograde. They only appear to do so from our earthly viewpoint. The effects of these apparent conditions on our lives, however, are quite real and significant.)

To properly understand Rahu and Ketu (Ketu is called the South Node in western astrology), it is necessary to consider the following story of Hindu mythology. During the beginning of time, Lord Vishnu was conferring immortality on the "planetary beings" by feeding them a special potion called *amrita*. Just as Venus, Mercury, Jupiter, and the others were drinking the *amrita* and gaining immortality, a *rakshasa*, or serpent-demon, entered the room and drank some of the potion. The Sun and Moon saw the demon and informed Lord Vishnu, who instantly grabbed His sword and severed the demon in half. Unfortunately, the demon did not die because it had already swallowed the *amrita* and become immortal. The creature, now cut in two, became two malefic beings that live in our birthcharts (and therefore in our lives). The beings are named Rahu and Ketu.

Rahu, the head of the serpent, represents insatiable cravings and desires for power and worldly accomplishment. Ketu, the bottom portion of the serpent, symbolizes the opposite of Rahu's significations. Ketu represents spirituality, psychic ability, detachment from the world, and the yoga of discrimination. The natal house position of Rahu indicates areas of life in which a person craves benefits. In Foster's case—Rahu in the ninth house—she craves higher knowledge and travel to foreign countries. If not for Rahu's strong, stationary retrograde position in the ninth house, Foster might have avoided college entirely or had serious problems in college life. This is because the ninth house governs higher knowledge, and is, aside from Rahu's powerful and beneficial placement there, seriously afflicted. The ninth house is afflicted because it contains "fallen" Mars (Mars in Cancer) and is aspected by Saturn. Ketu, the bottom half of the demon, occupies the third house in Jodie Foster's chart. This is a good placement because malefic planets are well-placed in the third, sixth, tenth, and eleventh houses (called *upachaya* or growing houses). Ketu in the third house gives excellent willpower, and this means Foster can fulfill desires easily. Because Ketu is so closely aspected by malefic Saturn, however, Ketu dasas and bhuktis may be difficult or frustrating. Rahu and Ketu will be described further in later charts.

The best dasa-bhukti during Jodie Foster's Moon period is that of Moon-Jupiter, which is under way as this book is being written. The

Moon-Jupiter period is auspicious because Jupiter aspects the Moon, thus bestowing its benefic energy onto the Moon. The Moon-Jupiter period in this chart brings remarkable happiness as well as great career benefits and success. In the lunar-based system of Hindu astrology, the Moon is the most important planetary influence. If the Moon is weak or afflicted in a person's chart, his or her life is generally filled with pain, suffering, struggle, and strife. If the Moon is well-placed and well-aspected, the person is blessed with abundance, comforts, happiness, and general good fortune. Wealthy, successful, and famous individuals typically have a well-placed, favorably aspected Moon in their chart (i.e., the Moon in the sign of Cancer or Taurus or in the fifth or ninth house, or the Moon aspected by Jupiter, Venus, or Mercury). To a Hindu astrologer, at first glance the Moon in Jodie Foster's chart looks weak because it is a waning Moon (growing smaller) and is not very bright. (To determine whether the Moon is waxing or waning in a birthchart, examine the Moon's relationship to the Sun. If the Moon, which is a faster moving planet than the Sun, is moving toward the conjunction of the Sun, it is a waning Moon. If it is moving toward the opposition of the Sun, the Moon is waxing or growing bigger.) However, the Moon is so strongly aspected by benefic Jupiter that its brightness and waning condition are quite irrelevant.

The most troublesome dasa of Jodie Foster's life is that of Mars, the one that follows the Moon dasa and begins in the year 2000. Mars is fallen in her chart because it is in the sign of Cancer. The Hindus have narrowed down the placements of "exaltations" and "falls" to their exact degrees (e.g., Venus is exalted in twenty-seven degrees Pisces and fallen in twenty-seven degrees Virgo, Moon is exalted in three degrees Taurus and fallen in three degrees Scorpio, and so forth). Mars is most extremely fallen in the twenty-eighth degree of Cancer, and Foster's Mars is in the twenty-fifth degree of Cancer. This is a bad condition that portends serious problems for seven years. As if the fallen Mars placement were not enough, Mars is aspected by malefic Saturn and Rahu. The worst dasa-bhukti will be Mars-Saturn, because Mars, the dasa planet, will pick up all of Saturn's harmful energy during that time. Mars rules the first house and is so afflicted that during Mars dasa Jodie Foster's confidence, reputation, and well-being will be extremely vulnerable. She might also have accidents that harm her appearance. Her health will be at risk because Mars rules the sixth house. Mars rules the bloodstream, so Foster may suffer illnesses caused by weak or impure blood. Because the sixth house rules enemies and competitors, Foster will be in danger from enemies and competitors. Because Mars occupies the ninth house, she will have problems with religious teachers, spiritual individuals, and foreigners. Travels may also bring unhappiness. If Foster were in contact with her father, she would likely suffer on his account (Jodie's father left before she was born —apparently due to the heavily afflicted ninth house, which contains two malefics and is aspected by Saturn). Regarding the signification of father, South Indian astrologers consider the ninth house to represent the father, while North Indian astrologers give this signification to the tenth house. I have seen some charts where the ninth house signifies the father, and others where the tenth house represents the father. In Foster's case, it is clearly the ninth house.

Hindu astrology provides a number of traditional remedies to alleviate karmic problems indicated by afflicted planets or bad dasas and bhuktis. During the Mars dasa, Jodie Foster should wear the gemstone of Mars—red coral. (Actually, because Mars rules her first house, red coral is her "birthstone", and should be worn her entire life. In the Mars dasa, however, the size of the red coral may be increased to five or ten carats.) More importantly, she should have a *yagya* performed. A *yagya* is a mantra-chanting ceremony that Hindu priests perform in order to alleviate karmic difficulties revealed by a person's birthchart. *Yagyas* are easily obtained by contacting Hindu temples in America or India. In Jodie Foster's case, the most crucial times to have *yagyas* performed are in the Mars dasa, Saturn bhukti and in the Mars dasa, Rahu bhukti. However, the wisest decision might be to have one *yagya* performed each year for the entire seven years of Mars dasa. Small *Yagyas*, such as a *nava graha yagya*, which generally take about two hours to perform, cost approximately $125 or $150 in America as of this writing. (In Foster's case, a larger *yagya* would be even better, one that might involve a priest chanting for several days and that would require a larger financial sacrifice.) Jodie Foster may also gain relief by chanting the Mars mantra daily throughout the entire dasa. A mantra is a two- or three-sentence Hindu prayer in Sanskrit. Because fallen Mars occupies the ninth house, the house of religion, philosophy, faith, and devotion, she is unlikely to gain help from religious sources during Mars dasa. Although Foster has a faithful and spiritual nature, indicated by Jupiter aspecting the Moon so strongly, she will have troubles in religious and spiritual matters in Mars dasa. She must also beware of charlatans and fraudulent gurus her whole life because of her afflicted ninth house.

The fallen Mars in Foster's natal chart indicates a lack of confidence (because Mars rules the first house). Any weakness in this area, however, is not obvious to the casual observer because the Sun and Mercury occupy the first house, and this gives a very powerful and confident appearance. Also, she may have good confidence in Sun and Moon periods because those planets are so well-aspected. But whenever Foster experiences Mars bhuktis or the Mars dasa, her confidence and inner strength may diminish quite significantly.

Determining Foster's confidence outside of periods relating to first house planets (Mars, Sun, and Mercury—the planets occupying and ruling the first house) is difficult because the ruler of the first house is weak but the occupying planets are strong. In Hindu astrology, where rulerships are monumentally significant, the perpetual question that exists in analyzing a birthchart house is whether to give more weight to planets in a house or to the condition of the house ruler. Even if the house ruler is slightly more significant, as I believe, it is crucial to consider the current dasa and bhukti.

Jodie Foster became famous for her performance in the 1976 film, *Taxi Driver*. She was in Venus dasa, Jupiter bhukti, and was nominated for an oscar. Although Venus dasa always brings some interest or activities in the arts, Venus in this chart does not portend fame in its dasa. Because Venus both rules and occupies the twelfth house, the twenty-year dasa is mainly connected to spiritual evolution, sexual experiences, debts and expenses, and travels to remote foreign countries. The dasa also relates to love relationships because Venus rules the seventh house. Although Venus is in Libra, its own sign, Venus is significantly afflicted because it is aspected by Mars and Saturn, two malefics. Whenever a house or planet is aspected by two malefic planets, serious damage results. It is likely that Foster had serious troubles in many of the areas mentioned above during her Venus dasa, which occurred in childhood. It is perhaps not coincidental that she became famous playing the role of a child with Venusian difficulties—a child prostitute.

Foster's chart is extremely career oriented, and she has been on television since the age of three. Because her natal chart is so powerful, prominence could be gained in the bhukti of any very well-placed and well-aspected planet. Jupiter bhukti, the subperiod during which she was honored with her first Oscar nomination for *Taxi Driver*, was very favorable because Jupiter in this chart is especially powerful and benefic. Jupiter is strong because it is in an angular house and is aspected within one degree by the benefic Moon. The Moon is benefic by nature and is also benefic because it rules the ninth house—the best house in a birthchart. Therefore, it throws an excellent aspect onto Jupiter, and the Jupiter bhukti would bring positive results for all of Jupiter's significations. In Foster's chart, Jupiter rules the second house (money) and the fifth house (art). (In Hindu astrology the fifth house represents painting and crafts while the third house rules music, dance, and drama.) The fifth house is also *poorvapunya* or past-life credit. Because Jupiter rules the house of past-life credit and is so well-aspected, during Jupiter periods and subperiods Foster gets abundant benefits because of efforts she has made in previous lifetimes. Because Jupiter occupies the fourth house, her past-life credit promises prosperous fourth house matters—land, homes, cars, boats, happiness, and so on.

In summary, Jupiter periods bring Jodie Foster artistic benefits, happiness, plenty of money, nice homes, cars, boats, conveyances, and abundant property. Because Jupiter is the planet of religion, philosophy, and higher knowledge, she also benefits in these areas every time she experiences a Jupiter period or subperiod.

In predicting the effects of dasas, the natal chart as a whole must be considered. For Jodie Foster, Mars dasa will be a rough one, and she will undoubtedly have her hands full during those seven years. But, in trying to determine whether her life will completely crumble and whether she will lose her prestige and fame, it is crucial to assess the entire natal chart. When a dasa of an extremely afflicted planet occurs in the life of an average or relatively powerless person, the damaging effects are usually more debilitating and incessant. In fact, the difference between bad dasas for common people and bad dasas for extraordinary people is that extraordinary people have greater resources to tap, and they therefore recover more quickly and gracefully (as long as the dasa does not predict such things as death or insanity).

Before concluding that Jodie Foster will lose her wealth, power, and reputation for seven straight years in Mars dasa, consider these natal chart conditions: two planets, Saturn and Venus, occupy their own signs, thus strengthening their significations and influence; Jupiter aspects the Moon to the exact degree, conferring all kinds of blessings, luck, fortune, and prosperity; the Moon is angular (tenth house), adding to its strength; Jupiter is also angular (occupying the fourth) and is exactly aspected by the benefic Moon (the ninth house ruler); and finally, the third house, which in Hindu astrology represents a person's courage, will power, and ability to focus, could not be stronger. Malefics in the third house are considered excellent and Foster has both Saturn and Ketu in the third! The Mars dasa will be Foster's most difficult one, but she will not roll over and die because the going gets tough. Her strength will be tested, but the natal chart indicates that she has more than enough ability to conquer adversity.

Experts in Hindu astrology will also notice that Mars attains *neechabhanga rajayoga*, a kind of cancellation of debilitation that occurs because 1) the ruler of the house holding the fallen planet, in this case the Moon, is angular, and 2) the planet which would be exalted in the sign holding the fallen planet, in this case Jupiter, is angular. Astrologers differ in their interpretations of *neechabhanga* planets. Some say that a fallen planet that gains *neechabhanga rajayoga* functions as if it were exalted. In my experience, and according to my mentors, some alleviation of affliction occurs, but never enough to remove all of the suffering indicated.

Marlon Brando has won Academy Awards during two dasa-bhuktis that clearly indicate fame, prominence, and recognition. The first oscar came in March 1954 for his performance in *On The Waterfront* during a Venus dasa, Jupiter bhukti. Although both Jupiter and Venus are "natural benefics," it is the natal conditions and placements of the planets that confer such good effects. First, look at the marvelous disposition of Venus, which occupies its own sign, Taurus, and is aspected by benefic Jupiter. (Jupiter throws an even more benefic aspect than usual because it rules the fifth house—the second best house in a Hindu chart.) Venus is completely free of aspects from malefic planets. Obviously, the Venus dasa was a favorable one for all Venusian matters, and these twenty years would produce excellent success in artistic endeavors, as well as conferring abundant comforts and pleasures on Brando. Because Venus occupies the seventh house, the Venus dasa also means he would have artistic and beautiful lovers and marriage partners.

The best dasa-bhukti during the twenty years of Venus dasa was Venus-Jupiter because Jupiter throws its benefic aspect directly onto Venus. Whenever two planets involved in a dasa-bhukti aspect each other natally, the effects are extremely good or bad, depending on the benefic or malefic natures of the planets. In this case, the dasa-bhukti is extraordinarily beneficial. Furthermore, Jupiter is placed in the first house, indicating recognition, promotion, great confidence, and general well-being. The Venus-Jupiter dasa-bhukti produced great fame for Brando in 1954, when he appeared in two giant hits, *The Wild One* and *On The Waterfront.*

Brando's fame began to grow in 1951, during Venus dasa, Rahu bhukti, when he was nominated for an Oscar for *A Streetcar Named Desire.* Rahu (called the North Node in western astrology) is extremely well-placed in the tenth house (career) in Brando's chart, and the power of Rahu brought his second Oscar for *The Godfather* during his Moon dasa, Rahu bhukti.

One benefic in the first house along with a benefic aspect thrown onto the first house creates a beautiful appearance, strong confidence, and a great likelihood of fame. Two other actors who have remarkably powerful first houses in their Hindu charts are Dustin Hoffman and Paul Newman. Hoffman has Jupiter in the first house in its own sign (Sagittarius) and Venus in the seventh house. Paul Newman has three benefics in the first house: Venus, Mercury, and Jupiter, which occupies its own sign, Sagittarius.

Brando's second Oscar was awarded in April, 1972 for his magnificent performance in *The Godfather.* Winning the Oscar occurred in a Moon dasa, Rahu bhukti that, in this chart, is excellent for career achievement. First, let us analyze the Moon dasa. At first glance, the Moon seems extremely afflicted because it is very dim and waning (a Sun-Moon conjunction indicates a new moon birth, while a Sun Moon opposition means a full moon birth). The Moon is also "combust" the Sun, a harmful condition that exists when a planet is conjunct within six or eight degrees of the Sun and becomes "burned" by the Sun's hot rays. (Remember that the Sun is a malefic in Hindu astrology.) These afflictions cause problems that are discussed further on. On the positive side, however, there is a condition that gives supreme strength to the Moon, despite its obvious problems. The Moon forms what is called a *rajayoga*, or "royal union" in the fifth house, the second best house of a Hindu chart and the house of *poorvapunya* or past-life credit. A *rajayoga* is an extremely rare and highly beneficial condition that occurs when two planets ruling good houses form a conjunction. The Moon's *rajayoga* status alone means that some excellent effects were predictable in Moon dasa, despite all the other afflictions to the Moon.

Regarding the *rajayoga* in Brando's chart, the Sun and Moon rule the ninth and tenth houses, which are both important and benefic houses. As if the *rajayoga* in the fifth house were not powerful enough, the Sun and Moon (and the fifth house) are aspected by benefic Jupiter. And because Jupiter throws its aspect onto Pisces, the sign that Jupiter rules, the aspect is a much more auspicious one than usual. The Sun's happy position (tenth house ruler—career planet) in the fifth (past-life credit) means that Marlon Brando gains tremendous career benefits in this life because of career efforts he has made in past lives.

A person's entire life is affected by positive or negative actions from past incarnations and this is reflected in the birthchart. However, astrological indications, connected to the fifth house specifically indicate events or conditions that must occur in this life because the karma has been building lifetime after lifetime and cannot be held back any longer. The more one studies Hindu astrology, the more obvious it becomes that individuals who are enormously famous or remarkably wealthy are reaping benefits of work from past lives. This certainly is true in Marlon

04-03-1924, 11:00 PM CST, Omaha, Nebraska
41° N 17, 96° W 01
Source: Doris Doane, Lois Rodden data base

RASI

5th ♓ ☉ 21° ☽ 20°	6th ♈ ☿ 4°	7th ♉ ♀ 6°	8th ♊
4th ♒ ☋ 8°			9th ♋
3rd ♑			10th ♌ ☊ 8°
2nd ♐ ♂ 24°	1st ♏ ♃ 27° Asc. 10° 52'	12th ♎ ♄ ℞ 7°	11th ♍

VIMSOTTARI

	DASA Mo. Day Year	BHUKTI Mo. Day Year
☉	09-01-1963	♀☊ 11-01-1950
		♀♃ 11-01-1953
☽	09-01-1969	♀♄ 07-01-1956
♂	09-01-1979	☽☊ 02-01-1971
		☽♃ 08-01-1972
☊	09-01-1986	☽♄ 12-01-1973
♃		☊♃ 05-13-1989
		☊♄ 10-07-1991
♄		☊☿ 08-13-1994
		☊☋ 03-01-1997
☿	04-03-1924	☊♀ 03-19-1998
☋	09-01-1936	
♀	09-01-1943	

NAVAMSA

6th ♃	7th	8th ☿	9th ☊
5th ♀			10th
4th ☉ ☽			11th
3rd ♄ ℞ ☋	2nd ♂	1st Asc.	12th

NORTH INDIAN

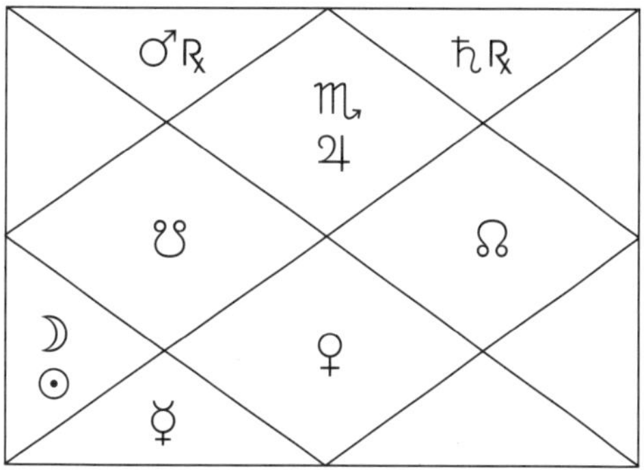

400 Brando's case. (Some astrologers consider the ninth house to govern *poorvapunya* because the ninth house signifies luck. There is a significant difference, however, between luck in general and specific past-life credit or debt that MUST occur this lifetime. The ninth house, in fact, represents something opposite of past-life effects—it signifies a person's FUTURE life. This includes the person's reputation on earth following his or her death. A good example is the supremely powerful ninth house of John F. Kennedy's Hindu chart. His ninth house contains Sun, Jupiter, and Venus in Taurus (Venus' sign) completely free from aspects of malefic planets. This is why, astrologically speaking, JFK's prestige increased so greatly after his death.)

The subperiod of 1972 was Rahu, the top portion of the demon and the so-called "shadowy planet", which represents worldly power and material benefits. Rahu is extremely well-placed in the tenth house (career). When a person's most intense cravings and desires (Rahu) are focused toward career success, the result is fame, prominence, and professional accomplishment. Also, in Hindu astrology, malefic planets cause very good effects when they occupy the third, sixth, and tenth houses (*upachaya* or "growing houses.") Note that in later years, during Mars dasa, Brando claimed to have retired from the limelight and indicated that he was not going to make more films. The dasa following Mars, however, is Rahu (which began in September 1986). Because Rahu occupies the tenth house, it is not surprising that he returned to prominence in one way or another during Rahu's eighteen-year period. He made a number of films during Rahu dasa, and even though he played the smallest of roles, he always managed to capture global media attention.

The Moon is the single most important planet in a Hindu chart and the house it occupies shows areas of life where a person will play out a great deal of karma. The Sun is called the *atmakaraka*, or indicator of the soul, and though not as important as the Moon, its house placement also indicates vital areas of interest. In Hindu astrology, the fifth house represents "kingship" or politics. Because the Sun-Moon rajayoga occupies the fifth house, Brando is extremely political. He refused to accept his second Oscar for political reasons relating to the plight of Native Americans. He has also been active in civil rights causes during his lifetime. The fifth house also rules the arts (painting, drawing, and crafts) and the mind. Having both the Sun and Moon in the fifth house creates artistic and mental leanings in life. Brando is clearly a thinker, and one of his greatest hobbies is said to be reading.

The Moon, which in Hindu astrology governs common sense, the memory, and the peace of mind, is afflicted in Brando's chart, despite its *rajayoga* status and its very strong aspect from benefic Jupiter. The Moon is combust the malefic, heat-producing Sun, as described above. It is also aspected by malefic Mars. Brando's mental happiness has always been disturbed, and he was persuaded by director Elia Kazan to see a psychiatrist early in his career (which he later claimed to be of some help). Mental calmness is also damaged because of Mercury's afflicted condition. Mercury, the planet ruling the intellect, is in the harmful sixth house (a *dusthana* or grief-producing house) and is aspected by malefic Saturn. (Whenever both planets of the mind—Moon and Mercury—are afflicted in a birthchart, incidentally, the person almost always suffers from headaches.)

Despite his fame during the Moon dasa, Brando's peace of mind must have been more disturbed than ever before. An angry state of mind was probably partly the cause of his refusing to accept his second Oscar. This was also responsible for the extremely disparaging remarks he made about his own artistry and the entire field of acting at a time when he could have been basking in the joy of fame and recognition. According to biographies, much of Brando's intense suffering and depression occurred because of his mother's alcoholism. The Moon, of course, represents one's mother. (Mercury is also a "*karaka*" or indicator of mother in Hindu astrology and Mercury is, as described above, quite afflicted.)

In order for Brando to lessen his mental disturbances and moodiness, he should wear a large, good-quality pearl, the gemstone of the Moon. (The "secondary stone" for pearl is moonstone, and this may be worn instead, although the healing effect may be somewhat weaker.) The most unfortunate period for Brando's mental state was Moon dasa, Sun bhukti starting in March 1979, the year *Apocalypse Now* appeared. This was a bad period because the Moon is harmfully aspected by the Sun. It would have been advantageous for Brando to have a *yagya* performed during the six months of the Moon dasa, Sun bhukti in order to ameliorate the almost certain problems (for an explanation of *yagyas* see the explanation of Jodi Foster's afflicted Mars dasa). Incidentally, the Moon dasa, Sun bhukti happens to be the period and subperiod of the two planets of the *rajayoga* and therefore some very good effects related to the houses that the Sun and Moon rule and occupy (fifth, ninth, and tenth—art, politics, children, luck, travel, religion, and career) could have been predicted.

From his birthchart, it appears absurd that Marlon Brando has been married more than once (he has had three wives). Venus occupies the seventh house and is in its own sign, Taurus. Furthermore, it is aspected by benefic Jupiter. There are, however, some important points to consider. First, Venus in the seventh house—even when well-aspected—may give too much passion and emotional craving to produce smooth married life. The person has such strong sexuality that "intrigues in love" (according to ancient Hindu sages) result. The benefit of a seventh house Venus in Hindu astrology is a tendency to attract beautiful, outstanding partners and the ability to attract any love partner one desires. It also means that the person is "skilled in the art of sensual pleasures," and that he or she fulfills cravings effortlessly.

The next and most severe problem with Brando's married life relates to his second house, which, in Hindu astrology, governs family life (in western astrology, family life is the fourth house.) The second house, as ruler of family life, must always be analyzed when diagnosing marital happiness and harmony. Brando has malefic Mars in the second house, which is further harmed by Saturn throwing its malefic aspect onto Mars and the house itself. This is a profoundly negative condition which causes a steady stream of fighting and bickering. In the same way that two benefics aspecting or occupying one house produce tremendous benefit, when two malefics bestow their energies onto a house, that house is badly harmed. (Note that there are no benefic planets aspecting the second house.)

Mars in the second house is a good influence for money matters, though usually the person with that placement makes money through extremely hard work or, in some cases, illegal means. What gives Brando such great earning ability, aside from an extraordinarily powerful chart as a whole, is the exchange of signs (mutual reception) between Mars and Jupiter—the rulers of the first and second houses, and even more importantly, his well-aspected eleventh house. The rajayoga planets, the Sun and Moon, throw their aspects onto the eleventh house. This causes something of a *rajayoga* effect on the eleventh house, the house of "gains and profits by any means," or in other words, money that may come from side ventures. All of Brando's acting jobs in later years have been side ventures because they are incredibly brief and sporadic and no longer constitute earnings from daily work. In the charts of exceptionally wealthy individuals, it is common for both the second house and the eleventh house to be very powerful.

Also, relating to the eleventh house reaping some *rajayoga* benefit, Brando was blessed with a remarkably close friendship with entertainer Wally Cox, whom he knew since childhood. After Cox died, Brando kept his ashes in his house, where they reportedly still reside. According to one biography, Brando talks to his deceased friend (via the ashes) regularly. It should be mentioned, incidentally, that the eleventh house of Brando's chart also contains a major affliction because Mercury, the eleventh house ruler, is so afflicted. Whenever one house of a chart is both extremely well-disposed and extremely afflicted, the result is that both very good and very bad effects can be expected, especially depending upon the transits and dasa-bhuktis. One good birthchart influence does NOT cancel out one bad birthchart effect. Therefore, Brando must certainly suffer on account of friends from time to time. Mercury periods and subperiods must also produce a great deal of distress.

The second house also rules speech, and malefics occupying or aspecting the second house indicate a propensity for foul language. The combination of Brando's anger (caused by the Moon's intense combustion with the Sun) and his constant use of expletives (because of his damaged second house) make for some very distinctive interviews on the rare occasions Brando gives them.

Ketu (called the South Node in western astrology) in the fourth house is a very bad placement for Brando's mother. Although he was extremely close to his mother (Sun-Moon conjunctions, when tight by degree, always cause an intense bond with the mother and a constant craving for the mother's affection), Ketu in the fourth house indicates weird problems with the mother. Alcoholism and mental afflictions are typical effects on the mother's part. Brando's Ketu dasa occurred between the age of twelve and nineteen, and during this period his mother's life deteriorated and her drinking became excessive. Brando, haunted by this, became rebellious and unmanageable during these years.

Ketu, the planet of spirituality, psychic ability, and discrimination, occupies the fourth house, the house of endings and the heart, among other things (the heart in western astrology is ruled by the fifth house). Ketu in Brando's fourth house means that he feels a detachment or spirituality deep within his heart, which will increase toward the end of his life. His last few years, therefore, are likely to be introspective, spiritual, and as isolated as possible during a materialistic, fame-craving tenth-house Rahu dasa.

Brando's excessive weight problem does not show up in his chart clearly. Hindu astrological sages declare that if the sixth house is strong and well-aspected, the person has "the blessings of a fine appetite." In present day, this translates into weight problems. Brando's sixth house, however, is weak because it is aspected by Saturn, and the aspect is worse than usual because Saturn aspects Aries, Saturn's fallen sign. Also on the negative side, Saturn aspects Mars, the ruler of the sixth house. In Brando's case, his hefty weight is caused by the nearly stationary retrograde condition of Jupiter (only two days before stationary). Jupiter, which has a mean motion of approximately five minutes

404   per day, moved about three SECONDS on the day of Brando's birth. When Jupiter is extraordinarily powerful, the person is very lucky, but he or she may indulge excessively in pleasures (food, drink, sex, and so on.)

This is the chart of a man who, if it were not for two malefics in the first house, would be far too spiritual and pure-hearted for the coarse activities of political life. The Moon is the most important planet in Hindu astrology and in this chart the Moon rules the first house, the most significant house of a birthchart. Notice that the Moon in Vice President Al Gore's chart is closely conjunct Jupiter in Jupiter's own sign, Sagittarius. This confers purity, a profound faith in God, and a never-ending sense of optimism, positivity, and idealism. It also indicates that Gore's life is charmed and that he will enjoy comforts and pleasures during his whole life. Next, the Sun (the *atmakaraka* or indicator of the soul) occupies the ninth house—the house of religion and philosophy. This means that Gore has tremendous faith and devotion, and that his soul is connected to issues of higher knowledge, religion, and philosophy. On top of all this, both Jupiter and the Moon throw beneficial aspects onto the twelfth house, the house of *moksha* (enlightenment or final liberation). This highly spiritual condition reveals that Gore is interested in raising his consciousness, and that during this lifetime he will make significant strides in his path toward perfection. It also means he gains great results from any spiritual techniques he practices.

The sixth house, the house containing the Moon-Jupiter conjunction, is one of the strongest houses in this chart. Two of the main significations of the sixth house are health matters and, according the ancient Hindu astrological scriptures, "enemies and competitors." This means Gore's health and recuperative powers are extremely robust, and that he will easily overcome enemies and competitors that get in his way. A person is favored in overcoming his or her rivals if the sixth house contains either benefic or malefics planets. Malefics in the sixth (i.e. Mars, Saturn, Sun, Rahu, or Ketu) indicate that a person defeats or destroys his or her enemies and competitors in a rather conscious or purposeful way. This does not mean that the person looks for trouble or enjoys vanquishing rivals. It means that when enemies appear, the person summons strong psychic energy to handle the problem quickly and effectively.

Benefics in the sixth house, though producing just as beneficial results, operate in a slightly different way. If benefics occupy the sixth house, the person rarely encounters enemies and is rather unaware that competitors exists, even as he or she effortlessly overcomes them. A person with a strong, well-aspected sixth house may win a particular position without ever finding out that twenty or thirty other applicants were also vying for the same post. More importantly, the person is exceptionally well-liked, and therefore others have no thoughts whatsoever of harming or taking advantage of the person. This is the case with Al Gore. Interestingly, during the vice presidential debates between Gore and ex-Vice President Dan Quayle, when Quayle became more and more mean-spirited in his attempts to crush his enemy, Gore barely seemed to notice Quayle's malevolent attitude and never even slightly resorted to similar tactics. What appeared to be southern gentlemanly behavior was, from the astrological perspective, the result of two major benefics in the sixth house. Consistent with his sixth house birthchart karma, Gore took the vice presidency away from Quayle without ever uttering a mean word.

As mentioned earlier in this text, the sixth house is known as an *upachaya* or "growing" house, along with the third, tenth, and eleventh houses. The planets occupying these houses signify energies in a person's life which gradually develop and increase with each passing year. For instance, if Mercury is in the third, sixth, tenth, or eleventh house of a Hindu chart, the person's intellectual and communicative abilities grow stronger with age. Likewise, if Venus is in an *upachaya* house, the person's artistic talents and aesthetic sensibilities increase over time. In Al Gore's case, with the Moon and Jupiter in the sixth house, his religious and spiritual nature (Jupiter) continues to grow as do his nurturing tendencies and his love for the masses (Moon).

Gore's sixth house, the house representing health and healing, is so powerful that his main political interest is to halt the environmental crisis now threatening human civilization, to heal the whole earth. Even before his ecological commitment, he was known for his involvement in health issues. In 1984 he sponsored the Organ Procurement and Transplantation Act. Later, he went on to become vice chairman of Congress' Biomedical Ethics board. With his healing ability (as indicated by his strong sixth house), Gore would probably have been quite successful in the medical profession, had he chosen so.

Unfortunately for Vice President Gore, his chart contains a malefic conjunction of Mars and Saturn in the first house. Both Mars and Saturn are extremely afflicted in this chart, because both malefic planets throw their harmful energy onto each other. Furthermore, Mars is in the twenty-fifth degree of Cancer, extremely close to its most intense "fallen" position—the twenty-eighth degree of Cancer. Terrible effects are pre-

AL GORE

03-31-1948, 12:53 PM EST, Washington,D.C.
38° N 54, 77° W 02
Source: birth certificate, Lois Rodden data base

RASI

9th ♓ ☉ 17°	10th ♈ ☊ 21°	11th ♉ ♀ 2°	12th ♊
8th ♒ ☿ 23°			1st ♋ ♄℞ 22° ♂ 25° Asc. 11° 06'
7th ♑			2nd ♌
6th ♐ ☽ 10° ♃ 5°	5th ♏	4th ♎ ☋ 21° 22'	3rd ♍

VIMSOTTARI

	DASA Mo. Day Year	BHUKTI Mo. Day Year
☉	12-14-1969	♂♄ 05-05-1988
		♂☿ 06-14-1989
☽	12-14-1975	♂☋ 06-11-1990
		♂♀ 11-08-1990
♂	12-14-1985	♂☉ 01-08-1992
		♂☽ 05-14-1992
☊	12-14-1992	
♃	12-14-2010	
		☊♃ 08-26-1995
♄		☊♄ 01-20-1998
		☊☿ 11-26-2000
☿		☊☋ 06-14-2003
		☊♀ 07-02-2004
☋	03-31-1948	☊☉ 07-02-2007
		☊☽ 05-26-2008
♀	12-14-1949	☊♂ 11-26-2009

NAVAMSA

6th	7th ☋	8th ☿ ♃	9th
5th ♂			10th ☽
4th ♀ ♄			11th
3rd ☉	2nd	1st ☊ Asc.	12th

NORTH INDIAN

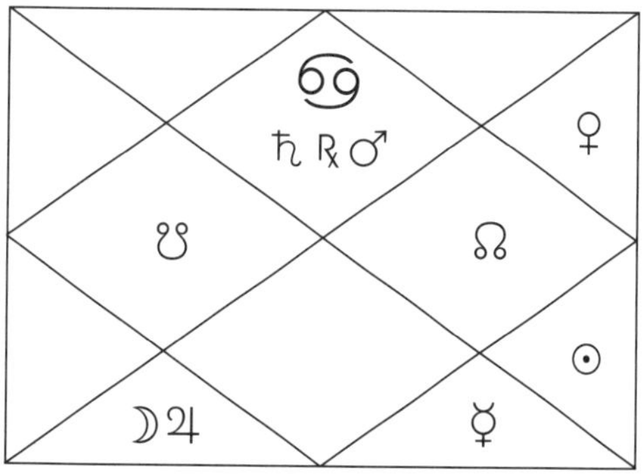

408 dictable in either a Mars dasa, Saturn bhukti or a Saturn dasa, Mars bhukti. In May 1988, Al Gore entered a thirteen-month Mars-Saturn dasa-bhukti which demonstrated the kind of dreadful effects a really bad dasa-bhukti can bring. Mars rules the fifth house (children) and during this ominous period, in April 1989, writes Gore, "I walked outside of a baseball stadium and saw my son Albert... get hit by a car, fly thirty feet through the air and scrape along the pavement another twenty feet until he came to rest in a gutter." (Miraculously, Albert Gore Jr. did not die and is now reported to be completely recovered.)

During Gore's Mars-Saturn dasa-bhukti, he was at risk in matters pertaining to the fifth, tenth, and first houses, the houses that Mars rules and occupies. Therefore, Gore's career was vulnerable, as was his health, peace of mind, children, etc. Considering the ominous astrological conditions, Gore was fortunate not to have encountered violence, a disfiguring accident, or a major career fall during Mars dasa, Saturn bhukti. His wonderful Moon-Jupiter conjunction in Sagittarius confers not only great luck but also protection from harm. Fortunately, he will not experience a Saturn dasa, Mars bhukti until June 2039 at the age of ninety-one!

Another excellent example of the efficacy of dasas as predictors is the Rahu dasa which began just as Gore ascended from senator to vice president. (The exact date Rahu dasa started was December 14, 1992.) Rahu (called the North Node in western astrology) occupies the tenth house, which portends a significant increase in fame and prominence for a full eighteen years. This bodes well for Gore, whose presidential aspirations are well known. In 1988, Gore was the youngest presidential candidate in U.S. history, and he was, according to *Current Biography Yearbook,* "the most aggressive" democratic candidate. Gore should do especially well in subperiods of Jupiter, Moon, Venus, and Sun because these planets are all very well-placed or well-aspected. Indeed, Rahu dasa, Jupiter bhukti, which starts August, 1995 and goes until January 1998, is likely to bring extraordinary success.

Unfortunately, however, Rahu, the planet representing insatiable desire and cravings for worldly power, rarely brings happiness and contentment. The term "insatiable desire" is extremely accurate for Rahu because in Rahu dasa, no matter how much a person accomplishes, he or she only craves more! And while Gore's star may continue to rise during the eighteen years of Rahu dasa, as the period progresses, Gore will almost certainly lose some of the spiritual sweetness of his life. (It will, of course, return during the immediately following Jupiter dasa.) Rahu's influence is very materialistic, and Gore, who is known to be a very religious man (*Current Biography* says "religious ties that are fervent but not fanatic," and conservative political commentator John McLaughlin calls him "too good to be true"), may find that the power of his prayer weakens. When he prays during Rahu dasa, he may no longer feel the usual connection to God he has always known. Or he may feel like his communications to God go unheard. Rahu is a very materialistic and earthy influence.

Although he graduated *cum laude* from Harvard with a degree in Government, at one time Gore felt (according to *Current Biography Yearbook*) "that Politics would be the last profession he entered." *Current Biography* also quotes Gore as saying that he enrolled at Vanderbilt University's Graduate School of Religion "to study the spiritual issues that were most important to me at the time." The astrological condition most responsible for Gore's life in politics, aside from Rahu in the tenth house—which gives an intense desire and ability to sway masses (the charts of Jimmy Carter, Mahatma Ghandi, and Johnny Carson all have Rahu in the tenth house)—is the Mars-Saturn conjunction in the first house. Whenever Mars is conjunct with Saturn (or when Mars is with Mercury), the person has an extremely practical nature. Technical ability, such as talent in architecture, drafting, engineering, and politics is often evident. In Gore's case the fifth house (the house of politics) is prominent because Venus aspects the fifth house and because the ruler of the fifth house (Mars) is in the first house.

The condition of Mars is both extraordinarily afflicted and extraordinarily powerful. As mentioned earlier in this text, one positive element does not cancel out a negative element. Both extremes can occur primarily dependent upon the current dasas and bhuktis. The astrological condition that confers enormous power and beneficial energy onto Mars (its negative indications were described above) is its *rajayogakaraka* (royal union indicator) status because it rules two excellent houses (the fifth and tenth). And, Gore was born about a day-and-a-half after Mars turned stationary direct! This means that Mars, which has an average motion of thirty-three minutes per day, was only moving one minute per day when Gore was born. There is almost nothing stronger than a stationary direct or extremely slow-moving planet in forward motion.

Having Mars and Saturn in the first house is one of the strongest indicators of selfishness in a horoscope (it also causes significant depression and unhappiness). Although a strong self-interest is needed for successful political life, Gore is otherwise quite fortunate that the rest of his chart confers such spiritual tendencies and refined qualities (Moon-Jupiter conjunction in Sagittarius, Sun in the ninth house in Pisces, Venus aspecting the fifth house, etc.). Interestingly, in addition to being called "the most aggressive" Democratic presidential candidate

Al Gore

of 1988 by *Current Biography Yearbook*, the *Wall Street Journal's* David Rogers said, "The consummate politician, Mr. Gore is fiercely competitive, but seems blind to the ambition that drives him." One of the chief criticisms of Gore, says *Current Biography*, is that he "pursues media coverage too aggressively." It goes on to quote a congressional aide who said, "If it's in the news, then young Albert will be there on television."

During the Vietnam war, Gore served as an army reporter, and upon returning home became a reporter with a newspaper in Nashville, Tennessee. In Hindu astrology, writing and journalism are seen from the second house. In Gore's chart, the ruler of the second house is strong because it occupies the ninth house, the best house of a chart, and is free from any malefic aspects. More important, however, the second house is aspected by Mercury, the planet of writing and speaking. Mercury in the second house or aspecting the second house gives good communication and literary talent. It also means the person makes good use of knowledge and may become an author or an authority figure in his or her field. Gore's 1992 book, *Earth In The Balance*, is packed from one end to the other with facts, figures, and statistics. Characteristic of Gore's elevated consciousness and innate spirituality, it is written with wisdom and broad perspective and contains anecdotes from gurus and religious lives such as Mahatma Ghandi.

Married life is difficult for Al Gore, as can easily be seen from his birthchart. In Washington, news articles have said that the Gores have sought marital counseling, and it is no wonder why. Saturn, the ruler of the seventh house (marriage) is conjunct within three degrees of fallen Mars (Mars in Cancer). Saturn does not function well in Cancer because Cancer is opposite Saturn's ownership sign, Capricorn. On top of this, two malefics, Mars and Saturn, aspect the seventh house. This latter condition is a subtle matter because it causes both good and bad.

As malefics, Mars and Saturn clearly throw harmful aspects onto the seventh house and cause marital problems. However, the aspects thrown are cast onto Capricorn, the exaltation sign for Mars and the ownership sign for Saturn and this causes good effects. Although it causes domestic strife, Mars' aspect onto its exaltation sign and seventh house gives power and special qualities to the spouse. Likewise, Saturn's aspect thrown onto the Capricorn seventh house causes marital problems but also bestows upon the spouse elevated Saturnian qualities such as responsibility, discipline, and the ability to be an authority figure in her field. The result of these combined influences in his birthchart means that Gore gets a wife who is powerful, special, authoritative, and successful but that he will have problems, friction, and fighting within his marriage.

Al Gore also has an astrological condition called *kujadosha* (pro-nounced koo-ja-doe-sha) or "Mars affliction" which harms married life and portends divorce. *Kujadosha* occurs when Mars occupies the first house (unless it occupies Aries), the fourth house (unless occupying Scorpio), the seventh house (unless in Capricorn or Pisces), the eighth house (unless in Cancer), and the twelfth house (unless in Sagittarius). (Western astrologers are cautioned to apply this information only to HINDU HOROSCOPES USING THE SIDEREAL ZODIAC.) A person with *kujadosha* is attracted to partners who eventually cause major problems and, in most cases, divorce. The antidote for a person who has *kujadosha* is to marry another who also has *kujadosha*. In this way, the person marries someone who is also paying karmic love debts and is uncon-sciously waiting to be victimized. Thus, neither person gets victimized and the difficult love karma is postponed until a future lifetime. In India, where marriages are prearranged, astrologers always match *kujadosha* individuals with other "Mars-afflicted" individuals.

Fortunately, Al Gore has done something that *Kujadosha* Western-ers rarely do. He has chosen a wife who also has *kujadosha*. Therefore, it is possible that the Gores can stay married. However, the basic afflictions to Gore's seventh house make it clear that he will be plagued with more than his share of trials in married life. Gore's most difficult periods for love matters are his Saturn bhuktis because Saturn rules the seventh house and is afflicted by its conjunction to fallen Mars (his next one, Rahu dasa, Saturn bhukti, occurs from January 1998 until November 2,000). Fortunately, for his domestic happiness, Gore's nineteen-year Saturn dasa doesn't begin until 2036, at the age of seventy-eight. Transits of Saturn through the seventh house of his chart will also be trying, but Saturn's next transit through the seventh house is not until around 2022.

The dasas in John Denver's birthchart are an excellent example of how a person can quickly go from superstardom to a much more introspective and secluded existence. But before saying anything about John Denver's dasas, it is crucial to examine the first house of this chart, which appears completely incongruous with smiley-faced, highly optimistic John Denver. As mentioned previously (in Al Gore's chart analysis), two malefics such as Mars and Saturn occupying the first house are one of the strongest indications of selfishness, unhappiness, and depression. Mars-Saturn conjunctions also confer tremendous technical ability such as talent in law, politics, architecture, engineering, and drafting. None of these descriptions remind of us the artistic, heart-felt, thrilled-to-be-alive singer John Denver. Yet Current Biography Yearbook says that "Denver enrolled at Texas Tech University in Lubbock to study architecture... In Los Angeles, Denver got a job as a draftsman and began making rounds..." Christopher Anderson, in *The Book Of People*, makes a point of describing Denver as a person who is far more serious and moody than he seems. He quotes Denver: "My rocky mountain highs have been balanced by incredible lows. When I get depressed, I question whether life is worth living." These are the results of Mars and Saturn in the first house. It should be noted, incidentally, that in Denver's chart the Mars-Saturn first house conjunction is less harmful than usual because Venus aspects the conjunction and Saturn carries much beneficial energy because of the auspicious houses it rules (Saturn's *rajayogakaraka* status is described a few paragraphs below).

The astrological indications of Denver's infectious buoyancy, charm, and happiness are found in the placements of Jupiter in the fourth house, Jupiter aspecting the Moon, Venus aspecting the ascendant, and the combined influence of three benefic planets in angular houses. The fourth house, in Hindu astrology, represents happiness (Venus is the planet of happiness). Jupiter's position in the fourth house is a great blessing conferring happiness, delight, and enjoyment of life. Whenever the all-important Moon is aspected by Jupiter (or Venus), as in this chart, the person is favored, charmed, and protected from harm. Finally, Venus' angular position gives even more bliss and positivity. Hindu sages say that when Venus is angular the person is so fulfilled that he or she can forgive anyone.

Fundamental birthchart factors indicate that John Denver is extremely career-oriented. Notice that the Moon, the most important planet in a Hindu chart (the Moon, along with the ascendant, represents the person, unlike western astrology where the Sun takes this honor), is in the tenth house (career) and is well-aspected by Jupiter. Also notice that the ruler of the tenth house (career) occupies the first house (personality). John Denver's life is clearly oriented toward profession and public life. However, he entered a seventeen-year Mercury dasa in August 1977 and Mercury in his chart indicates completely introspective, spiritual, and inward tendencies (Mercury's condition is analyzed several paragraphs below). This is why, astrologically speaking, he has disappeared from the limelight.

Denver gained his fame during Saturn dasa. Saturn is a malefic planet. However, because this is a Taurus ascendant, Saturn rules two very auspicious houses, the ninth and tenth. So Saturn becomes what is called a *rajayogakaraka* or "royal union indicator." A *rajayoga* is an extremely special condition which for most charts can only occur when two planets ruling good houses come together in one house to form a conjunction. In the case of a Taurus ascendant chart, an automatic *rajayoga* exists because Saturn rules two good houses—the ninth and tenth. (Libra and Cancer ascendants are the only other ascendants with one-planet rajayogas. Saturn rules the fourth and fifth houses for Libra ascendants, and Mars rules the fifth and tenth houses for Cancer ascendants, thereby causing royal unions). For Taurus ascendant birthcharts, such as John Denver's, Saturn dasas are generally the best periods of all (because Saturn is the *rajayogakaraka*) unless Saturn is afflicted in some serious, unalterable way.

The *rajayoga* caused by Saturn occurs in Denver's first house, the house signifying personality, appearance, and the ability to gain fame and recognition. Saturn is further strengthened because it is an angular house (angular houses are the first, fourth, seventh, and tenth). On top of this, Saturn receives an aspect from Venus, which is an even better than usual benefic aspect because Venus is throwing its aspect onto its own sign, Taurus. Finally, Saturn functions very well in Venus' signs (Saturn is exalted in Venus' other sign, Libra.) Because Saturn rules the tenth house and occupies the first house, Saturn dasa brought positive effects relating to the first and tenth houses, that is, fame and recognition. (Saturn also rules the ninth house and therefore the dasa also brought beneficial results in the area of religion and philosophy. These are described further on.) Denver's career success began in 1969 during Saturn dasa, Moon bhukti when his first record album appeared. The album contained the hit song "Leaving On A Jet Plane," originally made famous by Peter, Paul, and Mary. Denver's rise during the Moon bhukti

JOHN DENVER

12-31-1943, 3:55 PM MWT, Roswell, New Mexico
33° N 24, 104° W 32
Source: birth certificate, Lois Rodden data base

RASI

11th ♓	12th ♈	♂ ℞ 12° ♄ ℞ 28° ♉ Asc. 17° 41'	2nd ♊
10th ♒ ☽ 21°			3rd ♋ ☊ 13°
9th ♑ ☋ 13° ☿ ℞ 1°			4th ♌ ♃ ℞ 3°
8th ♐ ☉ 16°	7th ♏ ♀ 4°	6th ♎	5th ♍

VIMSOTTARI

	DASA Mo. Day Year	BHUKTI Mo. Day Year
☉		♄♀ 05-24-1965
		♄☉ 07-24-1968
☽		♄☽ 07-06-1969
		♄♂ 02-06-1971
♂		♄☊ 03-15-1972
		♄♃ 01-21-1975
☊		
		☋♀ 12-30-1994
♃	12-31-1943	☋☉ 02-30-1996
		☋☽ 07-06-1996
♄	08-03-1958	☋♂ 02-06-1997
		☋☊ 07-03-1997
☿	08-03-1977	
		♀♂ 08-03-2007
☋	08-03-1994	♀☊ 10-03-2008
♀	08-03-2001	♀♄ 06-03-2014
		♀☿ 08-03-2017

NAVAMSA

10th	11th ♂☽	12th ♃ ☋	1st Asc.
9th			2nd
8th ☿			3rd ☉ ♀
7th	6th ☊	5th	4th ♄

NORTH INDIAN

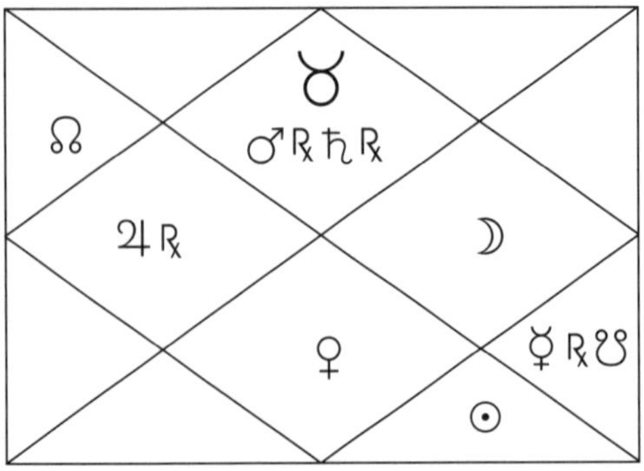

was fitting because the Moon, occupying the tenth house and being aspected by Jupiter, would naturally bring career benefits.

There are, incidentally, two drawbacks to Saturn's condition in Denver's chart, but they are minimal in comparison to Saturn's benefits. The drawbacks are Saturn's retrograde motion (although ancient sages say retrograde planets are strong, dasas of retrograde planets are weaker than normal) and the wide aspect (sixteen degrees) Saturn receives from Mars, the ruler of the evil twelfth house. (Hindu astrology uses the term "evil" simply to mean bad, not wicked or sinful.) These Saturn weaknesses are not, however, enough to significantly alter Saturn's *rajayogakaraka* status and strength.

The dasa that comes after Saturn is Mercury, and in Denver's chart Mercury clearly indicates a period of introspection, introversion, and religious or spiritual pursuits. Unlike his Saturn dasa, the Mercury period does not point at all to worldly desires or materialistic success. Mercury is a good planet in this chart because it rules the fifth house and occupies the ninth house. These are the two best houses in a chart and this condition confers some benefits relating to Mercury and the houses Mercury rules and occupies (the second, fifth, and ninth). These benefits are minor, though, compared to the strong spiritual, introspective, and mystical tendencies along with the assorted difficulties and obstacles indicated by Mercury's retrograde motion in the ninth house conjunct with "otherworldly" Ketu.

Ketu (known as the South Node in western astrology) is the bottom portion of the demon (for the story of how Rahu and Ketu were created, see the analysis of Jodi Foster's chart), and it represents psychic energy, the astral plane, *gnana yoga* (yoga of discrimination), and extreme introversion, among other things. Because Mercury is both retrograde and conjunct with Ketu, the likelihood for Denver to robustly pursue worldly success during Mercury dasa is slight, and even if he does so, he is unlikely to gain the support of nature to which he is accustomed. When asked during interviews about his declining musical success in recent years, Denver has said that when his musical style changed, the public simply did not wish to follow. The subperiods of Moon and Saturn (the well-placed and well-aspected planets ruling and occupying the tenth house) will help with success, and Denver can gain some prominence during these bhuktis. But the Mercury dasa as a whole is spiritual, mystical, and self-reflective at best. At worst, it is filled with obstacles, delays, mental troubles, and problems in business and worldly matters.

When planets are conjunct Ketu, they become harmed or impaired. The closer a planet is to Ketu, the more damaged it is. Planets near Ketu

416 function in an unconscious or uncontrollable way, and the difficulties signified by planets conjunct Ketu manifest strongly during the dasas and bhuktis of such planets. This is what has occurred in Denver's Mercury dasa. Fortunately, Denver's Ketu is twelve degrees away from Mercury, so Mercury is not completely ruined. But Mercury's dasa cannot be expected to produce much benefit in worldly affairs. To understand conjunctions with Ketu, a few examples may be helpful. If Venus, the planet of love, is close to Ketu, the person is likely to have love relationships with weird, mystical, alcoholic, or drug-addicted individuals. Or the person attracts partners who are married, unstable, or emotionally unavailable. If the Moon is conjunct Ketu, the person may suffer from emotional disturbances, a wavering mind, and a mother who is erratic, unstable, weird, or in the more unfortunate cases, mentally deranged. If the Sun is conjunct with Ketu, the person's confidence and leadership abilities are impaired, and he or she suffers on account of a father who is strange, unhealthy, absent, or emotionally removed.

On the positive side, Ketu represents psychic ability, metaphysics, otherworldly realities, and enlightenment through discrimination. When a planet is conjunct Ketu in a person's chart, especially a personal planet such as Sun, Moon, Mercury, or Venus, Ketu's significations are dramatically strengthened. Thus, the person benefits greatly in spiritual matters, metaphysical interests, and psychic tendencies. Because Rahu and Ketu, the top and bottom halves of a demon, are completely devoid of intellectual power and reasoning ability, the energy they benefit from most is that of Mercury. Rahu and Ketu flourish tremendously and begin to function in a more intelligent way when they acquire Mercury's energy. It is extremely typical to find Ketu in one of Mercury's signs (Gemini or Virgo) or Ketu conjunct with Mercury in the lives of dedicated spiritual seekers intent on enlightenment. (As a point of interest, Sun-Ketu and Moon-Ketu conjunctions often appear in the birthcharts of professional psychics.)

John Denver not only has the Mercury-Ketu conjunction, but he has it in the ninth house, the best house of a chart and the house that signifies religion and philosophy. Aside from giving great ability to discriminate and mystical and spiritual interests throughout Denver's life, the dasas and bhuktis of Ketu will be fortunate and powerful in producing spiritual growth and mystical experiences. Ketu dasa for him begins in August 1994, which will be a very favorable period in these realms. Denver may have some of his greatest encounters with gurus, he may learn more about religion and philosophy than ever before, and he may travel to far-off countries during these seven years.

Denver has engaged in spiritual practices and the pursuit of enlightenment for many years. He has spoken passionately and publicly in favor of Transcendental Meditation, Werner Erhard's *Est* seminar, and Zen macrobiotics, among other things. Aside from the Mercury-Ketu conjunction, spiritual and mystical tendencies are a recurring theme in his chart. Mars and Saturn, the rulers of the ninth house (religion and philosophy) and the twelfth house (enlightenment or final liberation), occupy the first house (personality), and they throw an aspect onto the ruler of the first house—Venus. Mercury's placement in the ninth house gives understanding of scriptures, as well as the ability to investigate or write them. Jupiter in the fourth house is considered an extremely spiritual influence because Jupiter represents religion, and the fourth house in Hindu astrology signifies the heart (the heart is associated with the fifth house in western astrology). Planets in the fourth house indicate things "dear to one's heart." On top of all this, Jupiter aspects the all-important Moon. As if all this were not enough, the Sun occupies the religious sign of Sagittarius in the mystical eighth house (in Hindu astrology the eighth house represents metaphysics) and receives an aspect from Jupiter. This Jupiter aspect is an even more beneficial aspect than usual because Jupiter throws its aspect onto its own sign— Sagittarius. John Denver is clearly a spiritually aware person and a seeker of enlightenment.

Denver's chart shows that he gains higher consciousness and evolution in the three different ways that are possible according to Hindu astrology. In Hindu life, there are three main gods (or energies) who bestow enlightenment. Lord Krishna is the god of devotion, represented by Jupiter. Lord Shiva is the god of destruction (the destroyer of ignorance), represented by Saturn. Lord Vishnu is the god of intelligence (evolution via discrimination and the intellect), represented by Mercury. If Jupiter occupies or aspects the first house, or if Jupiter throws an aspect onto the Sun, the Moon, or the planet ruling the first house, then the person evolves through devotion to God or devotion to a guru (members of devotional sects such as the Hare Krishnas almost always have one or more of the above-mentioned Jupiter features). If Saturn occupies or aspects the first house or if Saturn throws an aspect onto the Sun, the Moon, or the ruler of the first house, then the person gains higher consciousness through austerity, discipline, meditation, fasting, and "avoidance of the senses" (members of meditation groups such as the Transcendental Meditation movement almost always have one or more of the above-mentioned Saturn features). If Mercury occupies or aspects the first house, or if Mercury aspects the Sun, the Moon, or the ruler of the first house, then the person evolves through intellectual paths. These include practices such as Zen Buddhism, psychotherapy, self-improvement seminars, astrology, and disciplines based upon the precept that "the truth shall set you free."

418   John Denver gets evolution through all three different means because Saturn (Lord Shiva) occupies the first house and aspects Venus, the ruler of the first house. He is strongly devotional (to God or to gurus) and gains evolution through Jupiter (Lord Krishna) because Jupiter aspects both the Sun and Moon. Finally, he gets evolution through Mercury (Lord Vishnu) not because Mercury associates with the Sun, Moon, or first house, but because Mercury is in the ninth house, the house of religion and philosophy. Mercury's position is responsible for his involvement in seminars such as *Est* and his activities with Zen macrobiotics (macrobiotics appears to be a dietary regimen but is in fact a philosophy and evolutionary path).

John Denver married Ann Martel in June 1967 during a Venus bhukti (within Saturn dasa). This is astrologically fitting because Venus is the planet of love and it occupies the seventh house—the house of marriage. The marriage eventually ended in divorce. This is not hard to understand considering that two malefics, Mars and Saturn, aspect Denver's marriage house. Also, *kujadosha,* or "Mars affliction," the condition harming married life, exists. (For a full explanation of *kujadosha,* see the analysis of Al Gore.) Although Denver's marriage ended in divorce, his chart clearly indicates a very powerful bond with marriage partners, as well as marriages to partners he may have known in past lives. Whenever the ruler of the first house (the self) occupies the seventh house (the spouse) or the ruler of the seventh house is in the first house, the above-mentioned effects occur in the person's life.

In Denver's case, not only does the ruler of the first house occupy the seventh house, but the ruler of the seventh house occupies the first house. This is called "exchange of signs" ("mutual reception" in western astrology), and is a very significant and beneficial astrological condition. During the years the Denvers were married, their marriage was quite celebrated by the public and the press. One of Denver's most popular tunes, "Annie's Song," was a tribute to his wife and a testament to their love. It may seem odd to praise a marriage that ends in divorce. However, individuals whose charts contain the ruler of the first house in the seventh house or vice versa consistently say that their marriage bond is (or was) profound, whether or not divorce occurred. These individuals almost always stay in contact with their former spouse.

Despite such strong talent in technical fields and a very practical nature revealed by the Mars-Saturn conjunction in the first house, the astrological indications for Denver's musical career appear in several different ways. Venus, Mercury, and the third house (which represents music, dance, and drama in Hindu astrology—as does the fifth house in western astrology) are prominently placed or significantly aspected in this chart. The Moon, which rules the third house (music), occupies the **419** tenth house (career). Venus, the planet of art, aspects the first house (personality and self) as well as Saturn, the ruler of the career house (tenth). On top of this Mercury, a communicative and musical planet, aspects the third house (music). Rahu in the third house activates the house of art because Rahu is aspected by Mercury, the planet of intelligence. This beneficial aspect causes the ordinarily mentally-deficient Rahu to flourish. If Mercury did not aspect the house of music and if Mercury was not almost stationary retrograde at birth, John Denver would have a somewhat difficult time in any profession involving communications because of Mercury's debilitating conjunction to "otherworldly" Ketu. The Moon in the tenth house contributes to his career by creating a strong desire to be the center of attention and to perform for the public.

Accurately predicting dasa-bhukti effects of Rahu and Ketu, the "shadowy planets," is usually harder than predicting the results of planetary dasas and bhuktis. This is because Rahu and Ketu are more like masses of energy than directed forms of intelligence. Generally speaking, Rahu periods portend materialistic cravings and worldly benefits, and Ketu periods tend toward spiritual or mystical leanings. Ketu periods can also cause breakdowns in a person's outer circumstances, causing the person to question his or her existence and enter into spiritual, metaphysical, or ethereal domains. It is unlikely that Denver will have such problems during Ketu dasa (from August 1994 until August 2001), because he is already in touch with his inner, spiritual nature. Ketu dasa for Denver is likely to be especially spiritual and filled with long-distance travel and important experiences with foreign countries because Ketu occupies the ninth house and is very well-aspected by Mercury. (Note that Mercury is harmed by its conjunction to malefic Ketu while Ketu is powerfully strengthened by its conjunction to benefic Mercury. This is the way Hindu astrology works.)

Many astrologers predict the dasas and bhuktis of Rahu and Ketu by analyzing the condition of the dispositors of Rahu or Ketu. A dispositor of a planet is the ruler of the house that the planet occupies. In Denver's case, Ketu occupies Capricorn, and Capricorn is ruled by Saturn, making Saturn the dispositor of Ketu. In my own astrological practice I have had mixed results using dispositors to predict Rahu and Ketu periods. However, because they sometimes work quite well, they are worthy of analysis and further study. If this dispositor method works in his case, then Denver stands to gain great prominence and fame in Ketu dasa. Note that Ketu's dispositor, Saturn, is the *rajayogakaraka* and Saturn occupies the first house (ability to gain recognition and renown). Also, Saturn is aspected by Venus, and the aspect is a great one because

Venus throws its energy onto its own sign, Taurus.

In Denver's future, there are two dasa-bhuktis which are precarious at best, dangerous at worst. The periods are Venus dasa, Mars bhukti and Venus dasa, Saturn bhukti. The problem is not merely that Mars and Saturn are malefics, but both these planets throw damaging aspects onto Venus. Because Venus rules the first and the sixth houses, Denver's health and general well-being will be at risk, with a possibility of accidents or bodily harm. Venus-Mars is far more threatening than Venus-Saturn for several reasons. First, Mars aspects Venus within about eight degrees whereas the Saturn aspect occurs within about twenty-four degrees. Second, Mars is the planet that signifies accidents and violence. Third, even though Saturn is a malefic that can harm Venus, it also brings some very good effects to Venus because of its *rajayoga* status. Nevertheless, Denver should be very careful in both Venus-Mars and Venus-Saturn periods. Marital discord or relationship problems are also possible during these periods because Venus, the dasa planet, occupies the seventh house.

In order to protect himself during these dasa-bhuktis, Denver should wear a large, high-quality Venus gemstone. (The stone for Venus is diamond, which should be worn during his entire life, anyway, because Venus is the ascendant ruler.) Denver should also engage a Hindu priest to perform some *yagyas* to strengthen Venus. (For more information about *yagyas*, see the analysis of Jodi Foster's chart) And, as he is interested in spiritual matters himself, Denver may wish to chant the Venus mantra himself.

In the interest of providing more depth and subtlety of information regarding planetary periods, I have decided to present my own horoscope to describe how five dasas and several bhuktis have functioned in my life. While I certainly consider this unorthodox, bold, and slightly embarrassing, I believe the advantages far outweigh the drawbacks. By analyzing a chart and a life that I know especially well, I am able to address many astrological issues that I would be reluctant to write about in someone else's life. Naturally, my perceptions may be overly subjective. But the purpose of presenting my birthchart is to give a wider spectrum of astrological issues rather than to accurately examine my own life. I therefore ask the reader to forgive my boldness and to understand that the astrological conditions and life issues that I have chosen to discuss in this analysis are deliberately selective. Astrologers who are reading about Hindu astrology for the first time here should take note that from this point on the information about birthchart interpretations may be slightly more advanced and will go deeper into natal astrological conditions than in the previous charts. I will also diverge quite often from the birthchart analysis in order to explain important astrological conditions.

Analyzing birthcharts of enormously famous persons, those we do not know intimately can be a problem. By studying too many famous persons birthcharts, one can begin to make overly positive or negative predictions about dasas and bhuktis in the lives of ordinary folk. Also, it is nearly impossible to confirm what occurred in a famous person's life during mediocre planetary periods. Finally, because the charts of famous persons are so extraordinary, they may handle difficult periods more masterfully or successfully than the common person.

One of the most important principles I have learned during my years of practice with Hindu astrology is that the natal chart is more essential than the periods and subperiods. If a person's birthchart is generally weak and afflicted, with few angular and trinal planets, few planets in their own or exaltation signs, few planets receiving aspects from Jupiter or other benefics, too many planets tightly aspected by Saturn, and perhaps a dim or injured Moon, then even if the person enters the dasa of an exalted planet, the results are rarely great. Similarly, individuals with powerful natal horoscopes (such as famous persons) are usually not so badly traumatized by a bad dasa. Those with powerful charts may take a major fall at the onset of a bad dasa, but because so many other planets in their chart are strong and favorable, the bhuktis or subperiods of these well-placed and well-aspected planets provide fortitude and ameliorating effects. When a person with a weak and afflicted chart enters a highly favorable dasa, unfortunately, he or she keeps encountering weak and afflicted subperiods. It is far better to have a powerful chart with a few weak dasas than a weak and afflicted chart with a few good dasas.

Looking at the chart at hand, my first dasa-bhukti was Venus-Saturn. Venus is extraordinarily afflicted, first because it is conjunct with two malefics (Ketu and Mars), second because the aspects are within one and two degrees respectively, and third because the aspect to Mars is worse than usual because Mars rules the twelfth house—the most damaging house of a horoscope. Ordinarily, Venus periods and subperiods are quite good for individuals with a Taurus ascendant (see rulership graph on page 369), even if some afflictions to Venus exist. But in this case, Venus is far too injured to function well. Venus dasa was in effect for the first four years and eleven months and was fraught with all kinds of difficulties. Venus occupies the fourth house, which rules the mother. My worst and most immediate problems were related to instability at home because my mother was seriously ill constantly. Indeed, after my birth, the doctor advised my mother not to have any more children.

My first eleven months were during a Saturn subperiod, and while I have no details to relate about this early period, I mention it to address an important issue. Although it is not a basic premise of Hindu astrology, it is my experience that for the majority of individuals the first dasa-bhukti of one's life is critical. It is not hard to fathom that a soul's first impressions of a life should profoundly color his or her entire existence. In examining the charts of powerful people—presidents and the like—one often finds that the first period and subperiod specifically relate to power, authority, and leadership. Artists are often born in a Venus period or subperiod, or that of a planet ruling or occupying one of the houses of art (third house rules fine arts, fifth house rules painting and crafts). Those who spend their lives pursuing enlightenment are often born in a Ketu period, a dasa or bhukti of a planet occupying or ruling the twelfth house, or that of a planet conjunct Ketu. Individuals who are born in a dasa or bhukti of the Moon or a planet ruling their first house (personality) tend to be more self-centered and concerned with their own perceptions and experiences than others throughout their lives. They are also more likely to gain fame and recognition.

JAMES BRAHA

10-16-1951, 7:36 PM, Fort Lauderdale, Florida
26° N 07, 80° W 08
Source: birth certificate

RASI

11th ♓ ♃℞ 14°	12th ♈ ☽ 23°	1st ♉ Asc. 2° 33'	2nd ♊
10th ♒ ☊ 15°			3rd ♋
9th ♑			4th ♌ ♂ 14° ☋ 15° ♀ 16°
8th ♐	7th ♏	6th ♎ ☿ 2°	5th ♍ ♄ 14° ☉ 29°

VIMSOTTARI

	DASA Mo. Day Year	BHUKTI Mo. Day Year
☉	09-24-1956	♀♄ 10-16-1951
		♀☿ 09-24-1952
☽	09-25-1962	♀☋ 07-26-1955
♂	09-24-1972	☽♀ 07-26-1970
		☽☉ 03-25-1972
☊	09-25-1979	
♃	09-24-1997	
♄		
☿		
☋		
♀	10-16-1951	

NAVAMSA

3rd	4th	5th	6th
2nd ☊			7th
1st Asc.			8th ♂ ☋
12th	11th ☽ ♃℞	10th ☿	9th ☉ ♀

NORTH INDIAN

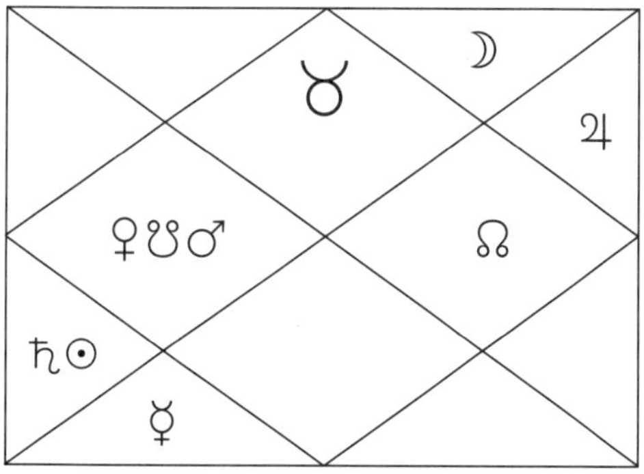

I also feel a strong connection between my first dasa-bhukti (Venus-Saturn) and the rest of my life. The greatest damage Venus dasa caused, aside from my suffering on account of my mother, were delicate health and difficulties with confidence. This is because Venus rules the first house (personality, ability to be recognized, and so on) and the sixth house (health and ability to defeat enemies and competitors). Fortunately, the sixth house is less afflicted because a benefic planet, Mercury, occupies the sixth house. Venus' placement next to otherworldly Ketu caused extreme introversion, excessive shyness, timidity, and constant fearfulness early in my life. These problems were doubled by Venus' tight conjunction with Mars because Mars rules the twelfth house—whose significations are nearly exactly the same as Ketu's.

The greatest benefits that Venus generates in this chart are a spiritual lifetime, mystical experiences, psychic ability, and tendencies to pursue enlightenment. When the Sun, Moon, Mercury, or the first house ruler is conjunct Ketu in the natal chart, a person's consciousness functions partly on the earth plane and partly on the astral or heavenly plane. The person becomes sensitive, introspective, reflective, and open to realities beyond the five senses. This same effect occurs when important personal planets are in any way related to the twelfth house. Both of these conditions exist in my chart because Venus, the first house ruler, is conjunct Ketu, and Venus is conjunct Mars, the twelfth house ruler. This is quite relevant to my work in astrology and mysticism. However, judging by Venus' afflictions alone, my first experience of life during the Venus dasa must have been horrendous for any sense of self, poise, and confidence. Venus rules the first house—one's self-image, ability to be recognized, and so forth. But let us look at the subperiod, Saturn.

Saturn is the most powerful and well-aspected planet in this horoscope for many reasons. First, it is the best planet for Taurus ascendant, a *rajayogakaraka* because of the excellent houses it rules (ninth and tenth). Second, it occupies the auspicious fifth house, the second best house of a chart. Third, it is aspected by benefic Jupiter within the exact degree. Even though Jupiter is not a good planet by virtue of rulership (see graph on page 369), it still throws a tremendous amount of positive energy because of its natural benefic energy. Saturn occupies the fifth house (the mind) and rules the ninth house (religion, philosophy, and higher knowledge) and the tenth house (career and professional activities). Although shyness, confidence, and the ability to gain recognition is an uphill struggle throughout life because of Venus' (as ruler of first house) natal implications, I have always managed to gain ground in these realms through the use of my intellect, religion and philosophy, and career success—all the significations connected to

Saturn in this horoscope. Saturn's extremely powerful natal disposition would cause this in any case, but I believe that being born in Saturn bhukti has had a fortunate effect on my psyche that has remained until this day. Being born in Venus dasa has intensified tendencies toward introversion, introspection, and spiritual and occult interests, as well as a weak sense of self. However, the experience of Saturn's energy at birth has, almost paradoxically, provided the potential for a serious, out-wardly-directed, and career-oriented life. Saturn, more than any other planet, is the indicator of career and happens to rule the tenth house (career) in this chart.

Every time I have entered a Venus bhukti, I have experienced rough periods characterized by first, fourth, and sixth house problems, the houses Venus rules and occupies. This has meant confidence problems; difficulties with homes, cars, and mother, and health problems relating to the throat and kidneys, the significations of Venus. (Venus, incidentally, also rules the thyroid, reproductive system, and skin, although Saturn may also have some bearing on the skin). During Saturn subperiods, I have always had great career success or prominence in school, wonderful support of nature, and other major benefits. Saturn has, however, also brought some suffering in the areas of its essential significations.

Over the years, I have observed that no matter how well-placed and well-aspected Saturn is in a person's birthchart, Saturn dasa and Saturn bhuktis always generate some restrictions, obstacles, delays, burden, and grief. Even for people with Taurus and Libra birthcharts in which Saturn becomes a *rajayogakaraka* and Saturn periods and subperiods are highlights of life, some serious misery almost always happens. The same is true within a person's natal chart. Saturn, when well-placed and well-aspected, in the natal chart, gives great benefits as well as problems to the houses and planets it associates with.

Perhaps the worst dasa-bhukti of my life was Venus-Ketu, which began at the age of three years nine months and lasted until four years eleven months. Whenever a person experiences a period and subperiod where the dasa planet is afflicted by the bhukti planet, major problems or suffering is a certainty. (Note that if the dasa-bhukti in this case were reversed, i.e. Ketu-Venus rather than Venus-Ketu, the results of the period would be favorable because Ketu would receive the beneficial energy of benefic Venus. The dasa planet always takes precedence over the bhukti planet. Naturally, the closer the aspect of affliction by degree, the worse the problems will be. Venus and Ketu in this chart are only one degree apart, a very intense injury. During my Venus-Ketu period, my mother's emotional state so deteriorated that she had to be hospitalized. To this four-year-old, the predicament did not appear temporary. To make matters worse, my two older brothers and I were then placed in a summer camp which was so unpleasant (I do not remember why) that my eight- and ten-year-old brothers decided to run away. Despite my pleas, my brothers said I was too young to accompany them. My mother was gone, my father off at work somewhere in another town, and now my last living relatives were leaving me in the hands of strangers. I felt overwhelmingly abandoned. Though slightly humorous in retrospect, this scene at the age of four was seriously traumatic.

It is worth noting that ancient Hindu scriptures indicate that a Venus-Ketu conjunction confers the ability to "cast spells." In modern times, this means ability with hypnotism or ability to powerfully influence others. Although I do not practice hypnotism and make no claims to cast spells, I have often been told that my lectures on astrology are remarkably effective—having an almost hypnotic power to influence even the most fervent nonbelievers.

The dasa following Venus was the Sun period which ran from the age of four years, eleven months until ten years, eleven months. Although the Sun is a good planet for Taurus ascendant, becoming a functional benefic by virtue of rulership, the Sun in this chart is weak. It is in an excellent *trikona* house, the fifth, but is, unfortunately, in the last degree of a sign. Hindu astrology describes "planetary zones" which are as follows:

PLANETS IN EVEN SIGNS	PLANETS IN ODD SIGNS
0 - 6 DEATH STATE	0 - 6 CHILDHOOD STATE
6 - 12 OLD AGE STATE	6 -12 BOYHOOD STATE
12 - 18 ADULTHOOD STATE	12 -18 ADULTHOOD STATE
18 - 24 BOYHOOD STATE	18 -24 OLD AGE STATE
24 - 30 CHILDHOOD STATE	24 -30 DEATH STATE

Although astrologers are not overly concerned about the planetary zone a planet occupies, the matter becomes critical when a planet occupies the first two or three degrees of a sign or the last two or three degrees of a sign. (The three exceptions to this rule are the exaltation positions of Venus, Moon, and Mars. Venus is exalted in the twenty-seventh degree of Pisces, the Moon in the third degree of Taurus, and Mars in the twenty-eighth degree of Capricorn.) In these cases, the planet becomes weak or powerless, almost completely dissipating the planet's ability to do good for the houses it rules. Two fine examples of how powerless a planet can be when occupying weak zones are Jupiter in John Kennedy's chart and Jupiter in Bill Clinton's chart. (Kennedy's Jupiter was in 0° 21' Taurus, Clinton's Jupiter is 0° 8' Libra). Both presidents' charts have (or had) Virgo ascendants, making Jupiter the ruler of the fourth house (homes) and seventh house (marriage). Both of these men reportedly have (or had) significantly weak marriages. I do not mean weak in the sense of being full of problems or tension. I mean weak in the sense of being without interest or fulfillment to them. John Kennedy is rumored to have married only because of political necessity, and his alleged affairs seem to bear out that theory. Based on news reports of Clinton's infidelities, his married life seems remarkably similar to Kennedy's. Regarding Jupiter's rulership of the fourth house, Kennedy, for all of his wealth, did not purchase his own home until four years after he was married! (In my own chart, the ruler of the fourth house is in the last degree of a sign, and I have never owned a house or any land.)

At any rate, the Sun in my chart occupies the final degree of a sign and is therefore very weak. (In the contemporary Hindu astrological house system, the Sun falls in the sixth house, which is a dusthana or bad house. This further weakens the Sun.) The Sun rules the fourth house (homes). It is typical to move to a new home or city in the dasa of a planet that rules or occupies the fourth house, and that is exactly what happened. Within a year after the Sun period began, our family moved to another part of the state. Because the Sun is so weak, the experience was painful rather than pleasant, and I distinctly recall being extremely upset at having to leave familiar conditions and a close friend. As for my mother's well-being, almost any period would have been better than the previous one, Venus-Ketu. Although it was better, the lack of energy that a 29° Sun (as fourth house ruler) provided was not particularly favorable.

My Sun dasa as a whole was difficult for reasons already mentioned. The most interesting developments were related to fifth house matters (the Sun occupies the fifth house) and the significations of the Sun. The Sun is known as the *atmakaraka*, or indicator of the soul. (The Sun is the "natural" *atmakaraka*. There is also another *atmakaraka* and that is the planet in the latest degree of a sign within one's horoscope. In my chart the Sun takes both these honors.) The areas of life governed by the house position of the Sun become important and vital realms "connected to one's soul." The fifth house represents the mind, among other things. During this period, I awoke to realize that intense thinking is part of my nature, and that intellectual activity connects me to my soul and purpose. During the previous dasa, Venus, as afflicted as Venus may be in my chart, my experience was entirely dictated by desires for pleasure and comfort. These are the significations of Venus. Now, however, I was beginning to use my mind (fifth house) more than before. Note also that in this chart, the two mental planets, Mercury and the Moon, aspect each other. In Hindu mythology, Mercury is the son of the Moon. When these two "relatives" aspect each other, an extremely intellectual or communicative nature is guaranteed.

Notice that the Sun, which occupies the fifth house, is aspected by the two spiritual planets, Jupiter and Saturn. (Because Uranus, Neptune, and Pluto are not used in Hindu astrology, Jupiter and Saturn are the most spiritual planets in a birthchart.) As mentioned in the birthchart analysis of John Denver, Jupiter is the planet of Lord Krishna, and it represents faith and devotion. Saturn is the planet of Lord Shiva, the God of destruction, who provides evolution through austerity, discipline, and avoidance of the senses. The traits of Jupiter and Saturn were extremely prominent in my father's life (Jupiter and Saturn aspect the Sun and Sun represents father), and they were now becoming part of mine. During the Sun dasa, I suddenly became aware of my father's intensely religious nature as well as innate spiritual tendencies within myself. As I began thinking more deeply about life, I discovered that the way my father dealt with his increasingly difficult life (on account of my mother's troubles) was through prayer and faith in God. My father practiced the traditional morning Jewish ritual every day since beginning at age thirteen. Because spiritual techniques, mantras, and rituals are represented by the fifth house, I became interested in my father's morning prayers during Sun dasa. I even contemplated becoming a rabbi, but dropped the idea when I found no evidence that prayer changed my father's circumstances or my own.

As the Sun dasa continued, my father's problems worsened as he suddenly lost his business and had to seek employment with others for the first time in his adult life. While on this subject of how my chart influenced (or reflected) my father's fortune, I would like to mention that in Hindu astrology, the physical conditions of a person's life are dramatically affected by the charts of those around him or her. My father's life was harmed by the weak position of my 29° Sun as well as the 15° conjunction of the Sun and Saturn, especially during the six years of my Sun dasa. To illustrate this point in another way, the significations regarding mother are so afflicted in my chart that my mother's life was scheduled to worsen soon after my birth (because of the Venus-Ketu dasa-bhukti) and remain difficult through my entire life.

Aside from the weak Sun ruling the fourth house, two malefics occupy the fourth house (Mars and Ketu), and one of these (Mars) rules the grief-producing twelfth house. (Benefic Venus also occupies the fourth house, and because Venus rules the first house, this produced a powerful love and very strong bond with my mother.)

It is common for individuals' lives to be altered by the karma of loved

ones, and Hindu astrologers often tell people that their lives will be better **429**
or worse when their spouse, parents, or other loved ones have departed
this world. As a point of interest, I once analyzed the charts of lottery
winners and observed that the most common significant factor of each
person was a phenomenally powerful eighth house (partner's wealth) in
the charts of their marriage partners! All of the charts of lottery winners
were favorable for wealth, but not in a particularly noticeable way. The
marriage partners of all these individuals, however, had the excellent
fortune to obtain extraordinary financial benefits from their spouses.

Back to the chart at hand, the fifth house is also *poorvapunya*, or
past-life credit. In the periods or subperiods of fifth house planets or
planets ruling the fifth house, a person gains credit or debts relating to
past-life karma that must be fulfilled in this life. Because the Sun in this
chart is weak, the *poorvapunya* related to the Sun becomes a debt from
the past rather than a credit. (There is also favorable credit relating to
well-aspected Saturn in the fifth house, which will be discussed further
on.) Aside from the Sun ruling the father, it also represents a person's
confidence, ego, and use of power. During the Sun dasa, I watched my
father's life seriously deteriorate, and felt my own power and confidence
weaken. Because the Sun in my chart is weak in the house of *poorvapunya*,
it can safely be concluded that I misused power and my ego in past lives
and now bear the consequences in this life.

It is important to determine one's *poorvapunya* when analyzing a
birthchart because these are benefits or problems a person is certain to
receive. If Venus occupies the fifth house, without affliction, the person
involved may have artistic talent because of artistic efforts made in
previous lifetimes. That person would also receive good karma in matters
of the heart from the past, which now generates a happy love life.
(Although if the seventh house happens to be afflicted, some bad marital
effects may occur simultaneously.) Venus afflicted, on the other hand,
means the person may have misused love in the past, and now he or she
has love problems that are specifically tied to negative actions in the
past. If Jupiter occupies the fifth house without affliction, then the
person gets good gurus and spiritual teachers, has great ability to get
higher knowledge, and so forth. This is the way to understand
poorvapunya.

The positive *poorvapunya* in my chart is connected to Saturn, which
occupies the fifth house, and Mercury, which rules the fifth house.
Because Mercury occupies the sixth house and is well-aspected by a
bright Moon (about two days after a full Moon), there is knowledge of
healing techniques or health matters (sixth house) because of work
performed in this realm in past lives. Saturn's placement in the fifth

430 house, very tightly aspected by benefic Jupiter and ruling such good houses—the ninth and tenth—indicates benefits relating to discipline, responsibility, patience, and all the affairs that Saturn signifies. Because Saturn rules the ninth house, there is abundant credit with spiritual teachers and the ability to gain higher knowledge whenever desired. Long distance travel is also guaranteed. Saturn's rulership of the tenth house means I gain fame or recognition in career because of diligent work in previous lives.

Although there is tremendous *poorvapunya* connected to my ninth house, Jupiter, the planet of higher knowledge and spiritual teachers, is aspected by two malefic planets, Mars and Saturn, and both planets make the aspect to Jupiter within the exact degree! Even though I have excellent religious karma, I also have, simultaneously, negative karma in this realm. It is very common when analyzing birthcharts to find a mixture of extreme good and extreme bad pertaining to a particular house. When this occurs to the ninth house, it almost inevitably means that the person loves religion, philosophy, and higher knowledge but will not stay with one guru. The person will be eclectic in the religious and philosophical realm. This has certainly been the case in my life.

Between the age of ten and eleven, in the last bhukti of the Sun dasa, something very upsetting occurred. (This was during Venus bhukti, the most afflicted planet of my chart.) During the six years of the Sun period, my greatest happiness came from sports. Sports is governed by the fifth house and Mars. The Sun occupies the fifth house, and the fifth house is enormously strong because of the combination of trinal and angular house rulers (Sun and Saturn) occupying the fifth house, the aspect from Jupiter to the fifth house, and the powerful *rajayoga* that occurs there. (Saturn alone makes a *rajayoga*.) On top of this, Mars (sports) is conjunct within two degrees of Venus, the ruler of the first house (self). Aside from my intensely intellectual interests, sports was my life, and baseball was my sport.

Oftentimes, having a dasa-bhukti of two weak planets is as devastating as encountering a dasa-bhukti of two planets that afflict each other. This was the case during the Sun-Venus period and the results were terrible. During the Sun dasa, I cared more about baseball than anything and (because of the incredibly prominent fifth house of my birthchart) hoped to eventually play professionally. Venus' placement so close to Ketu and twelfth lord, Mars, makes my personality nearly invisible and my ability to be recognized extraordinarily weak. This, combined with a 29° Sun, was all it took during the Sun-Venus dasa-bhukti to destroy my chances of fulfilling any desires. Out of over one hundred children who paid their fees to join littleleague, for some unknown reason, two were left out, and

I was one of them. Though my parents made valiant efforts, the teams, we were told, were simply too full. Missing the first year of little league, where children learn to play with fast pitching, put me out of step with my peers without any way to catch up. This effectively ended my hopes of a life in baseball. The ruler of my tenth house (career) occupies the fifth house (sports and the mind), and though I wound up doing mental work, I have often lamented over missing out on a career in sports.

In order to further illustrate how destructive two weak planets, though unrelated by aspect, can be during their dasa-bhukti, I would like to mention what occurred to Werner Erhard, the western guru and founder of the *Est* training. In 1981, Erhard entered a ten-year Moon dasa (see page 432), and the Moon in his chart is conjunct malefic Mars and is fallen (in Scorpio) in the seventh house, the house of marriage. The Moon dasa quickly caused deterioration of his marriage and a reportedly difficult, bitter divorce. The other affairs of his life, however, did not (to outsiders anyway) appear spoiled. In February 1989 Werner entered the Venus subperiod within Moon dasa, and Venus is the second most afflicted planet in his chart. Venus is retrograde in the fourth house, four degrees away from the malefic hot Sun (therefore "combust" or burned up), and aspected within ten degrees by malefic Saturn (even though Saturn is *rajayogakaraka*, it is still a "first class malefic" and still throws very harmful energy).

Venus rules both the first house (personality, self, and ability to be recognized) and the sixth house of Erhard's chart (health and ability to defeat enemies). During this terrible dasa-bhukti, his empire crumbled as he was publicly maligned on the weekly television news program "Sixty Minutes." The program alleged that he raped his daughter and committed other serious offenses. Interestingly, critics of the program charged that the attack on Erhard was orchestrated by Scientologists, supposed enemies (enemies are a sixth house signification, and Venus, the bhukti planet, rules the sixth house) of Erhard because he allegedly appropriated their techniques to use in his programs many years ago. Both of the dasa-bhukti planets, Moon and Venus, were so weak and afflicted that Erhard was powerless and defenseless. He sold his corporation under great duress.

In coming back to my own chart, before describing the effects of the next dasa, the Moon, I would like to address the peculiar condition of the ascendant lord (Venus) being conjunct Ketu and Mars, two planets of entirely different natures. Ketu is a mystical and otherworldly influence, causing introversion and introspection, while Mars is a planet of aggression and assertiveness. The greatest problem beginning astrologers of Hindu astrology have is trying to comprehend how two diametri-

WERNER ERHARD

09-05-1935, 10:25 PM EST, Philadelphia, Pennsylvania
39° N 57, 75° W 10
Source: Contemporary American Horoscopes, Lois Rodden Data Base

VIMSOTTARI

	DASA Mo. Day Year	BHUKTI Mo. Day Year
☉	04-06-1975	☽☿ 02-06-1987
		☽☋ 07-06-1988
☽	04-06-1981	☽♀ 02-06-1989
		☽☉ 10-06-1990
♂	04-06-1991	
		♂☿ 10-06-1994
☊	04-06-1998	♂☋ 10-03-1995
		♂♀ 02-30-1996
♃		♂☉ 04-30-1997
		♂☽ 09-06-1997
♄		
		☊♄ 05-12-2003
☿	09-05-1935	☊☿ 03-18-2006
☋	04-06-1948	
♀	04-06-1955	

RASI

11th ♓	12th ♈	1st ♉ Asc. 18°56'	2nd ♊ ☋ D 27°
10th ♒ ♄ ℞ 13°			3rd ♋
9th ♑			4th ♌ ☉ 19° ♀ ℞ 23°
8th ♐ ☊ D 27°	7th ♏ ☽ 20° ♂ 0°	6th ♎ ♃ 24°	5th ♍ ☿ 11°

NORTH INDIAN

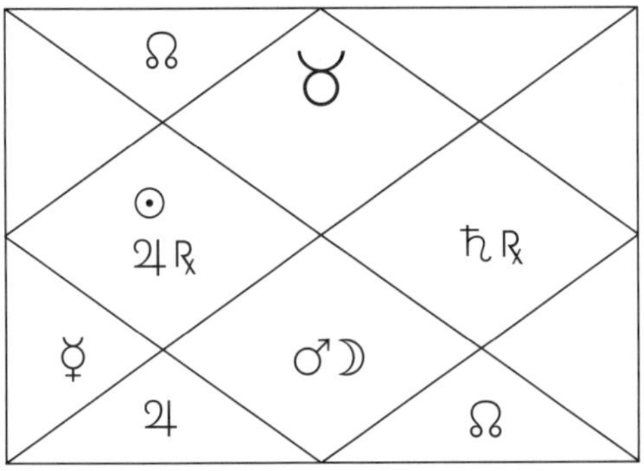

cally opposed astrological influences function. I hope that by addressing this issue over and over in this book with real life examples, my readers will begin to understand the coexistence of opposites.

Because the ruler of my first house is conjunct Ketu, my personality is shy, retiring, introspective, otherworldly, and lacking in a strong sense of self. Paradoxically, because Venus is conjunct hot and aggressive Mars, I am also bossy, aggressive, assertive, physical, and extremely determined. There is no doubt whatever that my general demeanor in life is reserved, sensitive, spiritual, and often timid. And yet I appear anything but shy when lecturing about astrology. As the years have passed, I have even begun to work at being less bossy when teaching classes and workshops. My personality is therefore an excellent example of how two entirely opposing influences prevail, without in any way nullifying each other.

If it is not yet obvious, the assertive writing style of my astrological textbooks is an example of the effect of a prominent and powerful Mars conjunct the ascendant lord. Not only does the Venus-Mars conjunction occur within two degrees, it occupies the fourth house, an angle of the chart (angular houses are one, four, seven, and ten). Hindu scriptures say that when a Venus-Mars conjunction occupies an angular house, the person will be a leader (Bill Clinton and Mahatma Gandhi have the conjunction in the first house, Hitler had it in the seventh house). In my case, the leadership ability conferred by the angular Venus-Mars conjunction is harmed by the extremely close association with Ketu. But as harmed as it is, leadership ability has still managed to show through. In 1986, when I published the first Hindu astrology text by a Westerner in recent years, I did so against the conventional belief that Hindu astrology could not take hold in the West. Furthermore, training astrologers to use both Hindu and western astrology (while maintaining the integrity of each system) for each chart interpretation, rather than one system or the other, is another example of leadership.

Conjunctions and seventh house aspects to Mars (opposition aspects) are very important to understand. These aspects almost always confer talent in such fields as architecture, engineering, drafting, law, and other technical fields. Also, the more positively Mars is aspected (i.e., aspected by benefic planets), the more likely the person is to be a leader. Nearly all military commanders, presidents, and other political leaders have either a benefic planet conjunct Mars or a benefic planet aspecting Mars from the opposite house. Some politicians and rulers even have Mars conjunct with malefics, suggesting that even when Mars is afflicted by malefic conjunctions, it may also be greatly energized.

Consider the placements of Mars in the Hindu charts of the following leaders (western astrologers beware that some of these conjunctions may not exist in these individuals' western charts. Conjunctions in Hindu astrology occur within thirty degrees, not eight or ten degrees.):

John Kennedy, Mars conjunct Mercury; Ronald Reagan, Mars conjunct Mercury; Bill Clinton, Mars conjunct Venus; Franklin Roosevelt, Mars conjunct Moon; Herbert Hoover, Mars conjunct Moon and Mercury; Lyndon Johnson, the bossiest and most powerful U.S. president ever (passed more legislation than anyone), Mars conjunct Mercury, Jupiter, Sun, and Moon; Richard Nixon, Mars conjunct Mercury, Jupiter, and Sun; Adolf Hitler, Mars conjunct Mercury, Venus, and Sun; Jimmy Carter, Mars is aspected by Venus and Mercury from the opposite house; Mahatma Gandhi, Mars conjunct Venus and Mercury and Mars aspected by Jupiter from the opposite house; Al Gore, Mars (a-day-and-a-half from stationary direct) conjunct Saturn; Dan Quayle (everyone wonders how he became Vice President), Mars conjunct Sun, and Mars aspected from its opposite house by Moon and Saturn.

In the chart of George Bush, a president who went to war more than once in only four years (Panama and Iraq), Mars forms a conjunction with Ketu within the exact degree. Over the years, I have observed that for some reason, Mars and Saturn are the only planets that are not consistently devastated by conjunctions with Ketu. Sometimes close Saturn-Ketu conjunctions destroy a person's discipline and patience and the houses Saturn rules, but not always. In the case of Mars-Ketu conjunctions, sometimes the person has weak blood or other types of Mars problems. But in nearly all the instances I have seen, the person is extremely aggressive or assertive in a way that is not necessarily obvious or aboveboard. This is certainly the case with George Bush. The most typical comments friends of George Bush make are about what a very nice man he is. Nice or not, one should never underestimate the power and warlike tendencies of person whose chart contains a close Mars-Ketu conjunction.

Regarding Mars–Rahu conjunctions, persons with this aspect are usually overly virile and sexual. Their spouses often report that they habitually have sex for several hours at a time.

The next dasa of my life was the Moon period, which ran from the age of ten years and eleven months until twenty years and eleven months. The Moon in my chart rules the third house, occupies the twelfth house, and is aspected by benefic Mercury. The effects of the Moon dasa were more connected to the third house, the house that the Moon rules, than the house the moon occupies (the twelfth). The third house represents the fine arts of music, dance, and drama. I began taking drama classes at thirteen and spent my high school years acting in all the school plays. From there, I went on to enroll in an intense professional acting school, where other academic subjects were for the most part ignored. During the entire Moon dasa, except for the first year or so, I lived and breathed theatre. Theatre replaced my interest in sports.

Dasas are not as dramatically influential for everyone as they have been in my life. Many individuals do not change so conspicuously from dasa to dasa, and it is difficult to say exactly why my dasas have consistently brought such clear and objective results relating to the significations of the dasa planet. (Critics of astrology like to say it is because I believe in the star language, but I knew nothing of astrology until the age of twenty-seven). To some extent I believe the reason I am more affected by dasas than others is because my purpose in life, as seen through the tenth house, is very changeable. The tenth house represents a person's *dharma*. *Dharma* means duty or life purpose, and when the tenth house is aspected by planets that rule *dusthana* houses, especially the twelfth, (six, eight, and twelve are *dusthanas*), the person either has trouble determining his or her proper *dharma* or has numerous careers throughout life which continually change. In 1984, Poputlal Padia, my second astrological mentor, noticed that the rulers of the sixth and twelfth houses throw aspects onto my tenth house (Venus and Mars in the fourth house cast the aspect), and he declared, "You have had many different careers. And you will have more after this one (i.e., after astrology)! I was about thirty-two years old when he made the statement and had already been an actor, a businessman (retail), a spiritual disciple and teacher of meditation, and an astrologer. Some months after leaving India, to my surprise, I began my writing work, which has continued for eight years now.

The Moon period was more emotional than the other dasas of my life because the Moon rules a person's feelings and emotions. In retrospect, the Moon years also seemed to be more personal than any other period. I felt intense desires to express myself, which I did through drama. This could have been the effects of the Moon dasa, because of my age, or because the communication planet, Mercury, aspects the Moon. Or it could have been a combination of all these influences. Nevertheless, the Moon is the most important and personal influence in a Hindu chart (the ascendant ruler is equal in importance to the Moon), and many people experience the Moon period as an extremely personal and emotional time of life.

Although my Moon is placed in the twelfth house, I noticed no spiritual effects or desires for enlightenment as might be expected during a dasa of a planet occupying the house of "*moksha*" (final liberation). However, there was a great deal of emotional suffering. The twelfth house is the worst house of a Hindu chart, and a sensitive influence like the Moon is badly harmed in this *dusthana* house. The Moon rules the emotions as well as peace of mind, and these domains were quite disturbed for ten years. I also felt extreme shyness and introversion, which is fitting for a dasa of a twelfth house personal planet (Sun, Moon, and Mercury are the most personal influences). However, these kinds of difficulties were nothing new. They existed from birth because of natal chart conditions. However, the increasing intensity brought on by the Moon dasa was unpleasant and unwelcome.

Notice that every natural benefic planet in my chart is significantly afflicted. Jupiter is aspected by both Mars and Saturn to the exact

436   degree, Venus is tightly conjunct Ketu and Mars, the Moon and Mercury are in the twelfth and six houses respectively (both *dusthana* or "grief-producing" houses). When all benefic planets are afflicted in a birthchart, the person usually suffers a good deal and has to work very hard for any benefits and pleasures. This has been the case in my life so far.

Aside from continuing problems in my mother's life (Moon rules mother), some of the biggest suffering during the Moon dasa occurred on account of women (at my age, girls). During the entire ten years of the Moon dasa (between age eleven and twenty-one approximately), I had almost no relationships with girls and all attempts were futile. For someone with an extremely tight, passion-producing Venus-Mars conjunction, the inability to enjoy intimacy with the opposite sex was painful. Having the ascendant lord (Venus) conjunct the ruler of the house of marriage (Mars) made the lack of love even harder to bear, because this natal condition means a person is looking to form an exceptionally strong bond with a member of the opposite sex.

My lack of love relationships was not simply related to the fact that I was in an afflicted Moon dasa and the Moon rules women. (Even though Venus is the *karaka* or indicator of love, the Moon has an effect on all women in a person's life. Likewise, the Sun represents all men in a person's life, and therefore has a special influence on a woman's love life.) The problem is that the Moon in my *navamsa* (marriage chart) rules the seventh house (relationships) and occupies its fallen sign—Scorpio.

Hindu astrology calculates sixteen charts for each individual. The natal chart is called the *rasi* chart, and the other fifteen are called *vargas*, or divisional charts. (In western astrology, these are known as harmonic charts. However, harmonic charts are sometimes calculated differently than *vargas* and are therefore not always the same.) The most important divisional chart is the *navamsa*, or one-ninth divisional chart, which represents a person's marriage and has power to positively or negatively affect the *rasi* or natal chart. Although the *rasi* chart provides essential information about all areas of life, the divisional charts provide more detailed information about particular realms. Looking at a *navamsa* chart is like looking at a person's marriage with a microscope. Analyzing a person's *dasamsa* (career chart) provides more particulars about a person's professional life.

Because the Moon rules the seventh house (marriage) of my *navamsa* or marriage chart (see page 423) and is fallen (in Scorpio, the worst sign for the Moon), I have always been overly sensitive, emotional, and vulnerable in relationships. During Moon periods and subperiods, the problem is greatly exacerbated. During the Moon dasa, the stronger my desires for emotional intimacy became, the more shy, scared, and **437** awkward I became.

The vargas or divisional charts can be quite useful both in providing more subtle information about a particular realm of life and in making more detailed predictions. *Varga* charts however, are *extremely* affected by the slightest error in birthtime. It is quite usual for a one- or two-minute birthtime discrepancy to completely alter the houses of a divisional chart. In fact, it is so common that I would never attempt to analyze a the *varga* chart of a Westerner without first making sure that the given birthtime accurately correlates TO THE PARTICULAR *VARGA* CHART BEING ANALYZED. Western astrologers have investigated birthtime hospital recording practices and determined that a huge number of recorded birthtimes are wrong by five or ten minutes. For these individuals, analyzing most of the *varga* charts provides entirely false information because house placements are completely thrown off (planets in the signs are not affected unless the time is wrong by hours, and then, in most cases, only the Moon is affected). I regret to say that many astrologers currently practicing Hindu astrology in the West use the *varga* charts without ever questioning the birthtime. Some astrologers will check to see if the birthtime tallies with information ascertained by the *navamsa* chart, and if it does they assume that the birthtime is exact and that all other *vargas* are correct. However, the *navamsa,* which in many cases is ruined by a two- or three-minute error in birthtime, is less vulnerable to birthtime error than most others *vargas!*

There are different opinions about how to use divisional charts once the astrologer is sure the *varga* chart is accurate. I use *varga* charts in two ways. Before explaining these ways, let me first describe a fundamental way to determine if the *varga* chart is correct. Simply find a predictive event, circumstance, or condition indicated in the divisional chart that is ABSOLUTELY not indicated in the natal chart and note whether the phenomenon has occurred as expected, especially in a dasa or bhukti related to that signification within the appropriate varga chart. For example, in my own chart I can safely conclude that the *navamsa* chart is accurate because every time I have entered a Moon period or subperiod, love relationships and married life has taken an obvious, objectively verifiable turn for the worse. The Moon does not relate to marriage in any way in the natal chart, but it rules the marriage house (the seventh house) of the marriage chart (*navamsa* chart) and is debilitated by its placement in the sign of Scorpio.

As another example, say a person has Jupiter ruling the tenth house of the *dasamsa* or career chart, and in that chart Jupiter is in Cancer, its exaltation sign. If the person has consistently had promotions or

A Lifetime of Dasas

438 major professional benefits in Jupiter periods or subperiods AND JUPITER IS UNRELATED TO THE TENTH HOUSE IN THE NATAL CHART (that is, Jupiter does not occupy or rule the tenth house of the *rasi* chart), then the person's *dasamsa* chart is very likely accurate.

My Indian mentors taught me to use *varga* charts in two ways. The first is to note how well or poorly each planet is placed in the signs of the *varga* charts. If a planet is exalted or in its own sign (the sign it rules) in a great many of all sixteen charts, then that planet is significantly strengthened in the natal or *rasi* chart. If a planet is in its fallen sign in many of the *varga* charts, then that planet is significantly weakened in the natal chart. As already mentioned, planets in the *varga* signs are not altered by a slight discrepancy in birthtime (except in extraordinarily rare cases). To estimate the strength or weakness of a planet by virtue of all its *varga* placements, I use a "*varga* chart summary," which a computer program calculates in an instant. The *varga* chart summary records exactly how many times each planet occupies very good or very bad signs.

My own *varga* chart summary, shown on page 439, is quite ordinary. Notice that the Sun is in its own sign (Leo) in two divisional charts; it is not exalted or fallen in any *varga* charts. The Moon is in its own sign (Cancer) once; it is not exalted in any *vargas,* and it is fallen (in Scorpio) twice. These *varga* placements do not affect the power of those planets in the natal chart significantly. Notice, however, the conditions of Venus and Jupiter in the chart summary. Venus is fallen in three *varga* charts and is only in its own sign once, causing extra damage to Venus in the natal chart. Jupiter is even more affected by its *varga* placements, because it is in its own sign (either Sagittarius or Pisces) three times and is exalted (in Cancer) three times. A planet well-placed in six out of sixteen charts is very strengthened.

Now consider the varga summaries of two extremely special people, Robert De Niro and Al Pacino. Note that in De Niro's varga chart summary (on page 439, the Sun is in its own sign ten times and is exalted twice. The Sun rules and occupies the third house of his chart (see page 441). The third house represents willpower and music, dance, and drama. (Even though the Sun is in a weak degree, it is tremendously strengthened by being exalted and in its own sign so many times. Also, notice the *rajayoga* in the third house produced by the Venus-Mercury conjunction.)

In Al Pacino's varga chart summary, Venus (the planet of art) is in its own sign in seven *vargas*. Rahu, which occupies the third house (drama) in Pacino's natal chart (see page 440), is exalted (in one of Mercury's signs) in six divisional charts. The Moon is fallen four times, which also occurs once in the natal chart. The Moon is well-placed only twice. Because the fallen Moon in the natal chart rules the first house (ability to be promoted and recognized) and is weakened by the Moon's *varga* placements, it has taken an absurdly long time for Pacino to win an Academy Award. Though he was nominated over and over again since 1973, it is only since entering Rahu dasa in January 1992 that Pacino finally won an Oscar. He won the award in 1993. Now that Pacino is in a Rahu dasa until 2010, his fame, power, acting ability, energy, and courage will increase tremendously because Rahu is exalted in the natal chart in the third house and is in Mercury's signs a total of six times.

The other way I was taught to use *varga* charts is to analyze the specific house that correlates to the meaning of the *varga* chart. For example, the most important house of the *navamsa* (marriage chart) is the seventh house because that is the house of marriage. The most important house of the *dasamsa* (career chart) is the tenth house because that is the career house. To obtain more detailed information about a person's karma with children, analyze the fifth house (children) of the *saptamsa* (children chart), and so on. This may not be the only way to understand *vargas*, but it is one that works quite well. I have already shown how the seventh house of my *navamsa* chart reveals my vulnerability and overly emotional tendencies in relationships. Now consider how the tenth

BRAHA VARGA CHART SUMMARY

	Occupies Own Sign	Occupies Exaltation Sign	Occupies Fallen Sign
Sun:	2	0	0
Moon:	1	0	2
Mercury:	2	1	0
Venus:	1	0	3
Mars:	1	1	1
Jupiter:	3	3	0
Saturn:	3	1	0
Rahu:	0	2	0
Ketu:	0	1	0

DE NIRO VARGA CHART SUMMARY

	Occupies Own Sign	Occupies Exaltation Sign	Occupies Fallen Sign
Sun:	10	2	0
Moon:	1	0	0
Mercury:	4	2	0
Venus:	2	0	0
Mars:	1	1	1
Jupiter:	3	1	2
Saturn:	1	1	0
Rahu:	0	1	0
Ketu:	0	2	0

PACINO VARGA CHART SUMMARY

	Occupies Own Sign	Occupies Exaltation Sign	Occupies Fallen Sign
Sun:	4	1	2
Moon:	1	1	4
Mercury:	2	2	2
Venus:	7	0	1
Mars:	3	3	1
Jupiter:	0	1	0
Saturn:	1	1	1
Rahu:	0	6	0
Ketu:	0	1	0

AL PACINO
04-25-1940, 11:02 AM EST, Manhattan, New York
40° N 46, 73° W 59
Source: birth certificate, Lois Rodden Data Base

house of my *dasamsa* (career) chart provides more details about my profession. My *dasamsa* chart is given on page 443.

Notice that Mercury occupies the career house. This means that on top of the indications for a mental career revealed by my natal chart, the career chart, which gives a microscopic look at profession, indicates Mercurial activities—lecturing, writing, teaching, and so on. Notice that

Mercury rules the ninth house. This means that my profession relates to foreign countries, religion, philosophy, higher knowledge, and travel. This relates to my work as an astrologer, my teaching meditation for seven years (during Mars dasa—described later), and also for my *dharma* of bringing the astrology of a foreign country to the West.

PACINO RASI

9th ♓ ☋ 26° ☿ 18°	10th ♑ ♃ 2° ♄ 11° ☉ 12°	11th ♉ ♂ 22° ♀ 27°	12th ♊
8th ♒			1st ♋ Asc. 11°57'
7th ♑			2nd ♌
6th ♐	5th ♏ ☽ 28°	4th ♎	3rd ♍ ☋ 26°

The ruler of the tenth house of my *dasamsa* or career chart occupying the first house indicates that I might approach my career in a very personal way. Or that I would somehow use my personality for career purposes. This seems astrologically accurate because this text is the second I have written in which I use my own life to illustrate the efficacy and greatness of astrology (the other book is called *Astro-Logos, Language of Life: The True Story of a Man and the People and Planets Around Him*).

PACINO NORTH INDIAN

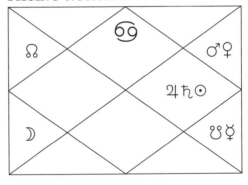

When analyzing the marriage chart, obtain the most information from the seventh house. When analyzing the children chart, look to the fifth house. For the chart of siblings (*drekana*), look to the third house. For the chart of parents (*dwadasamsa*), look to the fourth and tenth or fourth and ninth houses, and so forth. In analyzing the *saptamsa* or

08-17-1943, 3:00 AM EDT, Brooklyn, New York
40° N 38, 73° W 56
Source: Neil Marvell quotes him, Lois Rodden Data Base

children chart, if the ruler of the fifth house occupies its own or exaltation sign, then good results with children are likely. If the ruler of the fifth is in its fallen sign or in the sixth, eighth, or twelfth houses (*dusthanas*), some problems or grief with children may result. If a benefic planet occupies the tenth house of the *dasamsa* chart, good professional results are predictable, especially in the dasa or bhuktis of the particular planet involved. If Saturn or Mars occupies the seventh house of the marriage chart, karmic problems or fighting in married life are to be expected, no matter how good married life may appear from the natal chart. This is one reliable way to use the *vargas.*

DE NIRO RASI

10th ♓	11th ♈	12th ♉ ♂ 3°	1st ♊ ♄ 1° Asc. 22°21
9th ♒ ☽ 21°			2nd ♋ ♃ 17° ☊ 22°
8th ♑ ☋ 22°			3rd ♌ ☉ 0°27' ☿ 25° ♀ ℞27°
7th ♐	6th ♏	5th ♎	4th ♍

The effects of *varga* charts are not more significant or powerful than the conditions indicated in the *rasi* or natal chart. However, IN THE DASA OR BHUKTI OF A PLANET RELATING TO A PIVOTAL HOUSE IN A *VARGA* CHART (in the way I have described above), the person gets the results that the varga chart planet indicates. (The person also gets the natal chart effects that are indicated.)

DE NIRO NORTH INDIAN

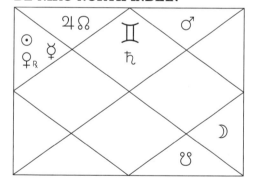

Regarding the use of planetary aspects in *varga* charts, it contradicts my experience and strains my common sense to use them. My Indian mentors did not use aspects or conjunctions in *varga* charts, and neither do I. I am aware that some very prominent Hindu astrologers use *varga* aspects, but this is not something I recommend.

To reiterate perhaps the most important point, astrologers analyzing charts of Westerners should be extremely wary of using any *varga* chart without first determining that particular chart is accurate. In Hindu culture, when a teacher wants to convey a message with utmost emphasis, he or she repeats it three times. Because so many astrologers in the West are making all kinds of predictions using *varga* charts without determining whether the divisional chart they are analyzing is correct, I will say this three times. The house placements (but not the sign placements) of *varga* charts are often ruined by a slight error in birthtime. The house placements of *varga* charts are often ruined by a slight error in birthtime. The house placements of *varga* charts are often ruined by a slight error in birthtime.

In January 1972, in the midst of my college theatre days, I began having spiritual feelings and was initiated into Transcendental Meditation. This was during Moon dasa, Venus bhukti. The Moon occupies my twelfth house (enlightenment and spiritual growth), and Venus, the bhukti planet, is closely conjunct the ruler of the spiritual twelfth house (Mars), as well as the metaphysical and otherworldly planet, Ketu. Nine months later, in September 1972, I entered Mars dasa, and my life started to shift subtly but dramatically. Suddenly, I became more and more fascinated with meditation and found myself able to have relationships with women for the first time. Mars rules the seventh house (marriage) and the twelfth house (enlightenment or final liberation). Mars is strengthened because it occupies the fourth house, an angular house, and is only two degrees away from benefic Venus. It is also tightly conjunct Ketu, but in this case Ketu is not quite as harmful as usual because it receives such good energy from its close conjunction to Venus.

Mars dasa was the happiest period of my life up to this point, and I credit this more to Mars' close conjunction to benefic Venus than anything else. In a dasa or bhukti of a planet that is closely conjunct with a benefic, positive results can almost always be expected. Likewise, a planet closely aspected by a malefic will bring suffering in its periods. Although I was not without problems in Mars dasa, I had a profound underlying feeling of happiness and well-being that was quite Venusian. I also felt a strong sense of detachment and discrimination because Mars is so close to Ketu.

Mars, in my chart, occupies the fourth house (homes, land, cars, and so forth), but the Mars dasa was more related to the seventh and twelfth houses—the houses that Mars rules. During the seven years of Mars, two areas of life dominated my consciousness—marriage and the pursuit of enlightenment. A year into Mars dasa, when I graduated from college in 1973, I went to Switzerland to meditate for extended periods and to train as a teacher of meditation. Two years later, I married a fellow classmate, an actress I had begun dating in the beginning of Mars dasa. Because

Mars, the ruler of my marriage house, conjuncts Venus, the likelihood of marrying an artist is strong. Because the ruler of the seventh house is conjunct two planets, Venus and Ketu (Rahu and Ketu are always considered planets when considering planetary unions), two marriages are likely. This, to western astrologers, may seem simplistic but that is the way Hindu astrology works. My second marriage came in 1993 during the writing of this book.

The same is true of planets that occupy the marriage house. If there are two planets in the seventh house, the person will probably marry twice, and each spouse will personify one of the particular planets involved. In other words, if Mars and Jupiter occupy the seventh house, the person will probably marry one partner who is assertive, fiery, aggressive, and argumentative, and one person who is religious, spiritual, or wealthy. Although this is a general rule and few general rules work 100 percent of the time, predicting the number of marriages by the number of planets in the seventh house or the number of planets aspecting the seventh house ruler is relatively reliable. There may also be numerous marriages if Mercury or the Moon alone occupy the seventh house, or if they aspect the ruler of the seventh house because Mercury and the Moon are planets of abundance (Mercury is dual-natured and fickle and the Moon is changeable because it is continually waxing and waning).

BRAHA DASAMSA

3rd ♃	4th	5th	6th
2nd ☉			7th ☋
1st Asc. ♀ ☊			8th
12th ♂	11th ☽	10th ☿	9th ♄

I have seen plenty of cases where the ruler of the seventh house is closely aspected by Mercury or a bright Moon, and the person has been married three times. In these cases, the seventh house of the chart is usually especially afflicted. In the western world, seventh house afflictions are extraordinarily common. Years ago when I studied astrology in India with R. Santhanam, we analyzed charts of my friends and family nightly for several months. Eventually Santhanam became startled and blurted out in broken English, "Doesn't anyone in America have happy married life?"

This brings up an interesting point, incidentally, about analyzing charts in foreign countries. Although I did not have the opportunity to peruse the charts of Indians while in India, I have practiced astrology in Switzerland and Iceland and have noticed that each county produces certain features peculiar to the culture that show up in the charts of inhabitants. For example, in Iceland a full eighty or ninety percent of the charts I analyzed had enormously powerful and well-aspected eighth houses. The eighth house rules longevity. Each time I told a person with one of these phenomenally strong eighth houses how remarkably long their life expectancy was, they told me that their grandparents had lived well into their nineties or longer! The eighth house also rules intuition and metaphysical subjects in Hindu astrology. In this country of eighth house miracle horoscopes, I achieved the greatest response to my introductory astrology lecture ever. Out of forty or fifty people who were present, twenty-seven signed up for birthchart readings! A powerful eighth house means a powerful interest in astrology.

In Switzerland, where I have visited several times to do chart readings, the horoscopes always contain an uncommon emphasis on money and abundance. Mind you, this occurs in the charts of common-ers as well as the rich. Switzerland has the highest standard of living in the world and wealth, or at the least a great interest in wealth, is reflected in nearly everybody's chart there.

Aside from marriage and the spiritual realm, the only other matter that seriously grabbed my attention during Mars dasa was making money. This was not due to Mars dasa but to an influence in my wife's chart. As stated earlier, people's lives are powerfully affected by the karma of those around them, and this becomes especially significant when a person gets married. This matter, to use an expression of my Indian astrology mentor, R. Santhanam, is not a joke. In my wife's chart, the ruler of the seventh house (marriage) occupies the second house (money) and is well-aspected. This means that it is her karma to marry a person involved in second house matters (education or money). Before getting married I told her that if she was interested in a life of money and comfort, I was not a particularly wise choice for marriage because I was fervent about gaining enlightenment. She, being a true artist, cared less about wealth than I did. Nevertheless, within months after marrying, I began having consuming desires to make money and opened a retail business that soon paid off well. (This ex-wife's next long-term suitor, incidentally, was not a moneymaker but a writer.)

Back to the dasa at hand. In the same way that the Moon dasa was emotional, Mars dasa was characterized by intense energy, drive, and passion. That is the nature of Mars. In my chart passion and sexual energy are intense because Mars is so close to Venus. I distinctly remember that during Mars dasa, trying to remain celibate on medita-tion courses was more than difficult—it was torture.

During the final year of Mars dasa, I entered the Moon subperiod **445** and married life quickly deteriorated. This is caused by the Moon's fallen placement in the *navamsa* or marriage chart described earlier. A few months after Mars-Moon dasa-bhukti ended and Rahu dasa began, my wife and I went our separate ways and eventually divorced. Divorce was something I had never before considered, and it was very painful. Ancient Hindu scriptures say that Rahu periods sometimes bring intense and destructive effects during both the first and last few years of the dasa. And that is exactly what occurred when my Rahu dasa began. As if divorce was not excruciating enough, only a few short months later, my father contracted cancer and died. This was the greatest loss of my life, and I grieved for a solid two years.

There are a few different possibilities as to why Rahu dasa brought such intense and dramatic effects. Some astrologers point to Rahu being so closely aspected by two planets that rule malefic houses (Venus and Mars rule houses six and twelve). Others would say it is because of the bad relationship between Rahu and Rahu's dispositor. The dispositor of Rahu is Saturn (because Saturn rules the house which Rahu occupies). Rahu is six houses away from Saturn and sixth house relationships are terrible (as are eighth and twelfth house relationships). Whether these are the reasons I am uncertain, but they are possibilities.

On the positive side, Rahu is well-placed in the tenth house because malefic planets flourish in *upachaya* houses (three, six, ten, and eleven). It is common to gain fame, recognition, and prominence in the dasa of Rahu in the tenth house. Furthermore, the dispositor of Rahu (Saturn) is in the auspicious fifth house and is aspected to the exact degree by benefic Jupiter. It is true that Jupiter rules the eighth house, thus causing harm, but Jupiter also carries its natural benefic energy. I have gained great recognition in the astrological community during Rahu dasa on account of my astrology books. My first text, *Ancient Hindu Astrology for the Modern Western Astrologer*, even sells in India.

Although the Hindu astrologers that I have worked with do not place a great deal of attention on sign placements, the signs do have an impact. Rahu occupies the sign of Aquarius, an occult sign relating to secretive subjects like astrology, tarot, and so on. Within a month or two of beginning Rahu dasa, I had the first astrological reading of my life and was completely enthralled with the subject. I soon began studying astrology, and the rest, as they say, is history. What is unfortunate, perhaps, is that my spiritual hunger has subsided, and I find prayer and meditation far less enchanting. Such is the nature of the serpent-demon Rahu.

446   Rahu represents cravings and desires for worldly success, and that has been my story for the last approximately fourteen years. While I have enjoyed important and successful professional accomplishments and have made spiritual pilgrimages to places like India, Israel, and Nepal, which Rahu in the tenth house often brings, I have not enjoyed a fraction of the spiritual contentment and divine sweetness I felt during Mars dasa. The effect of Rahu on my life has been, more than anything, an unrelenting desire for recognition, career success, and promotion of astrology. It is a thrill and an honor to make a contribution to the world of astrology, but I am more than eager to be done with Rahu's period and experience Jupiter dasa, which begins in a few short years.

Because my chart tends more toward the spiritual than the worldly, Jupitarian energy is far more enticing than Rahu's. The condition of Jupiter in my chart is an intense mixture of extremes. On the positive side, Jupiter occupies its own sign, Pisces, and is aspected by the *rajayogakaraka* or royal union maker, Saturn, to the exact degree. Also, in the *varga* charts, Jupiter is in its own signs three times and is exalted three times, thereby strengthening natal Jupiter. The negative conditions are that Jupiter is aspected by two first-class malefics, Mars and Saturn, and both planets make the aspect within the exact degree. Jupiter's rulership of the eighth house is harmful, because the eighth house is a *dusthana,* or grief-producing house. But the eighth house also rules astrology, and astrology is my career.

Jupiter is the planet of religion, philosophy, travel, and abundance. Jupiter both occupies and rules the eleventh house (financial gains and profits, groups and friends, major goals and desires). It also rules the eighth house (occult subjects, money from partners, inheritances, death, and so on). As described above, Jupiter is both extremely well-placed and extremely afflicted. What do you predict will be the effects of this Jupiter dasa?

Jai Lord Ganesh

Astrologers may find the following information helpful. Some of the material pertains to dasa and bhuktis and some to natal Hindu astrology. Western astrologers should not apply any of this information to western birthchart interpretation.

1. As mentioned earlier in this text, planets in the first or last few degrees are generally weak. If the ASCENDANT degree is one of the first or last few degrees of a sign (twenty-eight to twenty-nine degrees, or zero to one degree), the effects are very debilitating. Babies with weak ascendants such as these are often given up for adoption or are ignored during childhood because they could not command enough care and attention from their parents.

The weakening effects are somewhat mitigated if a benefic planet occupies the first house or there are powerful aspects to the ascendant. If the ascendant degree is weak, but there are benefic planets occupying or aspecting the ascendant, then the person usually exhibits good confidence while also feeling a void or strong insecurity within. A note of caution, however: use discretion with this information in the West, because birthcharts are often wrong by five or ten minutes. Usually four minutes of birthtime changes the ascendant by one degree.

2. In this text, I have not mentioned astrological *yogas* (planetary unions) except for the most basic *rajayogas*. There are literally thousands of planetary unions, both good and bad, mentioned in ancient Hindu astrological scriptures. Occasionally, what appears to be a good dasa turns out bad because the dasa planet forms a bad *yoga*. Likewise, an apparently afflicted or menacing dasa sometimes turns out well because the dasa planet is involved in a beneficial *yoga*. This phenomenon is rare but does occur from time to time.

During the years that Ronald Reagan enjoyed two of the most successful terms as U.S. president, he was in the midst of a Saturn dasa. Saturn occupies its fallen sign, Aries, in Reagan's birthchart. Even though Reagan has given out several different birthtimes (probably to throw his detractors off because he uses astrology himself), the Saturn dasa went on for several years during the Reagan presidency no matter

448   which of these birthtimes one uses. According to some highly respected Hindu astrologers, Saturn forms a special and beneficial yoga in Reagan's chart that ancient astrological seers describe as conferring "kingship," or what we today call political success.

Because there are thousands of astrological yogas that an astrologer must memorize in order to gain supreme predictive accuracy in Hindu astrology, a strong second house is especially desirable for anyone wanting to pursue astrology. The second house reveals the person's ability to memorize information and details. Hindu astrological scriptures constantly say that the best astrologers are those with a powerful second house.

3. Every planet enjoys what is called its "great year." the following are the great years of the planets:

The Great Year of Jupiter is the 16th Year
The Great Year of the Sun is the 22nd Year
The Great Year of the Moon is the 24th Year
The Great Year of Venus is the 25th Year
The Great Year of Mars is the 28th Year
The Great Year of Mercury is the 32nd Year
The Great Year of Saturn is the 36th Year
The Great Year of Rahu is the 42nd Year
The Great Year of Ketu is the 48th Year

During the great year of a planet, that planet matures or comes of age and gives its full effects. For example, many people suddenly begin to exhibit leadership qualities around their thirty-sixth year (age thirty-five)—the year of Saturn. Many people begin to write a great deal or to experience heightened self-expression around their thirty-second year (age thirty-one)—the year of Mercury, and so on.

During the great year of a planet, the person experiences an integrating effect relating to the nature of the planet, as well as to the houses that planet rules in the person's birthchart. For instance, if Saturn rules the first house (Capricorn or Aquarius ascendant), then during the thirty-sixth year (age thirty-five), the person experiences his or her personal power in a way never before fully grasped. If the person has a Cancer ascendant, then during the year Mars matures, the twenty-eighth year (age twenty-seven), the person suddenly becomes aware of his or her career potential, because Mars rules the tenth house (career). For that person, all the time leading up to the year that Mars matures seems to have been investigation and experimentation with Mars energy and the houses that Mars rules. Even if the person was successful in professional life before Mars matured, there is still an increase in professional power and a greater grasp of one's dharma (duty or purpose) when Mars, as ruler of the tenth house, matures.

If the planet that is maturing happens to be extremely afflicted, the great year of that planet may be terrible. For example, if Venus, the planet of love, is fallen (in Virgo) and is aspected by malefic planets like Mars and Ketu, the person may suffer terribly in love matters during his or her twenty-fifth year of life (age twenty-four). The person also experiences difficulties in the areas of life that Venus rules and occupies in the birthchart.

In my experience, maturity of planets is one of the most consistently accurate features of birthchart interpretation. It is extremely important to consider the year of maturity for the ascendant ruler because, in a great many cases, that is the year when a person begins to take responsibility for his or her destiny and dreams. Also, always note the great year of a planet forming a *rajayoga*, as that will generally bring a powerful rise in life. For instance, if Jupiter is involved in a *rajayoga* in a person's chart, then that person's life may flourish in the sixteenth year, Jupiter's great year. For people with Cancer ascendants, the year of Mars is especially good (unless Mars is extremely afflicted), because Mars alone is the *rajayogakaraka* (royal union indicator). For those with Libra and Taurus ascendants, Saturn alone is the *rajayogakaraka;* for these people the thirty-sixth year brings increase of prominence and power.

Without considering the great years of the planets (especially planets that rule the ascendant, planets that are extremely afflicted, or planets that form a *rajayoga*) some very significant years in a person's life will be missed. Moreover, ignoring planetary maturities can spoil predictive accuracy of dasa-bhuktis when a great year whose effects contradicts a dasa-bhukti occurs.

4. Retrograde planets are generally weaker in their dasas and bhuktis than direct planets. In *shadbala,* a highly technical computation system which determines the relative strengths and weaknesses of the planets, retrograde planets are considered strong. However, despite the *shadbala* appraisal, in natal birthchart interpretation retrogrades weaken the energy of the planet and the affairs of the houses the retrograde planets rule. In the cases of malefics like Mars and Saturn, these planets, when retrograde, do LESS DAMAGE THAN USUAL to the houses they occupy than if they are direct.

During a dasa or bhukti of a retrograde planet, the energy of the planet is held back, and the person needs to take action in order to reap whatever potential benefits the period promises.

5. Although it is not mentioned in Hindu astrological scriptures, planets that occupy signs opposite their rulership signs generally function poorly. In western astrology, these are called planetary detriments. For example, because the Sun rules Leo, it usually produces poor results in Aquarius. Likewise, Jupiter, which rules Sagittarius and Pisces, is poorly placed in Virgo, the sign opposite Pisces.

These placements do give some good results, however, because by being in the sign opposite their ownership, they throw an aspect onto one of the houses they own (because all planets aspect their opposite house in Hindu astrology). In the two examples above, the Sun in Aquarius throws an excellent aspect onto Leo because the Sun rules Leo. Jupiter in Virgo throws an aspect onto its own sign, Pisces, and this also is a special aspect. In this case, Jupiter's weak placement in Virgo would produce some damage to the house it occupies and also to Sagittarius, the house Jupiter rules. Jupiter's other house, Pisces, would not be harmed because of the special aspect Jupiter throws onto Pisces.

6. During a Venus dasa for a person with an extremely afflicted Venus, the person will likely have extra difficulties on Fridays, the day of Venus, throughout the dasa. A person in an afflicted Moon dasa will have problems on Mondays, and so on. It is a good idea to pray, fast, perform austerities, or practice religious ceremonies on the day ruled by the dasa planet.

7. Some astrologers believe that a malefic planet that transits its own sign produces good effects rather than bad. For example, if Saturn is transiting the fifth house of a person's chart, and that house happens to be Capricorn or Aquarius (Saturn's ownership sign), some astrologers predict good effects instead of Saturn's usual malefic influence. I have not found this to be the case. This predictive reasoning may work well for mundane astrology (predictions for countries and the world as a whole) but not for natal astrology (individual birthcharts).

Similarly, many beginning astrologers believe that a malefic planet occupying its exaltation sign will throw good aspects instead of its usual harmful energy. Such astrologers believe, for example, that if Mars is in Capricorn, its exaltation sign, that Mars will throw beneficial aspects onto the houses it aspects (Mars aspects the fourth, seventh, and eighth houses from itself). In my experience, this is simply inaccurate. Mars throws damaging energy even when it is powerful and well-placed by house or sign. The same is true of all other malefic planets.

Finally, some astrologers believe that in cases where Mars and Saturn become *rajayogakarakas* or royal union indicators (Mars is a *rajayogakaraka* for Cancer ascendant birthcharts and Saturn for Taurus and Libra ascendants), they will throw entirely beneficial energy onto the houses and planets they aspect. This is also untrue. *Rajayogakarakas* that are malefic by nature will throw some good energy because of the auspicious houses that they rule, but they simultaneously throw their usual damaging influence.

8. Saturn occupying the seventh house of a chart or Saturn ruling the seventh house can harm the accuracy of the astrologer. This is a principle of horary astrology which often applies in natal astrology. If Saturn OCCUPIES the seventh house or if Saturn RULES the seventh house of a birthchart, there is a strong chance that the astrologer will make mistakes either in his or her interpretation or in birthchart calculations. In certain cases, a person with such a birthchart may accidentally give a wrong birthtime to the astrologer.

9. Astrologers may have a difficult time interpreting a birthchart that contains an afflicted ninth house. If the ninth house of a person's chart is weak and badly aspected, that person has bad karma in gaining higher knowledge. This makes it difficult for the astrologer to provide the person with accurate and plentiful knowledge. Typically, the person with the afflicted ninth house may arrive late for an astrological session or behave arrogantly or act in some way that irritates the astrologer. Also, persons with an afflicted ninth house often have problems finding their correct birth time. Conversely, if the person has a beneficial ninth house, the astrologer has an easy time interpreting the chart. Information surfaces easily and the astrologer enjoys his or her interaction with the client.

10. Hindu scriptures state that a planet that is exalted and retrograde functions as if it were fallen, and that a fallen planet that is retrograde functions as if exalted. I have found this to be accurate only sometimes. Astrologers should be careful about making definitive positive or negative statements about dasas of exalted or fallen planets that are retrograde.

A good example occurs in Hugh Hefner's chart. Mercury is fallen (in Pisces) in the eighth house and retrograde in Hefner's chart, and Mercury gave results as if it were exalted during his Mercury dasa (between 1961 and 1978). This was when Hugh Hefner built his publishing empire. (Note—in Hindu astrology, Mercury is exalted in Virgo and fallen in Pisces. This is the only exaltation and fallen placement that differs with western planetary dignities.)

11. It is common to hear an Hindu astrologer say that if Saturn is in the twelfth house from Venus, the person may be an artist, or that if Saturn is in the twelfth house from Mercury, the person may be a writer or teacher. The reasoning behind this is that Saturn, more than any other planet, is a *karaka* or indicator of career and that because the first transit Saturn makes after birth is (in the examples above) to Venus or Mercury, these planets will color the person's profession. This technique works for all planets near Saturn and produces fairly good results.

Similarly, any planet in the twelfth house from Saturn will also color the person's profession, because in that planet's first transit after birth, it conjuncts Saturn. For instance, if Jupiter is in the twelfth house from Saturn, the person's profession may be connected to spirituality or law because Jupiter is the first planet to transit Saturn. These astrological techniques, which Hindu astrologers constantly use, are actually from a different astrological system. There are three major Hindu astrological systems in use today. The most popular system is called the *Parasara* system, originating from the ancient Hindu sage, Parasara, and that is the system taught in this book. The other astrological systems are called *Jaimini* and *Tajaka,* and these twelfth and second house transit techniques come from one of these two (I do not remember which one).

12. People often dislike gemstones that correspond to planets that are extremely afflicted in their charts (despite the fact that these are usually the gems they need most). They also have a tendency to lose such stones. On the other hand, people often receive as gifts the gemstones that correspond to powerful or well-aspected planets in their charts.

13. A dasa of an extremely powerful, well-placed, and well-aspected planet generally causes good effects in all areas of life, while a dasa of a weak and afflicted planet generally causes problems all around.

14. There is a school of thought that says that a dasa planet THROWS aspects, for better or for worse, during its period. In natal astrology, Jupiter throws its aspect onto the fifth, seventh, and ninth houses. Therefore, some say that in the dasa of Jupiter where Jupiter occupies, say, the first house, the fifth, seventh, and ninth houses will significantly benefit. As another example, such astrologers say that if Jupiter occupies the second house then in Jupiter dasa good effects will occur to the affairs of the sixth, eighth, and tenth houses because of the aspects that Jupiter throws onto those houses.

If Venus is combust or closely conjunct the Sun, this school of thought maintains that Venus and the houses Venus rules would be particularly harmed during the Sun dasa. Or, for example, during the dasa of a benefic planet that is closely conjunct the ruler of the seventh house, the person may marry or have beneficial love opportunities. I have seen cases where this analysis of dasas and bhuktis works, and I have seen others where it does not work. I present this material only for further study and investigation.

INSTRUCTIONS FOR DETERMINING
THE DASA-BHUKTI AT BIRTH

The dasa and bhukti a person is born into is determined by the degree of the Moon in the natal birthchart. The 360° zodiac is broken up into twenty-seven *nakshatras* (constellations or lunar mansions), each measuring thirteen degrees and twenty minutes. Each *nakshatra* is ruled by a particular planet, Rahu, or Ketu (North and South Nodes). The planet ruling the birth *nakshatra* is the dasa at birth. Given below are all twenty-seven nakshatras and their ruling planets.

NAKSHATRAS — LUNAR MANSIONS

	Degrees	Nakshatra	Ruled By
1.	00° 00' — 13° 20'	Aswini	Ketu
2.	13° 20' — 26° 40'	Bharini	Venus
3.	26° 40' — 40° 00'	Krittika	Sun
4.	40° 00' — 53° 20'	Rohini	Moon
5.	53° 20' — 66° 40'	Mrigishira	Mars
6.	66° 40' — 80° 00'	Arida	Rahu
7.	80° 00' — 93° 20'	Purnavasu	Jupiter
8.	93° 20' — 106° 40'	Pushyami	Saturn
9.	106° 40' — 120° 00'	Aslesha	Mercury
10.	120° 00' — 133° 20'	Makha	Ketu
11.	133° 20' — 146° 40'	Poorva phalguna	Venus
12.	146° 40' — 160° 00'	Uttara phalguna	Sun
13.	160° 00' — 173° 20'	Hasta	Moon
14.	173° 20' — 186° 40'	Chitra	Mars
15.	186° 40' — 200° 00'	Swati	Rahu
16.	200° 00' — 213° 20'	Vishakha	Jupiter
17.	213° 20' — 226° 40'	Anuradha	Saturn
18.	226° 40' — 240° 00'	Jeyshta	Mercury
19.	240° 00' — 253° 20'	Moola	Ketu
20.	253° 20' — 266° 40'	Poorva ashada	Venus
21.	266° 40' — 280° 00'	Uttara ashada	Sun
22.	280° 00' — 293° 20'	Saran	Moon
23.	293° 20' — 306° 40'	Dhanishta	Mars
24.	306° 40' — 320° 00'	Satabhish	Rahu
25.	320° 00' — 333° 20'	Poorva bhadra	Jupiter
26.	333° 20' — 346° 40'	Uttara bhadra	Saturn
27.	346° 40' — 360° 00'	Revati	Mercury

A person can be born into any part of the dasa-bhukti. In other **455**
words, a person may be born into the last three days of a Mercury-Sun
dasa-bhukti, after which follows the Mercury-Moon period and subperiod.
Or one can be born into the second week of Venus dasa, Venus bhukti,
and so on. In order to determine the dasa based on the position of the
Moon in your natal chart, refer to the tables on pages 457 and 458. To
show how to determine the exact part of a dasa-bhukti one is born into,
let us use the following example. Let us say the Moon is in two degrees
and twenty minutes of Taurus at birth. Now go to the left-hand column
of the table on page 457 and find the same longitude (degree and minute)
of the Moon's position at birth.

Next, go to the top of the table and find which column is to be used
for the Moon in Taurus and follow this down until the appropriate
longitude point is reached.

The numbers indicating years, months, and days which are found on
the same line as that of the Moon's longitude reveal the duration of time
still remaining in the *dasa* in operation. In this case the *dasa* in operation
is that of the Sun. The time remaining in that period is 3 years, 5 months,
and 12 days, after which the other successive *dasas* run their courses
(i.e., 10 years of Moon, 7 years Mars, 18 years *Rahu* etc.).

Now it must be explained what to do if the Moon's longitude falls
BETWEEN the 20 minute intervals listed in the left-hand column. In
such a case, locate the closest degree and minute to the Moon's position
and note the difference in minutes. This figure must be less than 10.

As an example, let us say the Moon was in Aries, 23 degrees 22
minutes. The closest longitude listed is 23 degrees 20 minutes, leaving
a difference of 2 minutes. Note that at the exact degree of 23 degrees 20
minutes, the *dasa* at birth is Venus and the duration of this period
remaining after birth is exactly 5 years. Now, in order to account for the
2 minute difference, go to the smaller table on the bottom of page 458
entitled "Proportional Parts for *Dasas* of Planets." First locate the column
for Venus and then the difference of minutes, which is listed in the far
left column. The appropriate figure in this case is 18 days. Since the 2
minutes was an INCREASE of time (22 is more than 20), the 18 days
must be SUBTRACTED from 5 years. When calculating *dasas* and
bhuktis. months are counted as 30 days. Therefore the time of Venus
dasa remaining at birth is 4 years, 11 months, and 12 days.

In cases where the degree of the Moon is some minutes LESS THAN
the closest longitude given in the far left column, the difference in days
or months would have to be ADDED to the duration of *dasa* remaining.

Appendix

456 DETERMINING THE BHUKTI

The next step is to determine the subperiod that is in effect. This is easily done by referring to the table on page 459, which gives the duration of all *bhuktis* within each *dasa*.

Continuing with the example above, subtract the balance of time remaining in the *dasa* at birth (4 years, 11 months, 12 days) from the FULL *dasa* (Venus = 20 years) to distinguish how much time has already passed. Note that in order to make the subtraction possible, reductions are necessary (20 yrs. = 19 yrs., 11 mos., 30 days).

yrs.	mos.	days
19	11	30
-04	-11	-12
15	00	18

Now locate the *bhukti* table for Venus and note that after 15 yrs., 0 mos., and 18 days all *bhuktis* through Jupiter are completed. Therefore the one underway (at birth) is Saturn.

ANTARA DASAS—The calculations for inter-subperiods take up several pages in tables alone, and therefore the reader may refer to Lahiri's CONDENSED EPHEMERIS or Grace Inglis' book HINDU DASA SYSTEM (see bibliography). The *dasa bhukti* tables in this book are from Lahiri's ephemeris. *Antara dasas* are especially important during extended bhuktis, which may last as long as two or three years in some cases.

Long. of Moon	Moon in Aries Leo, Sagittarius			Moon In Taurus Virgo, Capricorn			Moon in Gemini Libra, Aquarius			Moon in Cancer Scorpio, Pisces		
° '	y	m	d	y	m	d	y	m	d	y	m	d
0 0	Ketu 7	0	0	Sun 4	6	0	Mars 3	6	0	Jupiter 4	0	0
0 20	6	9	27	4	4	6	3	3	27	3	7	6
0 40	6	7	24	4	2	12	3	1	24	3	2	12
1 0	6	5	21	4	0	18	2	11	21	2	9	18
1 20	6	3	18	3	10	24	2	9	18	2	4	24
1 40	6	1	15	3	9	0	2	7	15	2	0	0
2 0	5	11	12	3	7	6	2	5	12	1	7	6
2 20	5	9	9	3	5	12	2	3	9	1	2	12
2 40	5	7	6	3	3	18	2	1	6	0	9	18
3 0	5	5	3	3	1	24	1	11	3	0	4	24
3 20	5	3	0	3	0	0	1	9	0	Saturn 19	0	0
3 40	5	0	27	2	10	6	1	6	27	18	6	9
4 0	4	10	24	2	8	12	1	4	24	18	0	18
4 20	4	8	21	2	6	18	1	2	21	17	6	27
4 40	4	6	18	2	4	24	1	0	18	17	1	6
5 0	4	4	15	2	3	0	0	10	15	16	7	15
5 20	4	2	12	2	1	6	0	8	12	16	1	24
5 40	4	0	9	1	11	12	0	6	9	15	8	3
6 0	3	10	6	1	9	18	0	4	6	15	2	12
6 20	3	8	3	1	7	24	0	2	3	14	8	21
6 40	3	6	0	1	6	0	Rahu 18	0	0	14	3	0
7 0	3	3	27	1	4	6	17	6	18	13	9	9
7 20	3	1	24	1	2	12	17	1	6	13	3	18
7 40	2	11	21	1	0	18	16	7	24	12	9	27
8 0	2	9	18	0	10	24	16	2	12	12	4	6
8 20	2	7	15	0	9	0	15	9	0	11	10	15
8 40	2	5	12	0	7	6	15	3	18	11	4	24
9 0	2	3	9	0	5	12	14	10	6	10	11	3
9 20	2	1	6	0	3	18	14	4	24	10	5	12
9 40	1	11	3	0	1	24	13	11	12	9	11	21
10 0	1	9	0	Moon 10	0	0	13	6	0	9	6	0
10 20	1	6	27	9	9	0	13	0	18	9	0	9
10 40	1	4	24	9	6	0	12	7	6	8	6	18
11 0	1	2	21	9	3	0	12	1	24	8	0	27
11 20	1	0	18	9	0	0	11	8	12	7	7	6
11 40	0	10	IS	8	9	0	11	3	0	7	1	15
12 0	0	8	12	8	6	0	10	9	18	6	7	24
12 20	0	6	9	8	3	0	10	4	6	6	2	3
12 40	0	4	6	8	0	0	9	10	24	5	8	12
13 0	0	2	3	7	9	0	9	5	12	5	2·21	
13 20	Venus 20	0	0	7	6	0	9	0	0	4	9	0
13 40	19	6	0	7	3	0	8	6	18	4	3	9
14 0	19	0	0	7	0	0	8	1	6	3	9	18
14 20	18	6	0	6	9	0	7	7	24	3	3	27
14 40	18	0	0	6	6	0	7	2	12	2	10	6
15 0	17	6	0	6	3	0	6	9	0	2	4	15
15 20	17	0	0	6	0	0	6	3	18	1	10	24
15 40	16	6	0	5	9	0	5	10	6	1	5	3
16 0	16	0	0	5	6	0	5	4	24	0	11	12
16 20	15	6	0	5	3	0	4	11	12	0	5	21
16 40	15	0	0	5	0	0	4	6	0	Mercury 17	0	0
17 0	14	6	0	4	9	0	4	0	18	16	6	27
17 20	14	0	0	4	6	0	3	7	6	16	1	24
17 40	13	6	0	4	3	0	3	1	24	15	8	21

Balance of Vimsottari Dasa continued

Long. of Moon	Moon in Aries Leo, Sagittarius			Moon In Taurus Virgo, Capricorn			Moon in Gemini Libra, Aquarius			Moon in Cancer Scorpio, Pisces		
° '	y	m	d	y	m	d	y	m	d	y	m	d
18 0	Venus 13	0	0	Moon 4	0	0	Rahu 2	8	12	Merc. 15	3	18
18 20	12	6	0	3	9	0	2	3	0	14	10	15
18 40	12	0	0	3	6	0	1	9	18	14	5	12
19 0	11	6	0	3	3	0	1	4	6	14	0	9
19 20	11	0	0	3	0	0	0	10	24	13	7	6
19 40	10	6	0	2	9	0	0	5	12	13	2	3
20 0	10	0	0	2	6	0	Jupiter 16	0	0	12	9	0
20 20	9	6	0	2	3	0	15	7	6	12	3	27
20 40	9	0	0	2	0	0	15	2	12	11	10	24
21 0	8	6	0	1	9	0	14	9	18	11	5	21
21 20	8	0	0	1	6	0	14	4	24	11	0	18
21 40	7	6	0	1	3	0	14	0	0	10	7	15
22 0	7	0	0	1	0	0	13	7	6	10	2	12
22 20	6	6	0	0	9	0	13	2	13	9	9	9
22 40	6	0	0	0	6	0	12	9	18	9	4	6
23 0	5	6	0	0	3	0	12	4	24	8	11	3
23 20	5	0	0	Mars 7	0	0	12	0	0	8	6	0
23 40	4	6	0	6	9	27	11	7	6	8	0	27
24 0	4	0	0	6	7	24	11	2	12	7	7	24
24 20	3	6	0	6	5	21	10	9	18	7	2	21
24 40	3	0	0	6	3	18	10	4	24	6	9	18
25 0	2	6	0	6	1	15	10	0	0	6	4	15
25 20	2	0	0	5	11	12	9	7	6	5	11	12
25 40	1	6	0	5	9	9	9	2	12	5	6	9
26 0	1	0	0	5	7	6	8	9	18	5	1	6
26 20	0	6	0	5	5	3	8	4	24	4	8	3
26 40	Sun 6	0	0	5	3	0	8	0	0	4	3	0
27 0	5	10	6	5	0	27	7	7	6	3	9	27
27 20	5	8	12	4	10	24	7	2	12	3	4	24
27 40	5	6	18	4	8	21	6	9	18	2	11	21
28 0	5	4	24	4	6	18	6	4	24	2	6	18
28 20	5	3	0	4	4	15	6	0	0	2	1	15
28 40	5	1	6	4	2	12	5	7	6	1	8	12
29 0	4	11	12	4	0	9	5	2	12	1	3	9
29 20	4	9	18	3	10	6	4	9	18	0	10	6
29 40	4	7	24	3	8	3	4	4	24	0	5	3
30 0	4	6	0	3	6	0	4	0	0	0	0	0

Proportional Parts For Dasa of Planets
(To be subtracted from the balance of dasa for increase by mlnutes of the longitude of moon)

min.	Ketu (7 yr.)		Venus (20 yr.)		Sun (6 yr.)		Moon (10 yr.)		Mars (7 yr.)		Rahu (18 yr.)		Jupiter (16 yr.)		Saturn (19 yr.)		Merc (17 yr.)		min
	m	d	m	d	m	d	m	d	m	d	m	d	m	d	m	d	m	d	
1	0	3	0	9	0	3	0	5	0	3	0	8	0	7	0	9	0	8	1
2	0	6	0	18	0	5	0	9	0	6	0	16	0	14	0	17	0	15	2
3	0	9	0	27	0	8	0	14	0	9	0	24	0	22	0	26	0	23	3
4	0	13	1	6	0	11	0	18	0	13	1	2	0	29	1	4	1	11	4
5	0	16	1	15	0	14	0	23	0	16	1	11	1	6	1	13	1	8	5
6	0	19	1	24	0	16	0	27	0	19	1	19	1	13	1	21	1	16	6
7	0	22	2	3	0	19	1	2	0	22	1	27	1	20	2	0	1	24	7
8	0	25	2	12	0	22	1	6	0	25	2	5	1	28	2	8	2	1	8
9	0	28	2	21	0	24	1	11	0	28	2	13	2	5	2	17	2	9	9
10	1	1	3	0	0	27	1	15	1	1	2	21	2	12	2	26	2	17	10
15	1	17	4	15	1	11	2	8	1	17	4	2	3	18	4	8	3	25	15
20	2	3	6	0	1	24	3	0	2	3	5	12	4	24	5	21	5	3	20

Dasa → Bhukti ↓	Sun—6 yrs. Sub Periods (y m d)	Sun Total (y m d)	Moon—10 yrs. Sub Periods (y m d)	Moon Total (y m d)	Mars—7 yrs. Sub Periods (y m d)	Mars Total (y m d)
Sun	0 3 18	0 3 18	—	—	—	—
Moon	0 6 0	0 9 18	0 10 0	0 10 0	—	—
Mars	0 4 6	1 1 24	0 7 0	1 5 0	0 4 27	0 4 27
Rahu	0 10 24	2 0 18	1 6 0	2 11 0	1 0 18	1 5 15
Jupiter	0 9 18	2 10 6	1 4 0	4 3 0	0 11 6	2 4 21
Saturn	0 11 12	3 9 18	1 7 0	5 10 0	1 1 9	3 6 0
Mercury	0 10 6	4 7 24	1 5 0	7 3 0	0 11 27	4 5 27
Ketu	0 4 6	5 0 0	0 7 0	7 10 0	0 4 27	4 10 24
Venus	1 0 0	6 0 0	1 8 0	9 6 0	1 2 0	6 0 24
Sun	—	—	0 6 0	10 0 0	0 4 6	6 5 0
Moon	—	—	—	—	0 7 0	7 0 0

Dasa → Bhukti ↓	Rahu—18 yrs. Sub Periods (y m d)	Rahu Total (y m d)	Jupiter—16 yrs. Sub Periods (y m d)	Jupiter Total (y m d)	Saturn—19 yrs. Sub Periods (y m d)	Saturn Total (y m d)
Rahu	2 8 12	2 8 12	—	—	—	—
Jupiter	2 4 24	5 1 6	2 1 18	2 1 18	—	—
Saturn	2 10 6	7 11 12	2 6 12	4 8 0	3 0 3	3 0 3
Mercury	2 6 18	10 6 0	2 3 6	6 11 6	2 8 9	5 8 12
Ketu	1 0 18	11 6 18	0 11 6	7 10 12	1 1 9	6 9 21
Venus	3 0 0	14 6 18	2 8 0	10 6 12	3 2 0	9 11 21
Sun	0 10 24	15 5 12	0 9 18	11 4 0	0 11 12	10 11 3
Moon	1 6 0	16 11 12	1 4 0	12 8 0	1 7 0	12 6 3
Mars	1 0 18	18 0 0	0 11 6	13 7 6	1 1 9	13 7 12
Rahu	—	—	2 4 24	16 0 0	2 10 6	16 5 18
Jupiter	—	—	—	—	2 6 12	19 0 0

Dasa → Bhukti ↓	Mercury—17 yrs. Sub Periods (y m d)	Mercury Total (y m d)	Ketu—7 yrs. Sub Periods (y m d)	Ketu Total (y m d)	Venus—20 yrs. Sub Periods (y m d)	Venus Total (y m d)
Mercury	2 4 27	2 4 27	—	—	—	—
Ketu	0 11 27	3 4 24	0 4 27	0 4 27	—	—
Venus	2 10 0	6 2 24	1 2 0	1 6 27	3 4 0	3 4 0
Sun	0 10 6	7 1 0	0 4 6	1 11 3	1 0 0	4 4 0
Moon	1 5 0	8 6 0	0 7 0	2 6 3	1 8 0	6 0 0
Mars	0 11 27	9 5 27	0 4 27	2 11 0	1 2 0	7 2 0
Rahu	2 6 18	12 0 15	1 0 18	3 11 18	3 0 0	10 2 0
Jupiter	2 3 6	14 3 21	0 11 6	4 10 24	2 8 0	12 10 0
Saturn	2 8 9	17 0 0	1 1 9	6 0 3	3 2 0	16 0 0
Mercury	—	—	0 11 27	7 0 0	2 10 0	18 10 0
Ketu	—	—	—	—	1 2 0	20 0 0

The following is a list of suggested reading on Hindu and western astrology.

WESTERN ASTROLOGY TEXTS

Arroyo, Stephen. *Astrology, Karma and Transformation.* Sebastopol, CA: CRCS Publications, 1978.

——— *Astrology, Psychology, and the Four Elements.* Sebastopol, CA: CRCS Publications, 1975.

——— *Relationships and Life Cycles.* Sebastopol, CA: CRCS PUblications.

Braha, James. *How To Be a Great Astrologer: The Planetary Aspects Explained.* Hollywood, FL: Hermetician Press, 1992.

Carter, C.E.O. *Astrological Aspects.* Wheaton, IL: Quest Books, The Theosophical Society.

——— *Essays on the Foundations of Astrology.* Wheaton, IL: Quest Books, The Theosophical Society, 1978.

——— *The Principles of Astrology.* Wheaton, IL: Quest Books, The Theosophical Society.

Hand, Robert. *Horoscope Symbols.* West Chester, PA: Whitford Press, 1981.

——— *Essays in Astrology.* West Chester, PA: Whitford Press, 1982

——— *Planets in Composite.* West Chester, PA: Whitford Press, 1975

——— *Planets in Transit.* West Chester, PA: Whitford Press, 1976.

——— *Planets in Youth.* West Chester, PA: Whitford Press, 1977.

Hickey, Isabel. *Astrology: A Cosmic Science*. Sebastopol, CA: CRCS 1992.   **461**

Lewi, Grant. *Astrology for the Millions*. St Paul, MN: Llewellen Publications, 1990.

Sasportas, Howard. *The Twelve Houses.* Great Britain: The Aquarian Press, 1985.

Soric, John. *The New Age Astrologer.*

Tompkins, Sue. *Aspects in Astrology.* Dorset, England: Element Books, 1989.

Zain, C.C. (a.k.a. Elbert Benjamin) - *Delineating the Horoscope.* Los Angeles, CA: Church of Light, 1950.

HINDU ASTROLOGY TEXTS BY WESTERNERS

Braha, James. *Ancient Hindu Astrology for the Modern Western Astrologer.* Hollwood, FL: Hermetician Press 1986.

Dreyer, Ronnie Gale. *Indian Astrology.* Wellingborough, Northamptonshire, England: The Aquarian Press, 1990

Frawley, David. *The Astrology of Seers.* Salt Lake City, UT: Passage Press, 1990.

Hopke, Tom. *How to Read Your Horoscope.* Honolulu, HI: Vedic Cultural Association, 1987.

Roebuck, Valerie *The Circle of Stars.* Rockport, MA: Element Books, 1992.

HINDU ASTROLOGY CLASSICS

Brihat Jatika - by sage Vahara Mihira

Brihat Samhita - by sage Varaha Mihira

Hora Sara - by sage Prithuyasas

Parasara Hora Shastra - by sage Parasara

Phaladeepika - by sage Mantreswara

Saravali - by sage Kalyana Varma

Ojah, Pandit Gopesh. Predictive Astrology of the Hindus. Bombay, India: D. B. Taraporevala Sons & Co. Pvt. Ltd., 1972.

Raman, B.V. *How to Judge a Horoscope.* Bangalore, India: IBH Prakashana, 1981.

——— *Three Hundred Important Combinations.* Bangalor, India: IBH Prakashana, 1979.

For a catalogue of Hindu astrology books, contact the 21st Century Bookstore in Fairfield, Iowa at 1-800-593-2665 or Passage Press in Sandy, Utah at 1-800-873-0075 or (801) 942-1440.

James Braha
Hermetician Press
P.O. Box 1961
Hollywood, FL 33022

- **Hindu birthchart interpretation by James Braha:** write for details or call directory assistance for Hollywood, Florida (305) 555-1212.

- **Hindu Astrology Software:** calculates all 16 varga charts; nakshatras, dasas, bhuktis, and sub-bhukti periods. Includes options for English or Sanskrit, North or South Indian chart methods, explanatory comments on all planets and houses. The most user-friendly program available. PC or Macintosh, $110.

BOOKS

- *Ancient Hindu Astrology for the Modern Western Astrologer* by James Braha, $21.95.

- *How To Be a Great Astrologer: The Planetary Aspects Explained* by James Braha, $19.95.

- *Astro-Logos, Language of Life: The true story of a man and the people and planets around him* by James Braha, $12.95.

FOR COMPUTER-CALCULATED HINDU CHARTS WITH DASA-BHUKTIS, CONTACT:

ACS - Astro Communications Services Inc.
P.O. Box 34487
San Diego, CA 92163-4487
(800) 888-9983

464   Astrogram
3600 N. Lake Shore Dr. #1817
Chicago, IL 60613
(312) 589-6314

FOR A CATALOGUE OF HINDU ASTROLOGY TEXTS, CONTACT:

21ST CENTURY BOOKS
401 N. 4th St.
Fairfield, IA 52556
(515) 472-5105 (800) 593-2665

PASSAGE PRESS
8180 S. Highland Dr.
Sandy, UT 84093
(801) 942-1440 or (800) 873-0075

TO OBTAIN YAGYAS IN THE UNITED SATES, CONTACT LOCAL HINDU TEMPLES OR CALL:

Pandu Malyala
3744 Old William Penn Highway
Pittsburgh, PA 15235
(412) 374-9244
(412) 823-1296

Hindu Temple of Greater Chicago
12 South 701 Lemont Rd.
Lemont, IL 60439
(708) 972-0300